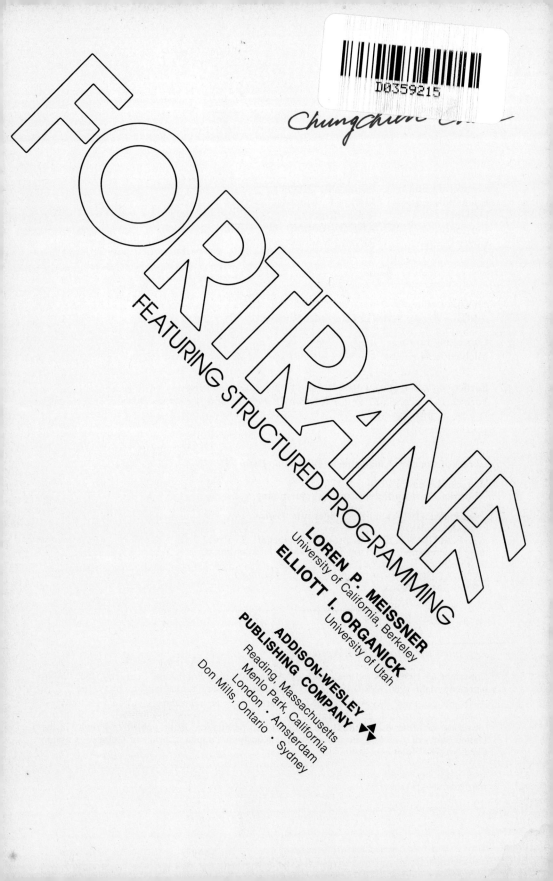

FORTRAN

FEATURING STRUCTURED PROGRAMMING

LOREN P. MEISSNER
University of California, Berkeley

ELLIOTT I. ORGANICK
University of Utah

**ADDISON-WESLEY
PUBLISHING COMPANY**
Reading, Massachusetts
Menlo Park, California
London · Amsterdam
Don Mills, Ontario · Sydney

D0359215

Sponsoring Editor: William B. Gruener
Production Editor: Martha K. Morong
Designer: Robert Rose
Illustrator: ANCO / Boston
Cover Design: Richard Hannus

This book is in the
Addison-Wesley Series in Computer Science.

Consulting Editor
Michael A. Harrison

Earlier editions of this work were published under the titles
Fortran IV, Second Edition, A Fortran IV Primer, and *A Fortran Primer.*

Library of Congress Cataloging in Publication Data

Meissner, Loren P., 1928–
   Fortran 77: featuring structured programming.

   Second ed. (1974) published under title: Fortran IV.
   Includes index.
   1. FORTRAN (Computer program language)   2. Struc-
tured programming.   I. Organick, Elliott I., joint author.
II. Title.
QA76.73.F25073   1979   001.6′424   78–74689
ISBN 0–201–05499–X

Reprinted with corrections, April 1982

Copyright © 1980, 1974, 1966, 1963 by Addison-Wesley Publishing Company, Inc. Philip-
pines copyright 1980, 1974, 1966, 1963 by Addison-Wesley Publishing Company, Inc.

All rights reserved. No part of this publication may be reproduced, stored in a retrieval
system, or transmitted, in any form or by any means, electronic, mechanical, photocopying,
recording, or otherwise, without the prior written permission of the publisher. Printed in the
United States of America. Published simultaneously in Canada. Library of Congress Catalog
Card No. 78–74689.

ISBN 0-201-05499-X
FGHIJK-HA-89876543

What is it about the Fortran language that keeps it going strong after more than 20 years? First of all, we must consider its contribution to the portability of programs. Fortran is the one language that is universally available, on large and small computers, in the United States, Europe, and the rest of the world. But Fortran would not have been able to achieve this leading position, and to maintain it for so many years, if it did not have some important fundamental characteristics, especially those features that make it possible for Fortran processors to generate very *efficient* running programs.

Of course the name Fortran has been applied, over these 20 years or more, to a number of different dialects. A major change occurred in the early 1960s with the introduction of Fortran IV: Such features as the logical IF and labeled Common blocks were included. After the first ANSI Fortran standard was adopted in 1966, some of the variations among Fortran IV dialects disappeared in favor of "standard conforming" processors. However, the Fortran standard permitted compatible extensions, and by the middle 1970s it became apparent that many of the most widely adopted extensions to Fortran IV could be incorporated into a new Fortran language standard. Accordingly, an updated standard language, known semiofficially as Fortran 77, was announced in 1977 and formally standardized in 1978 by ANSI. But even while this new Fortran standard (ANSI X3.9–1978) was still in press, several groups had begun working on further extensions and revisions to the language. By experimenting with compatible extensions to Fortran 77, those groups are contributing to the further development of Fortran.

The history of Fortran is to some extent paralleled by the history of this textbook. Beginning with *A Fortran Primer* in 1963, and continuing with *A Fortran IV Primer* in 1966 and *Fortran IV, Second Edition* in 1974, this book represents a continuing attempt to provide a comprehensive, yet not too technical, exposition of the Fortran language. The goal has always been to present the general principles of Fortran and structured programming with the aid of numerous specific examples. The 1963 text was unique in the "pre-structured programming" era. It was the first published Fortran text to emphasize the importance of good structure in programs. This was done by focusing on the mapping process from algorithms, in the form of flowcharts having structural clarity, to equivalent Fortran code.

The present book continues in the same tradition and aims to be a complete, modern Fortran textbook for both the engineer and nonengineer. This book presents Fortran 77, with its new character data type, *if-then-else* structure, zero-trip DO loop, list-directed (format-free) input and output, and numerous other features. The purpose is to suggest ways of using these new elements alongside the familiar Fortran features. Furthermore, this book indicates how Fortran 77 can be used to improve "program structure," while suggesting ways to surmount many of the remaining deficiencies of Fortran with regard to control structures.

Chapter 1 of this text is intended mainly as an introduction to programming for those students who have no previous computing experience. Those who are already familiar with BASIC, Pascal, PL1, or a similar language can begin with Chapter 2.

Because it attempts to provide comprehensive coverage of the Fortran language, this text includes material well beyond that needed for a single one-quarter or one-semester introduction to programming. Yet a serious attempt has been made to maintain an organization that will not suffer unduly from the omission of the more esoteric features. Each chapter progresses from the simpler to the more complicated parts of a given subject; thus most of the sections that can be omitted without undue hazard will be found near the ends of chapters. For example, in Chapter 2, Sections 2.6 and 2.7 (double precision and complex data types) could be skipped.

Again, the entire book progresses from the more essential to the less essential features of programming in general and of Fortran in particular. Thus a good simple introduction can be put together without going beyond Chapter 4, or possibly through Section 5.1. Formatted input and output can now be relegated to the background, with the introduction in Fortran 77 of list-directed (format-free)

READ and PRINT statements. Only the most comprehensive courses will likely wish to include Chapter 9 (which deals mostly with the input and output of files).

While most courses can be constructed by using this text from the beginning up to a certain point, there is one exception. Chapters 6 (Basic Input and Output) and 8 (Subprograms) are nearly independent of each other. Thus it is possible to introduce some of the concepts of "modular programming" (using parts of Chapter 8) while omitting the details of format construction (Chapter 6).

While conceding that there is a place for less comprehensive Fortran texts, the authors urge that consideration be given to the use of a comprehensive text-book even when only parts of the material it contains are to be covered in the course. The difference (if any) in cost to the student will be more than compensated by availability of the more advanced material for reference later on.

Part 3 (Chapter 10, Fortran Applications) consists of six different examples, each of which includes a program complete with flowchart, typical data, and results from a computer run. These worked-out examples can be used for reference, to tie together the language components from the earlier chapters in the context of complete programs. They can also be used for enrichment, along with the projects that are suggested for extending each of them.

A feature of this book is the summary of ANSI Standard X3.9-1978 that appears as Appendix C. Although of course it must be recognized that there is no authoritative description of Standard Fortran except the ANSI standard itself, this appendix provides basic coverage of the entire language (including such features as PAUSE, assigned GO TO, INTRINSIC, SAVE, CLOSE, and IN-QUIRE statements that are not mentioned elsewhere in the text). Appendixes on conventional computer systems and flowchart conventions have been included.

Although we boldly claim that the examples in this text represent good Fortran 77 usage, the authors recognize the difficulty of predicting the directions that Fortran 77 usage will take. It is obvious that no significant body of usage yet exists for many of the new features. Therefore, feedback is solicited from instructors who use this book. Let us know (by writing to us in care of Addison-Wesley) which examples and exercises you found most helpful, and tell us about other applications that you think should be covered. The experience of hundreds of instructors and thousands of students is incorporated into this text as it stands, and further feedback from users can continue to increase its usefulness.

A preliminary draft of the manuscript for this edition was reviewed in detail by Bruce Martin, who made many helpful suggestions for improvement. His assistance is greatly appreciated.

Berkeley, California   L.P.M.
Salt Lake City, Utah   E.I.O.
September 1979

CONTENTS

PART 1

COMPUTERS AND COMPUTING

CHAPTER 1

AN INTRODUCTION TO COMPUTING

1.1 UNDERSTANDING COMPUTERS

How does one learn to use a computer?

Even though computers are complex systems, they are surprisingly easy to understand. Why is this true? It is because we construct a *model* of a computer in our mind.

Let us draw an analogy with the process of learning to use some other complex system that is more familiar, such as an automobile. We are able to understand the principles of using automobiles by referring to a general model of an automobile. These general principles, in turn, help us to understand and to use any specific automobile.

The model that exists in our mind, that we use to understand the operation of automobiles, has been developing since we were very young. We have become familiar with such models, both miniature and full-sized ones, and we have ridden in automobiles and played with toy automobiles for many years. A good computer model, once we become familiar with it, should be no more difficult to understand and to use.

One characteristic that we look for in a good model of a computer is its ability to represent a variety of different specific kinds of computers. Computers vary much more widely than automobiles do, both in organizational plan and in internal detail. If a model is based too closely on one specific type of computer, it will not adequately represent computers of a different design that we may need to understand later on. Furthermore, excessive detail in our model causes unnecessary complication, and hides the essential properties that we are trying to understand. Our paramount objective, then, is to construct a model that is an *idealization* rather than a faithful *imitation* of specific computers.

The model used in this book is a deliberate idealization. In fact, we shall call it the *ideal computer,* though it may seem a bit arrogant to do so. The first step in our approach to the use of computers will be to learn what the ideal computer is and how it works. It will be easy to explain how a person can transmit instructions and data to this ideal computer, and how the computer can respond with useful results.

Fortran is itself based on an idealization of what a computer is and how it functions. The purpose of this first chapter is to present a rudimentary understanding of Fortran in terms of this model. The remaining chapters are intended to give a deeper understanding of the finer points of Fortran, so that the language can be used effectively with any particular system that is available.

1.1.1 Algorithms

Computers, including our idealized version, are machines that execute tasks on request, according to the way in which those tasks are described. The word *algorithm* has come into wide use during the past century to refer to any precise description of a task, but especially for a task that some computer is to perform. Our first objective in explaining the ideal computer is to discuss in some detail what algorithms are and how they are represented.

An algorithm may be defined as a list of instructions for carrying out some process step by step. Almost any complex process, such as the way a baker bakes a cake, the way a pharmacist fills a prescription, or the way a professional indexer prepares the subject index for a book, can be analyzed and subdivided into simpler subtasks and ultimately into a sequence of primitive steps.

The amount of detail needed for describing a task will depend strongly on what is assumed about the skill and competence of the person who is to use that description for carrying out the task. A more experienced baker, pharmacist, or indexer should need only a relatively short list of instructions, while a novice might use a longer list of simpler instructions resulting from a more detailed subdivision of the task. The size (degree of detail) of each step will depend on what constitutes a *primitive* step from the point of view of the executor of the algorithm. An algorithm should consist of steps of the proper size so that the person who uses the algorithm can comprehend each step *as a unit* during execution of the task.

Computer algorithms are subdivided according to this same principle. The computational task described by the algorithm is broken down into instructions, each of which is primitive in the sense that the computer can "understand" it as a unit. (Nothing mysterious or supernatural is implied by the statement that a computer "understands" instructions. This term merely indicates that some mechanism exists whereby a particular instruction step, given to the computer as part of an algorithm, results in the carrying out of appropriate actions by the computer.) In this book, we assume that the primitive instructions that can be understood by the ideal computer are exactly the statements of the Fortran programming language.

For example, here is a typical statement that might form part of an algorithm expressed in Fortran:

```
AVG = (X + Y) / 2.0
```

This statement is taken from a program whose purpose is to calculate the average, *Avg,* of a given pair of numbers *X* and *Y*. Such a statement represents a primitive step of the algorithm, expressed as a Fortran *assignment statement.* This is one of the statement forms of the Fortran language, and it specifies an *expression,* in this case

```
(X + Y) / 2.0
```

whose value is to be computed and *assigned* as the value of a designated variable such as *Avg.*

1.1.2   Information Storage and Information Processing

The most important characteristic of a computer, including our idealized computer model, is the ability to *store* and to *process* information. The primitive operations that are to be performed on an item of information will affect the way in which it must be stored in the computer. The ideal computer can store and process two principal forms of information: *numeric* information and *character* (textual, or verbal) information. Since these two kinds of information must be processed differently, they are also stored differently. The unit of numeric information is a single number, and the primitive operations that are performed on numeric information are operations of arithmetic. Verbal information, on the other hand, can be stored and manipulated in units as small as a single character (letter, digit, or punctuation symbol), and arithmetic operations are not appropriate for manipulating it.

The overview of Fortran presented in this chapter covers only the processing of numeric information. Character processing is no less interesting than the manipulation of numbers, but the traditional tasks for which Fortran programs have been designed in the past were principally numerical calculations, which used textual information only for such purposes as making printed numerical results more readable. It is likely that future uses of Fortran will more strongly emphasize character processing.

Storage cells

Numbers to be processed by a Fortran program are stored in *cells* of equal size (see Fig. 1.1). A cell may be visualized in our ideal computer as a *box* containing a strip of paper with a number written on it. Each cell to be used in a particular program is given a name; whenever this name appears in the program it refers to the number in the cell. The cell name is inscribed on a *sticker* glued to the top of the box. Each box has a *lid,* which is removed when the number stored in the cell is to be changed. Each box also has a *window* in the side, so that the present value of the number in the cell can be determined without removing the lid from the box.

The cells of an actual computer of course bear no physical resemblance to the windowed boxes described here. Cells in a real computer are assemblages of microelectronic devices that operate at extremely high speeds. In our model we are not trying to imitate these devices in precise detail. Our aim is to present a *conceptual* model that has the essential attributes of actual computer cells, but is easier to visualize. It is easy to understand the operation of a model in which each cell is a box with sticker, lid, and window. Thus we can avoid becoming distracted by questions relating to the microelectronics of the actual computer and its behavior as an electronic system.

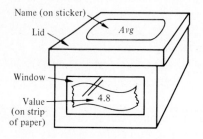

Name (on sticker)

Lid

Avg

Window

Value (on strip of paper)

4.8

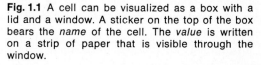

Fig. 1.1 A cell can be visualized as a box with a lid and a window. A sticker on the top of the box bears the *name* of the cell. The *value* is written on a strip of paper that is visible through the window.

1.1.3 Variables and Constants

A name used to identify a cell is a *variable*. This name remains fixed throughout the execution of a program, while the contents of the cell may *vary* from time to time. The contents (that is, the number in the cell at any given instant) is the *value* of the variable. Storing a number in the cell *assigns* a value to the variable.

When a new value is assigned to a variable, the old value is lost, and there is no way to retrieve the previous contents of the cell. In the ideal computer, the strip of paper containing the previous contents is removed and destroyed when the lid is removed for inserting the new strip of paper.

It is important to note the difference between what happens when a number is stored in a cell, and what happens when a number is retrieved from a cell for use in a calculation. When a number is stored, the *lid* of the box is removed and the old value is destroyed. By contrast, the number stored in a cell may be viewed through the *window* of the box when its value is needed; the lid remains firmly in place and the number inside remains unchanged. A number can be retrieved as many times as necessary from the cell where it has been stored, without being destroyed. The contents of a cell does not change until a new number is stored there. When a new number is stored, however, the old number is lost and the contents of the cell is changed. This operation is similar to that of an audio tape recorder. A signal that has been recorded on the tape remains there and can be played back repeatedly without being destroyed. The signal is lost only when a new signal is recorded. A cell in the computer can be compared to a portion of the tape: Only the *latest* signal recorded there can be retrieved at any specified time.

Example   Let us consider the Fortran statement

```
AVG = (X + Y) / 2.0
```

This statement uses three variables, *Avg, X,* and *Y.* Execution of the statement therefore involves three cells, which we visualize as three windowed boxes (Fig. 1.2). Stickers bearing these variables as names have been pasted on the three boxes, so that each name remains fixed throughout the execution process. Also, specific numerical values have been written on slips of paper and inserted in the boxes named X and $Y.$ Execution of the statement consists of retrieving the values of the variables X and $Y,$ using the values so obtained to compute the value of the expression

```
(X + Y) / 2.0
```

and assigning this computed value as the value of *Avg:* The value is written on a strip of paper and inserted in the box so named.

Note that the expression

```
(X + Y) / 2.0
```

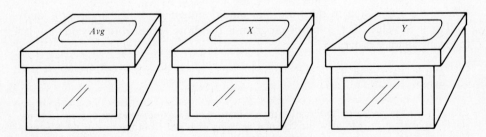

Fig. 1.2 Windowed boxes representing cells for variables.

contains some other symbols besides the variables X and Y. These include the *constant* 2.0, as well as a plus sign, parentheses, etc. A constant is like a variable,† in that a cell inside the computer is allocated for storing its value. However, the value of a constant is not allowed to change; a constant is a symbol that always represents the same specific numerical value. The value of a constant is obvious from the way the constant is written in the program, and the value is not changed after the name is affixed to the cell. It is as if the lid of the box corresponding to a constant were sealed and could never be opened (Fig. 1.3).

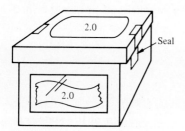

Fig. 1.3 Sealed box for constant.

1.1.4 Data and Results

We have seen that a Fortran statement called an *assignment statement* specifies an expression (involving variables and constants) whose value is to be computed and then assigned to a designated variable. It is possible to combine several assignment statements into a program, for example,

```
X = 4.7
Y = 4.9
AVG = (X + Y) / 2.0
END
```

Except for the END statement, whose role we shall discuss later, all the statements of this program are assignment statements. The expressions on the right-hand sides of the first two assignment statements are especially simple in form: Each consists merely of a single constant. Each of these first two statements assigns a value to the variable on the left, so that these values can be used for evaluation of the expression in the third assignment statement, which involves X and Y. The final value of Avg in this program is therefore identical to its value in the following simpler program:

```
AVG = (4.7 + 4.9) / 2.0
END
```

† This is not the only way to visualize the evaluation of an expression that contains a constant. An alternative is to view the constant as being obtained from the text of the Fortran statement itself, or as being materialized anew each time it is needed, rather than as being preserved in a storage cell.

Such a program is unsatisfactory for at least two reasons. First, these programs change the value of the variable *Avg* in a storage cell inside the computer, but they make no provision for making this value available outside the computer so that a person could use it. Furthermore, it is impractical to develop a program that will calculate the average of only these two constants. More useful would be a program that could compute the average of *any* two numbers, with the specific values of X and Y to be chosen after the program is written.

To permit development of more useful programs, statements are needed for producing *output* of results to an external device, as well as for requesting *input* of data from an external device. Fortran provides READ and PRINT statements for these purposes. Using these statements, we can write the following, more useful, complete program:

```
READ *, X, Y
AVG = (X + Y) / 2.0
PRINT *, X, Y, AVG
END
```

The first statement of this program† specifies that values for X and Y are to be obtained from a card reader or other input device in the external environment. The values so obtained are assigned to the designated variables when the READ statement is executed. For example, if the values obtained externally are 4.7 and 4.9, then execution of the READ statement results in the assignment of these values to X and $Y,$ respectively. The windowed boxes shown in Fig. 1.2 now appear as shown in Fig. 1.4. No value has been assigned to *Avg* up to this point.

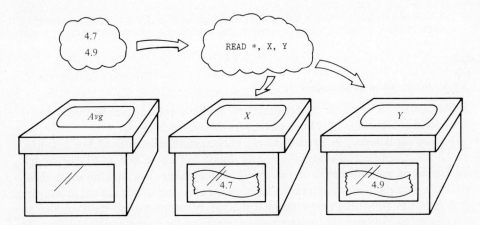

Fig. 1.4 As a result of execution of the READ statement, values have been assigned to the cells named X and Y. No value has been assigned to *Avg*.

† The use of the asterisk * in the READ and PRINT statements is explained in Section 1.2.2.

When the second statement is executed, the expression is evaluated and the value is assigned to *Avg* (see Fig. 1.5). The third statement specifies that the values of *X, Y,* and *Avg* are to be retrieved from the designated cells (without changing their values) and transmitted to a line printer or other output device in the external environment.

Note that the values to be supplied as input data to this program do not appear in any of the statements of the program itself. They are supplied later, at the time when the program is executed by the computer. It is useful to print the input data values along with the results, to give a complete record of the computation process.

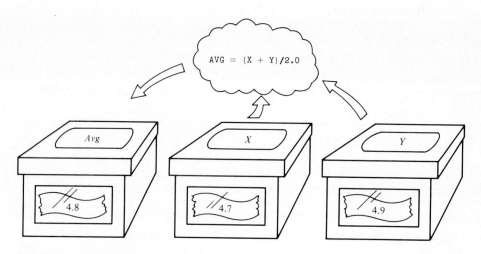

Fig. 1.5 When the assignment is executed, the values of *X* and *Y* are used to determine the value of the expression, and this value is assigned to *Avg*. Using the values of *X* and *Y* does not destroy those values.

1.1.5   Information in Storage

Before going on, we need to consider how numeric information is stored in the cells of an actual computer. First we must raise some questions.

How big is a cell, in terms of its capacity to store information? For example, can it hold an integer having a thousand digits? We know that hand calculators, adding machines, and similar devices work with numbers having a limited number of digits. Are the numbers stored in a cell of the ideal computer limited to integers and numbers with only a few decimal places? What about real numbers like *pi* (3.14159265358979 . . .), or the result of dividing 1 by 3 (that is, 0.333333 . . .)? Can such numbers, which in principle have an infinite number of digits, be stored in a cell?

In the ideal computer, there is no practical limitation on the size of the cells. Integers or real numbers of any size (with any number of digits) may be stored in them. No matter how long the number, we assume that it could still be stuffed into one of the ideal computer's cells.

However, when we use a Fortran program on an *actual* computer, we find that its cells each have a specific fixed capacity. The storage cell capacity is an important design feature of each particular actual computer. Cell capacity can be roughly expressed in decimal digits; however, the internal structure of most computers is *binary* rather than decimal. This means that numbers are represented internally in powers of two rather than ten. As a result, the capacity is not a whole number of decimal digits. For example, many computers provide 24 significant binary digits, or slightly more than 7 significant decimal digits, of precision. Others provide approximately 8, 9, 12, or even 15 significant decimal digits of precision in a single cell. It is because of these differences in cell capacity among various actual machines that we have bypassed this difficult issue and assumed that our ideal model computer has unlimited cell capacity.

Besides the differences among various actual machines, another factor involving cell capacity introduces differences between the results from an ideal calculation and those from a calculation performed on any actual computer. This problem arises because certain real numbers, such as the value of pi or of the quotient ⅓, have an "infinite" number of decimal digits that will never fit into a storage cell in any actual machine.

Abstract algorithms and programs are generally developed without taking cell capacity limitations into account. Nevertheless, the user of an actual computer must remember that the numerical values stored in actual cells are not necessarily the ideal or exact values that would be present in the ideal computer, and that this difference from the ideal will vary from one actual computer to another.

It is not the intent of this book to explore fully all of the consequences of limited cell capacity: That subject is treated at length in textbooks on numerical analysis. Rather, we wish to indicate why results from the same abstract algorithm or Fortran program may be different on various actual computers. The same algorithm expressed in Fortran on different actual computers may require minor changes in the Fortran language statements to account for differences in cell size.

Integer numbers and real numbers

In Fortran, a variable consists of up to six characters. The first character must be a letter, and the remaining characters (if any) may be letters or digits. A constant is a string of digits, possibly including a decimal point.

There are two fundamental numeric *types* in Fortran. *Integer* variables and integer constants are distinguished from *real* variables and real constants, and their values are stored differently in the cells of an actual computer.

The value of an integer variable or constant must be a positive or negative integer (whole number). Such values are especially useful for counting how many times a calculation is repeated, or for indicating a particular item in a sequence of several items. Real variables and constants need not have whole number values, and are used in calculations that may involve decimal fractions.

It is easy to tell by looking at a Fortran constant or variable whether its type is integer or real. A real constant must be written with a decimal point; an integer constant must not include a decimal point. By convention, the first character of an integer variable is one of the letters I, J, K, L, M, or N. A real variable begins with a letter *other* than these. (There are ways, which we shall not consider at this point, to change this convention.)

Examples   Integer variables:

```
IN      MI      JA      L
MAX     I3BOX2  ISAX    KOUNT
```

Integer constants:

```
0    1    356    2
123456789
```

Real variables:

```
X        R3       XY       YDEV
ALONGS   ABCDEF   SUPERC   COUNT
```

Real constants:

```
0.0    1.0    14.37    .00547
3.14159265358979
```

1.1.6   Exercises

1. Each of the following partial problem descriptions might be used as the basis for an algorithmic description of a calculation. For example, the sentence, "The average of two numbers is found by adding them together and dividing the sum by two," can be expanded and analyzed to obtain the following algorithm:

   Read two numbers, X and Y.
   Compute Avg by adding X to Y and dividing the sum by two.
   Print the values of X, Y, and Avg.
   Stop.

Expand and analyze each of the following, to produce an algorithm for each. In each case, tell which variables and constants are referred to, and how many storage cells would be needed for execution of the algorithm.

a) The area of a rectangle is determined by multiplying its length by its width.
b) The area of a triangle is one-half the product of its base and its altitude.
c) The middle note in a major triad is four semitones above the root.
d) To find the average of three numbers, add them all together and then divide by three.

2. Find out the capacity of the cells of the computer that you will be using during your study of the Fortran language. For example, how many decimal digits of precision can be included in the contents of a cell representing the constant pi (3.14159265358979 . . .)?

1.2   FORTRAN LANGUAGE AND FORTRAN PROCESSORS

Language

Fortran is a language that was developed for the purpose of making the description of algorithms easy and precise. An algorithm expressed in Fortran or a similar language is a computer program, and a computer can execute it. Fortran programs are composed of *statements*. We have seen how the steps of an algorithm may be expressed with Fortran assignment statements, READ statements, PRINT statements, and END statements. The Fortran programming language is made up of a small group of statement types. In forming these statements, one complies with a set of rules that are analogous to the grammatical and syntactical rules of a "natural language" such as English.

The Fortran language has evolved to its present form largely as a result of experience gained by many users of earlier versions on various computers. A group of closely related dialects, all of which were loosely called Fortran IV, were in extremely wide use from the early 1960s until the development of Fortran 77. This version was defined in 1977 by technical committee X3J3 of the American National Standards Institute, and was standardized as ANS X3.9-1978.

Processors

The primitive steps acceptable to our ideal model computer are Fortran statements. Before these can be executed by an actual computer, they must be translated into *machine code,* consisting of more primitive steps that can be directly processed by the simple devices that compose the actual machine. A user does not need to know any of the details of this translation process or of the machine code, but it is useful to know that some kind of conversion is performed. For each computer that will accept Fortran programs, a system of large supporting programs has been made available to control the translation of the Fortran statements into machine code and the execution of the translated code. This system of programs is collectively known as a *processor*.

The user furnishes a Fortran program, along with the required data, to the processor. If all goes well, the desired results are produced and returned to the user. However, there are two distinct points at which difficulty may appear. During the translation of the Fortran statements to machine code, the processor may detect program statements that fail to conform to Fortran language rules. If no such errors are detected, the processor will proceed to execute the machine code, and during execution other errors may become evident. These may be errors in program structure or control logic, or they may be caused by faulty preparation of data for the program.

It may be necessary to make successive corrections to the program and data until satisfactory results are produced. This process is called *debugging*. Statements that do not conform to the Fortran language rules are reported to the user at the conclusion of the translation phase. These errors, along with gross errors in data preparation, are relatively easy to detect and repair. Errors in program structure or control logic usually result from insufficient care during the design of an algorithm, and are often difficult to detect after the program statements have been written.

Many beginners find themselves looking for help when debugging their programs. The testing or debugging of a program is not unlike the checking of any other system or device. There is no substitute for careful work, the self-discipline that leads to complete analysis of a problem, and the faithful use of check lists. In short, good work habits are as necessary here as in any other endeavor.

1.2.1   Preparing the Program for Execution

As we have seen, the first step in solving a problem with the aid of a computer is to devise a method of solution, or *algorithm*. Next, the solution process is subdivided into primitive steps. The algorithm is then translated into a *program,* written in a language (such as Fortran) that the computer is prepared to accept. Before the computer can begin to process and execute the Fortran statements, however, a further step must be taken. The program must be prepared in a form that the computer can read.

Some Fortran systems permit the user to type the statements on a keyboard and display terminal connected directly to the computer. Other systems require that the program be prepared in advance, in the form of a deck of punched cards. In the remainder of this section we shall describe the preparation of a computer program as a sequence of *lines,* which may be either entered directly on a terminal or prepared in advance on punched cards.

Fortran statements (including the READ statements, PRINT statements, assignment statements, and END statements in the foregoing examples) are composed from characters in the Fortran character set. These are the 26 uppercase (capital) letters, the digits 0 through 9, the blank (space), and the 12 special characters

$$+ - * / . , ( ) = ' \$:$$

The special characters have a number of uses, which we shall encounter as we proceed. The asterisk * is used to indicate multiplication, and the slash / indicates division. It is extremely important to note the distinction between similar characters, such as the digit 0 (zero) and the letter O (oh), or the digit 1 and the letter I.

The processor includes a program that produces machine code corresponding to the Fortran statements. The Fortran statements are the input data that is read by this translation program. Therefore, the arrangement of the statements on the lines must conform to the expectations of the processor.

The format for lines containing Fortran statements is illustrated in Fig. 1.6. Typical Fortran statement lines are shown in Fig. 1.7.

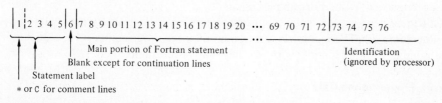

Fig. 1.6 Arrangement of Fortran statement lines.

FORTRAN Program Worksheet

1	2 3 4 5	6	7 8 9 10 11 12 13 14 15 16 17 18 19 20 21 22 23 24 25 26 27 28 29 30 31 32 33 34 35
			R E A D * , X , Y
			A V G = (X + Y) / 2 . 0
			P R I N T * , X , Y , A V G
			E N D

Fig. 1.7 A Fortran program may be written out on a worksheet, which can be checked before the program lines are finally generated in the proper form for transmission to the computer.

Lines that contain comments (interspersed among the program statements as an aid to the programmer, but otherwise ignored by the processor) must have an asterisk in column 1. (The letter C in column 1 is also accepted as an alternative indication of a comment.) Comment lines may also use lowercase letters or other characters that are not included in the Fortran character set.

The first six columns of a statement line are usually blank. Statements that are *labeled* (a concept that we shall discuss later) have the label in columns 1 to 5. Column 6 is used only when a statement is so long that it must be continued on more than one line. In this case, some character other than blank or zero is inserted in column 6 to indicate that the remaining columns contain a continuation of the statement begun on a preceding line.

The Fortran statement itself appears in columns 7 to 72. Except within a character constant (see Section 5.1.2), blank columns in a Fortran statement line have no meaning and may be used freely to improve the appearance of the program. For example, in this text we use extra blanks on each side of an operator such as + or *, and we indent some lines of the program to make its structure more evident. These extra blanks can make the program easier to understand, but they are ignored by the Fortran processor.

The processor also ignores any characters on a Fortran statement line beyond column 72. These columns may be used by the programmer for a sequential line number or other identification, or they may be left blank.

1.2.2   Preparing the Data

We have noted that the Fortran statements are read by the processor, and that they must conform to the column arrangement illustrated in Figs. 1.6 and 1.7. The data, on the other hand, is read by the user's program during execution, and it must be arranged according to the requirements of the READ statements in the program.

List directed input

For programs that process data in complicated ways, it is often essential that the *format* of the input and output be arranged according to specifications established by the programmer. Fortran data formats can be extremely flexible, but they can also be quite complicated. However, it is neither necessary nor desirable to learn all about ways of controlling this flexibility, before gaining some experience as a user of the Fortran language.

Fortran provides a simple alternative, namely, *list directed* input and output, whose format is controlled by the data and by the list of items to be read or printed. List directed input is specified in a READ or PRINT statement by an asterisk immediately following the initial keyword READ or PRINT (as illustrated in Fig. 1.7).

The data values for list directed input are arranged in "free format" on input data lines, and are separated by one or more consecutive blanks. Blank columns must not be embedded within a single data value. Values may appear anywhere in the data line.

Execution of a READ statement assigns data values in *sequence* to the variables in the input list. Thus, the sequence of data values must correspond exactly to the sequence of variables in the list. Several data values may be included in a single line; it is not necessary to fill the lines. However, a new line must be used to correspond to the beginning of each new READ statement list.

Figure 1.8 illustrates a typical input line that might be used with the input list of the Fortran program illustrated in Fig. 1.7. The data values on this input line are to be read by the statement

```
READ *, X, Y
```

The first number on the line is the value for X, and the second is the value for Y.

1	2	3	4	5	6	7	8	9	10	11	12	13	14	15
4	.	7							4	.	9			

Fig. 1.8 A typical input line that might be used to provide data for the program shown in Fig. 1.7.

1.2.3 Job Control Instructions: The Operating System

Most computers that execute Fortran programs operate under the control of a sophisticated program known as the *operating system,* which processes the jobs more efficiently than would be possible if a human operator handled each job individually. Typically, the user submits (delivers or transmits) to the computer center a *job file* (a sequence of lines prepared on a terminal) or a *job deck* (a self-contained package of cards). This consists of the Fortran statement lines and the data lines, plus some *job control instructions* to be executed by the operating system. These job control instructions contain all the necessary specifications to permit the job to be processed with a minimum of human intervention.

Although all Fortran processors use a common, standard line format for the statements of the Fortran program itself, the situation with regard to the job control instructions is not so well standardized. Two different installations, even if they have exactly the same computing equipment, may use different conventions for specifying some of the parameters that appear in the job control instructions. Therefore, before submitting a job to any computing center for the first time, the user should obtain the necessary specifications for preparing job control information to be used at that installation.

Although it is impossible for us to include detailed job control specifications here that will be generally applicable, we can indicate the kinds of information that may be required in job control instructions for a typical Fortran job. These include:

1. The programmer's name, to be used in returning the printed results to the originator;

2. An account number, assigned by the "customer" or by the computing center for allocating costs of the computing resources used (in a college or university, the customer is typically an individual instructor or student);

3. Resource limits, including estimates of the job's maximum execution time and maximum amount of output (for example, number of printed output lines expected);

4. Specification of the location of external files to be used by the job (for example, card reader, line printer, tape or disc files)—location of lines containing the Fortran program to be compiled, loaded, and executed; location of input data to be read by the program during execution; location to which the results of the computation are to be sent;

5. Special information, if needed, to identify the end of the Fortran program, the end of the data, and the end of the entire job.

The operating system may check the account number against an approved list and reject the job if it is unauthorized. It may use the resource limits in deciding the sequence in which jobs are to be run; for example, it may give priority to jobs that will be completed in a matter of seconds, over jobs that are expected to occupy a major portion of the computer's resources for several minutes. It also uses the resource limits to protect the user from unexpected charges, such as those that would result from a program error that could cause the limits to be exceeded.

1.2.4 Exercises

1. Prepare the following program and data for the computer, arranging the data as indicated in Fig. 1.8. Be extremely careful to copy all punctuation symbols exactly as they are shown. Remember that each program statement begins in column 7.

```
READ *, X, Y
AVG = (X + Y) / 2.0
PRINT *, X, Y, AVG
END
```

Data:

4.7   4.9

Find out what job control instructions are required at your computing center, and add them to make a complete job deck or file. Submit the job to your computer. If the computer does not print the results

4.7   4.9   4.8

you have probably made an error in preparing your program or data. Find and correct the errors, if any, and run the job again until the correct results are obtained.

2. Prepare a program based on one of the algorithms you developed for Exercise 1 of Section 1.1.6. Run the program on the computer, with data of your own choosing or data supplied by your instructor. Rerun the job, if necessary, until the correct answers are obtained. (Save the finished program for Exercise 3 of Section 1.3.4.)

1.3   PROGRAMMING WITH FORTRAN

1.3.1   Time Sequence of Program Execution

When there are two or more actions to be performed, the *time sequence* in which they are performed may or may not be important. When a customer makes two deposits at a bank, either deposit may be made first; but if there is a deposit and a withdrawal, it is often important that the deposit be made first. The instruction, "Put on your shoes and stockings," should certainly not be executed in the sequence that the words might imply. When a cook bakes a cake, the dry ingredients can be combined in any sequence, but the liquids are added later.

Several different techniques can be used to specify the time sequence for carrying out a group of instructions. We can use words that imply time relationships: *then, next, afterward, later*—for instance, "Put on your shoes *after* you put on your stockings." Or we can number the steps: "(1) Put on your stockings. (2) Put on your shoes." Or we can make a *flowchart* and use arrows to specify the sequence (Fig. 1.9).

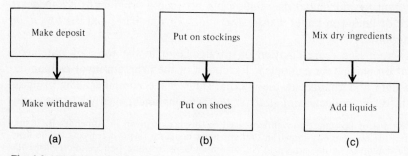

Fig. 1.9 Using flowcharts to specify the sequence of steps.

Flowcharts

Usually we arrange the boxes of a flowchart vertically, with arrows leading from each box to the one just below it; however, the arrows guarantee that there would be no confusion if we used a horizontal arrangement, as in Fig. 1.10, or even an arrangement with the arrows pointing upward or diagonally in some manner. In most cases, we must also indicate the *first* step to be performed, and we must say explicitly when the sequence of steps has been completed. Thus a "complete" flowchart for the process "Put on your shoes and stockings" might be that shown in Fig. 1.11. Note that we use certain conventions in drawing flowcharts: For example, the boxes indicating actions to be performed are enclosed in rectangles, while an oval shape is used for the Start and Stop boxes. Although such conventions are somewhat arbitrary, they should be followed consistently because they emphasize certain important aspects of the process.†

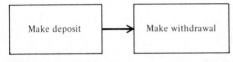

▲

Fig. 1.10 The use of flowchart arrows guarantees that the sequence will be clearly understood, even if the boxes are not arranged vertically in order.

▶

Fig. 1.11 Complete flowchart, including Start and Stop boxes.

1.3.2 Sequences of Program Statements

It is important to understand the relationship between a program as it *appears* in a sequence of lines (on paper, cards, a terminal, or the like), and the *execution* of the program.

A program is a representation of an algorithm in the form of statements written out on paper (for example). Execution of the program involves manipulations of data and changes in the internal state of the computer. The program itself—that is, the collection of statements—remains unchanged while these ma-

† A complete list of flowchart conventions used in this text is given in Appendix B. It may be noted that the conventions shown in that appendix conform in most respects to the flowchart standard adopted by the American National Standards Institute. See *Standard Flowchart Symbols and Their Use in Information Processing* (*X3.5*), ANSI, New York, 1970.

nipulations take place. Thus we say that the program is *static* (fixed) while the execution is *dynamic*. The statements of the program occupy *space* while the execution occurs in a *time* dimension.

We have seen how a flowchart can define a spatial relationship that represents a time relationship. The arrows on a flowchart clearly indicate the time sequence to be followed. Programming languages such as Fortran do not use arrows to indicate time sequence; instead, the "normal" execution sequence proceeds from top to bottom on the page. The first statement to be executed is assumed to be the one written at the top of the page; thus, no explicit START or BEGIN statement is needed in a program. As we saw in Section 1.1.4, the following program corresponds to the flowchart of Fig. 1.12.

```
READ *, X, Y
AVG = (X + Y) / 2.0
PRINT *, X, Y, AVG
END
```

The first step in the time sequence of execution is the reading of *X* and *Y* values. Then the assignment statement is executed, and finally the values of *X, Y,* and *Avg* are printed. The END statement corresponds to the Stop box in the flowchart.

Closer inspection of the assignment statement reveals an anomaly. Everything else in the calculation proceeds in exactly the same sequence that we follow when we read the program: The statements are executed from top to bottom, and processing within a statement (for example, within the list of variables in the

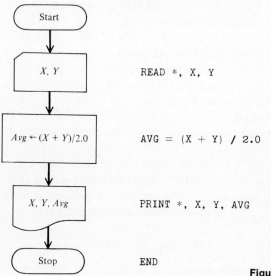

Figure 1.12

READ statement) proceeds from left to right. In the assignment statement, however, the expression on the *right* is evaluated *before* assignment to the variable on the *left* takes place. In flowcharts, and in some programming languages, this less familiar time sequence is made more explicit by the use of a left-pointing arrow instead of an equals sign for the assignment operator. Many people would find it less confusing if the assignment statement were written as

```
AVG ← (X + Y) / 2.0
```

The main reason for not using this symbol as the Fortran assignment operator is historical: The arrow was not available on most of the keypunches and other early input devices used to prepare programs for computers. However, we may mentally replace the equals sign by a left-pointing arrow in order to better understand the operation of an assignment statement.

1.3.3   Repeating the Steps of a Calculation

We have pointed out that a program to print the average of *any* two numbers can be prepared once for all, and then used on demand with data to be supplied at the time of execution. Such a program is much more useful than a program that can print only the average of a specific pair of numbers, decided on in advance and included in the program in the form of constants. Although this "improved" program is of some value to the novice programmer as an exercise in the preparation of program statements, data, and control instructions, its practical usefulness may still be questioned. Anyone who really wants to know the average of a pair of numbers would be unlikely to write (or find) this program, prepare data for it, and run it on the computer to obtain the average. There are much more convenient ways of getting the answer to such a simple problem.

The picture changes somewhat if there are *many* pairs of data values to be averaged. The user could submit the program to a computer several times, each time changing the data values, and so obtain the needed results. This still involves a fair amount of duplication of effort. The repeated handling of the program is laborious, and the processor must translate the program into exactly the same machine code each time it is submitted. Adding statements that cause some or all of the steps of the calculation to be *repeated* can eliminate all this redundant effort.

In the simplest case, the object is to repeat the entire calculation for a predetermined number of data values. For example, imagine that ten pairs of readings have been obtained from an instrument, and each pair of readings is to be averaged. How can such a computation be specified as a Fortran program?

Labeled statements

At this point we must digress to describe the labeling of statements, which is essential for repeating a group of Fortran program steps. A labeled statement simply consists of an ordinary statement of any valid form, with a number on the left. This number may have up to 5 digits, and is entered in columns 1 to 5 of the program statement line (see Fig. 1.6). If there are fewer than 5 digits, it is not necessary to begin in column 1.

The DO *statement*

A label (chosen arbitrarily) is associated with each group of statements in a Fortran program that are to be repeated. This label is used in a control statement that precedes the group, and the same label is placed at the left on a statement that terminates the group. The control statement is a DO statement, and the terminal statement is a CONTINUE statement (see also Section 4.3, concerning the use of other terminal statements).

```
       DO  Label, LOOP = 1, Limit
            group of statements
            to be repeated
 Label     CONTINUE
```

The keyword DO in Fortran is invariably associated with the idea of repetition (of a group of statements). The label that follows the keyword DO must match the identifying label of the terminal statement. All statements following the DO statement, up to and including the terminal statement (identified by the matching label), are to be repeated.

The *Limit* is an expression whose value indicates the number of times the group of statements is to be executed. Often, it is simply an integer constant, such as 10. Thus, if there are ten pairs of data values to be averaged, the following program can be written (see also the flowchart shown in Fig. 1.13).

```
 * Example 1.  Program to average ten pairs of data values.
       DO 7, LOOP = 1, 10
          READ *, X, Y
          AVG = (X + Y) / 2.0
          PRINT *, X, Y, AVG
 7        CONTINUE
       END
```

The group of statements (including the terminal statement), along with the initial DO statement, is called a loop, or DO loop. In the flowchart, the upward arrow at the right completes a flow loop. Note that we have used a hexagonal box to represent the DO statement, and a small circle at the lowest point of the loop to represent the terminal label. The flow line that emerges from the right side of the hexagon is to be followed so long as the loop is to be repeated. When the limit is reached, the line from the bottom of the hexagon is taken. This line leads to the flowchart box that corresponds to the program statement just beyond the terminal

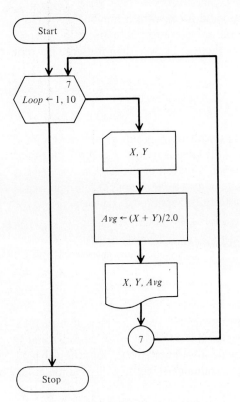

Fig. 1.13 Flowchart for the program in Example 1.

statement of the loop (the Stop circle, corresponding to the END statement, in this example).

Here are some more programs with DO loops.

```
* Example 2.  Areas of eight rectangles.
      DO 43, LOOP = 1, 8
         READ *, XLEN, WIDTH
         AREA = XLEN * WIDTH
         PRINT *, XLEN, WIDTH, AREA
   43    CONTINUE
      END
```

```
* Example 3.  Areas of five triangles.
      DO 176, LOOP = 1, 5
         READ *, BASE, ALT
         AREA = BASE * ALT / 2.0
         PRINT *, BASE, ALT, AREA
  176    CONTINUE
      END
```

```
* Example 4.  Squares and cubes of 20 integers.
      DO 5, LOOP = 1, 20
         READ *, I
         ISQ = I * I
         KUBE = ISQ * I * I
         PRINT *, I, ISQ, KUBE
   5     CONTINUE
      END
```

Examples 2 and 3 are based on some of the exercises from Section 1.1.6. The appropriate number of data cases would need to be prepared for each of these examples.

The terminal statement of a DO loop marks the first instance we have seen where the strict top-to-bottom sequence of execution of statements is not followed. When this terminal statement is reached, the next instruction to be executed is *not* the one following the terminal statement. Instead, the execution sequence returns to the loop control phase of the DO statement at the *top* of the loop: This includes keeping track of the number of times the statements have been repeated.

The hexagonal box is the first example we have seen of a box with more than one line emanating from it. Because more than one line leaves the flowchart box, a decision must be made as to which line to follow. This decision depends on whether or not the loop count limit has been reached. Correspondingly, in the program the choice of which statement is to be executed (following the loop control phase of the DO statement) depends on whether or not further repetition is required. If the statements have not yet been repeated the specified number of times, the execution sequence again continues with the first statement following the DO statement. But if the loop count limit has been reached, repetition ceases and execution continues with the statement immediately following the terminal statement of the loop.

The program examples illustrate some points relating to program readability. As noted in Section 1.2.1, a line with an asterisk at the extreme left is not a statement line, but a comment line. Comments should be used freely in the static program—for example, as explanations of the statements that follow. But they are ignored by the processor and do not become part of the dynamic process of program execution.

Note that we have *indented* all the statements to be repeated. This practice enables anyone to see at a glance which statements are part of the group.

Example 5: Computing a sum   How would you write a Fortran program to evaluate the *sum* or *total* of several input values? If there were two values, you might write

```
READ *, FIRST, SECOND
TOTAL = FIRST + SECOND
PRINT *, TOTAL
```

and if there were three values, you might write

```
READ *, FIRST, SECOND, THIRD
TOTAL = FIRST + SECOND + THIRD
PRINT *, TOTAL
```

But if there were 100 values, you might wish to find a general method.

A generalization, which can be adapted to Fortran, follows from a familiar style that one uses with ordinary adding machines or pocket calculators. The data items are entered *one at a time* and added onto a cumulative total. But recall which button must be pushed first. The first step is *not* to enter the first data value, but to push the *clear* button, which resets the total to zero. After this has been done, the process of entering each data value (including the first one) can be described as a repetitive group of steps.

A program to compute a sum in this way begins with a statement setting the *Total* to zero. This may be followed by a *loop* in which data values are read and added to the *Total*. Thus at any time (even before the first data value has been added on), the value of *Total* will be the sum of the data values read *so far*. (See also the flowchart in Fig. 1.14.) This summing technique should be studied carefully, until all the details of its operation are well understood.

```
* Example 5 (see Fig. 1.14).
* Program to read 100 data values, and to compute and print
* the current total after each data value is read.
      TOTAL = 0.0
      DO 7, LOOP = 1, 100
        READ *, DATUM
        TOTAL = TOTAL + DATUM
        PRINT *, DATUM, TOTAL
7       CONTINUE
      END
```

The statement

```
TOTAL = TOTAL + DATUM
```

should be considered with special care. Execution of this statement illustrates an important point about the sequence of execution *within* an assignment statement. Recall that execution of an assignment statement begins with evaluation of the expression on the right; this phase is *completed* before assignment of a new value to the variable on the left takes place. Therefore, there is no conflict in the use of the same variable, *Total,* on both sides of the assignment operator. The values of the variables *Total* and *Datum* will be retrieved (copied) from the cells in which they are stored, without changing those values; then they will be added together.

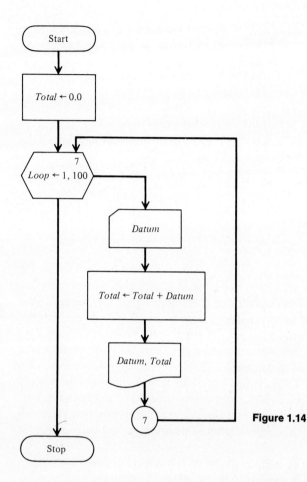

Figure 1.14

Only after the expression value has been calculated will the assignment of a new value to *Total* take place, thus changing the contents of that cell. The name *Total* on the right therefore refers to the *old* value of the variable, whereas the same name on the left refers to the *new* value. The left-pointing arrow that we use in flowcharts helps to serve as a reminder of this sequence of events.

1.3.4 Exercises

1. Modify the program in Example 5 to total eight values. Tell the value of *Total* at each repetition of the block.

   Data:

18.1	15.1	11.4	35.6	33.2	15.0	33.1	35.3

2. Prepare, and run on a computer, the program of Example 1 to average ten pairs of data values (see also the flowchart in Fig. 1.13). Use the following data values:

4.7	4.9	88.0	76.4
159.9	54.7	161.1	154.5
2.87	3.19	3170.0	3476.3
44.6	49.2	1940.4	1950.5
56.3	58.5	3.0	4.0

Be sure to check your results, to see that your program and your data have been prepared correctly.

3. Recall the program that you prepared for Exercise 2 of Section 1.2.4. Use the statements of that program in a new program that will repeat them four times. Prepare four sets of data. Run the program on the computer and check your results.

1.4 REFINEMENT

In Section 1.1, we defined an algorithm as "a list of instructions for carrying out some process step by step." Development of a computer program requires that some *process* be analyzed and subdivided into *steps* so small (primitive) that the computer can "understand" them and execute them directly.

The program examples that we considered first contained at most a half dozen statements. Once we had understood a simple repertory of statements (assignment, READ, PRINT, and END), it was not difficult to decompose the process into the program steps as required. But a more complicated process becomes correspondingly more difficult to analyze, and the corresponding program steps become more numerous so that their interrelationships are more difficult to keep in mind all at once.

A key to the management of complexity, when it begins to appear overwhelming, has long been known: It is expressed in the adage "Divide and conquer." If we can subdivide a task into a few large and relatively independent chunks, and then analyze each of the chunks without thinking too much about any of the others, we may be able to keep the overall problem organization in mind surprisingly well. The modern term for this "divide-and-conquer" approach is *refinement*—algorithm refinement, problem refinement, or program refinement, for example.

We can apply this principle to the loop examples of Section 1.3.3. A slightly modified version of Example 5 of that section will be used here to illustrate some further points concerning refinement.

Suppose we are given a set of data values to be averaged. The number of data values is not specified in the program, however, but instead is included with the input, on a separate line ahead of the values that are to be averaged. Thus we have the overall problem statement,

"Average some data values"

along with information on how to find out how many values there are. This problem statement is to be refined until primitive steps, each corresponding to a single Fortran statement, are obtained. But the problem statement does not directly suggest what these primitive steps might be. Therefore, we attempt a "divide-and-conquer" approach.

A search for an intermediate level of subdivision leads us to recall the process of computing an average. We must add the data values together and then divide the total by the number of values. Thus, the problem statement can be refined into three phases:

1. Find out how many data values there are.

2. Add all the data values together.

3. Divide the total by the number of values.

The first of these phases appears to consist of a single irreducible step:

1a. Read the *Number* of data items to be averaged.

The second phase is similar to the problem of Example 5 of Section 1.3.3. It can be refined into two steps:

2a. Set a *Total* to zero.

2b. Read each data item (*Datum*) and add it on to the *Total*.

In the third phase, we have forgotten to include an output step:

3a. Divide the *Total* by the *Number* of values, to find the the average (*Avg*).

3b. Print *Avg* (as well as *Number* and *Total*).

3c. Stop.

Except for Step 2b, each step now corresponds to a single Fortran statement. Guidelines for further refinement of Step 2b are found in Example 5 of Section 1.3.3. It is important to note that the overall problem can be understood at each successive level of refinement, even before the next refinement is achieved. The original one-line problem statement makes good sense, as does the first subdivision into three phases or subproblems. The complete outline as it has been developed to this point also makes sense, even before we decide how to decompose Step 2b into primitive steps or program statements:

Average some data values.

1. Find out how many data values there are.

1a. Read the *Number* of data items to be averaged.

2. Add all the data values together.

2a. Set a *Total* to zero.

2b. Read each data item (*Datum*) and add it on to the *Total*.

3. Calculate the average and print it.

   3a. Divide the *Total* by the *Number* of values, to find the average (*Avg*).

   3b. Print *Avg* (as well as *Number* and *Total*).

   3c. Stop.

1.4.1 Program Structures

The DO loop structure discussed in Section 1.3.3 is important because it permits us to comprehend the organization of a program in less detail than the individual statement level.

To illustrate this, we may continue the refinement of step 2b to the individual statement level:

2b. Perform the following steps the specified *Number* of times:
   i) Read the next *Datum*.
   ii) Add the *Datum* to the *Total*.

Refinement of a loop structure involves a shift in perspective, from the "collective" action that is to be achieved by the repetitive process *as a whole,* to the action involved in a "typical" *individual* execution of the steps. Conversely, the loop structure permits us to deliberately blur our perception of the individual steps and to concentrate on the repetitive process as a collective action. At this less detailed level of refinement, the problem description can be read (and easily understood) from top to bottom, since the repetitive process is condensed into a single line.

Structured programming

The term "structured programming" has been used widely, and with a variety of meanings, in recent years. The term is generally concerned with *how* computer programs are designed and developed. Some uses refer to the way in which groups of programmers are organized, especially for projects that require the cooperation of several people over many months. It has been found that certain good management practices can result in significant improvements in programmer productivity.

The term structured programming has also been used in relation to the appearance of the program itself and its readability, comprehensibility, or "style." †
A program should be viewed as a piece of creative writing; it should be elegant and aesthetically pleasing, somewhat like an "elegant" paragraph of prose, a sonnet or haiku, or a good mathematical proof. A program must be readable: One should be able to deduce the intent of the program fairly easily from the

† *The Elements of Programming Style,* by Brian W. Kernighan and P. J. Plauger (New York: McGraw-Hill, 1974), contains an excellent discussion of these ideas.

program text. At first it may seem that elegance or readability would have little to do with programmer productivity. But experience shows clearly that these concepts relate to the programmer's comprehension of the programming task. A program with good style, which is clearly understood by the designer, will contain fewer errors initially and will also be easier to understand later on when modifications are needed.

Again, experience has shown that program style is improved when a small number of different kinds of program patterns are used at each intermediate level of the problem refinement. We have seen how the concept of a DO loop as a unit (without undue emphasis on the individual statements within the loop) can be an aid to program comprehension. According to one definition, there are three basic program structures that should be used in this way at intermediate refinement levels: *sequence, repetition,* and *selection.* Selection, which will be discussed in Chapter 3, provides a means for choosing among alternative groups of statements. A sequence is simply a succession of repetition structures, selection structures, and individual statements (in any combination).

Fortran provides another program structure that is also very important with regard to the refinement process. This structure, which is discussed in Chapter 8, permits the decomposition of a complex problem into virtually *independent* segments, whose interactions can be strictly controlled. These independent segments or *subprograms* are called subroutines and functions.

Like literary style, of course, programming style cannot be achieved merely by slavishly following mechanical rules. It is far more important that programmers develop an awareness of the stylistic features of programs they read and of those they write. They should learn to identify program examples that seem unreadable and obscure, and should eventually be able to recognize program "elegance." In a textbook like this one, it is possible only to present some examples and to call attention to some of the tools that can contribute to proper programming style. Use of the tools, and development of good habits based on the examples, must be left to the individual programmer.

PART 2

THE FORTRAN LANGUAGE

CHAPTER 2
EXPRESSIONS AND ASSIGNMENT STATEMENTS

2.1 VARIABLES AND CONSTANTS

The *assignment* statement is one of the two basic kinds of Fortran statement that can be used to store a new value in a cell. (The other is the READ statement.) An assignment statement consists of two parts, separated by an equals sign: a *variable* appears on the left, and an *expression* on the right:

Variable = *Expression*

In Fortran, a variable is associated with a particular storage cell in the computer. Thus the left-hand side of the assignment statement tells which cell is to receive a new value. The computer executes an assignment statement by first determining the *value* of the expression on the right, and then assigning that value to the variable on the left of the equals sign. (The use of the equals sign here is misleading. The left-pointing arrow, which we use in flowcharts, would be much more appropriate, but unfortunately it is not available on the keyboards used for the preparation of many Fortran programs.)

The expression on the right side of an assignment statement may be very uncomplicated; it may consist of just a constant. Here are some examples of assignment statements of this simple form.

Example 1

```
A = 3.172        PI = 3.14159
MANY = 346021    N123 = 456
E = 2.71828      X = 4.5
K = 721          LOVE = 2
I = 721          THETA = 3.14159
```

There are two kinds of constants represented here: integer constants and real constants. An *integer* constant in Fortran is written without a decimal point, and a *real* constant is written with a decimal point. An integer constant is a simple example of an *integer expression,* and a real constant is a simple example of a *real expression.*

Each variable in a program also has a *type* (integer or real). Unless the program contains declarations (see Chapter 7) to override them, the *default implicit* type rules apply. According to these rules, a variable that begins with I, J, K, L, M, or N is an integer variable, and a real variable is one that begins with any other letter. In each of the assignment statements shown in Example 1, the variable on the left has the same type as the expression on the right.

The first step in execution of an assignment statement is *evaluation* of the expression on the right. When this expression is a constant, evaluation is trivial. Execution is completed by assigning the value represented by the constant (on the right) to the variable (on the left).

The next simplest form that an expression may take is illustrated in the following examples.

Example 2

```
X = Y
Y = X
THETA = PI
K = I
LOVE = MANY
HERE = THERE
```

Evaluation of the expression in each of these assignment statements consists of determining the value of a single variable. The contents of the cell designated by that variable is copied and stored in the cell designated by the variable on the left. Note the difference between the first two assignment statements in Example 2. In the first, the value of the variable Y is copied (the value of Y remains unchanged) and assigned as the new value of X; the result after this statement is executed is that the values of both variables, X and Y, will be the same as the former value of Y. In the second statement, on the other hand, the value of X is copied from the cell named X and assigned to Y, so that both variables end up with the value that X had originally. Throughout Example 2 we have consistently assigned the expressions (variables) on the right to variables of the same type, either *integer* or *real*.

We can form more complicated expressions by combining variables and constants arithmetically, using the operators for *addition, subtraction, multiplication,* and *division.* In Fortran, the asterisk * is used to indicate multiplication, and the slash **/** indicates division. Examples of assignment statements, with expressions consisting of variables and constants combined by means of arithmetic operators, are shown in the following example.

Example 3

```
I = J + 1                THETA = ALPHA - PI
THETA = Q * 3.14159      X = A / B
HALF = 0.5 * WHOLE       VOLUME = WIDTH * HEIGHT * DEPTH
```

Still more complicated expressions can be constructed in several ways. For instance, we can enclose an expression in parentheses and then use an arithmetic operator to combine the parenthesized expression with some other expression. Moreover, we can use the minus sign to indicate *negation.* (This operation differs from subtraction in that it involves only one expression as an operand, whereas in subtraction the minus sign appears between two expressions.)

Example 4

```
AVG = (A + B) / 2.0
AVG = 0.5 * (A + B)
IAVG = (I + J) / 2
NEG = -I * (-J / (-K))
```

We can also indicate *exponentiation* (the process of raising an expression to a power). The Fortran symbol for exponentiation is the double asterisk **. The assignment statements in Example 5 illustrate expressions involving this operation, as well as some miscellaneous composite expressions. Throughout each of the statements in this example, all variables and constants are of one type (except that a real expression is sometimes raised to an integer power).

Example 5

```
POWER = BASE ** EXP
PRES = (1.0 + PRT) ** (-N)
K = (M - (9 / L)) * N
Q = ((A + (12.0 / C)) + ((D ** E) * F)) - 17.0
CPND = (1.0 + RATE) ** N
ISQ = I ** 2
X = 0.5 * (X + (A / X))
```

A rule that must be followed in writing Fortran expressions is that no two operators may appear side by side in an expression. (The double asterisk, the symbol for exponentiation, is considered a single operator.) In practice, this restriction rarely presents any problem, except when a minus sign indicating negation appears in the middle of an expression. The difficulty can always be avoided by the insertion of an extra pair of parentheses:

A * (−B)   *not*   A * − B

2.1.1   The Importance of Numeric Types

The values of integer constants and variables are represented in computer storage in a different way than are real values. The computer must be instructed to perform either integer arithmetic or real arithmetic during any one step in the evaluation of an expression. The information that determines which type of arithmetic is to be performed is obtained by noting whether the constants and variables in the expression are of integer type or of real type. An expression consisting entirely of integer variables and integer constants (along with arithmetic operators, parentheses, etc.) is to be evaluated using integer arithmetic, whereas an expression consisting entirely of real variables, real constants, etc., is to be evaluated by means of real arithmetic.

In effect, then, each of the arithmetic operators does double duty. When a plus sign appears between a pair of integer expressions, it indicates the operation of *integer addition;* when it appears between real expressions, on the other hand, it indicates *real addition.* This distinction must be recognized by the language processor when it generates the instructions in machine code for the integer arithmetic or real arithmetic.

The distinction is particularly important in the case of division, since the result of *integer division* is truncated to a value of integer type; that is, the fractional part of the remainder is "chopped off." (No such truncation occurs during the evaluation of the real quotient expression 9.0 / 5.0, in spite of the fact that the real constants 9.0 and 5.0 happen to have values that are whole numbers. The result of evaluating 9.0 / 5.0 is 1.8, whereas 9 / 5 gives 1 because of truncation.) The quotient of any two expressions of integer type will be truncated to the next smaller (in absolute value) integer.

There is one special case to be observed. It involves a real expression, part of which may be of integer type. In exponentiation, raising a real expression to an integer power is simply a way of indicating repeated multiplication. For example,

A ** 5

(mathematically, A^5) means that five copies of the value of A are to be multiplied together, just as if we had written

```
A * A * A * A * A
```

The result is a real expression, even though the exponent is an integer constant. The exponent does not, of course, have to be a constant; it can be any integer expression, such as

```
A ** (I + 3)
```

An expression in the form A ** 5 is actually to be preferred over A ** 5.0, as we shall see.

2.1.2   A Closer Look at Constants

We now proceed to a closer examination of constants, as they are used in Fortran expressions. During the translation of expressions to machine code, the processor allocates a storage cell to each different constant that appears in an expression and stores the value of each constant in the corresponding cell before the machine code is executed. Thus, a constant appearing in an expression is actually associated with a cell in much the same way as a variable. Variables and constants are both *cell names*. The difference is that the *value* of a cell whose name is a variable is established *during* the execution phase and may change from time to time as execution proceeds, whereas the value of a cell whose name is a constant is established *before* execution begins and does not change during the execution phase. When a cell name occurs in a program, the processor determines whether it is a variable or a constant on the basis of its appearance. In particular, the first character of a variable must be a *letter,* but the first character of a constant is usually a digit. (Of course, a constant may also begin with a plus or minus sign or with a decimal point.)

Integer constants

An integer constant is written as a string of digits without a decimal point. A constant representing a negative integer must be preceded by a minus sign; the plus sign on a positive constant may be (and usually is) omitted. Extra nonsignificant zero digits may be included at the left without affecting the value of the constant.

Examples of integer constants

```
 1776    1492    −555    1234567890
 3       0       7       000022
```

Real constants

Real numbers may be written as constants in the ordinary way, with a decimal point. The decimal point *must not be omitted* from a real constant, even if its value happens to be an exact whole number. A negative constant must be written with a minus sign; the plus sign on a positive real constant is optional.

Examples of real constants

    2.0   3.14159   2.71828182846   −0.001293   39.37

Real numbers of astronomical or microscopic size usually have several zeros to the right or left of the decimal point, for instance,

    175000000.   or   0.0008761

It is possible to omit some or all of the nonsignificant zeros if we write an exponent to specify the position of the decimal point. For example, we can recognize that 1000000 (one million) is the sixth power of 10, or 10^6, and write $175. \times 10^6$ instead of 175000000. We could also write the same number as 17.5×10^7, or as 1.75×10^8, or as 0.175×10^9. The last of these is in *normalized* form, with the first significant digit immediately to the right of the decimal point. In Fortran, the exponent is written with the letter E replacing the "$\times 10$", and the exponent is not raised above the line. Thus, all the following are correct Fortran constants representing 175000000.

    175. E 6   17.5 E 7   1.75 E 8   0.175 E 9

In each case the exponent indicates the number of places to move the decimal point to the *right* to restore the indicated decimal value.

Very small numbers are written in an analogous way, except that a *negative* exponent is used, indicating that the decimal point must be moved *left* to obtain the proper interpretation of the number. For example, .0008761 could be written in normalized form as

    0.8761 E −3

or in other equivalent forms, such as

    8.761 E −4   or   0.08761 E −2   or   0.0008761 E 0

Negative numbers can also be written with an exponent. The minus sign appears to the left of the significant digits:

−0.5 E 5	means	−50000.
−0.56 E −4	means	−0.000056
−1. E 10	means	−10000000000.

Plus signs are optional and may be included if desired with a positive value or with a positive exponent. Extra nonsignificant zeros may also be included to the right or left of the significant digits or to the left of the exponent.

Constants of other types

Other types of constants that are sometimes used in Fortran, in addition to those of real and integer types, will be discussed later. There are double precision constants (Section 2.6), complex constants (Section 2.7), logical constants (Section 3.2), and character constants (Section 5.1).

2.1.3 Variables

A variable is a symbolic name associated with a storage cell in the computer. This symbolic name consists of from one to six letters (alphabetic characters) or digits. The first character *must* be a letter (A through Z).

Variable types

A variable is associated with data of a specific type. The type of a variable is determined in one of three ways.

In the absence of any declaration to the contrary, the type is determined according to the rules of *default implicit* type specification, depending on the first character of the symbolic name. If the initial letter is I, J, K, L, M, or N, the variable is of integer type; if the initial character is any other letter, the variable is of real type. For example, according to these rules the following variables are of integer type:

```
I15     J24K     IKE     LOOP
KIM     J123T    MASS    NY1
N       L3       LAST    KOUNT
```

and the following variables are of real type:

```
TEMP    XX    F55    P3ZK     RESULT
ALPHA   A     X      TOTAL    COUNT
```

The default implicit type rules may be superseded by a *declared implicit* type specification expressed in an IMPLICIT statement. For example, the declaration

```
IMPLICIT INTEGER (P - R), REAL (M)
```

changes the implicit type rules so that variables whose names begin with P, Q, or R are now also of integer type, while variables whose names begin with M are now of real type. The default rules remain in effect for variables beginning with letters that do not appear in the `IMPLICIT` statement. Thus, the following variables would be of integer type:

```
P3ZK    RESULT    KOUNT    LOOP    I    N1
```

while the following variables would be of real type if the `IMPLICIT` statement in the above example were included in the program:

```
TEMP    XX    MATRIX    F55    A    X    M
```

An *explicit* type declaration may be used to specify the type of individual integer variables and real variables. Such a declaration supersedes the default or declared implicit type rules with regard to the variables listed in the explicit declaration, but has no effect on names that are not listed. Examples of explicit type declarations are:

```
REAL LARGE, X, PRUNE, NUMBER, J22, Q
INTEGER BIG, SMALL, LEFT, RIGHT, M
```

The first of these declarations specifies that each of the six variables is of real type, and the second declares that each listed name represents an integer variable. Note that an explicit type declaration begins with a word specifying a particular type; this is followed by a list of the variables designated to be of that type. An explicit type declaration has no effect on the types of any other variables beginning with the same letter. For example, if both of the following statements were included in a program:

```
IMPLICIT REAL (M)
INTEGER M
```

all variables in the program *beginning* with the letter *M* would be of real type as specified by the `IMPLICIT` statement, except that the *particular* variable named *M* itself would be of integer type according to the explicit type declaration `INTEGER M`.

Variables of types other than integer and real are not covered by default implicit type specification rules, so these variables must have their types specified either by a declared implicit type specification or by an explicit type declaration. More will be said about these type declarations in Section 7.1.

2.1.4 Size Restrictions

Each processor imposes restrictions on the sizes of integer numbers and real numbers that can be stored in a cell. It is important to find out what these restrictions are, for the processor you are using, and to keep them in mind during preparation of programs to be executed by the processor.

For each processor there is a maximum number of digits acceptable in a number represented in integer form. Integer constants representing values beyond this range will not be accepted. The limit for some processors is as small as four or five decimal digits; for others it is as large as fifteen digits. Some processors use special hardware *index registers* for integers used in special ways (such as in counting repetitions of a group of statements, or in designating a particular item in a sequence of data values); there may be a more restrictive limit on the size of integers used in these ways.

Each processor may have separate size restrictions for those portions of a real number (in a storage cell) that represent the significant digits, the exponent, and the sign. When a real numerical value enters into an arithmetic operation, the computer interprets each of these portions correctly. Usually real numbers are stored in normalized form; however, since most computers operate in the binary (base two) number system, normalization is done in such a way that the significant digits form a fraction whose value is between one-half and one, and the internally stored exponent is a power of two rather than of ten. Numerical values assigned to real variables are stored in this form. Real constants, whether they appear in the program with an exponent or without one, are converted to this same internal form when the processor translates the program to machine code.

The maximum number of significant digits, and the amount of space available for the exponent portion, are characteristics of the processor representation of real numbers. These limits restrict the size and precision of numbers that can be stored. For algorithms that are sensitive to such size or precision restrictions, the programmer must know in advance what the limits are for the processor that is to be used. Precision limits can be extended by the use of double precision arithmetic (Section 2.6).

2.1.5 Exercises

1. Classify each of the following as

RV: a valid Fortran real variable,
IV: a valid Fortran integer variable, I, J, K, L, m, N
RC: a valid Fortran real constant, 2.01
IC: a valid Fortran integer constant, or 1171
N: none of the above.

123	$1.98	LOVE	X	BITE
1234	IJK	HATE	X3	MITER
123.4	I*J*K	3.	3X	12345678
LANDSCAPE	POLICEMAN	3.00000	3*X	A1B2
123,400,000	COMPUTER	0.00003	KITE	1A2B

2. Write each of the following real constants without an exponent.

3.08 E 0	−522.4 E −2	3. E 5
.291 E −4	99. E −1	.001 E +7

3.08°

3. Write each of the following real constants with an exponent, in normalized form.

.000276   −41900   3.08   6.023 × 10²³

4. Which of the following are not valid symbolic names of Fortran variables?

JOHNNIE	JOHNY	2JOHNY	JNOHY
J3OHY	J.OHY	ZZZZ	1234S
NN	N/4	A15AA	7G46H
ABLE	BAKER	G46	PHILIP

5. Which of the following are not valid symbolic names for integer variables according to the default implicit type rules?

MARY	2MARY	POLAR	ABLE
P	IPOOL	I15Z	I234
N−5	2Z	M22	N3
I1234TT			

6. Obtain the following information for the processor you will be using. Possible sources are your instructor, your computer center, or manuals for your computer or Fortran processor.

a) Range of *integers* in *bits*; in *decimal digits*.

b) Number of *significant digits* for *real* numerical values; for *double precision*.

c) Range of *exponents* for *real* and *double precision* numbers.

2.2 EXPRESSIONS

When we write A / B * C in Fortran, will it be interpreted as (A / B) * C or as A / (B * C)? How can we be sure, when we write a Fortran expression, that it will be interpreted in the way we had intended? Usually common sense, along with a little application of the everyday conventions of mathematics, is sufficient for us to tell unambiguously how the Fortran processor will interpret our expressions. Fortunately, in cases of doubt, we can always force the interpretation we have in mind if we use enough parentheses. However, there are no other enclosure symbols available for us to use in grouping parts of an expression in Fortran, and excessive use of parentheses may become more confusing than helpful.

2.2.1 Rules for Evaluating Expressions

Here we shall give a list of rules that will permit anyone to determine just how a Fortran expression will be evaluated.

Rule 1. Quantities within parentheses are computed first, before the parenthesized subexpression is combined with other parts of the expression. If there are parentheses within parentheses, the innermost parenthesized subexpression is evaluated first.

Rule 2.   The arithmetic operations within any expression or parenthesized subexpression are performed in the following order of precedence:

first, exponentiation;

second, multiplication and division;

third, addition, subtraction, and negation.

Rule 3.   When an expression (or parenthesized subexpression) involves two or more operations that are on the same level in the precedence list, their position within the expression determines the order in which these operations are performed. *Multiplication* and *division* operations, or *addition, subtraction,* and *negation* operations, are performed in order from left to right: Thus A **/** B ***** C means $(A \div B) \cdot C$ (see Example 2 below). However, the rules of mathematical notation require that two or more consecutive *exponentiation* operations be performed in order from right to left, so that A ****** B ****** C is interpreted as $A^{(B^C)}$.

In analyzing an expression, we apply these three rules to determine which operation will be performed first. We then proceed by assuming that the first operation has been performed, and that the operator and its operands have been replaced by a single numerical result, which we may call $\mathcal{R}_1$. At this point we go back to the rules to decide which operation is to be performed next, and we replace the next operator and its operands by a new result, which we may call $\mathcal{R}_2$. In this way we eventually obtain a single result as the value of the entire expression.

Example 1   (See Fig. 2.1.) The statement

    Q = A + B / C ** F

contains no parentheses, so we apply Rule 2.

Step 1.   The exponentiation, C ****** F, is performed first. We replace this subexpression by $\mathcal{R}_1$, obtaining

    Q = A + B / $\mathcal{R}_1$

Step 2.   The division operation, B **/** $\mathcal{R}_1$, is performed next. We replace this subexpression by $\mathcal{R}_2$, and obtain

    Q = A + $\mathcal{R}_2$

Step 3.   The final addition operation is performed, and we replace A + $\mathcal{R}_2$ by $\mathcal{R}_3$ to obtain

    Q = $\mathcal{R}_3$

Q = A + B / C ** F

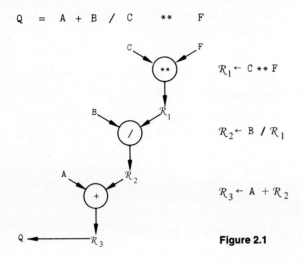

$$\mathcal{R}_1 \leftarrow C \ {**} \ F$$

$$\mathcal{R}_2 \leftarrow B \ / \ \mathcal{R}_1$$

$$\mathcal{R}_3 \leftarrow A + \mathcal{R}_2$$

Figure 2.1

The expression has now been entirely evaluated, and the assignment can take place. Thus the value of the expression is the same as if we had written the following equivalent assignment statement, using a parenthesized expression.

Q = A + (B / (C ** F))

Example 2   (See Fig. 2.2.) Rule 3 is a *tie-breaking* rule. Note that multiplication and division are both on the second level of the precedence list. Addition, subtraction, and negation are all on the third level. In this example, the left-to-right rule is applied in the evaluation of an expression containing two operations on the same level.

Q = A / B * C

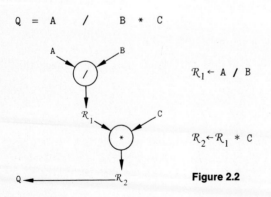

$$\mathcal{R}_1 \leftarrow A \ / \ B$$

$$\mathcal{R}_2 \leftarrow \mathcal{R}_1 * C$$

Figure 2.2

The statement

```
Q = A / B * C
```

contains no parentheses, and both operations are on the second level of the precedence list, so we apply Rule 3.

Step 1.   The operation on the left is performed first. We replace the subexpression A **/** B by $\mathcal{R}_1$ to obtain

```
Q = R₁ * C
```

Step 2.   The remaining operation is performed. We replace $\mathcal{R}_1$ * C by $\mathcal{R}_2$ and obtain

```
Q = R₂
```

The assignment can now take place. It is clear from this example that the Fortran expression

```
A / B * C
```

means the same as (A **/** B) * C, and *not* A **/** (B * C), because of the tie-breaking Rule 3.

Example 3   (See Fig. 2.3.) To evaluate the expression in the statement

```
Q = A + B / C + D ** E * F - G
```

we must apply both Rule 2 and Rule 3. The steps may be summarized as follows:

```
Q = A + B / C + D ** E * F - G
Q = A + B / C + R₁ * F - G
Q = A + R₂ + R₁ * F - G
Q = A + R₂ + R₃ - G
Q = R₄ + R₃ - G
Q = R₅ - G
Q = R₆
```

Thus the expression is equivalent to the parenthesized expression

```
((A + (B / C)) + ((D ** E) * F)) - G
```

The following examples include parentheses, so we apply Rule 1. Within each subexpression enclosed in parentheses, we proceed according to Rules 2 and 3.

$$Q = A + B \quad / \quad C + D \quad ** \quad E * F \; - \; G$$

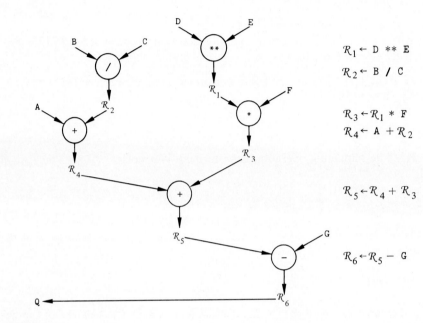

$$\mathcal{R}_1 \leftarrow D ** E$$
$$\mathcal{R}_2 \leftarrow B / C$$

$$\mathcal{R}_3 \leftarrow \mathcal{R}_1 * F$$
$$\mathcal{R}_4 \leftarrow A + \mathcal{R}_2$$

$$\mathcal{R}_5 \leftarrow \mathcal{R}_4 + \mathcal{R}_3$$

$$\mathcal{R}_6 \leftarrow \mathcal{R}_5 - G$$

Figure 2.3

Example 4   (See Fig. 2.4.)

$$Q = A * (B + C * D)$$
$$Q = A * (B + \mathcal{R}_1)$$
$$Q = A * \mathcal{R}_2$$
$$Q = \mathcal{R}_3$$

Example 5   (See Fig. 2.5.)

$$Q = A + (B + C - (D * E + F))$$
$$Q = A + (B + C - (\mathcal{R}_1 + F))$$
$$Q = A + (B + C - \mathcal{R}_2)$$
$$Q = A + (\mathcal{R}_3 - \mathcal{R}_2)$$
$$Q = A + \mathcal{R}_4$$
$$Q = \mathcal{R}_5$$

Note that the innermost parentheses have been removed first, in accordance with the last sentence of Rule 1.

Q = A * (B + C   *   D)

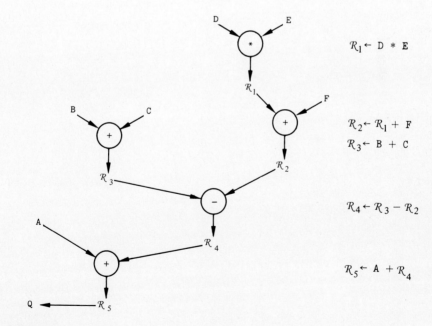

$\mathcal{R}_1 \leftarrow C * D$

$\mathcal{R}_2 \leftarrow B + \mathcal{R}_1$

$\mathcal{R}_3 \leftarrow A * \mathcal{R}_2$ **Figure 2.4**

Q = A + (B   +   C   −   (D   *   E + F))

$\mathcal{R}_1 \leftarrow D * E$

$\mathcal{R}_2 \leftarrow \mathcal{R}_1 + F$
$\mathcal{R}_3 \leftarrow B + C$

$\mathcal{R}_4 \leftarrow \mathcal{R}_3 - \mathcal{R}_2$

$\mathcal{R}_5 \leftarrow A + \mathcal{R}_4$

Figure 2.5

Example 6 (See Fig. 2.6.)

```
CK + A3 * BJ / 9.7 + 3.5 * P
CK + R₁ / 9.7 + 3.5 * P
CK + R₂ + 3.5 * P
CK + R₂ + R₃
R₄ + R₃
R₅
```

CK + A3   *   BJ / 9.7   +   3.5   *   P

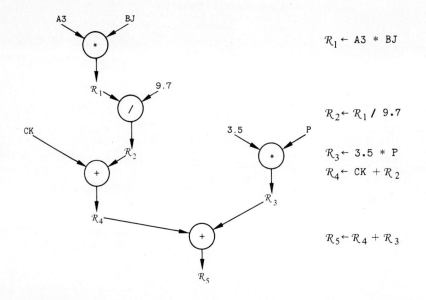

$$R_1 \leftarrow A3 * BJ$$

$$R_2 \leftarrow R_1 / 9.7$$

$$R_3 \leftarrow 3.5 * P$$
$$R_4 \leftarrow CK + R_2$$

$$R_5 \leftarrow R_4 + R_3$$

Figure 2.6

Example 7   (See Fig. 2.7.)

```
CK + A3 * BJ / (9.7 + 3.5 * P)
CK + A3 * BJ / (9.7 + ℛ₁)
CK + A3 * BJ / ℛ₂
CK + ℛ₃ / ℛ₂
CK + ℛ₄
ℛ₅
```

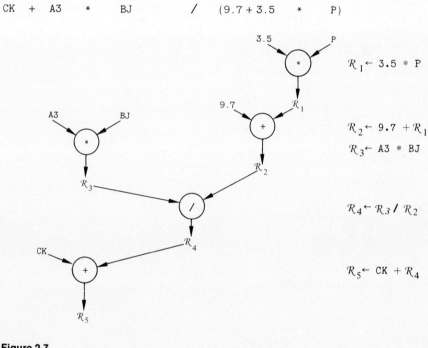

Figure 2.7

Example 8   (See Fig. 2.8.) Note that the expressions in the two following examples, as interpreted by Fortran, are algebraically equivalent.

```
A * B / C * D / E * F
R₁ / C * D / E * F
R₂ * D / E * F
R₃ / E * F
R₄ * F
R₅
```

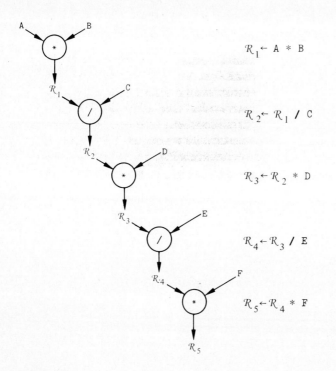

Figure 2.8

Example 9   (See Fig. 2.9.)

$(A * B * D * F) / (C * E)$
$(\mathcal{R}_1 * D * F) / (C * E)$
$(\mathcal{R}_2 * F) / (C * E)$
$\mathcal{R}_3 / (C * E)$
$\mathcal{R}_3 / \mathcal{R}_4$
$\mathcal{R}_5$

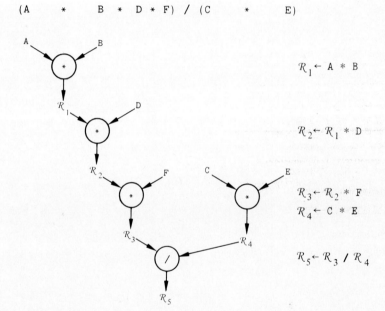

$(A \qquad * \qquad B * D * F) / (C \qquad * \qquad E)$

$\mathcal{R}_1 \leftarrow A * B$

$\mathcal{R}_2 \leftarrow \mathcal{R}_1 * D$

$\mathcal{R}_3 \leftarrow \mathcal{R}_2 * F$
$\mathcal{R}_4 \leftarrow C * E$

$\mathcal{R}_5 \leftarrow \mathcal{R}_3 / \mathcal{R}_4$

Figure 2.9

Example 10 (See Fig. 2.10.) The first pair of parentheses in Example 9 could have been omitted.

```
A * B * D * F / (C * E)
A * B * D * F / R₁
R₂ * D * F / R₁
R₃ * F / R₁
R₄ / R₁
R₅
```

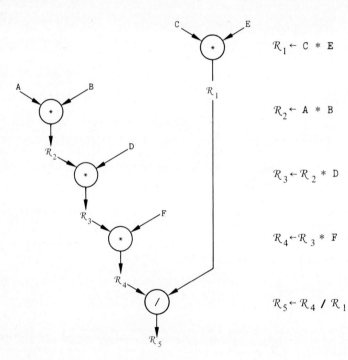

$R_1 \leftarrow C * E$

$R_2 \leftarrow A * B$

$R_3 \leftarrow R_2 * D$

$R_4 \leftarrow R_3 * F$

$R_5 \leftarrow R_4 / R_1$

Figure 2.10

Example 11   (See Fig. 2.11.) Note that according to Rule 2, the minus sign in the following example applies to the *entire expression,* and not just to the variable A. The same would be true for the assignment statement $Q = -3.0 ** 2$ as well.

$$Q = - A ** 2$$
$$Q = - \mathcal{R}_1$$
$$Q = \mathcal{R}_2$$

$$Q = - A \quad ** \quad 2$$

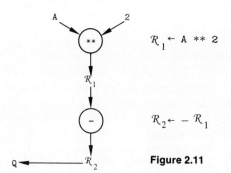

$$\mathcal{R}_1 \leftarrow A ** 2$$

$$\mathcal{R}_2 \leftarrow - \mathcal{R}_1$$

Figure 2.11

A similar effect will occur with such expressions as

$$F - A ** 2 \quad \text{and} \quad G * (- A ** 2)$$

Example 12   (See Fig. 2.12.) The variable on the left may also appear in the expression on the right, as in the following example.

$$X = X + 1.0$$
$$X = \mathcal{R}_1$$

The effect of this statement is to *increase* the former value of X by 1.0.

$$X = X \quad + \quad 1.0$$

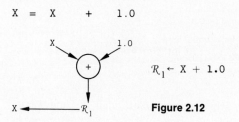

$$\mathcal{R}_1 \leftarrow X + 1.0$$

Figure 2.12

A fourth rule for determining precedence in the evaluation of expressions will be discussed in Section 2.3.1. It applies to expressions that require evaluation of a function, such as

```
ABS (A) * B / C
```

or

```
0.5 * (SQRT (X) + A / SQRT (X))
```

This fourth rule simply specifies that function evaluation takes precedence over all arithmetic operations.

Special note on integer division

It is important to recall that integer division produces an integer result; any fractional part of the quotient is discarded. Thus 3 **/** 4 would yield the quotient zero; 5 **/** 2 would yield the quotient 2. Consequently, the meaning of integer expressions depends on the *order of computation* much more than for real expressions. In algebra, the following two expressions would have the same value, regardless of the values of the variables J, L, M, and N.

    a) `(L − M) / N * J`   b) `J * (L − M) / N`

Nevertheless, the two expressions are likely to yield different numerical results in Fortran. For example, if the values of the variables are

    J: 5
    L: 7
    M: 4
    N: 5

then expression (a) yields zero, but expression (b) yields 3.

```
a) (7 − 4) / 5 * 5          b) 5 * (7 − 4) / 5
   3 / 5 * 5                   5 * 3 / 5
   0 * 5                       15 / 5
   0                          3
```

This truncation of the quotient occurs in any expression (or subexpression) where both operands in a division operation are of integer type.

2.2.2 Statements with Mixed Types

In all the assignment statements in the foregoing examples, each statement contained variables and constants of integer type throughout, or of real type throughout (except for the special case of arithmetic expressions involving a real expression raised to an integer power).

Fortran permits mixed types in *assignment;* that is, an expression of one type may be assigned as the value of a variable of a different type. In translating a mixed-type assignment statement, the processor automatically incorporates the necessary steps to convert the value of the expression *after it has been completely evaluated* to the same type as the variable to which the value is being assigned. If the assignment statement has the form

Real variable = Integer expression

the processor computes the value of the expression, using integer arithmetic. Then the representation of this result is changed to that of a real number of equivalent value. (In effect, we could say that the processor inserts a decimal point. Actually, it generates a number in the real internal form, complete with significant digits and exponent, having the equivalent value.) This value is then stored in the cell designated by the variable on the left.

If the assignment statement has the form

Integer variable = Real expression

on the other hand, the expression is first evaluated by means of real arithmetic. In order to represent this result as an integer value and store it in the cell designated on the left, the processor must truncate the real value. This amounts to deleting both the decimal point and all digits that would have appeared to the right of it. (The integer internal form has no provision for a decimal point or for a fractional part.)

Mixed-type *expressions* are also permitted in Fortran. Any operation having one operand of integer type and the other of real type produces a result of real type. Except for exponentiation of a real expression to an integer power (which is interpreted as repeated multiplication; see Section 2.3.4), the integer operand is converted to real type automatically, by the processor, before the operation is performed.

Explicit type conversion

Many Fortran programmers quickly discover that the use of mixed types within an expression or a statement can be a source of programming mistakes that are hard to locate. The conversion process is so "automatic" that the programmer finds it difficult to understand precisely what operations will be performed when the program is executed.

Fortran provides the *explicit type conversion* functions *Real* and *Int*. In the remainder of this section, we introduce these functions and use them to further explain the pros and cons of automatic type conversion. In the next section we consider these functions in greater detail, along with a somewhat superior explicit type conversion function *Nint,* which rounds a real value instead of truncating it.

The explicit type conversion function *Real* may be applied to an expression of integer type to produce an expression of real type. The integer expression whose representation is to be converted is written in parentheses following the function name:

REAL (*Integer expression*)

The function *Int* produces a result of integer type, when applied to an expression of real type:

INT (*Real expression*)

Truncation, of the same form that occurs automatically with integer division or mixed-type assignment, is applied to the value of the real expression so that the function value can be represented as an integer.

It should be noted that statements with explicit type conversion such as

```
X = REAL (I + 3)
J = INT (X)
AVG = TOTAL / REAL (NUMBER)
```

are *not* actually mixed-type statements. Type conversion occurs only as a result of evaluating the functions *Real* and *Int;* the arithmetic operations and assignment operations in these statements do not require that any further "automatic" conversions be introduced by the processor.

Interpreting statements with mixed types

It is especially important to observe the order of evaluation of subexpressions in a statement that involves mixing of types. For example, consider the two groups of assignment statements

```
a) A = K                    b) A = K
     M = (A / 4) * K             M = (K / 4) * A
```

which, at first glance, might be expected to produce identical results; and suppose that *K* has the value 3 initially. In both group (a) and group (b), the first assignment is interpreted as if it were written

```
A = REAL (K)
```

Thus the value of *A* is 3.0. In the second statement of group (a), the subexpression A / 4 is to be evaluated first, according to Rule 1. This is an expression of mixed type, so it is evaluated as if it were written as A / REAL (4). In other words, the integer operand is converted to real type before the division is performed. Since *A* is 3.0, the result of this first operation is 0.75. No truncation occurs during the division, because the operands are expressions of *real* type. The next operation is the evaluation of 0.75 * K. This is again a mixed expression, so the integer operand *K* has its value converted to a real representation (3.0). Thus, the final product is 2.25: No truncation has occurred up to this point. The final result is truncated to the integer 2 and assigned as the value of *M*. We see that the assignment statement is interpreted as if it were written

```
M = INT ((A / REAL (4)) * REAL (K))
```

On the other hand, the first subexpression to be evaluated in (b) is the expression K / 4, which is entirely of integer type and is therefore computed according to the rules of integer division. Truncation will occur, and since *K* is 3, the result will be zero. The expression 0 * A is then evaluated as if it were written REAL (0) * A; the result is zero, which is then converted back to integer form and assigned to *M*. Thus the assignment statement in (b) is evaluated as if it were written

```
M = INT (REAL (K / 4) * A)
```

and the final result is zero, rather than 2 as in case (a).

Another example is the sequence of assignment statements

```
I = R
R = I
```

which is executed as if it were written

```
I = INT (R)
R = REAL (I)
```

The value of the expression consisting of the variable *R* is first truncated and stored in integer representation as the new value of *I*. The second assignment step takes a copy of the value of *I*, generates the real representation having the equivalent value, and stores it as the new value of *R*. The effect is to truncate the value of *R* to the next smallest (in absolute value) whole number. An equivalent expression for the final value of *R* is REAL (INT (R)).

Note that truncation may occasionally produce unexpected results, because many numbers cannot be represented exactly in a computer with finite cell size. For instance, the result of dividing 1.0 by 3.0 (using real arithmetic) is 0.33333 . . . , which is slightly less than one-third. Multiplying this result by 3.0 will not produce 1.0 but rather 0.99999 . . . ; truncating this value, we obtain 0 rather than 1. Thus, if we use assignment statements such as

```
R = 3.0
X = 1.0 / R
L = 3.0 * X
M = R * X
N = X + X + X
```

the values of *L, M,* and *N* will all be zero because of the truncation that occurs along with the automatic type conversion.

Particularly insidious is the fact that, since most computers use a binary number representation, simple decimal fractions such as 0.1 or 0.02 are represented in the computer by approximations that are slightly smaller numbers (which we may think of as 0.0999999 . . . , 0.0199999 . . . , etc.). Thus in binary arithmetic, the following Fortran assignment instructions will also give zero as the values of *L, M,* and *N.*

```
R = 10.0
X = 1.0 / R
L = 10.0 * X
M = R * X
N = X + X + X + X + X + X + X + X + X + X
```

The same truncations occur, of course, even when explicit type conversion (by means of the functions *Real* and *Int*) is used. But the appearance of the conversion functions in a statement calls attention to the fact that truncation may be taking place, so that the programmer may be able to avoid hidden errors that might have occurred with expressions of mixed type. It takes very few seconds longer to write

```
(A / 4.0) * REAL (K)
REAL (K / 4) * A
```

and these expressions are in a form that makes evident the difference between their values. The shorter mixed-type expressions

```
(A / 4) * K
(K / 4) * A
```

may seem more convenient at first, but if an error of interpretation results, the time saved may be spent in attempting to locate the error.

It is important to remember that the rules of mixed-type expression evaluation do not apply to exponentiation of a real expression to an integer power, such as R ** I. As we have seen, such a subexpression is already of real type, and it is interpreted merely as repeated multiplication. In an expression of the form I ** R, however, *I* is converted to real type before the exponentiation is carried out.

A related problem, which does not actually involve mixing of types, occurs when we write an exponent expression involving integer division. If we try to compute the cube root of *X*, for example, by writing

```
X ** (1 / 3)
```

the integer division will be performed first, with truncation, and the effect will be the same as if we had written

```
X ** 0
```

instead. To obtain an approximation to the cube root of a real expression, we may use a real exponent, such as

```
X ** 0.33333
```

(See also Section 2.3.4.)

2.2.3 Exercises

1. Using the variable values

   J: 2
   K: 2
   KK: 7
   L: −3

   evaluate the following Fortran expressions.
   a) J * (K − KK) / (9 + L)
   b) J * ((K − KK) / (9 + L))
   c) (J * (K − KK) / 9 + L)
   d) (J * (K − KK)) / (9 + L)

2. Using the variable values

   A: 2.0
   B: 3.0
   C: 2.0
   D: 3.0

   evaluate the following Fortran expressions.
   a) A * B / C ** D
   b) (A * B / C) ** D
   c) A * (B / C) ** D

3. Using the variable values

> *A*:   1.0   *I*: 5
> *B*:   3.5   *J*: 7
> *Theta*: 10.0   *K*: 3
> *XYZ*:   5.0

evaluate the following Fortran expressions.

a) − (A + THETA)
b) (B + (XYZ / THETA)) / (4.0 * A)
c) (I * J) / K
d) I * (J / K)
e) (I / K) * J
f) − (K + 7) / J

4. Replace each of the following assignment statements by a statement that avoids the use of mixed-type expressions and of mixed-type assignment through the use of the explicit type conversion functions *Int* and *Real*.

a) R = A + I
b) W = I − 1.3 + J
c) K = 2 / 3 * 6.6
d) I = 123456789 + B
e) P = X ** 5

5. A man wishes to make a multicolored rug by sewing together one-foot squares of carpet. He plans to use the rug in his living room, and he wants at least 2.0 but less than 2.5 feet of wood floor to show on all sides of the rug. He has measured the living room and found that its length and width, in feet, are the values of the variables *RL* and *RW*. Write an expression whose value is the integer number of squares that he will have to sew together to make his rug.

2.3 FUNCTIONS

A number of operations, which are more complicated than the simple arithmetic operations of addition, subtraction, division, negation, and exponentiation, are so useful that they are provided in the Fortran language as functions that are always available to the user.

Table 2.1 lists the predefined functions available in Fortran (omitting those that involve types other than integer and real; see also Table 8.1).

Table 2.1 Predefined functions in Fortran 77

(See Table 8.1 for a more complete list.)

Function	Name	Definition
Group 1: Type conversion, rounding, and truncation		
Conversion to real type	**REAL**	The argument may be of real or integer type. The result has the same numerical value as the argument, and is of real type.

Table 2.1 (cont.)

Rounding to *nearest* whole number	NINT	The argument is of real type. The result is of integer type, and its value is the whole number nearest to the value of the argument.
	ANINT	The argument is of real type. The value of the result is the same as for NINT, but its type is real.
Truncation to *next smaller* whole number (in absolute value)	INT	The argument may be of real or integer type. The value of the result is of integer type, and its value is the nearest whole number that is not greater in absolute value than the argument.
	AINT	The argument is of real type. The value of the result is the same as for INT, but its type is real.

Group 2: Other functions with real or integer arguments

For functions in this group, the argument may be of integer or real type, and the type of the result is the same as the type of the argument. If there are two or more arguments, all must be of the same type.

Absolute value	ABS	The value of the function is obtained by ignoring the sign of the argument. (The result is always positive or zero.)
Remainder (two arguments)	MOD	The result is the remainder that would result from integer division ("long division") of the first argument by the second. (The value of the second argument must not be zero.)
Transfer of sign (two arguments)	SIGN	The magnitude of the result is obtained from the first argument, and the sign of the result is obtained from the second argument. (The sign of the first argument is ignored.)
Positive difference (two arguments)	DIM	Subtract the second argument from the first. If the difference is positive, it is taken as the value of the function; if the difference is negative, the value of the function is zero.
Largest or smallest (two or more arguments)	MAX MIN	The function takes on the value of the largest or smallest of its arguments.

Group 3: Mathematical functions (real arguments)

Square root	SQRT	Function values are defined as in mathematics.
Exponential (power of *e*)	EXP	Arguments of the trigonometric functions are
Natural logarithm (base *e*)	LOG	in radians.
Common logarithm (base 10)	LOG10	Also available are inverse trigonometric func-
Sine	SIN	tions ASIN, ACOS, ATAN (with one argument;
Cosine	COS	function value between $-\pi/2$ and $\pi/2$), ATAN2
Tangent	TAN	(with two arguments; function value between $-\pi$ and π), and hyperbolic functions SINH, COSH, and TANH.

Examples   In the following function reference expressions, assume that the value of J is 3, K is 5, X is -2.4, and Z is 7.3.

Function reference	**Value**
REAL (J)	3.0
NINT (5.999)	6
ANINT (5.999)	6.0
INT (5.999)	5
AINT (5.999)	5.0
ABS (X)	2.4
MOD (K, J)	2
SIGN (1.0, X)	-1.0
DIM (Z, 8.0)	0.0
MAX (X, 0.0, Z)	7.3
MIN (J, −K)	-5
SQRT (9.0)	3.0

2.3.1   Using Predefined Functions in Expressions

To invoke any of the functions listed in Table 2.1, we write the function name followed by a list of arguments *enclosed in parentheses*. (For most of these functions, the list will consist of a single argument. If there are two or more arguments, they must be separated by commas.) It is essential that the number and type of arguments agree with the specifications in the table.

Each argument may be *any expression* of an acceptable type; it may include arithmetic operations, other functions, or even the same function.†

The function name, along with the arguments in parentheses, forms an expression. This expression can be used in the same way as a variable or a constant, as part of a more complicated expression or as the right side of an assignment statement.

In the evaluation of expressions that contain functions, we might add another rule similar to Rule 1 of Section 2.2.1.

Rule 4.   Function evaluation always occurs *before* the function value is combined with other parts of an expression.

This means that expressions that occur as function arguments will be completely evaluated as the first step in evaluating any subexpression. If an argument expression includes a function, such a function again takes precedence.

---

† Some restrictions apply to the argument *values* for mathematical reasons. For example, the argument of *Sqrt* must not be negative, the second argument of *Mod* (getting the remainder from long division) must not be zero, and the argument of *Log* (logarithm) must be positive.

Examples of expressions that require function evaluation

```
ABS (A) * B / C
SQRT (REAL (M - 9 / L) * N)
A * SIN (THETA)
0.5 * (SQRT (X) + A / SQRT (X))
ABS (I - 5)
MOD (MINUTE, 60)
MAX (ABS (I - 5), I, 1)
SQRT (SQRT (A))
SQRT (B ** 2 - 4.0 * A * C) / (2.0 * A)
NINT (SQRT (REAL (ABS (J))))
```

Type of function arguments and values

Some of the predefined functions will accept arguments of either integer or real type, while other functions will accept only one type. The functions may be divided into three groups, as follows.

The type conversion functions always produce a result of one particular type. *Real, Aint,* and *Anint* produce a real result, while *Int* and *Nint* produce an integer result. The argument of *Aint, Anint,* or *Nint* must not be of integer type; *Real* or *Int* may have an argument of either type. (However, *Real* applied to a real argument, or *Int* applied to an integer argument, accomplishes nothing.)

For the next group of functions, *Abs, Mod, Sign, Dim, Max,* and *Min,* arguments of real or integer type are acceptable, but all arguments must be of the same type. The type of the result is the same as that of the arguments. (See also Table 8.1.)

The third group consists of the mathematical functions, for which arguments and results are of real type. As we shall see, these functions can also be used with double precision or complex arguments to produce a result of the same type as the argument. However, arguments of integer type are not accepted by functions in this third group.

An argument of the wrong type will *not* be converted automatically to an acceptable type. Some processors will not even detect such errors, but merely produce unexpected results. For example, SQRT (2) and SQRT (I) are not valid Fortran expressions (when *I* is of integer type). Explicit type conversion, as in SQRT (REAL (I)), will produce a valid expression.

2.3.2   Rounding

Except where it is important to simulate the truncation that occurs automatically during implicit type conversion, it is usually preferable to use the "nearest integer" or *rounding* function *Nint* rather than *Int* to perform conversions from real to integer type. This function requires an argument of real type, and produces a result of integer type. The value of the result is the whole number *nearest* to the value of the argument. (If the argument is exactly midway between two integer values, it is rounded up if positive and down to a more negative integer if negative.)

Use of this function avoids some of the more troublesome situations that were mentioned in Section 2.2.2. The statements

```
R = 3.0
X = 1.0 / R
L = NINT (3.0 * X)
M = NINT (R * X)
N = NINT (X + X + X)
```

will result in the values of *L, M,* and *N* all being set to 1, as expected. On the other hand, automatic type conversion or use of the function *Int* will produce zero values for *L, M,* and *N.*

Similarly, reasonable results will be obtained from the assignment statements

```
R = 10.0
X = 1.0 / R
L = NINT (10.0 * X)
M = NINT (R * X)
```

As another example, the integer nearest the square root of *N* may be obtained as the value of the expression `NINT (SQRT (REAL (N)))`.

2.3.3   Other Uses of Predefined Functions

Integer division with remainder

We often need the *remainder* from integer division. For instance, the easiest way to test whether one integer can be divided exactly by another is to perform the division and see if the remainder is zero. This idea suggests the possibility of breaking down an integer into its prime factors, or of finding the greatest common divisor of two integers.

A less mathematical example is a cyclical number system, which repeats after a certain number is reached, such as the hours in the day. For example, to find the time 2 hours later than the hour of 11 o'clock, we may add 2 to 11 and find the remainder after dividing by 12.

To find the lowest digit of a decimal number, we need the remainder upon division by 10; similarly, the remainder from integer division by 100 or 1000 gives the lowest two digits or three digits, respectively.

The remainder from integer division of *J* by *K* is given by the Fortran expression

```
MOD (J, K)
```

For example, the value of MOD (59 + 2, 60) is 1. Regardless of the signs of the arguments (so long as *K* is not zero), the values of

```
J / K    and    MOD (J, K)
```

form a "matched pair," one giving the (truncated) integer quotient and the other giving the remainder. The remainder given by the *Mod* function will correspond exactly to the integer division as indicated. In other words, in the following sequence of assignment statements

```
IQ = J / K
IR = MOD (J, K)
I = K * IQ + IR
```

it will always be true (except if *K* is zero), that the final value of *I* will be identical to the original value of *J*.

To see precisely what result will be produced by the *Mod* function, we may calculate the remainder in the following way.

1. Divide the first argument by the second.
2. Take the integer part of the quotient by truncating it to the next smallest integer (in absolute value).
3. Multiply the integer quotient by the second argument, and subtract the product from the first argument.

This process may be recognized as analogous to the process of long division taught in elementary arithmetic. The integer quotient corresponds to the successful trial divisor in the long division process.

The arguments of the *Mod* function need not be of integer type. However, the two arguments in any particular reference to the function must both be of the same type. For integer arguments, Step 2 may be thought of as occurring "naturally," due to the truncation that accompanies integer division in Fortran. For arguments of real type (or of other types, see Table 8.1), some extra attention must be given to that step.

Disconnecting the algebraic sign of a number

To obtain the magnitude of a number (of integer or real type) while ignoring the algebraic sign, we may use the *Abs,* or absolute value, function. The *Sign* function, on the other hand, can be used where we wish to ignore the magnitude and obtain a result that depends only on the algebraic sign of a number.

Storing and processing a disembodied sign would be difficult and awkward, however. Accordingly, the *Sign* function *transfers* the sign of its second argument to another number specified as the first argument. In many useful applications, the first argument is 1, so the function value is $+1$ if the second argument is positive, or -1 if the second argument is negative. (Both arguments must be of the same type, and the type of the result is defined to be the type of the arguments.)

What happens if the value of the second argument is zero (integer or real)? In most applications, either sign would be satisfactory, but we would like to know in advance what result will be produced in this case. Fortran arbitrarily chooses to handle a zero as though it were positive. Thus, the value of SIGN (X, 0.0) is exactly the same as the value of ABS (X).

In mathematical applications, there is sometimes a need for a *signum* function. As defined in mathematics, the signum function has one argument; the function value is -1 if the argument is negative, 0 if the argument is zero, or $+1$ if the argument is positive. Except for the zero case, the value of *signum X* is the same as the value of SIGN (1.0, X). A more complicated expression that will give the desired mathematical result for all real argument values, including zero, is

SIGN (0.5, X) $-$ SIGN (0.5, $-$X)

An application of the positive-difference function

The positive-difference function, *Dim,* is useful in applications that require the evaluation of the *excess* of one quantity over the other, where the desired value is *zero* if there is no excess. In a payroll calculation, we might compute gross pay, including overtime, with the expression

GPAY = BRATE * (MIN (THRS, 40.0) + 1.5 * DIM (THRS, 40.0))

The value of MIN (THRS, 40.0) is the number (40 or less) of "regular" hours, and DIM (THRS, 40.0) is an expression giving the number of hours in excess of 40—that is, the number of "overtime" hours to be paid at 1.5 times *Brate*. If *Thrs* is 40.0 or less, the value of this latter function will be zero.

2.3.4 Concerning Integer versus Real Exponents

We have noted that a real expression may be raised to an integer power. Does this differ from raising a real expression to a real power? How, for example, do the two expressions

A ** 2   and   A ** 2.0

differ? If *A* were 5.0, the value of each of these expressions would be 25.0. However, the use of integer exponents (wherever there is a choice) is to be preferred.

In translating the expression A ** 2, the Fortran processor will generate the same machine code as for A * A. Similarly, for A ** 3 it will generate the equivalent of A * A * A. If the power is an integer expression other than a constant, it will be evaluated and used to determine the number of times to repeat the multiplication operation.

By contrast, evaluation of an expression with an exponent of real type (even if the value of the real exponent is a whole number) involves the application of the logarithm and exponent functions. If $\mathcal{R}$ and $\mathcal{P}$ represent any real expressions, the operation $\mathcal{R}$ ** $\mathcal{P}$ is evaluated in the form

```
EXP (𝒫 * LOG (ℛ))
```

Compared with repeated multiplication, the use of the logarithm and exponential functions normally leads to much longer (and therefore more costly) computation and greater round-off error as well. For this reason, it is advisable to use exponents of integer type wherever possible.

Further restrictions on the *values* of expressions used in exponentiation are imposed to avoid inherent mathematical difficulties. For example, an expression whose value is zero must not be raised to a negative or zero power, and a negative expression must not be raised to any real power. These restrictions are necessary because the values of such expressions are not well-defined real numbers in the mathematical sense.

2.3.5 Exercises

1. In the following expressions, check for arguments of unacceptable type. Write the expressions correctly by using explicit type conversion, or in some other way.

   a) ABS (I + 1)
   b) SQRT (J)
   c) SQRT (REAL (NINT (Y) + 1.0))
   d) ABS (NINT (J + 3))
   e) MOD (Y, NINT (Z))
   f) EXP (REAL (LEG + 3.0))

2. Write Fortran expressions equivalent to each of the following mathematical expressions.

   a) $A \sin (\theta - t)$

   b) $\sin \dfrac{y}{\sqrt{x^2 + y^2}}$

   c) $\tan \theta$

   d) $\sin 2\pi L$

   e) $\sin \left(\tan^{-1} \dfrac{\sqrt{a^2 + b^2}}{|c|} \right)$

3. What is the value of the variable appearing on the left-hand side in each of the following assignment statements?

   a) `R7 = REAL (720)`
   b) `SR7 = SQRT (REAL (720))`
   c) `ISR7 = NINT (SQRT (REAL (720)))`

4. What is the value of the variable Z after the following sequence of assignment statements is executed?

   ```
   X = 3.0
   Y = 4.0
   Z = SQRT (X ** 2 + Y ** 2)
   ```

5. How many towels, each 1.8 feet wide, can be hung on a clothesline 15.7 feet long? How long is the piece of clothesline that must remain unused because it is too short to hold another towel? Write Fortran expressions giving the answer to each of these questions.

2.4   SIMPLE PROGRAMS WITH ASSIGNMENT STATEMENTS

When we write a program consisting of several statements, the sequence of statements in the program corresponds to the time sequence during execution of the program. If more than one of the statements refers to a particular cell, the contents of the cell at any time will be the last number that was stored there. For example, if we write

```
X = 1.2
Y = 3.4
X = Y
Y = 5.6
```

then the value assigned to X when the third statement is executed will be the value of Y *at that time,* namely, the value 3.4 that has been assigned to it during execution of the second statement. The final value of Y, however, will be 5.6 after the fourth statement has been executed. Note that the execution sequence of the statements proceeds from top to bottom, according to the way we are accustomed to reading. However, the sequence of execution *within* a statement does not necessarily proceed uniformly from left to right. The expression on the right is evaluated before assignment to the variable on the left, and within an expression the evaluation proceeds according to several rules, which may modify the strict left-to-right sequence (as we have seen).

The two sequences of statements in the following example have the same effect.

```
a) Y = A + B          b) Y = A + B
   X = A + B + C          X = Y + C
```

In (b) we have recognized that part of the expression has already been calculated and that only the new term, C, must be added. Similarly, if we have just assigned the value of A^3 to X and want A^4 for Y, we can save computation time if we write $Y = X * A$.

Interchanging the contents of a pair of cells is slightly more complicated than might be expected. To interchange the values of A and B we cannot simply write

```
A = B
B = A
```

because execution of the first of these statements destroys the original value in the cell named A; but this value is needed to provide the final value for B. Instead of the foregoing, we may use an "auxiliary" variable in the following manner.

```
AUX = A
A   = B
B   = AUX
```

Similarly, to cyclically permute the values of three variables, A, B, and C, we may write

```
AUX = A
A   = B
B   = C
C   = AUX
```

2.4.1   Initialization of Variable Values

We have said that the creation of a variable occurs when a symbolic name is associated with a storage cell. However, no value is associated with the variable at this time; we say that the variable's value is initially *undefined*. The value of a constant, on the other hand, is in effect stored in the cell at the time the cell is allocated.

Thus, if the first reference to a variable occurs as the left side of an assignment statement, with the expression on the right consisting wholly of constants, then the proper value can be determined and assigned. However, we must be careful to avoid using a variable in an expression on the right side of an assignment statement before it has been given a value in some valid manner. Such a practice would require reference to a cell whose value has not yet been defined.

Example 1   Suppose that we wish to form the sum of a number of variable values. By analogy to the way we would use an adding machine, we specify a separate operation for each variable to be added.

```
TOTAL = TOTAL + FIRST
TOTAL = TOTAL + SECOND
TOTAL = TOTAL + THIRD
. . .
```

The form ("syntax") of each of these statements is correct. However, in the first statement the expression on the right includes the variable *Total,* whose value is undefined so far as this sequence of statements is concerned. In order to compute the total correctly, we should include another step to initialize the value of that variable, for example by placing the statement

```
TOTAL = 0.0
```

ahead of the group of statements, so that it will be executed before any of the statements that include the variable *Total* in the expression on the right side.

Example 2 The variable *Kount* is to increase in value by 1 at various points in the program; thus its value at any time will indicate the number of times it has been incremented. The value of *Kount* should be initialized, perhaps by being set to 1, near the beginning of the program.

```
. . .
KOUNT = 1
. . .
KOUNT = KOUNT + 1
. . .
KOUNT = KOUNT + 1
. . .
```

2.4.2 Simple Input and Output Statements

Most programs, including even the simplest ones, involve the *reading* of data and the *printing* of results. Fortran input and output statements to accomplish these actions can also control the arrangement of input and output data values for a wide variety of numeric and nonnumeric applications. Later we shall see how to control this flexibility. At this point, however, we shall consider only the simplest form, called *list directed* input and output. Fortran statements calling for this input or output form are especially simple. The input data is prepared in "free form," and the arrangement of the results on a printer is determined by the data types of the results.

A list directed input statement has the form

```
READ *, list
```

and a list directed output statement is

```
PRINT *, list
```

The list used with either a READ or a PRINT statement consists of a variable (or an array element name; see Section 2.5), or of several such symbolic names separated by commas; a PRINT list may also include constants or expressions. Note the asterisk and the comma that separate the word READ or PRINT from the first item of the list.

Examples

```
READ *, DIAM
PRINT *, DIAM, 3.1416 * DIAM
READ *, X, Y
PRINT *, X, Y, (X + Y) / 2.0
READ *, X1, X2, X3, X4
PRINT *, 1, X1, 2, X2, 3, X3, 4, X4
```

The output list in the last example includes constants that are printed to help identify the results.

Data for list directed input is prepared in the form of constants of the proper type (corresponding to the type of the list items) on one or more data input lines (for example, punched cards). A comma or a blank space (plus as many additional spaces as desired) must be used to separate individual data input items on a line.

A pair of commas with no data value between them indicates a "null" data item. (There may be spaces between the commas, but no digits or other characters that represent data.) An input list item that corresponds to a null data item remains *unchanged* in value; if it has not been previously assigned a value, it remains undefined.

Printing explanatory text

Words or short phrases of text may be printed along with the numerical values specified by an output list. All that is necessary is to include a *character constant* among the items of an output list. A character constant consists of any Fortran or non-Fortran characters (see Section 1.2.1) enclosed in apostrophes (single quotes).

```
READ *, DIAM
PRINT *, 'Diameter[]is', DIAM, '[]Circumference[]is', 3.1416 * DIAM
```

Blank characters in the character constant (indicated by []) will be included in the printed output. The enclosing apostrophes will not appear. More details concerning output of character data are discussed in Chapter 5.

2.4.3 Exercises

1. Which of the following are valid Fortran assignment statements?

   a) `RP = 2.0 * (RL +  RW)`
   b) `I = I + 1`
   c) `I + 1 = I`
   d) `L = I + J + K`
   e) `3.14159 = PI`
   f) `SQRT (4.0) = 2.0`

2. Write a group of statements to perform each of the following tasks.

   a) *Diagonal of a box:* Read real values *A, B, C*; compute

   $$D = \sqrt{A^2 + B^2 + C^2}.$$

   Data:

A	B	C
3.0	4.0	12.0
2.4	3.2	3.0

   b) Read integer values *I1* and *I2*; print the quotient *I1 / I2* and the remainder (use MOD function), as well as *I1* and *I2*.

   Data:

I1	I2
17	4
25	6
18	3
5	4

   c) Read real values *X* and *Y*; compute and print their average.

   Data:

X	Y
8.6	9.4
104.3	127.5

3. The position of the minute hand of the clock at a certain instant is *Min1* minutes after the hour, where *Min1* is an integer between 0 and 59, inclusive. Write an assignment statement that will set the value of the variable *Min2* to the position of the minute hand *More* minutes later. (Hint: Use the function MOD.) Incorporate this assignment statement into a program, reading the values of *Min1* and *More* and printing *M2*.

   Data:

Min1	More
7	12
56	8
45	15
16	59
23	60
18	120

4. *Making change:* An interesting calculation, which can be programmed using the statements described in the foregoing sections, gives the amount of change for a purchase of 99 cents or less when the customer presents a dollar bill. Here are some hints on designing the program.

  i) It is probably simpler to work with cents than with dollars and to use integer variables.

 ii) First find the amount of change, in cents:

```
ICH = 100 - IPUR
```

iii) Find the number of 50-cent pieces (the largest coin) by integer division:

```
N50 = ICH / 50
```

iv) Find the remainder by using the MOD function. MOD (ICH, 50) is the amount of change that remains after taking out as many 50-cent pieces as possible. It is probably just as well to use the same variable *Ich* for this value:

```
ICH = MOD (ICH, 50)
```

 v) Continue using steps similar to (iii) and (iv) to find *N25, N10,* and *N5*; that is, find the number of pieces of each coin in order of decreasing value.

 vi) The remainder, after as many five-cent pieces as possible have been taken out, is the number of one-cent pieces.

 a) Write the necessary statements to read *Ipur* and to compute and print *N50, N25, N10, N5,* and *N1.*

 b) Rewrite the program for the case in which there are no 50-cent pieces available; that is, start with 25-cent pieces.

 c) Modify the program to take care of amounts up to $19.99 when the customer presents a $20 bill; that is, compute and print *N1000, N500,* and *N100* in addition.

 d) Rewrite the program to read both the amount of the purchase and the size of the bill presented (up to $20.00), assuming that the amount presented is more than the amount of the purchase. The same program should still work when more than one bill or coin is presented, provided that the change is less than $20.00 (see *IBill* in data below).

 e) Rewrite the program, keeping all calculations in integer cents, but doing all input with real numbers.

Data for (a) and (b):	Data for (c):	Data for (d) and (e):	
IPur	*IPur*	*IPur*	*IBill*
17	13.09	16.95	20.95
9	19.99	29.99	39.98
1	16.95	19.99	33.08
75			

2.5 ARRAYS AND ARRAY ELEMENTS

The compartmented box model

As a conceptual model, we may visualize a single box with one name, corresponding to an entire group of cells. This box is divided into compartments, one for each cell.

Such a group of cells is an *array*, and its name is the *array name*. An array name in Fortran has the same symbolic form as a simple variable. That is, it consists of from one to six letters or digits; the first character must be a letter. The type of an array name is determined in the same way as for a variable, either from the initial letter of the array name (by default or declared implicit type rules), or from an explicit type declaration (see Section 7.1). Each compartment within the box represents an *array element*. The type of each array element is the same as the type of the array name.

We shall first consider the case in which the compartments of the box are arranged in a single linear sequence, so that the array elements form a *linear array* or *list*. In mathematical applications, such an array is also called a *vector*.

2.5.1 Lists (Linear Arrays)

When a group of cells is arranged in a linear sequence, a particular cell of the array is identified by a sequential (ordinal) number: For example, a compartment might be designated as the *seventh* cell of a given array. Thus, an *array element name* appearing in a Fortran statement (within an expression, for example, or on the left side of an assignment statement) consists of the array name together with a *subscript* whose value uniquely designates a particular element within the array. In mathematical notation and in our flowcharts, the subscript is written in a lower position than the array name—for example:

$$Sam_1 \qquad \text{or} \qquad Line_{17}$$

The value of the subscript is interpreted as an *ordinal* number, giving the position of the designated element with relation to the other elements of the array. The examples given above are interpreted to mean "the first element of the list *Sam*" and "the seventeenth element of the list *Line*." In Fortran, the corresponding notation is

```
SAM(1)     or     LINE(17)
```

The expression enclosed in parentheses, which is to be interpreted as an ordinal number, is again called a subscript by analogy to the mathematical notation.

In order that the processor may create a list (that is, associate the array name with an appropriate number of cells of storage) before execution of the program begins, it must be provided with an *array declaration*. This declaration

indicates that the array name is not just an ordinary variable; furthermore, it
specifies the number of elements in the list. An array declaration for a list may
have any of the following three forms:

    REAL *Array name* (*Length*)
    INTEGER *Array name* (*Length*)
    DIMENSION *Array name* (*Length*)

For example,

    INTEGER X(20)
    REAL JOHN(3), DOE(16)
    DIMENSION ABLE(6), BAKER(120)

Note that declarations for two or more arrays can be combined into one declaration. Array declarations are discussed in more detail in Chapter 7.

Subscript expressions

The subscript, which is enclosed in parentheses and adjoined to the array name,
need not be a constant. It may be any integer expression whose value is *not less
than one* and *not greater than the Length* listed in the array declaration.†

   The particular array element to be referenced is determined by the *name* of
the array along with the *value* of the subscript expression. The form of the subscript expression is of no consequence.

Examples of array element names

    A(3)
    A(K)
    A(JOHN + 2)
    A(LOVER − 1)
    A(2 * MARY)
    A(73 * I + 4961)
    A(3 * JIM −1)
    A(50 * LINE + LETR)
    A(NINT (SQRT (0.5 * X) + A(K)) + 7)

   Note that a real expression can be included within a subscript if explicit type
conversion is applied. Use of the rounding function *Nint* is preferable to *Int* for
this conversion, because small errors in the representation of the real expression
can cause its value to be just less than the expected integer.

---

† As we shall see (Section 7.1), an array declaration can include a lower bound on the subscript value as well as an upper bound. However, at this point we consider only the simpler
"default" case in which the lower subscript bound is one.

Example 1 The 12 cells of the array *Acct* contain account balances for a very small bank. A program to process these bank accounts includes the following statements:

```
READ *, IDENT, VALUE
ACCT(IDENT) = ACCT(IDENT) + VALUE
PRINT *, IDENT, VALUE, ACCT(IDENT)
```

The data to be read consists of an account identification number, which is an integer between 1 and 12, as well as a value signifying the amount of money (dollars) to be deposited in the designated account. For example, if the value of *Ident* is 7 and the amount of *Value* is 100.00, then 100 dollars is to be deposited in account number 7.

2.5.2 Rectangular Arrays (Matrices) and Other Arrays

In some problems, we have a group of items that are ordered according to two or more independent index numbers. For example, each square of a chessboard can be identified by a row number and a column number. An array for which two indexes are required to specify an individual element is usually called a *rectangular array* or, in mathematical applications, a *matrix*. The first index identifies the row and the second identifies the column, according to the standard notation of matrix algebra. In Fortran, the two index numbers are again called subscripts, and they are written (as before) in parentheses and are separated by a comma. Referring to Fig. 2.13, we see that $Chek_{5,8}$ is the element in the fifth row and the eighth column of the array named *Chek*.

Rectangular arrays are often used in statistical analysis, economics, and other applications where individual numbers are identified by two parameters. For example, in the analysis of musical forms, the "transition probabilities," or the relative frequency with which one form is followed by another, may be represented in a rectangular array. For sales analysis, a shoe store might use an array showing how many shoes of category *i* were sold during a given month by employee *j*.

The following are some names that might appear in a Fortran program in reference to specific elements of a rectangular array.

```
CHEK(5, 8)
CHEK(3 * I + 1, K)
SHOES(I, J)
SHOES(17, M + 3)
FORM(L1, L2)
FORM(MUSIC, LIT)
```

Fortran also provides for arrays arranged according to three index values, such as a stack of cubes forming a large block (parallelopiped). An array name would apply to the entire stack of cubes, and an individual element (cube) would

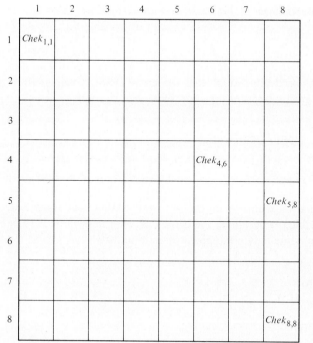

Figure 2.13

be identified by appending three ordinals to the array name. Although in the vast majority of applications linear and rectangular arrays are sufficient, there are applications in which arrays of three or even more dimensions can be used advantageously. For example, we might identify the positions on a board used for playing three-dimensional tic-tac-toe as elements of a 3 by 3 by 3 array. Economic analysis or statistics relating to any quantity considered as a function of three or more parameters can use three or more subscripts advantageously. For example,

```
A(2, 5, 3)
B(3, 2, 2)
SHOES(ISTORE, KATEG, MAN)
TABLE(I, J, K)
ALPHA(K, 3, 4 * I − 2)
```

Fortran permits as many as seven subscripts to be used with an array name. A declaration for an array with multiple subscripts must include the maximum value for each of the subscripts. In the declaration, as well as in the name for an element of such an array, commas are used to separate the individual subscript expressions. (Array declarations are discussed further in Section 7.1.)

2.5.3 Using Array Element Names

An array element name can be used at any place in an expression where an ordinary variable can be used. In particular, array element names may be used as function arguments, or as either operand of an exponentiation operation. The subscript expression must first be evaluated, so that the array element value can be determined and combined with the rest of the expression. For example,

```
A(K(3) − 1) + X
SQRT (ABLE(73 * I + 4961, JOHN + 2))
X ** LIST(I + 3)
A(I) ** A(J)
PRINT *, CHEK(NINT (SQRT (0.5 * X) + A(K)) + 7, 73 * I + 4961)
```

An array element name may appear on the left in an assignment statement, in the same way as a variable, to designate the cell to which a new value is to be assigned. An array element name may also appear in an input list.

```
LIST(3) = 14 * K
A(1, J) = SQRT (2.0)
READ *, A(1), A(2), A(3)
```

2.5.4 Exercises

1. Each of the following describes a sequence of five array elements. Write a subscript expression involving the variable *J*, which will designate each of the five elements in turn as *J* takes on the sequence of values 1, 2, 3, 4, 5.

    a) Each of the five elements of the linear array *Beta* in turn.
    b) The third through seventh elements of the linear array *Alpha*.
    c) The odd-numbered, first through ninth, elements of the linear array *Gamma*.

2. Write array declarations for the linear arrays mentioned in Exercise 1.

3. Write an array declaration for an array *Carton* arranged according to three index values, where the value of the first subscript ranges from 1 to 5, the value of the second subscript ranges from 1 to 4, and the value of the third subscript ranges from 1 to 17.

4. Write a program based on Example 1. Include an array declaration for *Acct*. Read beginning balances into $Acct_1$, $Acct_2$, $Acct_3$, . . . , $Acct_{12}$. Process one transaction.

    Data:

    Beginning balances:

    50, 0.0, 3.98, 700.00, 8.00, 0.0, 50.0, 75.00, 17.50, 88.88, 950.00, 0.0

    Transaction:

    Ident   7
    Value   100.00

5. Referring to Fig. 2.14, give the value of each of the following array elements.

   a) B(1)   b) J(3)
   c) B(62)   d) J(K)
   e) B(K − 2)   f) J(11)
   g) B(K + 56)   h) J(9)
   i) J(K + 6)   j) J(10)

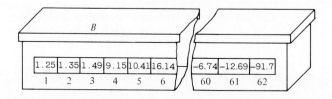

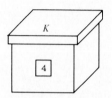

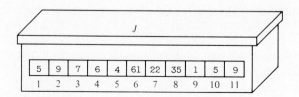

Figure 2.14

6. Referring to Fig. 2.14, give the value of each of the following array elements.

   a) J(K)
   b) J(J(K))
   c) B(K)
   d) B(J(K))
   e) B(J(J(K)))
   f) J(NINT (SQRT (B(K))))

2.6 DOUBLE PRECISION NUMBERS IN FORTRAN

Occasionally, the precision offered by arithmetic with real numbers proves to be insufficient, because of errors introduced by the need to store approximations to the true values of quantities in cells that can contain only a limited number of digits. Calculations that are sensitive to such limitations on precision can be performed with greater precision than that provided for expressions of real type. Fortran permits numbers to be stored in a *double precision* internal representation that includes approximately twice as many significant digits as ordinary real numbers contain. Such numbers are said to be of double precision type.

Double precision *constants* look just like real constants written with an exponent, except that the letter D is used in place of the E in the exponent. For example, the constant

    12.543210009876 D 3

means

$$12.543210009876 \times 10^3.$$

(The D, like the E in a real constant, indicates that the following integer constant is an exponent to be applied as a power of 10.)

Variables and *arrays* of this type must always be specified by a declared implicit type specification or in an implicit declaration, since there is no default implicit type specification for double precision type. For example,

    IMPLICIT DOUBLE PRECISION (D - E)
    DOUBLE PRECISION A, BETA, Q(6, 10), M

These statements declare that *A, Beta, M,* and *Q,* as well as all names beginning with D or E, refer to values of double precision type.

Arithmetic *expressions* involving double precision constants, variables, and array elements will have values of double precision.

An expression may contain subexpressions of integer, real, and double precision types. When one operand in any addition, subtraction, multiplication, or division operation is of integer or real type, and the other is of double precision type, automatic conversion of the integer or real subexpression to double precision type will take place before the operation is performed. Exponentiation of a double precision expression by an integer expression is permitted in Fortran, and is equivalent to repeated multiplication.

As shown in Table 8.1, predefined double precision functions are available corresponding to most of the real functions. The functions *Real* and *Int* may be used to explicitly convert a double precision argument to real or integer type (with truncation in the latter case), and *Dble* will convert a real or integer argument to double precision. Note also the function *Dprod* (with two real arguments and a result that is their double precision product), whose use is important in many mathematical applications.

Mixed assignment between integer or real types and double precision type is permitted. Fortran does not require that numerical values be rounded when they are reduced from double to single precision, either by mixed assignment or by explicit type conversion (using *Real* or *Int*). Most processors reduce the precision by "chopping," or simply ignoring the less significant part.

List directed *input* and *output* of double precision data presents no special problems. For input, some flexibility is permitted: Data values corresponding to double precision list items may appear as double precision constants (with exponent indicated by the letter D) or as real constants written with or without an E exponent.

2.7 COMPLEX NUMBERS IN FORTRAN

The Fortran language provides for variables, constants, and expressions of *complex* type. A complex number, *z*, consists of a pair of real numbers, *x* and *y*, called the *real part* and the *imaginary part*, respectively. Thus a number of complex type occupies a pair of cells; in terms of our conceptual computer model introduced in Chapter 1, it is stored in a box with two compartments.

A complex *constant* is written as a pair of real constants (of any valid form) separated by a comma and enclosed in parentheses. The first of the real constants is the real part of the complex constant, and the second real constant is the imaginary part.

A complex *variable* or *array* must be declared explicitly, since there is no default implicit type association for complex variables; for example,

```
IMPLICIT COMPLEX (C)
COMPLEX Z1, Z2, Z3
```

Operations of addition, subtraction, multiplication, or division of a pair of expressions of complex type are automatically interpreted by the Fortran processor according to the rules of complex arithmetic (Table 2.2). Complex exponentiation is also permitted.

Example 1 The statement

```
Z1 = (6.94, -5.9) + (3.941, 2.5 E -3)
```

assigns to *Z1* the complex value whose real part is $6.94 + 3.941$ or 10.881, and whose imaginary part is -5.8975.

Table 2.2 Rules of complex arithmetic

Let z_1 and z_2 be defined as follows:

Complex number	Real part	Imaginary part
z_1	x_1	y_1
z_2	x_2	y_2

Then the result of performing arithmetic operations on z_1 and z_2 will be the following (with the assumption that r is a real number).

Operation	Result	
	Real part	Imaginary part
$z_1 + z_2$	$x_1 + x_2$	$y_1 + y_2$
$z_1 - z_2$	$x_1 - x_2$	$y_1 - y_2$
$z_1 \times z_2$	$x_1 \times x_2 - y_1 \times y_2$	$x_1 \times y_2 + y_1 \times x_2$
$z_1 \div z_2$	$\dfrac{x_1 \times x_2 + y_1 \times y_2}{x_2^2 + y_2^2}$	$\dfrac{x_2 \times y_1 - y_2 \times x_1}{x_2^2 + y_2^2}$
$r \times z_1$	$r \times x_1$	$r \times y_1$
$|z_1|$	$\sqrt{x_1^2 + y_1^2}$	zero

Example 2

```
Z2 = (6.94, -5.9) ** 2
```

or the equivalent statement

```
Z2 = (6.94, -5.9) * (6.94, -5.9)
```

assigns to *Z2* the square of the complex value whose real part is 6.94 and whose imaginary part is −5.9. The real part of this product, according to the definition of multiplication (Table 2.2), is $6.94^2 - 5.9^2$, and the imaginary part is $2 \times (6.94 \times -5.9)$.

Example 3

```
Z3 = Z1 / Z2
```

assigns to *Z3* real and imaginary parts computed according to the rules for complex division given in Table 2.2.

Arrays and functions of complex type may also be declared and used in Fortran.

Expressions of mixed type are allowed in Fortran, except that no expression may include subexpressions of *both* complex and double precision types. An operand of integer or real type will be converted automatically to a complex form with a zero imaginary part, and then the operation will be performed in complex arithmetic.

As shown in Table 8.1, predefined complex functions are available for computing square roots, logarithms, exponentials, and trigonometric functions. The function *Abs* may be applied to a complex argument to produce a real result; the function *Conjg* is also provided. Explicit conversions between real and complex types use the functions *Cmplx, Real,* and *Aimag.* For example, the complex quantity whose real part is zero and whose imaginary part is $f(x, y)$, where f is a real function of two real arguments, can be constructed by means of the function *Cmplx.*

```
Z = CMPLX (0.0, F (X, Y))
```

Variables and array elements of complex type may appear in an input or output list; constants and other expressions of complex type may also appear in an output list. For list directed input, a data value corresponding to a complex list item is prepared as a pair of real constants (of any valid form) separated by a comma and enclosed in parentheses.

CHAPTER 3
PROGRAM STRUCTURES FOR SELECTION

All of the program examples in Chapter 2 illustrate *sequential execution* of program statements. In each of those examples, the statements are executed in sequence from top to bottom, as they are written on the page.

In the analysis of algorithms and in the construction of Fortran programs, we find that two other program structures (in addition to sequential execution) are needed. These are *selection* and *repetition*. A selection structure is needed when there are two (or more) alternative sequences of statements, and a decision is required during execution of the program in order to select a particular alternative. This chapter covers selection structures in detail. Program structures for repetition (of a group of program statements) are discussed in Chapter 4.

3.1 ALTERNATIVE STATEMENT SEQUENCES

We present some examples involving two alternative sequences of statements, showing how one sequence or the other may be selected on the basis of data values that can be recognized during execution of the program.

Example 1: Payroll with overtime   Employees are to be paid at $1\frac{1}{2}$ times their normal hourly rate, for hours worked in a given week in excess of 40 hours. Therefore, if the number of hours worked is 40 or less we simply multiply the number of hours worked by the hourly pay rate to find the employee's gross pay. But if the employee has worked more than 40 hours, a more complicated calculation is required. We compute regular pay by multiplying the hourly rate by 40, and we compute overtime pay by multiplying $1\frac{1}{2}$ times the hourly rate times the overtime hours (that is, hours worked minus 40). The employee's gross pay is then the sum of regular pay and overtime pay.

The payroll program includes separate statement sequences for these two cases, along with a *control statement* to select one or the other of the two statement sequences, depending on whether or not the employee worked more than 40 hours. The program, including the control statement and the two alternative statement sequences (along with input and output statements), appears as follows:

```
* Example 1. Payroll with overtime.
      READ *, RATE, HOURS
      IF (HOURS .GT. 40.0) THEN
         REGPAY = RATE * 40.0
         OVTPAY = 1.5 * RATE * (HOURS - 40.0)
       ELSE
         REGPAY = RATE * HOURS
         OVTPAY = 0.0
       END IF
      PAY = REGPAY + OVTPAY
      PRINT *, RATE, HOURS, REGPAY, OVTPAY, PAY
      END
```

The control statement

```
      IF (HOURS .GT. 40.0) THEN
```

indicates that the selection is to be based on whether or not the *assertion*

```
      HOURS .GT. 40.0
```

is true. If it is true, the statements immediately following the control statement are to be executed; if it is false, the statements between ELSE and END IF are to be executed.

General selection structure

Example 1 illustrates the general form of a program structure for selection between two alternative sequences of statements, on the basis of an assertion that is to be tested during execution of the program. Such a program structure has the general form

```
IF (Assertion) THEN
      Then block
   ELSE
      Else block
   END IF
```

The statements in the *Then* block are to be executed if the *Assertion* is true, and the statements in the *Else* block are to be executed if the *Assertion* is false. Figure 3.1 is a flowchart corresponding to this general program structure, and Fig. 3.2 shows how this structure applies to the payroll calculation of Example 1.

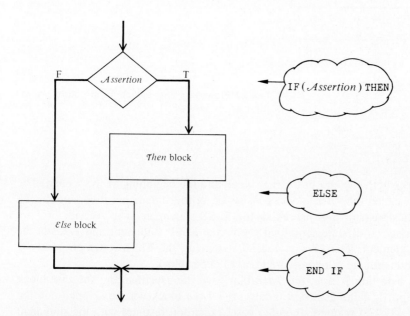

Fig. 3.1 Flowchart for general selection structure. The *Then* block will be executed if the *Assertion* is true; the *Else* block will be executed if the *Assertion* is false.

The selection structure begins with the **IF ... THEN** statement, and terminates with the **END IF** statement. In the middle of the structure is

```
ELSE
```

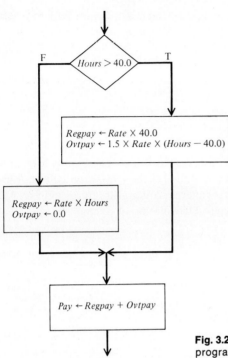

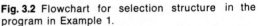

Fig. 3.2 Flowchart for selection structure in the program in Example 1.

which marks both the end of the first block and the beginning of the second. The first block, called the *Then* block, consists of all the statements *following* the IF ... THEN statement and *preceding* the ELSE statement. The second, or *Else,* block consists of all statements that *follow* the ELSE statement and *precede* the END IF statement. The IF ... THEN statement, the ELSE statement, and the END IF statement are not considered part of either block.

If the assertion is true, the *Then* block will be executed and the *Else* block will be skipped; if the assertion is false, the *Then* block will be skipped and the *Else* block will be executed. In either case, execution resumes with the statement immediately following the END IF statement.

In a program containing a decision structure, we emphasize the alternative statement blocks by indenting each statement four spaces. The amount of this indentation is arbitrary, and is ignored by the processor, but the indentation should be consistent.

Example 2: Small ships and large ships The Port Authority produces a monthly report concerning the ships that entered the harbor during the month. In the harbor there are some small piers, which can handle "small" ships of 3500 tons displacement or less, as well as some large piers, which are used for "large" ships of more than 3500 tons. The report is to indicate the number of small ships and the number of large ships, as well as the total weight of the ships in each category. Thus, in preparing the report, the following steps are required (see also the flowchart in Fig. 3.3).

```
* Example 2. Small ships and large ships.
      NSMALL = 0
      NLARGE = 0
      WSMALL = 0.0
      WLARGE = 0.0
      ...
*     .. Steps to process data for each ship.
      READ *, TONS
      IF (TONS .LE. 3500) THEN
          NSMALL = NSMALL + 1
          WSMALL = WSMALL + TONS
        ELSE
          NLARGE = NLARGE + 1
          WLARGE = WLARGE + TONS
        END IF
      ...
```

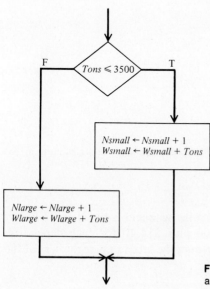

Fig. 3.3 Flowchart for selection structure in Example 2.

Example 3: Average displacement   After the input data for all ships has been processed, we wish to calculate the *average* displacement (weight in tons) for small ships and for large ships. However, it may happen that in a certain month no ships with a displacement greater than 3500 tons entered the harbor. To avoid dividing the *Nlarge* when its value is zero, we provide a separate statement sequence to be executed in this case. (See also Fig. 3.4.)

```
* Example 3. Average displacement of large ships.
      ...
      IF (NLARGE .EQ. 0) THEN
         AVLRG = 0.0
      ELSE
         AVLRG = WLARGE / NLARGE
      END IF
      PRINT *, NLARGE, WLARGE, AVLRG
      ...
```

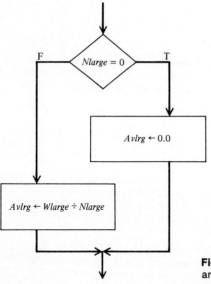

Fig. 3.4 Flowchart for selection structure in Example 3.

Example 4: Income tax withholding   Income tax withheld is based on gross pay minus a weekly exemption, which is $11.00 plus $14.40 for each dependent. However, the exemption must not be greater than the gross pay, regardless of the number of dependents. (See also Fig. 3.5.)

```
* Example 4. Income tax withholding base.
     READ *, GRPAY, DEPEND
     EXEMP = 11.00 + 14.40 * DEPEND
     IF (EXEMP .LE. GRPAY) THEN
         WHBASE = GRPAY - EXEMP
       ELSE
         WHBASE = 0.0
       END IF
     PRINT *, GRPAY, DEPEND, EXEMP, WHBASE
     END
```

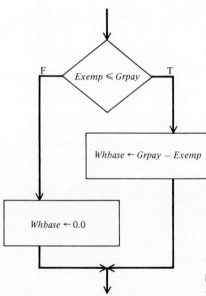

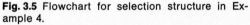

Fig. 3.5 Flowchart for selection structure in Example 4.

Example 5: Ranking two numbers   Two data values, X and Y, are given. We wish to set the values of corresponding integer variables Rx and Ry to indicate the relative sizes of the X and Y values: The integer variable corresponding to the larger variable is to be set to 1 and the integer variable corresponding to the smaller value is to be set to 2. We assume that the values of X and Y are not equal. (See also Fig. 3.6.)

```
* Example 5. Ranking two numbers.
     INTEGER RX, RY
     READ *, X, Y
     IF (X .GT. Y) THEN
          RX = 1
          RY = 2
     ELSE
          RY = 1
          RX = 2
     END IF
     PRINT *, X, Y, RX, RY
     END
```

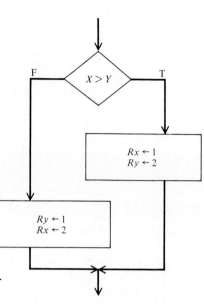

Fig. 3.6 Flowchart for selection structure in Example 5.

Example 6: Value swapping   We shall use the following rather trivial example throughout this chapter, to illustrate a number of points concerning selection structures.

Assume that the value of I is either 1 or 2. If it is 1, change it to 2; if it is 2, change it to 1.

In the first place, the desired result can be achieved with a single expression —no selection is actually required. The value of the expression $3 - I$ is 2 when I is 1, and is 1 when I is 2. Therefore, the statement

```
I = 3 - I
```

is all that is required.

However, we may use this problem to illustrate the basic selection structure, as follows. (See also Fig. 3.7.)

```
* Example 6. Swap the values 1 and 2.
     READ *, I
     IF (I .EQ. 1) THEN
          I = 2
     ELSE
          I = 1
     END IF
     PRINT *, I
     END
```

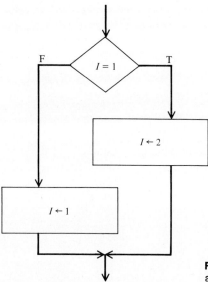

Fig. 3.7 Flowchart for selection structure in Example 6.

3.1.1 The Assertion

We return to examine the opening statement of a selection structure in greater detail. The most important component of this statement is the assertion. In its simplest form, an assertion is a *relational expression,* consisting of a pair of expressions separated by a *relational operator:*

$$\mathcal{E}xpression_1 \qquad \mathcal{R}elational \ operator \qquad \mathcal{E}xpression_2$$

Each of the expressions may be any valid expression of integer, real, or double precision type. The relational operator is one of the following:

Symbol	Customary notation	Meaning
.EQ.	$=$	Equals
.NE.	$\neq$	Is not equal to
.LT.	$<$	Is less than
.LE.	$\leq$	Is less than or equal to
.GT.	$>$	Is greater than
.GE.	$\geq$	Is greater than or equal to

The following are some further examples of relational expressions.

Example 7

```
TONY .LE. ALPHA
```

Meaning: The current value of *Tony* is less than or equal to the current value of *Alpha.* (This assertion at any time is either true or false.)

Example 8

```
X .GT. Y + 3.0
```

Meaning: *X* is greater than the quantity $Y + 3.0$.

If the expressions to be compared in a relational expression are of different types, their *difference* is computed as a mixed-type expression (Section 2.2.2) and the result is compared with zero. Thus,

```
I + J .LE. SQRT (X)
```

is computed as if it were written

```
I + J - SQRT (X) .LE. 0.0
```

Because there is no mathematical ordering among the complex numbers, only the relational operators `.EQ.` and `.NE.` are permitted with complex expressions. As we shall see in Chapter 5, relational expressions can also be written to compare character strings.

A pitfall to avoid

Because of the finite precision of the number representation used in computers, the value of a real expression may deviate slightly from its expected value. This means, in particular, that two expressions that are expected to have the same value may differ by a small amount. (In fact, we should consider it unusual when any two real expressions have *exactly* the same computed value.) A test for the exact equality of such a pair of expressions may, therefore, produce unexpected results. Any relational expression that requires the comparison of two *real* expressions for *equality* or *inequality,* such as

```
X .EQ. 2.0
A .EQ. B
```

should therefore be viewed with suspicion. Such expressions will often be false, when on mathematical grounds we would have expected them to be true.

In particular, the values of simple decimal constants such as 0.1 or 0.02 are not represented exactly on computers which use a binary (base 2) number representation. They are represented by slightly smaller values, just as the constant 1/3 is represented by a slightly smaller value when carried out to any finite number of decimal places as 0.3333333 .... Therefore, the result of adding 10 copies of the constant 0.1, for instance, will not be equal to the value of the constant 1.0 but will be slightly smaller on any binary computer.

Instead of asking whether two expressions are exactly equal, or whether an expression is exactly equal to zero, we should instead test for *approximate* equality, using some small tolerance, such as 1.0×10^{-6}. (The tolerance value must be chosen carefully in each specific case, to avoid an unacceptably broad definition of approximate equality.) We could write a relational expression such as

```
ABS (A - B) .LT. 1.0 E -6
```

that will be true whenever the two expressions are approximately equal to within the stated tolerance.

Compound relations

Relational expressions can be combined to express more complicated assertions consisting of compound relations.

Example 9   *I* is either 1 or 2.

```
(I .EQ. 1) .OR. (I .EQ. 2)
```

Example 10   *A* is zero and *B* is not zero.

```
(A .EQ. 0.0) .AND. (B .NE. 0.0)
```

The connectives *or, and,* and *not* are used to form compound relations. In Fortran, these connectives are written as `.OR.`, `.AND.`, and `.NOT.`. These connectives are used to combine *entire relations* (complete relational expressions and compound relations). They must not be used to combine the arithmetic expressions that form *parts* of a relation. In Example 9, for instance, it would be unacceptable to write

```
I .EQ. 1 .OR. 2
```

Further examples

```
(X .GT. 3.0) .AND. (X + 2.0 .GT. Y)
((A .LE. X) .AND. (B .GE. Y)) .OR. (C .GT. Z)
((I .GT. 3) .OR. (J .LE. 2)) .AND. (GAMMA .LT. EPS)
(ABS (X1 - X2) / X1 .LE. EPS) .AND. (LOG (X1) .GT. EPS)
.NOT. ((X .LT. Y) .OR. (G .GT. GG) .OR. (P ** 2 .LT. PL))
```

3.1.2   Nested Selection

A block of statements within a selection structure may, in turn, contain another such structure.

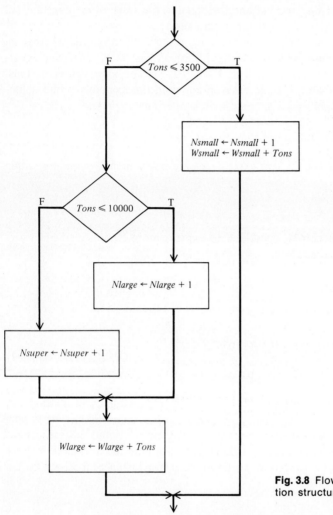

Fig. 3.8 Flowchart for nested selection structure in Example 11.

Example 11 Suppose that the report discussed in Example 2 is to be further refined. Besides the total number and weight of small ships and large ships, it is now necessary to subdivide the total number (but not the total weight) of large ships into "ordinary" large ships and "super-large" ships.

```
* Example 11. Small ships, large ships, and super ships.
      NSMALL = 0
      NLARGE = 0
      NSUPER = 0
      WSMALL = 0.0
      WLARGE = 0.0
      ...
```

```
*        .. Steps to process data for each ship.
        READ *, TONS
        IF (TONS .LE. 3500) THEN
            NSMALL = NSMALL + 1
            WSMALL = WSMALL + TONS
         ELSE
            IF (TONS .LE. 10000) THEN
                NLARGE = NLARGE + 1
             ELSE
                NSUPER = NSUPER + 1
             END IF
            WLARGE = WLARGE + TONS
         END IF
        ...
```

The flowchart in Fig. 3.8 shows the relation between the two selection structures in this program. The outer selection structure is based on the assertion TONS .LE. 3500. If this assertion is true, the *Then* block consisting of two statements is executed and the *Else* block is skipped. If this assertion is false, the *Else* block is executed. This block contains an inner selection structure based on the assertion TONS .LE. 10000, followed by a statement adding *Tons* to *Wlarge*. Thus this final statement will be executed as part of the outer *Else* block, regardless of which statement sequence of the inner selection structure is executed.

Example 12　The program in Figs. 3.9 and 3.10 reads an "old" bank account balance, a transaction value, and a code, which is 1 for a deposit and 2 for a withdrawal. If the transaction is a deposit, the program increases the balance by the transaction amount. If it is a withdrawal, it first checks to see that the old balance is sufficient, and then subtracts the transaction amount from the old balance. (See also Exercise 11 on p. 113.)

```
* Program to post bank account transactions, based on Kode
* which is 1 for deposit and 2 for withdrawal.
        READ *, BAL1, VALUE, KODE
        IF (KODE .EQ. 1) THEN
*            .. Deposit.
            PRINT *, 'Deposit.'
            BAL2 = BAL1 + VALUE
         ELSE
*            .. Withdrawal (after test for overdraft)
            IF (BAL1 .GE. VALUE) THEN
                PRINT *, 'Withdrawal.'
                BAL2 = BAL1 - VALUE
             ELSE
                PRINT *, 'Overdraft.'
                BAL2 = 0.0
             END IF
         END IF
        PRINT *, BAL1, VALUE, KODE, BAL2
        END
```

Figure 3.9

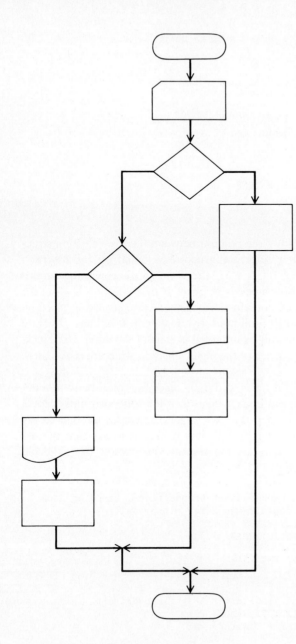

Fig. 3.10 Skeleton flowchart.

Example 13   (Compare Example 6.) If the value of *I* is 1, change it to 2; if it is 2, change it to 1. However, if the value of *I* is neither 1 nor 2, print an error message. (See Fig. 3.11.)

```
* Example 13. Swap the values 1 and 2.
      IF ((I .EQ. 1) .OR. (I .EQ. 2)) THEN
          IF (I .EQ. 1) THEN
              I = 2
            ELSE
              I = 1
            END IF
          PRINT *, I
        ELSE
          PRINT *, 'The□value□of□I□is□incorrect.'
        END IF
      END
```

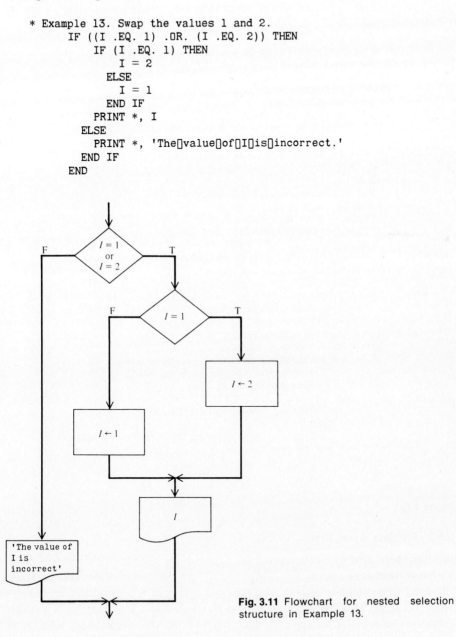

Fig. 3.11 Flowchart for nested selection structure in Example 13.

Example 14   The program and flowchart in Figs. 3.12 and 3.13 illustrate the use of selection in a longer program. This program finds all the roots of the quadratic equation $Ax^2 + Bx + C = 0$, given the coefficients A, B, and C. Several tests are required to handle special cases that arise when one or more of the coefficients is zero.

```
* Program to find all roots of a quadratic equation,
* given the coefficients A, B, and C.
      READ *, A, B, C
      PRINT *, 'Coefficients□are', A, B, C
      IF (A .EQ. 0.0) THEN
          IF (B .NE. 0.0) THEN
              PRINT *, 'Not□a□quadratic.□□Root□is', −C / B
          ELSE
              PRINT *, 'Equation□has□the□form□C = 0.□□C□is', C
          END IF
      ELSE
*         .. A is not zero. Find discriminant.
          PART1 = −B / (2.0 * A)
          DISC = B ** 2 − 4.0 * A * C
          PART2 = SQRT (ABS (DISC)) / (2.0 * A)
          IF (DISC .LT. 0.0) THEN
*             .. Discriminant is negative. Roots are complex.
              PRINT *, 'Complex□roots', PART1, '□+□or□−□i', PART2
          ELSE
*             .. Discriminant is zero or positive. Roots are real.
*             .. For maximum accuracy, change sign of PART2,
*                if necessary, to agree with sign of PART1.
              PART2 = SIGN (PART2, PART1)
              R1 = PART1 + PART2
*             .. For maximum accuracy, compute second root as
*                C / (A * R1) rather than as PART1 − PART2,
*                unless R1 is zero.
              IF (R1 .NE. 0.0) THEN
                  PRINT *, 'Real□roots', R1, C / (A * R1)
              ELSE
                  PRINT *, 'Real□roots', R1, PART1 − PART2
              END IF
          END IF
      END IF
      END
```

Figure 3.12

3.1.3 Multiple Alternatives

We have seen how to create a program structure for selecting either of two alternative sequences of statements. We now turn to a discussion of the case in which there are three or more alternatives. Any multiple selection problem can, in principle, be recast as a combination of two-way selections. However, such a transformation introduces an apparent hierarchy among the alternatives, whereas in the original problem all the alternatives may be equally important.

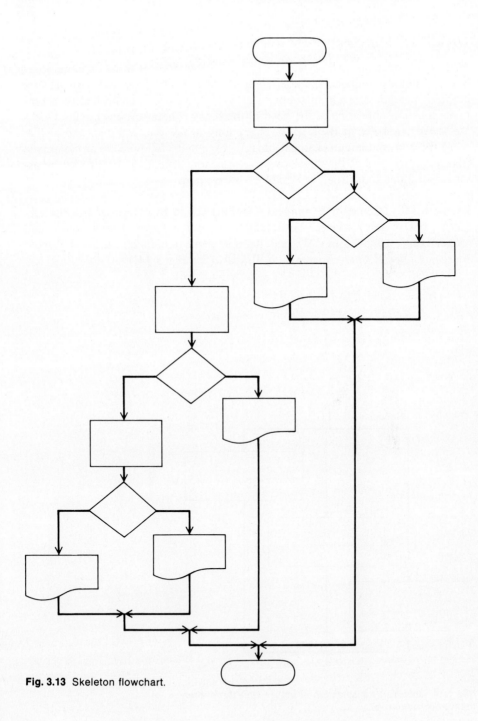

Fig. 3.13 Skeleton flowchart.

The ELSE IF *statement*

A selection structure in Fortran can include a sequence of three or more alternative statement sequences, rather than a single *Then* block and a single *Else* block. Execution of each alternative statement sequence is controlled by a separate assertion appearing at the head of the block. The assertions for the blocks are tested (in order of their appearance) until a true one is found, and at that point the corresponding statement block is executed (followed by an automatic transfer to the end of the entire multiple selection structure). If none of the assertions is found to be true, the *Else* block is executed.

Example 15 (Compare Example 11.) Ships are to be categorized as "small" (3500 tons or less), "large" (over 3500 tons but not over 10,000 tons), and "super" (over 10,000 tons). We omit the statements to initialize the totals *Nsmall, Nlarge, Nsuper, Wsmall, Wlarge,* and *Wsuper*. (See Fig. 3.14.)

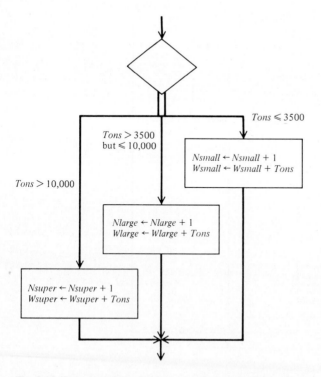

Fig. 3.14 Flowchart for selection structure with three alternatives (Example 15).

```
*  Example 15. Small ships, large ships, and super ships.
      ...
*        .. Statements to process data for each ship.
      READ *, TONS
      IF (TONS .LE. 3500) THEN
          NSMALL = NSMALL + 1
          WSMALL = WSMALL + TONS
        ELSE IF (TONS .LE. 10000) THEN
          NLARGE = NLARGE + 1
          WLARGE = WLARGE + TONS
        ELSE
          NSUPER = NSUPER + 1
          WSUPER = WSUPER + TONS
      END IF
      ...
```

Although the effect of this program and that of Example 11 are similar, there is an essential difference in viewpoint between the two programs. In Example 11, the ships are first divided into two categories, and then one of these is further subdivided. In Example 15, on the other hand, the basic selection structure treats the three categories as being equally important.

Example 16   The value of Y is to be computed by one of three formulas, depending on the value of X. If X is negative, then Y has the constant value 1. If Y is between 0 and 1, inclusive, then the value of Y is obtained from the formula $4X^3 + 1$. If X is greater than 1, the formula is $12X^2 - 12X + 5$.

```
      IF (X .LT. 0.0) THEN
          Y = 1.0
        ELSE IF (X .LE. 1.0) THEN
          Y = 4.0 * X ** 3 + 1.0
        ELSE
          Y = 12.0 * X ** 2 - 12.0 * X + 5.0
      END IF
```

The first assertion, X .LT. 0.0, is tested and if it is found to be true, the value of Y is set to 1; execution then proceeds from the END IF statement. If the first assertion is false, however, the next assertion is tested in turn to determine whether X is less than or equal to one; if so, the value of Y is computed according to the second formula. If neither of these assertions is found to be true, it may be concluded that X is greater than one. The $\mathcal{E}lse$ block will be executed in this case, and the third formula will be used to compute Y.

It is important to note that *exactly one* of the assignment statements in this example will be executed. When a true assertion is found, the corresponding block is executed, followed by a transfer to the end of the selection structure. The $\mathcal{E}lse$ block covers the case in which none of the assertions is found to be true.

Example 17 A transaction code is expected to have the value 1, 2, or 3. Some special action must be taken if any other value is encountered.

```
READ *, KODE
IF (KODE .EQ. 1) THEN
    [Process transaction code 1.]
  ELSE IF (KODE .EQ. 2) THEN
    [Process transaction code 2.]
  ELSE IF (KODE .EQ. 3) THEN
    [Process transaction code 3.]
  ELSE
    [Take special action.]
END IF
```

3.1.4 Complete and Incomplete Selection Structures

The most general selection structure available in Fortran is that discussed in Section 3.1.3—namely, an overall structure that opens with a control statement of the form

```
IF (Assertion) THEN
```

and ends with the statement END IF; between these two statements, there may be at most one ELSE statement, and there may be any number of statements of the form

```
ELSE IF (Assertion) THEN
```

all of which must precede the ELSE statement (if there is one). The IF . . . THEN, ELSE IF . . . THEN, and ELSE statements may be followed by sequences of statements to be executed under certain conditions determined by the truth of the assertions.

The assertions are tested in sequence, in the order of their appearance. When an assertion in an IF . . . THEN or ELSE IF . . . THEN statement is found to be true, the block of statements immediately following is executed, after which execution proceeds with the statement following END IF. As a consequence, if more than one of the assertions is true, the first one encountered will control the execution of the selection structure. If none of the assertions is true, the block of statements following ELSE will be executed: This block acts as a catchall to handle cases not covered by any of the assertions.

As we shall see, the ELSE statement (and the *Else* block that follows it) may sometimes be omitted. But in a complete selection structure, where the ELSE statement is not omitted, we can be sure that exactly one of the alternative blocks will be executed.

Missing statement sequences

It may happen that there is *no action* to be taken (no statements are to be executed) under certain of the conditions specified in a selection structure. In such a case, it is permissible to have no statements following an IF . . . THEN, ELSE IF . . . THEN, or ELSE statement.

Example 18 (Compare Example 6.) If the value of *I* is 1, change it to 2; if it is 2, change it to 1. If the value of *I* is neither 1 nor 2, leave it unchanged.

```
READ *, I
IF (I .EQ. 1) THEN
    I = 2
  ELSE IF (I .EQ. 2) THEN
    I = 1
  ELSE
  END IF
PRINT *, I
END
```

The "empty" *Else* block will be executed if *I* is neither 1 nor 2; thus, no change will be made in the value of *I* in this case. (See Fig. 3.15.)

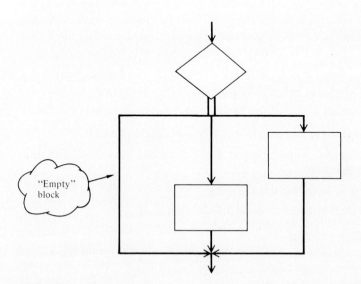

Fig. 3.15 Skeleton flowchart for Example 18, showing the missing third alternative.

Example 19: Small ships   Reporting requirements for the Port Authority have
now changed, so that it is necessary to keep track of only the ships of 3500 tons
or less entering the harbor. Thus the statements in the *Else* block of Example 2
may now be omitted. (See Fig. 3.16.)

```
. . .
IF (TONS .LE. 3500) THEN
    NSMALL = NSMALL + 1
    WSMALL = WSMALL + TONS
  ELSE
  END IF
. . .
```

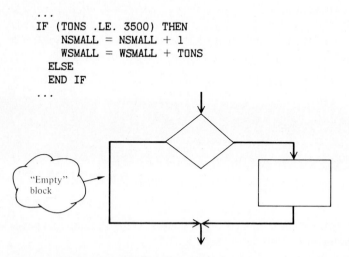

Fig. 3.16 Skeleton flowchart for Example 19, showing the missing *Else* block.

The *Then* block or the *Else* block in a two-way selection structure, or any one
or more blocks in a multiple selection structure, may be empty. A nested selection
structure may also include empty statement sequences, as illustrated by the following example.

Example 20   Given three values, *A*, *B*, and *C*, rearrange them, if necessary, so
that *A* is less than or equal to *B*, which in turn is less than equal to *C*.
We may refine the statement of this problem into two main steps:

1. Arrange the values of *A* and *B* so that *A* is less than or equal to *B*.
2. Arrange the value of *C* with respect to *A* and *B*, so that the values of all three
   variables are in the desired order.

Further refining Step 1, we obtain the following:

   1a. If *A* is less than or equal to *B*, no action is required.

   1b. If *A* is greater than *B*, interchange the values of *A* and *B*.

Refinement of Step 1b results in the following program steps (compare Section
2.4):

```
AUX = A
A = B
B = AUX
```

Step 2 is a bit more complicated:

  2a. If *B* is less than or equal to *C*, then all three values are now in the desired order, so no further action is required.

  2b. If *B* is greater than *C*, interchange the values of *B* and *C*. In this case, since the original value of *C* was less than *B*, it may also be less than *A*. So, while we know that *C* now contains the largest of the three values, it is necessary to make another comparison:

      i) If *A* is less than or equal to *B*, no further action is required.

     ii) If *A* is greater than *B*, interchange the values of *A* and *B*.

The steps that require no action correspond to empty statement sequences in the following program, and to flow lines containing no boxes in the flowchart, Fig. 3.17.

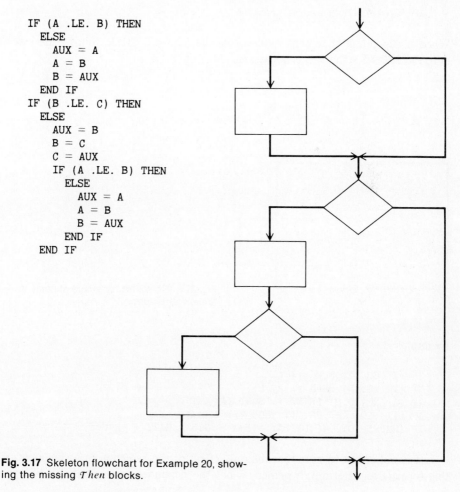

```
IF (A .LE. B) THEN
  ELSE
     AUX = A
     A = B
     B = AUX
  END IF
IF (B .LE. C) THEN
  ELSE
     AUX = B
     B = C
     C = AUX
     IF (A .LE. B) THEN
       ELSE
          AUX = A
          A = B
          B = AUX
       END IF
  END IF
```

Fig. 3.17 Skeleton flowchart for Example 20, showing the missing *Then* blocks.

Omitting the ELSE statement

When the *Else* block is empty, the **ELSE** statement may be omitted. Nevertheless, there is a good reason for including an empty *Else* block in the program. As we pointed out in the discussion of Example 16, when there is an *Else* block in the selection structure, we can be sure that *exactly one* of the alternatives will be selected. This assurance can contribute significantly to program reliability and readability.

A simple special case

It sometimes happens that there is only a *single statement* that is to be executed or skipped, depending on the truth of some assertion. A single-statement form is available for specifying this particular selection structure in Fortran:

IF (*Assertion*) *Dependent statement*

When a dependent statement, rather than the keyword **THEN**, follows the assertion, the **END IF** statement is not needed. See Fig. 3.18.

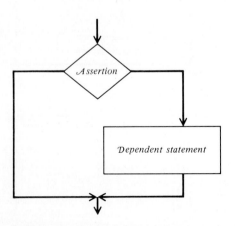

Fig. 3.18 Flowchart for single-statement selection structure.

Examples

```
IF (I .EQ. 1) SUM = 0.0
IF (I .LE. N) READ *, A, B
IF (A .GE. 0.0) PRINT *, SQRT (A)
IF ((I .EQ. 1) .OR. (I .EQ. 2)) I = 3 - I
IF (HOURS .GT. 40.0) PAY = PAY + 0.5 * RATE * (HOURS - 40.0)
```

It is important to note that the only effect of the assertion in a statement of this form is to determine whether or not the dependent statement will be executed. The statement following the IF statement will be executed in either case; see Exercise 19. (In Section 3.4, we discuss the situation in which the dependent statement is itself a control statement.)

This simple, single-statement selection structure is precisely equivalent in its effect to the following four-line structure.

```
IF (Assertion) THEN
     Dependent statement
ELSE
END IF
```

(Even if we chose to omit the ELSE statement, three statement lines would be required.) Thus, the single-statement form may be regarded as a convenient shorthand notation for the longer form. Where it is important to emphasize the precise structure of the algorithm, however, it may be preferable to write out the longer form.

3.1.5 Exercises

1. Correct any errors you can find in the following assertions.
   a) I = N
   b) X + Y .GR. 3.4
   c) (G .GE. 3) .OR. (A = 3.6)
   d) X + Y
   e) A .LE. LIST(1)

2. Write compound relations corresponding to the following assertions.
   a) X exceeds Y, and either F is less than 2 or G equals 4 or both.
   b) X lies between zero and three times A; that is, X is greater than zero and X is less than 3 times A.
   c) P exceeds X or it exceeds Y or it exceeds Z.
   d) A is not equal to B, and C is not equal to G nor to H nor to J.
   e) The absolute value of F is less than or equal to 3 times G.
   f) A and B each lie between 1 and 8, inclusive.
   g) A lies between 1 and 8 inclusive, but B does not.
   h) X exceeds 4 while Y is less than 5, or X is less than 5 while Y is greater than 4.
   i) The distance between the points in the plane having coordinates (x_1, y_1) and (x_2, y_2) is greater than the distance between (x_1, y_1) and (x_3, y_3).
   j) A and B are both negative or both nonnegative.
   k) Either A or B is zero, but not both.

3. Correct any errors you can find in the following assertions.
   a) (C .GT. D) .OR. (.NOT. (A + B .LT. D)
   b) A .OR. B .LT. 99.0
   c) (A .LT. B) .AND. (B .LT. A)
   d) A = B

  e) A .EQ. 1 .OR. 2
  f) X .LT. J

4. Write assertions corresponding to the following.

   a) The number of dependents, Nd, is greater than 3 and not greater than 6, and the number of years of service, N, is between 35 and 50 (inclusive).

   b) X lies between 0 and 1 (inclusive) or it lies between 3 and 4 (inclusive).

5. Consider Example 5.

   a) What will be printed if the values of X and Y happen to be equal?

   b) Modify the program to set both Rx and Ry to 1 in this case.

6. a) In the program of Example 6, what will be the final value of I if its original value is 0? If its original value is 3?

   b) In each of these cases, what would be the final value of I if the decision structure were replaced by the single assignment statement

   ```
   I = 3 - I
   ```

   c) What result will be produced (in each case) by the program in Example 13?

   d) What result will be produced (in each case) by the program in Example 18?

7. Write a program to read the values of two real variables and print the larger of the two variables.

Data:	First variable	Second variable
Case 1:	123.4	14.3
Case 2:	−0.930	−0.931
Case 3:	0.0	1111.1

8. Write a program to read two values, A and B, and print the quotient A/B only *if* B is not zero. (If B is zero, do not print anything.)

9. *Area of a triangle.* If the lengths of the three sides of a triangle are the values of the three variables A, B, and C, the area is given by

$$\sqrt{S \times (S - A) \times (S - B) \times (S - C)},$$

where S is one-half the sum of the lengths of the sides. However, the quantity whose square root is to be computed will be negative if the values of A, B, and C are incorrect and do not represent the sides of a real triangle (for example, 1, 2, and 4). Write a program that will read values for A, B, and C, and will print the area of the triangle; however, if the values are incorrect, print an error message instead.

Data:

Case 1:	7.0	8.0	9.0
Case 2:	3.0	4.0	5.0
Case 3:	123.4	432.1	399.9
Case 4:	1.0	2.0	4.0

10. Write Fortran statements to accomplish each of the following.

   a) If the *I*th element of the array *X* is larger than *Big*, assign this element's value to *Big* and assign the value of *I* to *Ibig*.

   b) Set the value of *Big* to the larger of the values of the variables *X* and *Y*, and set the value of *Small* to the smaller of those values. (If *X* and *Y* have equal values, it will not matter how these values are assigned. However, you should be sure that your program performs properly in this case.)

   c) Find the largest of three real variable values. Your program should work properly even if two or three of the values are identical.

11. Consider the program in Fig. 3.9 (Example 12).

   a) What will be the effect if *Kode* has some value other than 1 or 2?

   b) Modify the program to print an error message in this case.

12. Write a program to set *Signx* to −1.0 if *X* is negative, to 0.0 if *X* is zero, or to 1.0 if *X* is positive.

13. Construct complete flowcharts corresponding to the skeleton flowcharts in the following figures.

   a) Figure 3.10
   b) Figure 3.13
   c) Figure 3.15
   d) Figure 3.16
   e) Figure 3.17

14. Rewrite each of the five examples of single-statement selection structures (in the paragraphs headed "A simple special case"), using complete two-branch selection structures with IF...THEN, ELSE, and END IF statements.

15. In a nested selection structure, there should be as many END IF statements as there are statements ending with the keyword THEN. State a similar rule for a selection structure with multiple alternatives (that is, a structure containing ELSE IF...THEN statements).

16. Write a program to read three integers, and print them on one line in descending order. (Compare Example 20.)

   a) Data:

Case 1:	7 8 9
Case 2:	7 9 8
Case 3:	8 7 9
Case 4:	8 9 7
Case 5:	9 7 8
Case 6:	9 8 7

   b) Use data of your own choosing, designed to test the operation of the program when two or three of the data values are equal.

17. Some of the examples in this section can be programmed without the use of selection structures, by taking advantage of the power of predefined functions such as *Max, Min,* and *Dim* (see Table 2.1). For instance, a program to produce the same result as Example 1 is shown in Section 2.3.3 as an application of the function *Dim.* Write a program without using a selection structure, corresponding to each of the following.

    a) Example 4
    b) Exercise 7
    c) Exercise 10(b)
    d) Exercise 10(c)
    e) Exercise 12 (*Hint:* See Section 2.3.3.)
    f) Print the value of *A* if it is positive, zero if *A* is zero, and −*A* if *A* is negative. (Thus, if *A* is negative, a positive number with the same magnitude as *A* is to be printed.)

18. Read three integers and compare them. If no two are alike, print 0. If there is a pair, identify the pair; for instance, if the first and third are equal, print

    > 1   3

    If all three are identical, print 3.

    Data:

Case 1:	7	8	7
Case 2:	99	89	79
Case 3:	1	3	3
Case 4:	6	6	6

19. In Section 3.1.4 we pointed out that when a selection structure includes an *Else* block, it is guaranteed that exactly one of the alternative blocks will be executed. What is the disadvantage of the following program, as compared to those in Examples 6, 13, and 18, or to the method suggested in Exercise 6(b)?

    ```
    IF (I .EQ. 1) I = 2
    IF (I .EQ. 2) I = 1
    ```

    Hint: If the original value of *I* is 1, what will its value be after the *first* IF statement is executed? In this case, will the second assertion be true or false?

3.2 LOGICAL EXPRESSIONS

Logical expressions are used as assertions in the control statements of selection structures, or for other purposes in which a program must produce the value *true* or *false*. The simplest logical expressions are the relational expressions that have been used in the examples in this chapter. We shall now see that it is possible to form expressions that involve logical variables, constants, or functions. The connectives `.AND.`, `.OR.`, and `.NOT.` are used as *logical operators* to combine logical variables, relational expressions, or any other logical expressions.

Logical expressions are characterized by the fact that they may take on either one of the two possible values *true* or *false*. Although the primary use for logical expressions is as assertions in selection structures, we shall give some examples of other uses as well.

3.2.1 Logical Variables and Constants

The values of relational expressions and other logical expressions may be assigned to variables of logical type. Such variables must be specified in a declared implicit type specification or in an explicit type declaration, since there is no default implicit type rule for logical variables. A logical variable is the name of a cell, whose value at any time is either *true* or *false*. For example,

```
LOGICAL G
G = P .LT. S
```

The relational expression P .LT. S will be evaluated, and its value (*true* or *false*) will be assigned as the value of the logical variable *G*. Thus, if *P* is 7.0 and *S* is 6.0 when the assignment is executed, the value *false* will be assigned to *G*.

There are two logical constants, written as .TRUE. and .FALSE.. These constants can be used in the same way as other logical expressions. For example, we may assign the value *true* to the logical variable *G*, and assign the value *false* to the logical variable *H*.

```
IMPLICIT LOGICAL (G – H)
G = .TRUE.
H = .FALSE.
```

Or, we might wish to set a certain variable to *true* if *X* is greater than *Y*, and to *false* otherwise:

```
LOGICAL XGTY
IF (X .GT. Y) THEN
   XGTY = .TRUE.
 ELSE
   XGTY = .FALSE.
 END IF
```

Arrays and functions of logical type may also be used.

3.2.2 Expressions Involving Logical Variables and Constants

Logical expressions may be composed of the following elements.

1. Relational expressions, such as P .LT. 7.0, consisting of a pair of arithmetic (or character: see Chapter 5) expressions connected by a relational operator.

2. Logical constants, .TRUE. or .FALSE..

3. Logical variables (including array elements) or function references.

4. Combinations of the above, produced by means of the logical operators `.AND.`, `.OR.`, and `.NOT.`.

Suppose that we have declared *Flag, Gtest,* and *Lgcl* to be variables of logical type:

```
LOGICAL FLAG, GTEST, LGCL
```

(Of course, in a program containing this declaration we cannot use these variables for data of real, integer, or any other type.) We can now write statements such as the following:

```
FLAG = (X .EQ. 0.0)
```

If the value of X is zero, *Flag* will be assigned the value *true;* otherwise, *Flag* will be given the value *false*.

```
LGCL = FLAG
```

This statement will assign to *Lgcl* the current value (*true* or *false*) of *Flag*.

```
GTEST = (GTEST .OR. LGCL)
```

The new value of *Gtest* is *true* if its old value is *true* or if *Lgcl* is *true* (or both); otherwise, the new value of *Gtest* is *false*.

```
GTEST = G .GE. 0.0 .AND. G .LE. 5.0 .AND. .NOT. FLAG
```

Gtest will be set to *true* only if the value of the real variable G is between 0.0 and 5.0 inclusive, and *Flag* is *false*. Note that in this statement relational expressions are combined with logical variables.

```
LGCL = .TRUE.
```

Assign the value *true* to the logical variable *Lgcl*.

```
IF (FLAG) X = 0.0
```

Set the value of X to zero if *Flag* is *true*.

The logical operators

The logical expression

$$\varepsilon_1 \ .AND. \ \varepsilon_2$$

is *true* if both $\mathcal{E}_1$ and $\mathcal{E}_2$ are *true;* otherwise, it is *false.* The expression

   $\mathcal{E}_1$ .OR. $\mathcal{E}_2$

is *true* if either expression is *true* or if both are *true;* otherwise (that is, only if both $\mathcal{E}_1$ and $\mathcal{E}_2$ are *false*), the composite expression is *false.* The expression

   .NOT. $\mathcal{E}$

is *true* when $\mathcal{E}$ is *false,* and it is *false* when $\mathcal{E}$ is *true.*

The logical operators .AND., .OR., and .NOT. must be used only with logical expressions; any other use of these operators is invalid. Note that the expression

   $\mathcal{E}$ .AND. .FALSE.

is always *false,* whereas the expression

   $\mathcal{E}$ .OR. .TRUE.

is always *true,* regardless of the truth value of the logical expression $\mathcal{E}$.

Precedence

A logical expression may involve logical operators, relational operators, and (within the arithmetic expressions in a relational expression) arithmetic operators. Rules of precedence may be taken into account to establish the meaning of an expression such as

   LGCL .OR. A .GT. B + C

(assuming that *Lgcl* is of logical type and that *A*, *B*, and *C* are real).

1. Arithmetic expressions are evaluated first, according to the rules set forth in Chapter 2.
2. Relational expressions are evaluated next.
3. The logical operators are applied last. Among the logical operators, .NOT. is applied first, then .AND., and finally .OR.. Thus,
   $\mathcal{E}_1$ .OR. $\mathcal{E}_2$ .AND. $\mathcal{E}_3$
   means $\mathcal{E}_1$ .OR. ($\mathcal{E}_2$ .AND. $\mathcal{E}_3$) rather than ($\mathcal{E}_1$ .OR. $\mathcal{E}_2$) .AND. $\mathcal{E}_3$.

3.2.3   Using Logical Data

As we have seen, a logical expression may be used as the assertion in a selection structure. The assertions in the examples of Section 3.1 are simple relational expressions or compound relations consisting of two or more relational expressions connected by logical operators. We now see that other forms of logical expressions can also be used as assertions, for example (assuming that *Flag* and *Lgcl* are declared to be of logical type):

```
IF (FLAG) THEN
IF (LGCL .AND. X .GT. Y) THEN
IF (LGCL .AND. .NOT. FLAG) THEN
```

Logical data may also be used in other ways. Variables and array elements of logical type may appear in an input or output list; constants and other expressions of logical type (including relational expressions) may also appear in an output list. For list directed input, a data value corresponding to a logical list item may consist simply of the unquoted letter T for *true* or the unquoted letter F for *false*.

Many operations with logical data are analogous to those that apply to data of other types. As we have seen, there are logical constants and variables, logical functions, logical expressions, and input or output list items of logical type. However, it should be noted that there are some restrictions. Although expressions of integer, real, double precision, complex, or character types may be used in *relational* expressions that are components of a logical expression, "mixed-type" expressions are not permitted to include one operand of logical type and the other of numeric (integer, real, double precision, or complex) or character type. Such mixed expressions make no sense. Moreover, *relational* operators cannot be used to compare logical expressions—an expression such as FLAG .EQ. .TRUE. would not be permitted.†

3.2.4 Exercises

Tell whether the given compound logical expression is *true* or *false*, based on the given variable values. Assume that the program contains the declaration

```
IMPLICIT LOGICAL L
```

1. (G * P / Q .GT. 4.0) .OR. (.NOT. (A .GT. B))

$G:$ 5.0 $A:$ 32.0
$P:$ 9.0 $B:$ 41.5
$Q:$ 10.0

---

† However, there are two other *logical* operators that we have not mentioned, which can be used to determine whether or not two logical expressions have the same truth value. These are .EQV. and .NEQV., and both of these operators have lower precedence than any of the other logical operators. If $\mathcal{L}_1$ and $\mathcal{L}_2$ are logical expressions, then $\mathcal{L}_1$ .EQV. $\mathcal{L}_2$ is *true* when $\mathcal{L}_1$ and $\mathcal{L}_2$ are both *true* or both *false*, and $\mathcal{L}_1$ .NEQV. $\mathcal{L}_2$ is *true* when one is *true* and the other is *false*.

2. `(I ** 2 .NE. J + K) .AND. (3.0 .LE. B + ABS (C - 20.0))`

   I: 3   *B:* 1.0
   J: 5   *C:* 15.0
   K: 2

3. `.NOT. ((A + C * B .LT. 5.0 E 1) .AND. (J .LT. (4 + K) / M))`

   A: 0.0   *J:* 17
   B: 21.0   *K:* 44
   C: 0.042 *M:* 8

4. `L .OR. .NOT. A .GT. B + C`

   L: true   *A:* 5.0
              B: 1.0
              C: 2.0

5. `L1 .AND. .NOT. L2`

   L1: true   *L2: false*

6. The last example in Section 3.2.1 sets the logical variable *Xgty* to *true* if *X* is greater than *Y*, and to *false* otherwise. Assuming that *Xgty* has been declared a variable of logical type, write a single assignment statement that accomplishes the same effect. *Hint:* Assign to *Xgty* the value of a relational expression that is *true* or *false* under the required conditions.

3.3 PROGRAM TERMINATION: THE STOP AND END STATEMENTS

For a program that contains no control structure other than straight sequential execution of all its statements, the last statement to be executed will be the END statement, which terminates execution. However, when there are selection or repetition structures in the program, termination of execution at some point other than the last statement may be required. For example, we may wish to terminate program execution after printing an error message, when a data error is encountered. A STOP statement indicates that execution of the program is to cease.

Example 1

```
* Compute and print square root of input value.
* Stop if input value is negative.
      READ *, VALUE
      IF (VALUE .LT. 0.0) THEN
         PRINT *, 'Invalid value', VALUE
         STOP
      ELSE
         PRINT *, SQRT (VALUE)
      END IF
      ...
```

Execution of a STOP statement terminates the algorithm represented by the program, but does not stop the operation of the computer. As we saw in Section 1.2, most computers operate under the control of an *operating system,* which deals with a queue of jobs and attempts to schedule the available computing resources in an efficient manner. The effect of the STOP statement is to return control to the operating system, so that it can reallocate the resources that were used during the execution phase by this program.

The last line of a program, in its physical form on the lines of a computer readable file, must have the form

    END

If this line is reached during execution of the program, it is treated as a STOP statement. Although a STOP statement may appear anywhere in a program, the last line (even if it is immediately preceded by a STOP statement) must be an END line. Even though the END statement is not always executed, it serves as a signal to the processor during the translation phase, indicating that there are no more lines in the program to be translated.

3.4 EXPLICIT CONTROL OF PROGRAM EXECUTION SEQUENCE

The selection structures described in Section 3.1, along with the repetition structures to be discussed in Chapter 4, satisfy almost all of our requirements for control of program execution sequences. However, there are some cases that are not completely covered by those structures in their pure form. For example, it may happen at a point deep within a nested selection structure that the program can detect that the remaining statements of the entire nest will not need to be executed. Either the desired result has been achieved already due to some special circumstance, or it can be detected that the result will never be achieved for some reason such as data errors or divergence. What is needed is an *exit* from the structure. As another example, we shall see that the DO statement, which specifies repetition, cannot be used for a nonterminating loop, such as may be required by a program that monitors an industrial process.

It may be expected that additional structures will eventually be added to the Fortran language to accommodate these further control structure requirements. Meanwhile, however, the programmer may rely on specific *explicit* control statements, including the GO TO, the computed GO TO, and the arithmetic IF.

Each of these explicit control statements permits deviation from the normal execution sequence, and requires that a specific point in the program be specified, at which execution is to continue. For this purpose, *statement labels* are provided.

Statement labels

A label consists of one or more digits written at the left of the statement. (See Section 1.2.1 for the manner of placing labels on program lines.) Here are some statements with labels:

```
10     J = J + 1
4      READ *, A, B
376    D= SQRT (A ** 2 + B ** 2 + C ** 2)
73     IF (X .GT. Y) XGTY = .TRUE.
```

A statement should not be given a label unless it is referred to by an explicit control statement. Except for FORMAT declarations (Section 6.1), labels on non-executable statements are unnecessary and should be avoided.

3.4.1   The GO TO Statement

This statement has the form

```
GO TO  label
```

and specifies that the sequence of execution of the statements of the program is to be interrupted, and that the next statement to be executed is the one with the specified label; for example,

```
GO TO 10
```

The labeled statement may appear in the program either above or below a GO TO statement that refers to it.

The GO TO statement and program comprehension

Labels and GO TO statements can be used in ways that severely interfere with program comprehension. If they are used indiscriminately, transfers of control within the execution sequence can proliferate until it is impossible to analyze the flow of control or to determine which program paths lead to a given statement. Therefore, GO TO statements should be used only in certain restricted ways, or according to certain prespecified patterns. Unfortunately, Fortran language processors are of little help in enforcing such restrictions, so that proper principles of programming style must be enforced by the user's self-discipline.

As we have noted, one situation in which the use of GO TO statements may be acceptable is for conditional exit from a selection structure or a repetition structure, especially from an inner structure within a nest. Another situation is the creation of a nonterminating loop, by means of a "backward" GO TO statement, that is, one which transfers to a statement earlier in the program. Such transfers can also inadvertently create an "infinite loop" with no exit where this was not intended. Furthermore, such backward jumps are especially easy to misuse in ways that can make analysis of the program control flow almost impossible.

The CONTINUE statement

We may use a labeled CONTINUE statement to mark a point in the program where we need a label, but where we do not wish to associate the label with any particular computational action. Some programmers find that they achieve greater flexibility in making later modifications in a program, if nearly all labels are attached to CONTINUE statements (rather than to assignment statements, READ statements, etc.). CONTINUE statements are used far more often than any other statements for terminating repetition structures written with DO statements, as described in Section 4.3.

The CONTINUE statement is simply

```
CONTINUE
```

and is usually written with a label—for example,

```
876  CONTINUE
```

Using a GO TO statement in a selection structure

GO TO statements may appear in any of the alternative statement sequences of a selection structure. However, a warning is in order. One of the assumptions that we would like to make, when using a selection structure, is that (after one or another of the alternative statement sequences is completed) the execution sequence will *always* continue with the statement following the end of the structure. We can no longer make this assumption if we permit GO TO statements to appear within the structure. Therefore, extra care is required in order to maintain program comprehensibility and reliability when a structure contains explicit control statements.

The same warning applies when a GO TO statement is used as the dependent statement in a single-statement selection structure. We would like to assume that the statement following such a single-statement structure will be executed whether or not the assertion is true. But we cannot make this assumption when the dependent statement is a GO TO statement. If the assertion is false, the following statement will be executed as we would like to expect. But if the assertion is true, the GO TO will be executed, and the statement sequence will continue with the statement having the label that is referenced in the GO TO statement. The difference between these two cases is illustrated in Fig. 3.19.

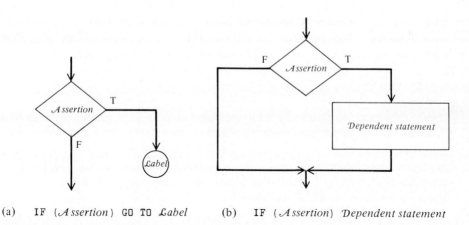

(a)   IF ($\mathcal{A}$ssertion) GO TO $\mathcal{L}abel$ (b)   IF ($\mathcal{A}$ssertion) $\mathcal{D}ependent\ statement$

Fig. 3.19 Effect of a single-statement selection structure on program control flow.

One restriction, imposed by the Fortran language, should be noted. In a selection structure, Fortran prohibits explicit transfer of control into any of the alternative blocks. (Jumps into a repetition structure are also forbidden.) However, a jump from within a selection structure to the END IF statement is permitted.

3.4.2   The Computed GO TO Statement

In most examples of selection structures with multiple alternatives (see Section 3.1.3), all the selections are based on the value of a single expression, which appears in the assertion of the IF ... THEN statement and reappears in all the ELSE IF ... THEN statements of the selection structure. Some programming languages include a CASE statement to handle such a situation, which permits the controlling expression to be written just once using a statement form that emphasizes its special role. The various values that the expression can be expected to take on are then clearly listed, and each value is followed by the statement sequence that is to be selected in case the control expression is found to have that value. Properly used, such a CASE selection structure can provide better program comprehensibility and reliability than the corresponding selection written with a sequence of ELSE IF ... THEN statements.

Fortran does not have a CASE selection structure. However, it does have an explicit control statement form that provides some of the features of the CASE structure when one of several alternatives is to be selected on the basis of the value of an integer expression. But, as we shall note, this control form has at least one major disadvantage (as compared with the use of a sequence of ELSE IF ... THEN statements).

In Fortran, we may use a *computed* GO TO statement, which has the form

GO TO ($\mathcal{L}_1, \mathcal{L}_2, \ldots, \mathcal{L}_m$), ε

The $\mathcal{L}$'s represent labels of statements elsewhere in the program, and $\mathcal{E}$ is an integer expression. Execution of this statement results in a branch to the statement labeled $\mathcal{L}_1$ if the value of $\mathcal{E}$ is 1, to $\mathcal{L}_2$ if the value of $\mathcal{E}$ is 2, etc. For example,

```
GO TO (30, 42, 50, 9), K
```

results in a jump to statement 30 if the value of K is 1, to statement 42 if K is 2, to 50 if K is 3, and to statement 9 if K is 4.

If the value of the integer expression $\mathcal{E}$ is less than 1 or greater than m (the number of listed labels), none of the branches is selected; instead, control proceeds to the statement immediately following the computed GO TO. (This effect is similar to that of an ELSE statement.)

The program of Example 18 in Section 3.1.4 can be rewritten using a computed GO TO statement. If the input value is 1 or 2, it will be changed to 2 or 1, respectively; otherwise, it will remain unchanged. (See also Fig. 3.20.)

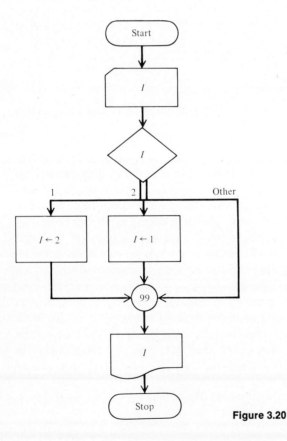

Figure 3.20

```
* Example 1. Program to interchange the values 1 and 2.
      READ *, I
      GO TO (10, 20), I
*          .. This point is reached if I is not 1 or 2.
      GO TO 99
*          .. The following statements will be executed if I is 1.
  10       CONTINUE
           I = 2
      GO TO 99
*          .. The following statements will be executed if I is 2.
  20       CONTINUE
           I = 1
*      .. All cases continue from here.
  99  PRINT *, I
      END
```

The expression controlling the computed GO TO is simply the variable I. If the value of I is 1, control is transferred to statement 10; if I is 2, control is transferred to statement 20.

If I is neither 1 nor 2, the computed GO TO does not transfer control to any of the statements whose labels appear in the list; instead, the normal execution sequence proceeds with the statement following the computed GO TO. This takes care of the case where I is zero, as well as any stray values of I that might appear (due to errors in data preparation or the like).

It is especially important to include the two statements

```
GO TO 99
```

which cause all the separate flow branches to rejoin and continue together from statement 99. It is one of the major advantages of the IF . . . THEN selection structure, that no such extra statements are needed. Control proceeds automatically from the end of the *Then* block to the END IF statement. No matter which branch is taken, control will eventually resume at the END IF statement after the statements in the *Then* or *Else* block have been completed. No such automatic aid is available with the computed GO TO. It is the programmer's responsibility to ensure that the branches rejoin—this usually means that a GO TO statement is needed at *each* of the separate branches (except the last one).

The following example involves "rational arithmetic"; that is, it provides for arithmetic operations on the numerators and denominators of fractions as *separate* integers. The program reads the numerators and denominators of two fractions, as well as a code K indicating whether the sum, difference, product, or quotient of the two given fractions is to be calculated. In each of the four cases, the numerator and denominator of the resulting fraction are again to be computed as separate integers, according to the conventions of arithmetic and algebra applied to fractions (see Fig. 3.21).

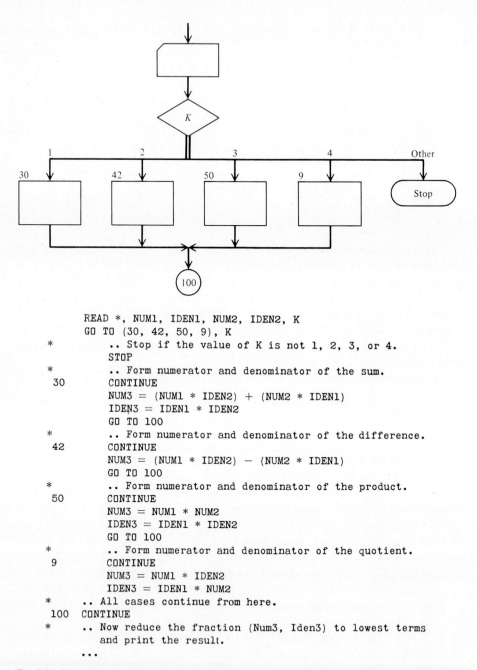

```
          READ *, NUM1, IDEN1, NUM2, IDEN2, K
          GO TO (30, 42, 50, 9), K
*             .. Stop if the value of K is not 1, 2, 3, or 4.
          STOP
*             .. Form numerator and denominator of the sum.
   30     CONTINUE
          NUM3 = (NUM1 * IDEN2) + (NUM2 * IDEN1)
          IDEN3 = IDEN1 * IDEN2
          GO TO 100
*             .. Form numerator and denominator of the difference.
   42     CONTINUE
          NUM3 = (NUM1 * IDEN2) - (NUM2 * IDEN1)
          GO TO 100
*             .. Form numerator and denominator of the product.
   50     CONTINUE
          NUM3 = NUM1 * NUM2
          IDEN3 = IDEN1 * IDEN2
          GO TO 100
*             .. Form numerator and denominator of the quotient.
    9     CONTINUE
          NUM3 = NUM1 * IDEN2
          IDEN3 = IDEN1 * NUM2
*         .. All cases continue from here.
  100     CONTINUE
*         .. Now reduce the fraction (Num3, Iden3) to lowest terms
          and print the result.
          ...
```

Fig. 3.21 Program to compute the numerator and denominator of the sum, difference, product, or quotient of two given fractions.

For example, when this program is applied to the data listed below, the printed results will be as shown.

Data

Num1	*IDen1*	*Num2*	*IDen2*	*K*
5	9	1	16	1
5	9	1	16	2
15	30	8	32	1
1	2	1	6	1
1	2	1	6	3
1	2	1	6	4
1	2	1	6	2
7	8	7	4	4
5	8	2	3	3
0	0	0	0	0

Results

Num3	*IDen3*
23	48
17	48
1	1
2	3
1	12
3	1
1	3
1	2
5	12

3.4.3   The Arithmetic IF Statement†

When selection is to be based on an arithmetic expression whose value is negative, zero, or positive, an arithmetic IF statement may be used. This control form has all the disadvantages of the computed GO TO, but it has the advantage that control need not be based on a sequence of integer values. The arithmetic IF statement has the following form.

IF (*Expression*) *Label*₁, *Label*₂, *Label*₃

---

† In contrast to the arithmetic IF, a single-statement selection structure is often called a *logical* IF statement.

This statement can be represented by a three-branch flowchart box (Fig. 3.22). The *Expression* is an ordinary arithmetic expression of integer, real, or double precision type. If the value of the expression is negative, the effect of the arithmetic IF is the same as GO TO $\mathcal{L}abel_1$; when it is zero, the effect is GO TO $\mathcal{L}abel_2$; and when it is positive, the effect is GO TO $\mathcal{L}abel_3$. Note that a jump to one of the three labels always occurs. Of course, any two of the labels may be the same.

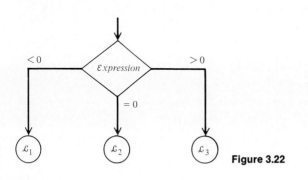

Figure 3.22

Example 2   (See Fig. 3.23.)

        IF (K(I, J) − 1) 20, 40, 30

Meaning: If the array element $K_{I,J}$ has a value less than 1, proceed to statement 20; if the value is 1, go to statement 40; if it is greater than 1, go to statement 30.

We might use such a three-way branch in a problem involving a checkerboard, represented as a rectangular array of values coded as follows:

    0   represents the absence of a checker:

    1   represents the presence of a black checker;

    2   represents the presence of a red checker.

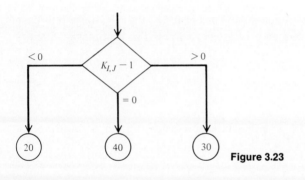

Figure 3.23

The value of the expression $(K_{I,J} - 1)$ is then negative, zero, or positive, respectively, in these three cases.

Further examples

```
IF (Z) 51, 20, 61
IF (Z - 0.1) 20, 71, 71
IF (ABS (A ** 2 + B ** 2 - C ** 2) - 0.1) 20, 5, 5
IF (B(I) - A(J)) 15, 15, 16
IF (B ** 2 - 4.0 * A * C) 12, 17, 17
IF (LS + LH - 2) 11, 51, 51
```

Note that the expression may be a valid arithmetic expression of integer, real, or double precision type.

All the precautions that apply to the use of statement labels with GO TO statements also apply, of course, to their use with the arithmetic IF. Nevertheless, the arithmetic IF statement is particularly useful in special situations for choosing among exactly three different execution sequences.

3.4.4 Exercises

1. Rewrite the rational arithmetic program of Fig. 3.21, using a multiple alternative selection structure (see Section 3.1.3).

2. In Example 1 of Section 3.4.2, suppose that the two GO TO 99 statements were omitted. If the original value of I is 1, 2, or 3, what would be the final value (in each case)?

3. Show how to modify the "rational arithmetic" program of Fig. 3.21 as follows.

   a) Instead of having separate statement sequences for sum and difference, merely change *Num2* to $-Num2$ when K is 2, and transfer to the sequence of statements that is executed when K is 1. (Note that this way of combining parts of conditional blocks is difficult to achieve with a selection structure.)
   b) In the sequence of statements beginning at 100, print a warning message and stop if *Iden3* is zero.

4. Write a program, using an arithmetic IF statement, based on a variation of Example 6 of Section 3.1. Read the value of I. If I is less than 1, leave it unchanged. If it is equal to 1, change it to 2. If I is greater than 1, change it to 1. After setting I to the correct final value, transfer (using GO TO statements as required) to a common point where the final value of I is printed. *Hint:* $I - 1$ is negative, zero, or positive.

CHAPTER 4
PROGRAM STRUCTURES FOR REPETITION

It is hardly possible to do any serious programming without encountering groups of statements that are to be executed *repeatedly*. Programs to merely read a single set of data values, perform a calculation, and print a single set of results, occur rarely in practical applications. Much more common are programs in which a sequence of statements is repeatedly executed. For example, it may be that at each repetition a new set of data values is read, the calculation is performed, and results based on those data values are printed.

4.1 COUNT-CONTROLLED REPETITION

For many applications, the number of repetitions of a group of statements is known in advance. Often the repetition is associated with a linear (singly subscripted) array, and the calculation is to be performed once for each array element. For example, it might be desired to compute the total (that is, the sum) of all the array element values, as in the following example (see also Fig. 4.1).

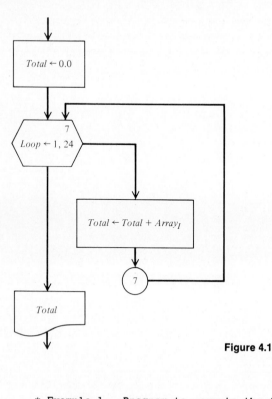

Figure 4.1

```
* Example 1.  Program to compute the total of the values
* of all elements of an array.
      REAL ARRAY (24)

      statements to assign values to array elements

      TOTAL = 0.0
      DO 7, I = 1, 24
        TOTAL = TOTAL + ARRAY(I)
7       CONTINUE
      PRINT *, TOTAL
      END
```

The array in this program has 24 elements. Values are assigned to these elements (for example, by means of READ statements). Then the statement

TOTAL = TOTAL + ARRAY(I)

is executed 24 times, once for each value of *I* between 1 and 24. Finally, after the last element of the array has been added on, the value of *Total* is printed.

This example illustrates the general program pattern known as a *loop* or DO loop. This pattern consists of a DO statement containing the necessary information to control a repetition, followed by the group of statements to be executed repeatedly, and finally a labeled terminal statement. In this section, we use a CONTINUE statement as the terminal statement; other possibilities are discussed in Section 4.3. This program pattern corresponds to the general flowchart in Fig. 4.2.

> DO *Label*, *Index* = *Initial value*, *Limit*
>   group of statements
>   to be repeated
> *Label*   CONTINUE

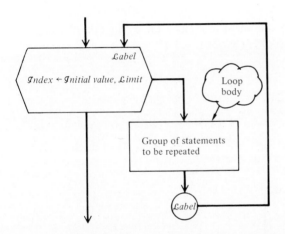

Fig. 4.2 Flowchart pattern for a group of statements to be repeated.

The *Label* following the word DO is, of course, the same as the identifying label on the CONTINUE statement. The *Index* is a variable (not an array element name), and the *Initial value* and *Limit* are expressions. The *Index*, *Initial value*, and *Limit* are of integer type in most applications, although they are also permitted to be of real or double precision type. The comma in the DO statement between the *Label* and the *Index* is optional, but its use is to be encouraged because it helps to make the statement more readable.

The terminal statement is included in the group of statements to be repeated. This group, along with the controlling DO statement, has the effect of the following sequence of steps.

1. Set the index to its initial value.

2. Compare the index with the upper limit. If the index exceeds the limit, terminate the iteration; otherwise, continue with Step 3.

3. Execute the group of statements.

4. Increase the index by 1, and return to Step 2.

When the index is found to exceed the limit at Step 2, execution of the program proceeds with the statement following the terminal statement.

Often the initial value is 1. Quite often the limit is the same as the number of elements in a linear array, and the index is used within the group of statements as a subscript. In this case, all the statements in the group will be executed once for each element in the array. On the other hand, there is no requirement that the index be used at all within the repeated group of statements.

The parts of the loop concerned with control, namely parts 1, 2, and 4 of this pattern, are concentrated in the DO statement, and are thus separated from the main calculation specified in part 3. This program structure makes the loop control easy to find and to check.

Example 2 We might use a DO statement to control the evaluation of a sum of products, $X_1Y_1 + X_2Y_2 + \cdots + X_nY_n$. (See Fig. 4.3.)

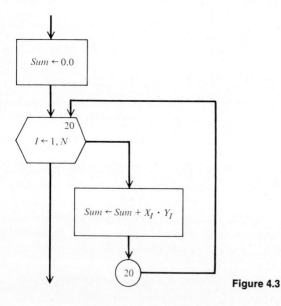

Figure 4.3

```
      SUM = 0.0
      DO 20, I = 1, N
         SUM = SUM + X(I) * Y(I)
20       CONTINUE
```

Example 3   We might wish to compute a sequence of values of a polynomial, $aX^2 + bX + c$, for equally spaced values of X, and store them in an array Y having *Many* elements.

```
      DO 15, J = 1, MANY
         X = XMIN + DELX * REAL (J - 1)
         Y(J) = (A * X + B) * X + C
  15     CONTINUE
```

4.1.1   The Parameters of a DO Statement: General Form

The *Label, Index, Initial value,* and *Limit* that appear in a DO statement are parameters (describers) of the repetitive process. The DO statement may also include a fifth parameter, the *Increment,* whose value indicates the amount by which the index variable is to be increased each time the loop is traversed. This more general form of the DO statement is the following.

DO *Label, Index = Initial value, Limit, Increment*

When the increment is not expressed, the index variable will be increased by 1 each time the loop is traversed, as we have seen.

Here is a summary of the discussion up to this point concerning the parameters of the DO statement.

- The *Label* is the label of the terminal statement of the DO loop. It indicates the end of the group of statements that are to be repeated.
- The *Index* is a variable whose value depends on the number of times the loop has been traversed. The value of the *Index* during the jth traversal will be equal to the *Initial value* plus $(j - 1)$ times the *Increment.*
- The *Initial value* is the value given to the *Index* prior to the first traversal of the loop.
- The *Limit* determines the number of times the loop will be traversed.

If the initial value is 1 and the increment is 1 (or is omitted), the number of traversals will be equal to the value of the limit, and the index value will be j during the jth traversal. More generally, the "trip count," or number of traversals, is calculated from the limit, the increment, and the initial value as follows. Find the value of the expression

$$(\textit{Limit} - \textit{Initial value}) \div (\textit{Increment})$$

Then add 1 to the largest integer that does not exceed this quotient. The result will be the number of times the loop is to be traversed. If the value of the trip count is less than 1, the repetition will terminate when the loop control phase of the DO statement is first executed, so that the group of statements controlled by the DO is not executed at all.† For example, the statement

        DO 5, I = 1, 10, 4

gives 2.25 as the value of $(10 - 1) \div (4)$; the largest integer that does not exceed 2.25 is 2; and adding 1 we find that the loop will be traversed 3 times (with 1, 5, and 9 as the values of *I* during these 3 traversals of the loop body). As another example,

        DO 17, J = 10, 9, 2

gives -0.5; the largest integer that does not exceed this quotient is -1, so the loop will be traversed 0 times. Note that when the initial value is the same as the limit, the quotient will be 0 and the trip count will be 1. For example, the body of a loop headed

        DO 21, K = 2, 2

will be traversed just once.

The basic iteration pattern described above can now be understood using the following computational model.

1. Set the index to its initial value. Compute the "number of traversals remaining" using the trip count procedure just described.
2. If the number of traversals remaining is less than one, terminate the iteration; otherwise, continue with Step 3.
3. Execute the group of statements.
4. Add the increment to the index value, decrease the "number of traversals remaining," and return to Step 2.

When the iteration is terminated at Step 2, execution of the program proceeds with the statement immediately following the terminal statement.

---

† Most versions of Fortran IV (the predecessor to Fortran 77) executed the statements in the loop once before performing any loop control test. Thus the minimum trip count would be 1, whereas for Fortran 77 it is zero.

Example 4 Recalling that the limit of a DO loop may be an expression, and need not be a constant, we see that it is not necessary to know the number of repetitions at the time a program is written. In this example, the total of a number of data items is computed. A separate item of data, inserted ahead of the values to be totalled, indicates the number of items to be totalled. (Compare Example 5 in Section 1.3.3.)

```
* Example 4.  Program to compute the total of N data values,
* where the value of N is provided as the first data item.
        TOTAL = 0.0
        READ *, N
        PRINT *, N
        DO 7, LOOP = 1, N
          READ *, DATUM
          TOTAL = TOTAL + DATUM
          PRINT *, DATUM, TOTAL
7         CONTINUE
        END
```

Example 5 As a further variation, the *average* of N data items could be computed by the following program.

```
* Example 5.  Program to compute and print the average of N
* data values, where the value of N is provided as the first
* item of data.
        TOTAL = 0.0
        READ *, N
*
        DO 7, LOOP = 1, N
          READ *, DATUM
          TOTAL = TOTAL + DATUM
          PRINT *, DATUM, TOTAL
7         CONTINUE
*
        IF (N .NE. 0) THEN
            AVG = TOTAL / REAL (N)
            PRINT *, 'Summary', TOTAL, N, AVG
        ELSE
            PRINT *, 'N⎵is⎵zero.'
        END IF
        END
```

Representing DO loops with flowcharts

The DO statement itself is represented in a flowchart by a hexagonal box as shown in Fig. 4.2. As we have seen, the actions performed when this statement is executed include Steps 1, 2, and 4 of the general iteration model. A more detailed flowchart, as in Fig. 4.4, can be drawn to expose these steps in full. The simplified flowchart in Fig. 4.2 may be thought of as a shorthand version of the detailed flowchart in Fig. 4.4. Thus the detailed flowchart is a *refinement* (see Section 1.4) of the simplified flowchart, to a level of detail beyond that represented by a single statement in Fortran.

Note that the *Label* component of the DO loop is not part of the model. It is required when we express the loop structure using the DO statement shorthand.

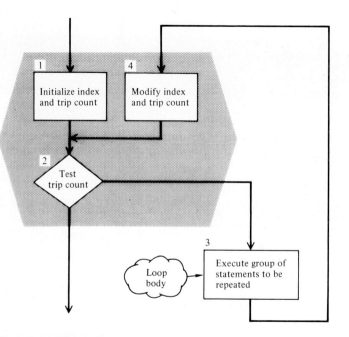

Fig. 4.4 Refinement of iteration flowchart, showing detail beyond the Fortran statement level.

Examples of DO statements

```
DO 23, I = JMIN, JMAX
DO 1492, KOLUMB = KING, KWEEN, ISABEL
DO 101, I = 1, 7
DO 15, LOOP = 1, ISPY, 3
DO 21, K = J, 9
```

Example 6 A program loop uses an array to store values F_K consisting of the last three digits of the Kth term in the Fibonacci sequence. (See Fig. 4.5.)

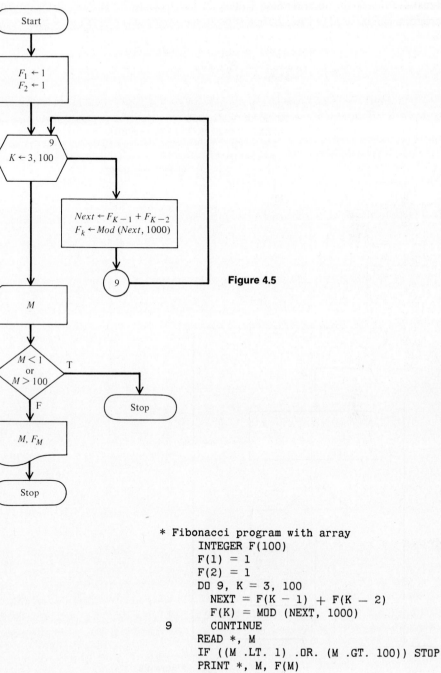

Figure 4.5

```
* Fibonacci program with array
      INTEGER F(100)
      F(1) = 1
      F(2) = 1
      DO 9, K = 3, 100
        NEXT = F(K - 1) + F(K - 2)
        F(K) = MOD (NEXT, 1000)
9     CONTINUE
      READ *, M
      IF ((M .LT. 1) .OR. (M .GT. 100)) STOP
      PRINT *, M, F(M)
      END
```

Example 7 If the intermediate values do not need to be stored, the following program can be used to save the space occupied by the array (see Fig. 4.6).

```
* Fibonacci program without array.
      INTEGER FI, FJ
      READ *, M
      FI = 1
      FJ = 1
      DO 9, K = 3, 100
        NEXT = MOD (FI + FJ, 1000)
        FI = FJ
        FJ = NEXT
        IF (K .EQ. M) PRINT *, NEXT
9       CONTINUE
      END
```

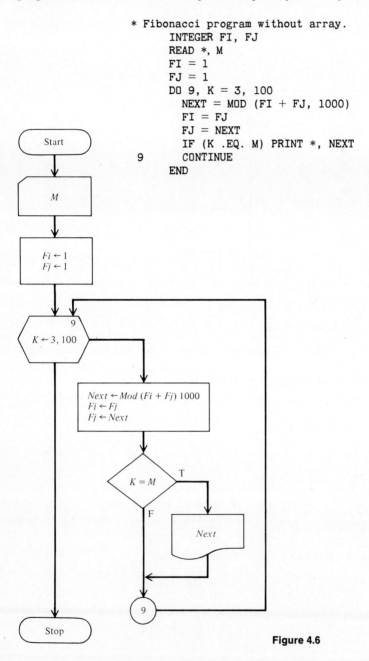

Figure 4.6

Example 8   This program reads two values, X and Y, from each of N data cards, and computes the sum of the XY products.

```
* Sum of products of pairs of data values.
      READ *, N
      SUM = 0.0
      DO 217, I = 1, N
        READ *, X, Y
        SUM = SUM + X * Y
  217   CONTINUE
      PRINT *, N, SUM
      END
```

Example 9   The next example reads values of the four elements of an array A and uses the predefined function *Min1* to find the smallest element. The index is used as a subscript, and each of the elements of the array in turn, beginning with the second, is examined.

```
* Largest element of an array
      REAL A(4)
      READ *, A(1), A(2), A(3), A(4)
      SMALL = A(1)
      DO 99, INDEX = 2, 4
        SMALL = MIN1 (SMALL, A(INDEX))
  99    CONTINUE
      PRINT *, SMALL
      END
```

Example 10   A loop may be used to "clear" (set to zero) the values of all the elements of a linear array.

```
      INTEGER LIST(25)
      ...
      DO 9, I = 1, 25
        LIST(I) = 0
  9     CONTINUE
```

Example 11   Here the PRINT statement causes four elements of a linear array to be printed on each line. This illustrates the use of an increment value greater than 1.

```
* Print four array element values per line.
      REAL X(100)
      ...
      DO 783, L = 1, 100, 4
        PRINT *, X(L), X(L + 1), X(L + 2), X(L + 3)
  783   CONTINUE
```

In the trip count calculation, the value of $(100 - 1) \div (4)$ is 24.75; the next lower integer is 24 and the trip count is one greater, that is, 25. The loop is first executed with 1 as the value of L, and X_1, X_2, X_3, and X_4 are printed. The second time the loop is executed, the value of L is 5 and the values of X_5, X_6, X_7, and X_8 are printed. The value of L during the 25th and last traversal is 97, and X_{97}, X_{98}, X_{99}, and X_{100} are printed.

Example 12 This program calculates the *factorial* of K, that is, the product of all positive integers not exceeding K.

```
* Factorial of K
      INTEGER FACT
      READ *, K
      IFACT = 1
      DO 33, I = 2, K
        FACT = FACT * I
33      CONTINUE
      PRINT *, K, FACT
      END
```

This example illustrates another point concerning the trip count. If the value of K is 1, the trip count calculation gives 0 as its final result. Therefore, the loop is never traversed and *Fact* retains the (correct) value, 1.

Example 13 The increment value may be negative, as illustrated in the following example.

```
      DO 20, I = J, 1, -1
        IF (NEXT .GE. L(I)) GO TO 30
        L(I + 1) = L(I)
20      CONTINUE
```

The first step in the trip count calculation gives $(1 - J) \div (-1)$. Assuming that J is greater than 1, this is equivalent to $(J - 1) \div (+1)$ (that is, we may change the signs of both numerator and denominator). The next smaller integer is $J - 1$, and we then add 1 to obtain J as the trip count value. Thus the loop will be traversed J times, with the value of I starting at J and decreasing by 1 at each traversal.

Some precautions

The loop index variable must not be redefined (assigned a new value) by means of the statements within the loop. For example, suppose that we wish to move elements C_1 through C_N from the linear array C to corresponding positions in the linear array A, except for the two elements C_8 and C_9, which we do not wish to move. The following statements might have been designed to accomplish such a move.

```
* Invalid redefinition of loop index variable
      DO 10, I = 1, N
        A(I) = C(I)
        IF (I .EQ. 7) I = I + 2
10     CONTINUE
```

This program is incorrect because it assigns a new value to I within the loop. The loop index variable must not be given a new value within the loop, by means of an assignment statement, an input statement, or in any other way except by the automatic loop control implied in the DO statement.

The desired effect might have been achieved by a selection structure within the loop.

```
      DO 10, I = 1, N
        IF ((I .LE. 7) .OR. (I. .GE. 10)) A(I) = C(I)
10     CONTINUE
```

In each of the foregoing DO loop examples, all of the parameters following the equals sign in the DO statements are of integer type. Fortran permits real and double precision DO parameters, but some precautions are necessary due to the possibility of truncation. As an example, consider the statement

```
DO 76, X = 0.1, 3.1, 0.5
```

which will cause the loop to be traversed with the sequence of X values

0.1, 0.6, 1.1, 1.6, 2.1, 2.6, 3.1.

The trip count calculation begins with the evaluation of $(3.1 - 0.1) \div (0.5)$, which gives 6.0; the next lower integer is 6 and we add 1 to find that the loop will be executed 7 times, as expected. Or will it? As we noted in Section 2.2.2, many computers represent decimal fractions with a slight error; thus, the value of $(3.1 - 0.1)$ may turn out to be slightly less than 3.0 in which case the quotient would be smaller than 6.0. If this happens, the final traversal of the loop with 3.1 as the value of X will not occur. In general, then, the only proper uses of real and double precision DO parameters are in cases where it is immaterial whether or not the loop is executed precisely the correct number of times.

4.1.2   The Range of a DO Loop

The group of statements to be repeated, including the terminal statement (but not the DO statement itself), is called the *range* of the iteration or of the DO loop.

Transfer to a point outside the range

The following example illustrates an "exit" from the loop, when it is found that no further traversals are needed in order to accomplish the intended purpose. The loop in this example is used to determine whether any element of the real array *A* is negative. Each element is examined in turn; as soon as a negative element is found, the repetition can be terminated because the remaining elements do not need to be examined (see Fig. 4.7).

```
      DO 10, I = 1, 40
         IF (A(I) .LT. 0.0) GO TO 100
10       CONTINUE
      PRINT *, 'No␣negative␣values.'
      STOP
100   CONTINUE
      PRINT *, 'Negative␣value␣at␣element', I
```

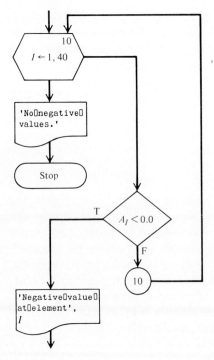

Fig. 4.7 Transfer out of the range of a DO loop.

The value of the loop index is preserved when an exit from the range of the loop is executed. Thus, the value of I that is printed will be the subscript of the first negative value in the array. If there are no negative values, the dependent statement GO TO 100 will never be executed and the loop will continue until it terminates normally.

Here is a similar example, in which a loop is used to "search" the integer array *List* until an array element is found whose value matches that of the variable *Look*. (This method of searching an array is called *linear search,* and is not so efficient as some other methods, such as the *binary search* algorithm described in Exercise 3 in Section 4.4.2.)

```
* Linear search for an element of the array List
* whose value matches that of the variable Look.
      ...
      DO 10, I = 1, 40
         IF (LIST(I) .EQ. LOOK) GO TO 100
  10     CONTINUE
      PRINT *, 'No[]match[]found.'
      STOP
 100  CONTINUE
      PRINT *, 'Match[]found[]at[]element', I
      ...
```

Value of the index variable at normal termination

If we carefully examine the sequence of steps of the basic iteration pattern (Section 4.1.1), we see that the index variable is always set to a new value just before the test for termination occurs. Thus, upon normal termination (when the number of traversals remaining is found to be less than one), the index variable will have the value we would have expected *if* the loop had been traversed one more time. Consider the following example.

```
      DO 10, I = 1, 40
         IF (A(I) .LT. 0.0) GO TO 100
  10     CONTINUE
 100  CONTINUE
      PRINT *, I
```

As we have seen, the value of I is preserved when the dependent statement GO TO 100 is executed in order to exit prematurely from the loop. Now we see that when *normal termination* occurs, the value of I will have been set to 41 just before the termination test was made. Therefore, the value printed will be between 1 and 40 if one of the elements of A is negative, and it will be 41 if there are no negative values.

Conditional execution of a part of the range

During execution of the statements in the range of a DO loop, we may detect that the remaining statements do not need to be executed. This situation can of course be handled with a selection structure of the following form:

```
DO  Label,...
    . . .
    IF (Assertion) THEN
          statements to be executed conditionally
       END IF
Label   CONTINUE
```

On the other hand, we noted in Section 3.4 that there are some situations in which *explicit* control of the execution sequence is required. As an example, suppose that an error is detected during execution of a statement at an inner level in a nested structure. The most appropriate way to handle such an exit may be with a GO TO statement.

For example, consider a program containing a loop to process a sequence of bank account transactions. The body of the loop contains a nested selection structure, to control the processing of each transaction on the basis of a transaction code as well as other tests. At some point inside this nested selection structure, it may be detected that an amount to be withdrawn from an account exceeds the account balance, or that an account number is invalid. After printing an error message in such a case, we wish to discontinue the further processing of the faulty transaction. Rather than continuing to make the tests implied by the selection structures in the remainder of the loop body, we use a GO TO statement to skip over the remaining statements and proceed to the next data case.

There is one point that needs to be noted. A transfer to the *terminal* statement of the loop will properly cause execution to continue with the next traversal of the loop. A transfer to the DO statement, on the other hand, is a transfer *outside* the range of the loop; this will cause the program to repeat the DO statement from the beginning, including a new initialization of the loop control parameters.

Whereas it is permissible to jump from a point within the range to a point outside, or to transfer from one point in the range to another (including transfer to the terminal statement), it does not make sense to jump *into* the range of a loop from a point outside. Such a jump would not permit the loop control to be established and executed correctly.

4.1.3   Implied DO Loops

Certain Fortran statements may contain a *list* that refers to a sequence of data items. Input and output lists, which were mentioned in Section 2.4.2, and certain lists in a DATA statement, which will be encountered in Chapter 7, may incorporate notation analogous to the specification in a DO statement:

    (*Sublist*, *Index* = *Initial value*, *Limit*, *Increment*)

The *Sublist* consists of a sequence of items of any form that is permitted in the list. The *Index, Initial value,* and *Increment* are subject to the same rules that apply to DO loops. The increment, if omitted, is given the default value 1.

Example 14 The following two lists are equivalent.

```
(A(I), I = 1, 6)
A(1), A(2), A(3), A(4), A(5), A(6)
```

Example 15 The following two statements are equivalent.

```
PRINT *, (C(2, J), J = 1, 5)
PRINT *, C(2, 1), C(2, 2), C(2, 3), C(2, 4), C(2, 5)
```

Example 16 An implied DO loop may appear along with other items in a list, as we see in the following example. The sequence specified by a list is based on a left-to-right scan of the entire list. When an implied DO loop is reached during the scan, all the elements it specifies are included in the sequence before the scan continues with the next item beyond the group. The following two lists are equivalent.

```
A, B, (P(K, K), K = 1, 3), D, E, F
A, B, P(1, 1), P(2, 2), P(3, 3), D, E, F
```

Example 17 The following equivalent lists illustrate a sublist consisting of more than one item.

```
K, L, M, (A(1), B(I), I = 1, 3)
K, L, M, A(1), B(1), A(2), B(2), A(3), B(3)
```

Example 18 The index variable does not have to be used as a subscript with any or all of the items of the sublist. Sublist items not involving the index variable will simply be repeated in the list sequence. The following are equivalent.

```
(C, A(4), T(I), D, I = 1, 3)
C, A(4), T(1), D, C, A(4), T(2), D, C, A(4), T(3), D
```

A form that is valid for use in an input list is the following.

```
N, (A(I), I = 1, N)
```

For example, if the first data value read is the integer 4, this list is equivalent to the following.

    N, A(1), A(2), A(3), A(4)

A list of this form should be used only with extreme caution, however, since a small error in data preparation could have a rather dramatic effect. Unless it is absolutely necessary to include N in the same list, it would be better to read N with a separate statement, make a check to ensure the validity of the data value just read, and then use another statement to read

    (A(1), I = 1, N)

The major difference between a DO loop and an implied DO loop is that the former consists of a group of *statements* to be repeated, while the latter consists of a group of *list items* within a single statement (that is, a *sublist*) to be repeated. The beginning and end of a DO loop are established by a DO statement that specifies a label, and a correspondingly labeled statement, respectively. The beginning and end of an implied DO loop are indicated by a pair of matching parentheses. The trip count, and the successive values of the index variable, are established identically in the two cases. A negative increment value for an implied DO loop, for example, will cause the index value to decrease. Certain values of the initial value, limit, and increment may result in a trip count less than one, so that the sublist is scanned zero times; for example,

    J = 5
    READ *, (A(I), I = J, 4), X

Since the trip count for the implied DO loop is zero, the first value read will be assigned to X.

A rule for input lists

We noted in Section 4.1.1 that a loop index variable must not be assigned a new value during execution of a loop. By analogy, the index variable of an implied DO loop must not appear as a sublist item in an input list. Thus, the implied DO loop

    (I, A(I), B(I), I = 1, 3)

would not be valid in an input list. It could be used in an output list, however, and would be equivalent to the list

    1, A(1), 2, A(2), 3, A(3)

4.1.4 Exercises

1. Write a program to copy all the elements of the linear array A into the corresponding positions in the linear array B. There are N elements.

2. Write a program to set each element of the linear array *Item* to a value indicating its position within the array; that is, assign the value I to the array element $Item_I$. There are N elements.

3. Write a program that will examine a real array A, having 40 elements, and locate the last I such that A_I is negative. (Hint: Compare Fig. 4.7. Use a negative increment.) What will be the final value of I if none of the array elements is negative?

4. Write a program to find the *product* of all the N elements of the linear array *Factor*. (Compare Example 1. Do not initialize the product to the value 0. What initial value should you use instead?)

5. Let *Tax* be a linear array having 22 elements. Assume that the first 20 elements have been assigned values, but the last two are undefined. Move each element down two places, and set Tax_1 and Tax_2 to zero.

6. Write programs for each of the following.

   a) Move the N elements of the linear array *Pig* to the array *Poke,* storing them in reverse order; that is, set $Poke_{N+1-I}$ to the value of Pig_I.

   b) Reverse the elements of the linear array A, without using more than one cell of auxiliary storage. (There is a possible pitfall in this problem.)

7. Correct any Fortran language errors you find in the following statements.

   a) `DO 52, I = 1, N`
   b) `DO 13, FOR I = 1 TO N`
   c) `DO 22, JOLLY .EQ. 12, 62, I`
   d) `DO 39, 1 = I, H`
   e) `DO 15, K(1) = K(2), K(3), K(4)`

8. *Arithmetic mean.* In statistics the arithmetic mean of a set of numbers X_1, X_2, ..., X_N is defined as the sum of the numbers divided by N. Write a program to compute the arithmetic mean of the elements of a linear array. (You may assume that the values of the array elements are already stored in the array. Include a declaration for the array, choosing some reasonable value for N.)

9. *Standard deviation.* We may compute the standard deviation of a sequence of numbers by first finding their sum, *Sum,* and the sum of their squares, *Sumsq.* Then we compute their arithmetic mean, *Avg,* as in Exercise 8. Next we find their variance, *Var,* according to the formula

$$Var = (Sumsq/N) - Avg^2.$$

The standard deviation, *Dev,* is merely the square root of *Var.* Write a program to compute the standard deviation of the elements of a linear array.

10. *Covariance and correlation.* When we have two linear arrays of numbers, X and Y, we can compute not only the individual averages, $Xavg$ and $Yavg$, and the individual standard deviations, $Xdev$ and $Ydev$, but also the covariance and correlation. To do this, we must first find the sum of the elements in each of the separate arrays, $Xsum$ and $Ysum$, the sum of the squares of the elements in each array, $Xxsum$ and $Yysum$, the sum of products of corresponding elements, $Xysum$, and the number of elements, N. We can evaluate all these sums at once, during a single pass through the two arrays. The covariance is given by

$$Covar = (Xysum/N) - Xavg \times Yavg$$

and the correlation is

$$Corr = Covar \div (Xdev \times Ydev).$$

Write a program to compute the correlation between a pair of linear arrays already in storage.

11. Write a program to compute the correlation as in Exercise 10, but assume that the X and Y values are read from cards, each card containing one value of X and the corresponding value of Y. (Do not use arrays. Thus, this program could be used for any number of data items.) Devise a method of detecting the end of the data. Run the program with one or more of the following data cases.

Suggested data for use with Exercise 11.

Case 1. Thickness of tree rings versus amount of rainfall

Year	1	2	3	4	5	6	7	8
Amount of rainfall, cm	18.1	15.1	11.4	35.6	33.2	15.0	33.1	35.3
Thickness of tree rings, mm	7.0	3.5	2.0	7.3	6.9	3.5	5.7	5.1

Case 2. Height versus weight of individuals

Height, cm	159.9	154.7	157.4	150.5	154.1	150.7	163.0	161.1	154.5
Weight, kg	88.0	76.4	92.0	66.3	80.6	75.3	105.6	106.1	88.2

Case 3. Test scores of students

Student	A	B	C	D	E	F	G	H	I	J	K	L	M	N	O
Math score	27	10	82	80	45	25	66	47	58	41	67	30	87	25	52
English score	70	22	71	57	47	45	46	40	24	31	67	55	42	25	59

Case 4. Sales versus year

Year	1	2	3	4	5	6	7	8	9	10
Sales	2.87	3.19	3.06	3.31	3.26	3.39	3.61	3.56	3.82	3.96

Case 5. Population of world (logarithm) versus time

Year	1	2	3	4	5	6	7	8
Population	9.465	9.471	9.472	9.479	9.484	9.488	9.490	9.491

Case 6. Inflation versus increase in money supply

Year	1	2	3	4	5	6
Increase in money supply, %	5	8	10	6	8	15
Inflation, %	5	6	8	5	7	10

Case 7. Deaths from lung cancer (thousands) versus U.S. tobacco production ($ million)

Year	1	2	3	4	5	6	7	8
U.S. tobacco production	1319	1326	1387	1406	1390	1354	1293	1228
Deaths from lung cancer	26.7	27.4	28.4	28.7	28.6	27.5	26.1	24.7

Case 8. Motor vehicle fatalities versus number of vehicles registered (millions)

Year	1	2	3	4	5	6	7	8
Vehicles	44.7	49.2	51.9	53.3	56.3	58.6	62.7	65.2
Fatalities	31,701	34,763	36,996	37,794	37,955	35,586	38,426	39,628

Year	9	10	11	12	13	14	15
Vehicles	67.6	68.8	72.1	74.5	76.4	79.7	83.5
Fatalities	38,702	36,981	37,910	38,137	38,091	40,804	43,564

Case 9. Exponential public debt growth (logarithm) versus time

Year	1900	1910	1920	1930	1940	1950	1960	1970
U.S. public debt	9.10	9.06	10.39	10.21	10.68	11.41	11.46	11.52

12. *Linear regression.* We may suspect a linear relation between two measured variables, for example, the thickness of tree rings during a sequence of years, as compared with the amount of rainfall. If there were such a relation, it could be expressed in the form

$Y = a + b \cdot X$.

The problem of determining the "best" values for a and b for a relation of this form (the coefficients of linear regression) is closely related to the foregoing statistical problems.

Making one pass through the data (or processing it during input), we compute (as before) *Xsum, Ysum, Xsqsum,* and *Xysum,* and we determine the number of elements, *Rn.* After these sums have been computed, we then determine the following statistics (as before):

$Xavg = Xsum/Rn,$
$Yavg = Ysum/Rn,$
$Xvar = (Xsqsum/Rn) - Xavg^2,$
$Covar = (Xysum/Rn) - Xavg \ Yavg.$

The regression coefficients, a and b, are then obtained from those statistics:

$b = Covar/Xvar,$
$a = Yavg - b \cdot Xavg.$

Write a program to compute the regression coefficients as described above. Run the program with one or more of the data cases that were suggested for Exercise 11.

13. Compute the product

$(Y - X_1) \times (Y - X_3) \times (Y - X_5) \times \cdots \times (Y - X_N),$

where N is some odd number. Store the result as the value of P.

14. *Divisors of an integer.* Write a program to read an integer N (larger than 1), and print all its divisors. *Hint:* A first approach is to test each integer, I, between 1 and N, to see whether it divides N.

IF (MOD (N, I) .EQ. 0) . . .

A little thought, however, suggests that if I divides N, then $(N \div I)$ also divides N. Therefore, the divisors can be found two at a time, and only those integers that do not exceed the square root of N need be tested. (Compare I^2 with N.)

15. *Tabulate votes in a bond election.* For each precinct there will be three integer data items on a card: the precinct number, the number of "yes" votes, and the number of "no" votes.

    Your program should print the total number of "yes" votes, total number of "no" votes, and total number of all votes cast, as well as the percentage of "yes" votes. Note that the last result will be a real number.

Data:

Precinct	"Yes" votes	"No" votes
1	946	321
2	1267	588
3	855	1443
4	1298	741
5	1039	780
6	819	599

16. You are working as a laboratory assistant for Professor Smythe-Heppelwaite, and you are helping him prepare data to be processed at the campus computer center. The professor gives you a deck of 100 cards, each containing the measured thickness of the wing of one of the 100 butterflies in his rare butterfly collection. The professor states that he has arranged the cards so that the variable values are in ascending order, but from past experience you have reason to be skeptical.

    Write a program to read the cards one at a time (without storing the data values in an array) and, for each card after the first, test for a "stepdown" in the sequence of data values, that is, for a card containing a smaller data value than the previous card.

    When a stepdown or sequence error is detected, print the location within the deck of the card on which it occurred, as well as the two data values involved. Also count the stepdown errors.

    After the entire deck has been read, print the total number of stepdowns (sequence errors) that were found.

Data:

1393	1394	1418	1429	1437	1465	1445	1455
1463	1497	1565	1578	1584	1585	1591	1597
1610	1657	1658	1673	1685	1707	1711	1717
1723	1730	1733	1738	1757	1765	1811	1842
1853	1879	1881	1887	1903	1905	1906	1909
1913	1920	1931	1946	1961	1976	1977	1986
1994	1987	2009	2024	2025	2026	2040	2041
2048	2049	2050	2072	2073	2074	2075	2088
2096	2089	2099	2101	2105	2120	2129	2135
2141	2142	2144	2145	2162	2167	2169	2170
2173	2176	2181	2189	2183	2221	2229	2233
2258	2264	2269	2272	2277	2288	2296	2309
2310	2352	2368	2377				

17. *Linear interpolation.* You are given a pair of linear arrays named *Height* and
Weight. The array *Height* contains numbers representing possible heights of persons. For each subscript value *J*, the array element $Weight_J$ has a value representing the average weight of individuals whose height is $Height_J$. (We say that
arrays which can be used in this way, in that elements of the two arrays which
have the same subscript value contain related information, form a *table*). Assume
that the heights are arranged in ascending order.

   Given the height of a particular individual, which might or might not coin-
cide with one of the tabulated values, we wish to estimate the corresponding
weight. We *search* the array of heights until we locate a value near the specified
height, *H*. That is, we find a value of *J* such that *H* is greater than or equal to
$Height_J$ and is less than $Height_{J+1}$. Then we estimate the corresponding weight
according to the following formula (see Fig. 4.8).

$$W = Weight_J + \frac{(H - Height_J)}{(Height_{J+1} - Height_J)} \cdot (Weight_{J+1} - Weight_J)$$

Data:

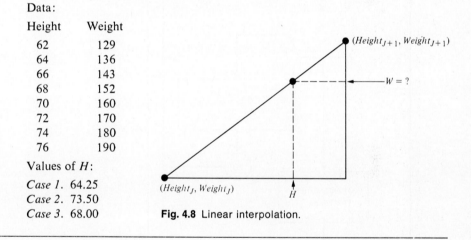

Height	Weight
62	129
64	136
66	143
68	152
70	160
72	170
74	180
76	190

Values of *H*:

Case 1. 64.25
Case 2. 73.50
Case 3. 68.00

Fig. 4.8 Linear interpolation.

4.2 NESTED ITERATIONS

Some common tasks of a repetitive nature prove, on close inspection, to consist
of one loop that is totally nested or embedded inside another loop. Here is an example of such a "nested iteration."

Example 1 We have a rectangular array of numbers, and we wish to form the
sum of all the numbers in each row, as well as a grand total. (Row *I* consists of
all the array elements whose first subscript value is equal to *I*.) We will need a
linear array of row sums; element *Row* of this array will be used to store the sum
of the elements in row *Row* of the rectangular array (see Figs. 4.9 and 4.10).

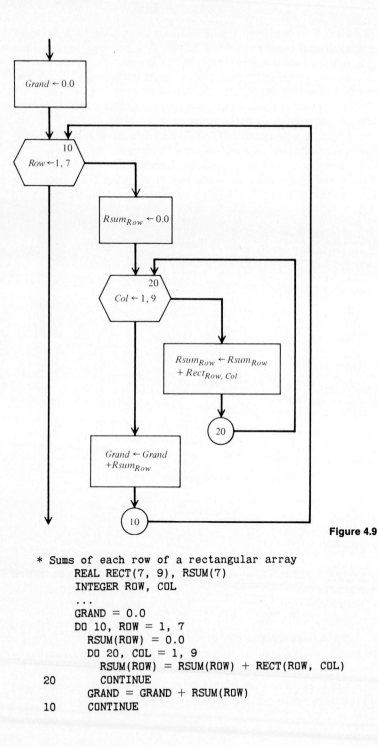

Figure 4.9

```
* Sums of each row of a rectangular array
      REAL RECT(7, 9), RSUM(7)
      INTEGER ROW, COL
      ...
      GRAND = 0.0
      DO 10, ROW = 1, 7
        RSUM(ROW) = 0.0
        DO 20, COL = 1, 9
          RSUM(ROW) = RSUM(ROW) + RECT(ROW, COL)
20        CONTINUE
        GRAND = GRAND + RSUM(ROW)
10      CONTINUE
```

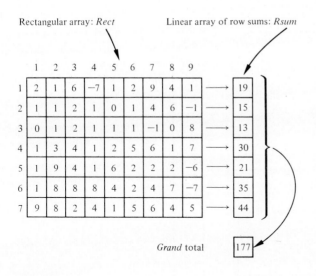

Figure 4.10

Here the outer loop is controlled by the statement DO 10, ROW = 1, 7. For each value of *Row*:

1. We initialize the row sum for row *Row*, that is, $Rsum_{Row}$, to zero;

2. We perform an iteration (inner loop) controlled by the statement DO 20, COL = 1, 9, which adds each $Rect_{Row, Col}$ to this row sum; and

3. When this inner iteration is complete, we add the sum for row *Row* to the *Grand* total.

Note the sequence of steps of this nested iteration. Each time the outer loop is repeated, its index, *Row,* is set to the new value and *retains* that value while the inner loop goes through all the values of its index, *Col.* After the inner loop has been repeated the proper number of times, the execution sequence proceeds to the terminal statement of the outer loop, thus causing the outer loop index to take on its next value and the entire inner loop to be repeated.

A general pattern for nested loops is shown in Fig. 4.11 in "skeleton" form. The symbol *y* represents the block of statements constituting the computational part of the inner loop, whose terminal statement is labeled $\mathcal{L}_1$. The outer loop, whose terminal statement is labeled $\mathcal{L}_2$, contains the inner loop and may also include a block of statements (indicated by *x*) to be executed before entering the inner loop and another block of statements (indicated by *z*) to be executed after completing the inner loop. Either or both of blocks *x* and *z* may be absent.

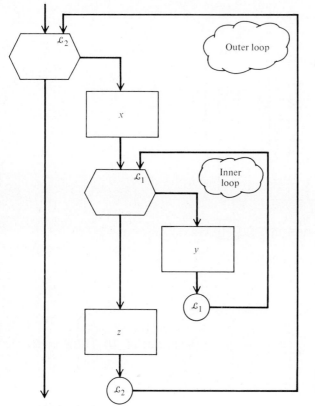

Fig. 4.11 General pattern for a two-level nest.

Depth of nesting

Example 1 and the general pattern in Fig. 4.11 show two levels of loops in a nest. It is possible to include another loop inside the inner loop of a two-level nest to create a nest with three levels: For example, the block y in Fig. 4.11 could also contain an entire DO loop inside it. Thus, there is no practical limit on the number of levels permitted in a nest of loops in Fortran.

Legal and illegal nesting

Two or more complete DO loops may appear at the same level in a nest. For example, the block z could contain another DO loop (as in Fig. 4.12a), or the block y could include two or more separate loops (Fig. 4.12b). However, the ranges of DO loops at different levels, or of two loops at the same level, must not partially overlap. If any part of the range of one loop overlaps the range of another, then one of the two loops must entirely contain the other (thus creating an additional nesting level).

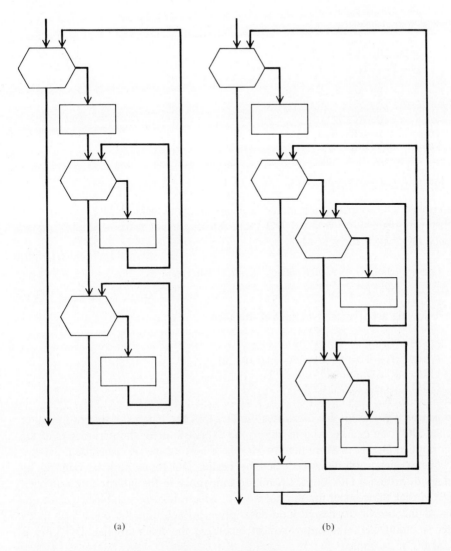

(a)   (b)

Fig. 4.12 Further examples of nested loop structures.

Perhaps the most common cause of improper nesting is simply the misnumbering of the terminal statements. For example, the following loops are illegally nested:

```
        DO 10, I = 1, 4
          DO 20, J = 1, 3
            ...
10        CONTINUE
20          CONTINUE
```

and so are the following:

```
        DO 10, I = 1, 4
           DO 20, J = 1, 3
           . . .
              DO 30, K = 1, 5
              . . .
20            CONTINUE
30               CONTINUE
10         CONTINUE
```

Nested implied DO loops

An implied DO loop may be included in a statement inside a DO loop, or in a sublist within an outer implied DO loop. An important form of doubly nested implied DO loop is the following.

$$((List_1, \ Index_1 = Initial \ value_1, \ Limit_1, \ Increment_1),$$
$$Index_2 = Initial \ value_2, \ Limit_2, \ Increment_2)$$

The following are specific examples of this form.

```
((B(I, J), J = 1, 7), I = 1, 5)
((B(I, J), J = 1, 7), I = 2, 10, 2)
((D(L, M), L = 1, 5), M = 7, 1, −1)
((C(I, J), I = 1, J), J = 1, 3)
```

The last of these examples illustrates the fact that the index variable of the outer implied DO loop can be used in any of the expressions for the parameters of the inner implied DO loop. More than two levels of nesting are also permitted.

The sequence of items specified by nested DO loops may be inferred by analogy to ordinary DO loops. (A minor annoyance in the interpretation of such a nest is that the control for the outer loop, which must be established first, appears at the *end* of the nested loop description.) Each time the outer loop index value is established, the entire sublist including the inner implied DO loop is scanned. For example,

```
(A, B(J), (C(J, I), I = 2, 3), D, J = 1, 2)
```

is equivalent to the list

```
A, B(1), C(1, 2), C(1, 3), D, A, B(2), C(2, 2), C(2, 3), D
```

That is, the value of J is set to 1 and the list is scanned as though it were written

```
A, B(1), (C(1, I), I = 2, 3), D
```

Then the value of *J* is set to 2 and the list is scanned as though it were written

```
A, B(2), (C(2, I), I = 2, 3), D
```

Example 2   The following statements provide a flexible way to accomplish the input or output of a rectangular array, or of a major section of a rectangular array, by using an implied DO loop to transmit the elements in a single row of the array, and then enclosing the READ or PRINT statement with this list in a DO loop that is executed once for each row. (We shall continue to assume that the variables *Row* and *Col* are declared to be of integer type.)

```
      DO 50, ROW = 1, 5
         READ *, (ARRAY(ROW, COL), COL = 1, 8)
   50    CONTINUE
```

We see that the READ statement will cause input of row *Row* of *Array,* while the DO statement permits *Row* to vary from 1 to 5. Thus, five complete rows of eight elements each will be transmitted. It is important to note that a *new input record* will be read for each row, since each traversal of the DO loop causes a new READ statement to be executed. Similarly, for output of an *M* by *N* matrix (rectangular array), we can write the completely general sequence of statements

```
      DO 50, ROW = 1, M
         PRINT *, (ARRAY(ROW, COL), COL = 1, N)
   50    CONTINUE
```

which will cause each *row* of the matrix to be printed, starting on a new line.
These statement sequences should be compared with the nested implied DO loop forms

```
READ *, ((ARRAY(ROW, COL), COL = 1, 8), ROW = 1, 5)
PRINT *, ((ARRAY(ROW, COL), COL = 1, N), ROW = 1, M)
```

which will transmit the identical sequence of array elements, but will not advance to a new line on the external medium for each row.

4.2.1 Exercises

1. Rewrite Example 1:
   a) For a square array of 5 rows and 5 columns;
   b) To compute column sums instead of row sums, along with the grand total.

2. Write a program involving two linear arrays of integers, one containing 15 elements and the other containing 20 elements. After reading data to obtain values for all the items in each array, your program should print the values of only those integers that appear in *both* arrays.

3. Write a program involving an array of three dimensions, for use in a biological analysis problem, concerning genetic factors: four different hair colors, four different eye colors, and four different skin color tones. The program should read a line of data for each individual, consisting of:

   a) An integer (1, 2, 3, or 4) identifying hair color,
   b) An integer (1, 2, 3, or 4) identifying color of eyes, and
   c) An integer (1, 2, 3, or 4) identifying skin color tone.

   As each set of data is read, the program should add 1 to the appropriate cell of the array. After all the data has been read, the program should print, for each cell in the array, the number of individuals found to have the corresponding set of genetic factors. (Note: Before starting the input phase, the program should set all the cells of the array to zero.)

4. A musical melody has been coded as a sequence of integers representing the notes (ignoring time values), and this sequence is stored in a linear array. Write a program to count, for each different possible pair of notes, how often the first note of the pair is followed by the second note of the pair. Assume that all the notes are within one octave of middle C: Thus there are 25 different notes, including sharps and flats. The melody consists of not more than 100 notes.

5. A checkerboard is represented by a rectangular array with 8 rows and 8 columns whose elements are denoted by $Chek_{I,J}$. If the value of $Chek_{I,J}$ is 1, there is a checker in row I and column J of the checkerboard; a 0 denotes the absence of a checker. Scan the entire board and determine the number of checkers on it.

6. As in Exercise 5, the value 0 denotes an empty square. However, the value 1 denotes an ordinary checker and the value 2 denotes a king. Scan the board and determine the number of ordinary checkers and the number of kings.

7. Expand the previous exercise to make the values 1, 2, 3, and 4 denote, respectively, a red man, a red king, a black man, and a black king. Scan the board and determine the number of checkers of each type.

8. Consider the following program.

```
      REAL A(6, 6)
      DO 12, I = 1, 6
        DO 11, J = 1, 6
          A(I, J) = REAL (I + J - 8)
11        CONTINUE
12      CONTINUE
      READ *, K, L
      TOTAL = 0.0
      DO 22, I = L, K
        DO 21, J = 1, I
          IF (A(I, J) .GT. 0.0) TOTAL = TOTAL + A(I, J)
21        CONTINUE
22      CONTINUE
      PRINT *, TOTAL
      END
```

In each of the following cases, tell (a) how many times the IF statement in the inner loop will be executed; and (b) what will be the final value of *Total*.

Case 1:   K = 6, L = 3.
Case 2:   K = 4, L = 5.

4.3 THE TERMINAL STATEMENT OF A DO LOOP

In all the examples we have presented so far, the label in the DO statement has referred to a CONTINUE statement. This statement causes no computational action, and therefore costs nothing in terms of execution time; thus, it is ideal for use as the terminal statement of a DO loop. In our examples, therefore, we will continue to follow the practice (which we highly recommend) of using a CONTINUE statement as the terminal statement of every DO loop, except when we want to demonstrate the effect of using some other statement form.

Fortran permits most other statements to be used to terminate a DO loop. Assignment statements and input or output statements, in particular, may be used in this position.

It was pointed out in Section 4.1.2 that a jump to the terminal statement will skip the remaining statements in the range of the loop and proceed with the next traversal of the loop. If the terminal statement is not a CONTINUE statement, however, the effect is not quite so simple. The terminal statement will be executed before the loop control processing begins, and this may have undesirable effects.

Some control statements are permitted in the terminal position,† but even those that are permitted according to the rules of Fortran can cause undesirable actions. Therefore, we reiterate our more conservative recommendation that leads to clearer program structure: A control statement should not be used to terminate a DO loop. The desired effect can be achieved, and a more readable program obtained, if the control statement is followed by a CONTINUE statement, which is then used as the terminal statement of the loop.

Nested loops with a common terminal statement

Another practice that is permitted by the rules of Fortran but leads to obscure program structure is the use of a single label (and thus a common terminal statement) for two or more DO loops in a nest. For example, Fortran rules permit

```
      DO 20 ROW = 1, 6
         DO 20 COL = 1, 6
            IF (A(ROW, COL) .LT. 0.0) GO TO 20
            . . .
20          TOTAL = TOTAL + A(ROW, COL)
```

---

† The rule is that a control statement may be used if there is some possibility that it will *not* result in a transfer of control. Thus a logical IF statement is acceptable but an unconditional GO TO is not permitted. Because nesting rules must be respected, a DO statement or any of the control statements of an IF ... THEN selection structure is also unacceptable.

Although we recommend against this practice, most programmers will at some time encounter a program that has been written disregarding (or in ignorance of) this recommendation. Thus it is useful to know how such a program will be interpreted according to Fortran rules.

We obtain the correct interpretation if we view the labeled terminal statement as a part of the *innermost* loop of the nest. All references to this label, in GO TO statements or elsewhere in any of the DO loops that include it, *except* for the references in the DO statements at the top of those loops, refer to the terminal statement in this innermost loop context. We then mentally insert an unwritten "loop control processing" step *after* the terminal statement, for each loop in the nest that has this common label.

> *Label*   [Execute terminal statement.]
> [Perform loop control processing for innermost loop.]
> [Perform loop control processing for next inner loop.]
>
>   . . .
>
> [Perform loop control processing for outermost loop.]

Therefore, the program in the above example is interpreted as follows:

```
       INTEGER ROW, COL
       DO 20b ROW = 1, 6
         DO 20a COL = 1, 6
           IF (A(ROW, COL) .LT. 0.0) GO TO 20
           . . .
20         TOTAL = TOTAL + A(ROW, COL)
20a        CONTINUE
20b      CONTINUE
```

Of course, the labels 20a and 20b are not valid in Fortran; we use them merely to illustrate the correct interpretation of the program in the example.

This same way of viewing the terminal statement of a DO loop also gives the proper interpretation when the terminal statement is a control statement. Note that it also gives the correct answer to the question, "From which points in the nest is one permitted to jump to the terminal statement?" Since the terminal statement is part of the innermost loop, a jump to that statement from an outer loop in the nest would be prohibited.

4.3.1   Exercises

1. We have a linear array of N integers, $K_1, K_2, \ldots, K_N$, some of which may be zero. We wish to count those that are positive and even and those that are negative and even, producing the separate tallies *Npos* and *Nneg*. Zeros and odd numbers are to be ignored.

2. *Polynomial arithmetic* (compare Fig. 3.20 in Section 3.4.2). Read the coefficients of two polynomials.

   a) Compute and print the coefficients of their sum, difference, and product.
   b) "Divide" the first polynomial by the second; that is, calculate the coefficients of the quotient polynomial and of the remainder polynomial. The degree of the quotient polynomial should equal the difference between the degrees of the two given polynomials, and the degree of the remainder polynomial should be one less than the degree of the second given polynomial, except when the degree of the second given polynomial exceeds that of the first. In this case, the quotient polynomial consists simply of the "zero polynomial" (having nothing but a constant term, with value zero), and the remainder polynomial is the same as the first given polynomial. Note that in any case some or all of the coefficients of the remainder polynomial may be zero. (See also D. E. Knuth, *The Art of Computer Programming,* Vol. 2, "Seminumerical Algorithms," p. 364.) Make up your own data, or use data given by your instructor. Check that your program will work in special cases—for example if the second polynomial consists simply of a nonzero constant term.

3. *Sorting.* Write a program to read a number of records, each containing a different integer value, arrange them in ascending order in a linear array, L, and print the sorted array.

   Here is a sorting method that you may use. This method, which is one of several denoted by the term "bubble sorting," is also called the *insertion* method, by analogy to the way a person might arrange a hand of cards at bridge. He arranges the first two cards in order, then picks up the third card and moves it past the second (and the first, if necessary, searching in decreasing order) until he finds its proper location; he then does the same with the fourth card, the fifth card, and so on.

   Details (see also Section 10.2.1): Read the first record into L_1. Then, starting with $J = 1$, read the next data value into an auxiliary cell named *Next*. Compare this value with L_J, L_{J-1}, and so on, until an element smaller than *Next* is found. When the value of *Next* is compared with L_I, if *Next* is larger or equal, the value of *Next* is stored at L_{I+1} and we exit from this inner loop to take the next value of J. If *Next* is smaller, however, we store the value of L_I in the cell L_{I+1} and continue the inner search loop. If no element smaller than *Next* is found, the loop will terminate with zero as the value of I (as explained in Section 4.1.2), so we store the value of *Next* at L_1 and proceed to the outer loop (Fig. 4.13).

   Data:

   Case 1 (5 data items).   19, 13, 5, 27, 1
   Case 2 (45 data items).   −9, 67, 116, 6157, 778, 634, −22, 61, −147, 1639, 496, 4208, 2170, 631, 1949, 277, 5718, 412, 220, 461, 3025, 1495, 13418, 248, 1025, 4094, 16, 373, 4067, 1, 1781, 6238, 1, 372, 258, 958, 984, 1104, 167, −122, −64, −32, 509, 175, −93

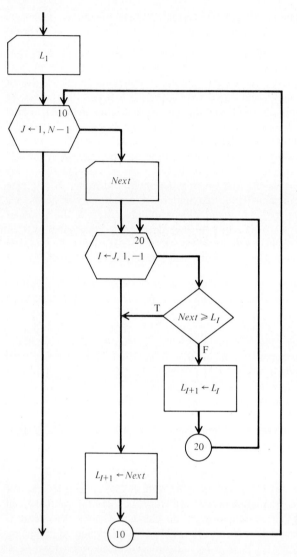

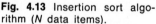

Fig. 4.13 Insertion sort algorithm (*N* data items).

4.4 CONDITIONAL LOOPING

Most modern high-level programming languages have a construct that permits *conditional looping,* or repetition of a block of statements an indefinite number of times, so long as some condition holds. (This condition may involve values of some of the variables in the program, for example.) Experience has shown that this feature in the programming language greatly encourages development of programs possessing elegance and style. Many programmers who have used only count-controlled loops (repeated a predetermined number of times) conceive of all repetitions in those terms. These programmers seem to develop a mental block that keeps them from perceiving other ways of controlling loops, which could be more appropriate and more natural for the problem.

For example, many mathematical algorithms consist of a loop in which some variable is modified according to a process of successive approximations, becoming closer at each step to some "ideal" value. The approximation process continues until the difference from the ideal becomes "insignificant" in comparison to a predetermined tolerance. The important idea is that the number of repetitions is not known in advance, since the rate of progress toward the ideal value may involve some parameters whose values have not been established when the program is designed.

Another example where the number of repetitions is not known when the program is designed is a data processing program such as a payroll, which applies the same calculation repeatedly to a variable number of items of data. We have seen how to insert an initial data item, to provide a limit for a DO statement that controls the input loop. For many such problems, however, it would be more convenient to go on reading until the data is exhausted.

A general flowchart for conditional looping is shown in Fig. 4.14. Note especially the *condition* that is tested each time the loop is traversed. Repetition is to continue until this assertion is found to be true. One block of statements precedes this condition, and another block follows it. Although some conditional looping problems may require only one or the other of these two blocks, a general

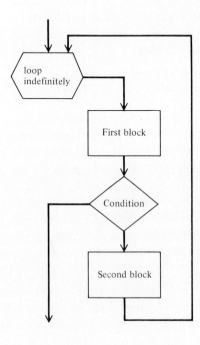

Fig. 4.14 General conditional looping structure, based on an indefinite loop with a conditional exit.

conditional looping structure must provide for both of them. This permits detection of the termination condition at whatever point in the loop is most appropriate for each specific application.

For instance, in a data processing problem it is important to be able to read an item, to test to see if the data is exhausted, and to perform the desired manipulations only in case there is actual data to be processed. In such a problem, the input operations form the first block, and the data manipulations form the second block.

This general looping construct is very elegant, easy to understand, and easy to use. Nevertheless, it has one major weakness. It can easily happen, because of a mistake in the program or in preparation of the data, that the condition for terminating the iteration is never satisfied. In an approximation process the tolerance level may have been set too tight, or incorrect preparation of the data may prevent the detection of the signal indicating that the data has been exhausted.

In practice, the programmer or the user almost always has some idea of an ultimate *maximum number* of times a loop should be repeated. The exact number of steps required by an approximation process may be impossible to determine in advance, but it may be known that if the process goes beyond twenty steps there is something wrong and further repetition is of no interest. Or, when the program is written the exact number of employees on the payroll may not be known, but it may be known that there cannot be more than three thousand. Thus, in practice the programmer will wish to take into account the possibility that something may go wrong. What is generally needed, then, is a "bounded" conditional loop construct—one that will terminate when a condition is satisfied *or* after a specified maximum number of iterations. Such a construct is easily available in Fortran.

4.4.1 Fortran Programs for Bounded Conditional Looping

The Fortran bounded conditional loop construct consists of an ordinary DO loop to establish the *maximum* number of repetitions, along with a *conditional exit* from the range of the loop.

In case the maximum number of repetitions is exceeded, the statement following the labeled terminal statement of the DO loop will of course be executed. In our examples, we put a STOP statement at this point; in practice, some other steps to be taken in this unexpected case would appear at this point in the program.

When the conditional exit occurs, the program will proceed to execute some other statements. These are written below the STOP statement that follows the DO loop, and are preceded by a *labeled* statement such as

```
8    CONTINUE
```

It is then necessary to provide a *transfer of control* to this labeled statement from within the loop when the termination condition is satisfied. This transfer provides the conditional exit from the loop (see Fig. 4.15).

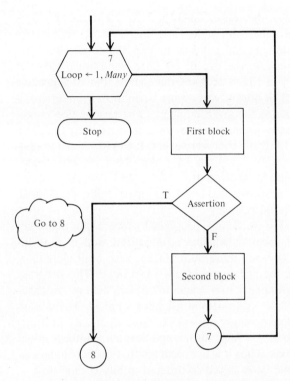

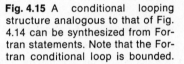

Fig. 4.15 A conditional looping structure analogous to that of Fig. 4.14 can be synthesized from Fortran statements. Note that the Fortran conditional loop is bounded.

We have already seen some examples of loop exits (including Fig. 4.7 in Section 4.1.2, and Fig. 4.13 relating to Exercise 3 in Section 4.3.1). The exit is usually implemented as a single-statement selection structure with a GO TO statement as its dependent statement:

    IF (*Assertion*) GO TO *Label*

A special form of the READ statement is used to set a "flag" indicating that the data has been exhausted:

    READ (*, *, IOSTAT = *Integer variable*), *List*

The special symbols in this READ statement are explained in Section 6.1.1, and in more detail in Section 9.1. The *List* is an ordinary input list. The *Integer variable* will be set to zero (automatically, by the processor) as the final step of execution of the READ statement in the normal case; a positive value for this variable indicates that the data has been exhausted. Thus a pair of statements such as

```
READ (*, *, IOSTAT = JSTAT) EMPNO, HOURS
IF (JSTAT .NE. 0) GO TO 8
```

will result in a jump to the statement numbered 8 when the data is exhausted.

As we noted in Section 3.4.1, the use of labels and GO TO statements does little violence to the ideas of elegance and style, provided these statements are used only in accordance with fundamental patterns such as the conditional exit.

The following examples illustrate the use of bounded conditional loops in Fortran programs. The program in Fig. 4.16 finds the square root of a positive real number by Newton's method. A normal exit occurs when the current approximation is close to the square root of the given number. (The termination condition is actually based on the square of the approximate root, divided by the given number; this ratio would equal 1.0 if the root were exact. It can be shown mathematically that this ratio will never be less than 1.0.) An abnormal exit is provided, in case the root is not found within 20 steps.

The program in Fig. 4.17 processes a payroll for up to 3000 employees, terminating when the input data is exhausted.

A final example, shown in Fig. 4.18, is a program for processing bank account transactions. An array of account balances is initialized, and then an indefinite number of transactions (but not more than 100) is read until the data is exhausted. When this occurs, all the account balances are printed. This program assumes that the transactions will appear in a "random" order, such as the chronological order of appearance of the customers at a teller's window. There is no reason why the same account number might not appear more than once in transactions scattered arbitrarily among the data; also, some account numbers might not occur in any of the transactions. Thus it is not assumed that the account numbers for the transactions will have been sorted or ordered in any special way.

```
* Read X and find its square root by Newton's method.
      MANY = 20
      EPS = 0.00001
      READ *, X
      PRINT *, 'Find□square□root□of', X
      IF (X .LT. 0.0) THEN
          PRINT *, 'X□is□negative.'
          STOP
        END IF
*
      R = 1.0
      DO 7, LOOP = 1, MANY
        R = 0.5 * (R + X / R)
*         .. Normal exit from loop, if R is close to square root of X.
        IF (R ** 2 / X - 1.0 .LT. EPS) GO TO 8
7       CONTINUE
*       .. Abnormal exit, in case root is not found in many steps.
        PRINT *, 'Root□not□found□in', MANY, '□steps.'
        STOP
*
*       .. Normal exit point.
8       CONTINUE
        PRINT *, 'Root□is', R
        END
```

Figure 4.16

```
* Process payroll for up to 3000 employees.
* N1 counts the number of non-overtime employees;
* N2 counts the number of employees with overtime.
      MANY = 3000
      N1 = 0
      N2 = 0
      DO 7, LOOP = 1, MANY
*         .. Terminate loop when data is exhausted.
         READ (*, *, IOSTAT = J) RATE, HOURS
         IF (J .NE. 0) GO TO 8
*
*         .. Basic payroll calculation.
         IF (HOURS .LE. 40.0) THEN
            PAY = RATE * HOURS
            N1 = N1 + 1
          ELSE
            PAY = RATE * (40.0 + 1.5 * (HOURS - 40.0))
            N2 = N2 + 1
          END IF
         PRINT *, RATE, HOURS, PAY
    7    CONTINUE
*      .. Error: more than 3000 employees.
      STOP
*
*      .. Normal exit point, when data is exhausted.
    8    CONTINUE
      PRINT *, N1, N2
      END
```

Figure 4.17


```
* Program to process deposit transactions,
* for a small bank with only 12 accounts.
* There should be no more than 100 transactions.
      REAL ACCT(12)
      NACCT = 12
      MANY = 100
*      .. Read initial balances for the accounts.
      READ *, (ACCT(I), I = 1, NACCT)
*      .. Now read and process all transactions.
      DO 7, LOOP = 1, MANY
        READ (*, *, IOSTAT = J) IDENT, VALUE
        IF (J .NE. 0) GO TO 8
        ACCT(IDENT) = ACCT(IDENT) + VALUE
    7    CONTINUE
*      .. Too many transactions
      STOP
*
*      .. End of data has been reached.
    8    CONTINUE
*      .. Now print all account balances.
      DO 13, I = 1, NACCT
        PRINT *, 'Account□number', I, '□Balance□is', ACCT(I)
   13    CONTINUE
      END
```

Figure 4.18

4.4.2 Exercises

1. Read some data items and add them together, continuing until the sum exceeds 24.0. Assume that the total will reach this value within the first 50 data items. Print the number of items added, and the total.
   Data:

1.9	1.3	0.5	2.7	0.1	2.6	3.1	1.6	0.2	0.9	1.1	2.1	0.2
0.1	0.4	0.3	0.6	0.5	0.8	0.7	1.0	0.9	1.9	1.3	0.8	2.7
0.3	1.4	0.7	1.6	1.7	0.6	2.4	1.2	1.8	1.2	0.8	0.7	3.1
1.6	1.1	3.3	2.3	3.3	2.3	3.0	3.6	1.5	1.7	1.9		

2. Modify the bank account program (Fig. 4.18) to process withdrawals as well as deposits, and to test for overdraft. (Compare Fig. 3.9 in Section 3.1.2.)

3. *Binary searching.* You are given a linear array of elements stored in ascending order. You are then given another item, and you are required to find the elements in the original array whose values are closest to the new item. In other words, if the array is A and the new item is X, you are supposed to find a subscript value, j, such that

   $A_{j-1} \leq X \leq A_j$.

   Instead of comparing X with all the elements of A in turn, it is more efficient (especially when the array is long) to perform a *binary search*.

   Method: Examine the middle element of the linear array, and thus determine whether the desired item is in the upper or the lower half. Subdivide whichever half it is in, and determine which quarter of the linear array contains the element sought. Continuing in this way, narrow the search to half as many elements each time until it converges on a single element.

   Use two variables, *Min* and *Max*. Set these initially to 0 and to $N + 1$, where N is the number of elements in the linear array. Each time a test is made, change one of these variables in such a manner that the value of X always lies between elements of the array A having subscripts equal to *Min* and to *Max*.

   If there is an element in the array whose value exactly equals X, the procedure will terminate with both *Min* and *Max* having the same value, equal to the subscript of the desired element of the array. (If several array elements exactly match X, an arbitrary one will be chosen.) If no array element exactly matches X, the final values of *Min* and *Max* will differ by 1, and the value of X will be between A_{Min} and A_{Max}. (If X is smaller than A_1, the final values of *Min* and *Max* will be 0 and 1; if X is larger than A_N, the final values will be N and $N + 1$.) See Fig. 4.19. For data, see Exercise 17 in Section 4.1.4.

4. Root finding by the *bisection*, or *midpoint*, method.
   a) *Fun* is a function of a single argument, X. If the sign of the function value for $X = A$ is opposite to the sign of the function for $X = B$, then proceed to step (b); otherwise, stop. (*Hint:* The signs are opposite if the value of the expression FUN (A) * FUN (B) is less than zero.)
   b) Repeat the following steps at most 20 times. (If the loop exit has not occurred by the time the iteration has been traversed 20 times, stop.)

      Set the value of C to the average of the values of A and B, and compute $Fun(C)$. If the absolute value is less than 0.001, exit from the loop (and print the value of C as the approximate root). If $Fun(C)$ has the same sign as $Fun(A)$, assign the value of C to the variable A; otherwise, assign the value of C to the variable B; in either case, continue the iteration.

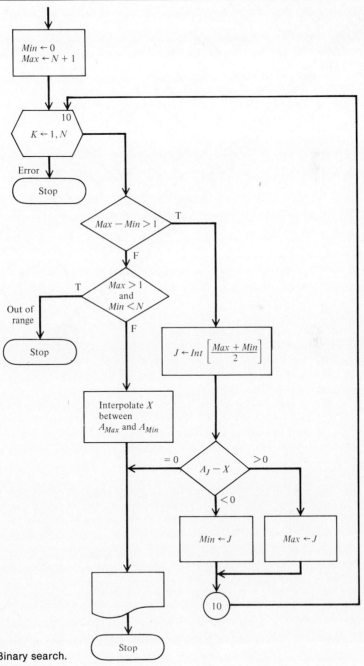

Fig. 4.19 Binary search.

CHAPTER 5
USING INFORMATION OF CHARACTER TYPE

Computers can store and process two principal forms of information: *numeric* information and *character* (textual, or verbal) information. Since these two kinds of information must be processed differently, they are also stored differently. The unit of numeric information is a single number, and the primitive operations that are performed on numeric information are operations of arithmetic. Verbal information, on the other hand, can be stored and manipulated in units as small as a single character (letter, digit, or punctuation symbol), and arithmetic operations are not appropriate for manipulating them. Up to this point we have covered only the processing of numeric information. Now we are ready to turn to the discussion of manipulations applied to words of text.

Character processing is no less interesting than the manipulation of numbers, but the traditional tasks for which Fortran programs have been designed in the past were principally numerical calculations, which used textual information only for such purposes as making printed numerical results more readable. In recent years, however, the processing of character information (sometimes referred to as "word processing") has assumed increasing importance among computer applications, and this importance has been reflected in improvements to the character manipulation features of the Fortran language.

5.1 CHARACTER EXPRESSIONS AND ASSIGNMENT

5.1.1 Storage of Character Information

The unit of storage for information of integer, real, or logical type is the cell or *numeric storage unit.* Character information, on the other hand, is subdivided and stored in *character storage units,* each of which holds a single character item of information. Because of the wide variety of representations of numeric and character data on actual computers, it is extremely difficult to establish universally acceptable conventions for sharing numeric and character storage. Therefore, Fortran assumes that the two forms of storage are incompatible. Thus, there is no way in Fortran to reuse a group of character storage units to hold numeric information, or to store character items in cells that have been used for numeric storage.

5.1.2 Character Constants

A constant of character type is written in Fortran as a sequence of characters enclosed between apostrophes (single quotes). The enclosing apostrophes are not included in the character information represented by the constant. There must be at least one character between the apostrophes. Blanks in character data are just as significant as other characters. (In this book, we use the symbol ⎕ to represent a blank character within a sequence of characters. Results printed by a computer would of course have a blank space in these positions.) Non-Fortran characters, as well as Fortran characters, are permitted in character constants.

To represent an apostrophe that occurs among the characters in a character constant, a special convention is needed: Each apostrophe is represented by a *pair* of consecutive apostrophes in the constant. Thus, for example, the word DIDN'T is written as a character constant in the form `'DIDN''T'`.

Examples of character constants

```
'FORTRAN⎕77'    '123'    'HELLO⎕THERE.'    'DIDN''T'
'THE⎕ANSWERS⎕TO⎕THE⎕EXERCISES⎕ARE⎕IN⎕THE⎕BACK⎕OF⎕THE⎕BOOK.'
'Non-Fortran⎕characters⎕are⎕also⎕permitted⎕in⎕character⎕constants.'
'%&;<>?'    'Didn''t⎕you⎕see⎕Mary''s⎕book?'
```

The character constant `'123'` represents the sequence of three characters 123. The enclosing apostrophes guarantee that this character constant will not be confused with the integer 123. Even if all the characters represented by a character constant are numeric digits, it is still not a numeric constant, because of the enclosing apostrophes.

The *length* of a character constant is the number of individual characters between the enclosing apostrophes, except that a double apostrophe used to represent an apostrophe character is counted only once (for the character actually represented). Remember that blank characters are counted. Thus, the lengths of the four constants in the first line of the examples above are 10, 3, 12, and 6, respectively. The constant `'DIDN''T'` consists of the 6 characters D, I, D, N, ', and T, so its length is 6 in spite of the fact that the constant occupies 9 columns in a Fortran program line.

5.1.3 Character Variables

Variables of character type must be explicitly or implicitly declared, because there is no default implicit type specification for types other than integer and real. A character type declaration must include a length specification (unless the variable is to have the default length one). In its simplest form, the length specification consists of an asterisk followed by an integer constant.

Examples of character variable declarations

```
CHARACTER*10 PR, STRING, TEXT
CHARACTER*80 LINE
```

The first declaration specifies that the three names *Pr, String,* and *Text* each refer to a character variable of length 10, and the second declaration specifies a single character variable *Line* of length 80.

An `IMPLICIT` statement may be used to declare an implicit character type for names beginning with certain letters. For example,

```
IMPLICIT CHARACTER*16 (A - C)
```

specifies that names beginning with the letter A, B, or C refer to a character variable of length 16. (All names specified by an `IMPLICIT CHARACTER` statement have the same length.) Of course, an explicit type declaration can specify a different type, or a different character length, for certain names beginning with these same letters—for example:

```
IMPLICIT CHARACTER*16 (A - C)
REAL BILLY, AXE, B
CHARACTER*3 ABEL, C
```

If all three of these declarations appear in a program, the two explicit type declarations *override* the implicit specification: *Billy, Axe,* and *B* are real variables; *Abel* and *C* are character variables of length 3; and all other names beginning with A, B, or C represent character variables of length 16.

Assignment

The value of a character constant or variable may be assigned to another variable of character type and of the same length, with no difficulty:

```
CHARACTER*7 FIRST, SECOND
FIRST = 'Summary'
SECOND = FIRST
```

Mixed length assignment is also possible (see Section 5.2.4).

5.1.4 List Directed Input and Output of Character Data

We have already seen some examples using list directed output to print a short message along with numerical results. The form of a list directed input or output statement does not change when character data is included in the list.

```
CHARACTER*7 FIRST, SECOND
READ *, FIRST, SECOND
SECOND = FIRST
PRINT *, FIRST, 'and', SECOND, 'are[]equal.'
```

Constants are permitted in the output list of a PRINT statement, but not in the input list of a READ statement.

An input or output list may include references to character data intermixed with references to data of other types, as illustrated in the following program example.

```
* Example 1.
* Input and output including character data.
      CHARACTER*7 FIRST, SECOND
      DOUBLE PRECISION BIGONE
      COMPLEX PIEYE
*
      READ *, KODE, X, FIRST
      SECOND = 'Payroll'
      BIGONE = 1.0D9
      PIEYE = (0.0, 3.14159)
      PRINT *, BIGONE, SECOND, KODE
      PRINT *, X, 2, FIRST, PIEYE
      END
```

Data for input with the READ statement in this program must of course be pre-pared with care. Note that the input list contains three variables, and that they are a mixture of integer, real, and character types. The types of the data items must correspond exactly to the types of these list items. The data items in this example must be prepared in the proper input forms for the type sequence integer, real, character, corresponding to the sequence of types in the input list. Integer data will consist of a string of digits without a decimal point, real data will contain a decimal point or an exponent (or both), and character data will be a sequence of characters (of the proper length) between apostrophes. Blank characters between the apostrophes are of course permitted and become part of the character data value; blanks elsewhere among list directed input data items are treated as separators.

When character values are printed using list directed PRINT statements, the enclosing apostrophes do not appear in the output, and only a single apostrophe appears for each apostrophe in the actual data value. For example, the output produced by the statement

```
PRINT *, 'Didn''t[]you[]see[]Mary''s[]book?'
```

would appear as follows:

```
Didn't[]you[]see[]Mary's[]book?
```

5.1.5 Summary

The following facts about character processing have been discussed so far in this chapter.

1. Character information is stored in character storage units rather than in numeric storage cells.

2. A character constant is a sequence of Fortran or non-Fortran characters enclosed between apostrophes. An apostrophe within the character value is represented by a pair of consecutive apostrophes in the constant.

3. Variables of character type must be explicitly or implicitly declared.

4. Each character constant or variable has a fixed length.

5. The value of a character constant or variable can be assigned to a character variable of the same length. (See also Section 5.2.4.)

6. Character data may be referenced in an input or output list, and may be interspersed with data of other types.

5.1.6 Exercises

1. Write a program to read employee name, pay rate, and hours worked, and to print employee name and gross pay. (Optional: Include provision for overtime pay.) Assume that 20 characters are sufficient to contain the longest employee name. Use the program to process the following data:

```
'Christopher[]Winters[]'      4.85      40.0
'Vernon[]Q. []Demerest[][]'   3.86      40.0
'Tanya[]Livingston[][][]'     3.62      32.0
'Carol[]Logan-Forbes[][]'     4.15      41.0
'Roger[]Chillingworth[]'      4.19      40.0
```

2. Write a program to read and print the following character data, using list directed input and output. [In data case (d), process the digits as characters; do not treat them as numbers.]

   a) `THE□QUICK□BROWN□FOX□JUMPS□OVER□THE□LAZY□DOG.`

   b) `TO□BE,□OR□NOT□TO□BE,□-□THAT□IS□THE□QUESTION:□-`

   c) `THE□MOVING□FINGER□WRITES□-□AND,□HAVING□WRIT,□MOVES□ON.`

   d) `PLEASE□REMIT:□$19.25□(CASH).`

3. What is the length of each of the following character constants?

   a) `'NO□I''M□NOT□ARMSTRONG-JONES.'`

   b) `'''TWAS□BRILLIG.'`

   c) `'IT''S□TOO□LATE□-'□I□CAN''T□GO.'`

   d) `''''''''`

5.2 CHARACTER ARRAYS, SUBSTRINGS, AND EXPRESSIONS

5.2.1 Character Arrays

Lists of character strings are exceedingly useful in applications. For example, a list might consist of employee names or other alphabetic and symbolic information concerning each employee.

```
CHARACTER*20 NAMES(5)
NAMES(1) = 'Christopher□Winters□'
NAMES(2) = 'Vernon□Q.□Demerest□□'
NAMES(3) = 'Tanya□Livingston□□□□'
NAMES(4) = 'Carol□Logan-Forbes□□'
NAMES(5) = 'Roger□Chillingworth□'
```

The declaration specifies that each element of the array is of character type and of length 20, that the array name is *Names,* and that there are five elements in the array. Thus, *Names* is declared to be an *array* of five twenty-character *strings*.

Note that all the elements of a character array have the same length. There is no way to create a Fortran character array containing some elements of one length and others of a different length.

In the example, assignment statements are used to store character information in each of the five array elements. Each element holds the name of one person. As usual, an array element name consists of the array name followed by a subscript expression in parentheses. The declarations

```
IMPLICIT CHARACTER*20 (N)
DIMENSION NAMES(5)
```

would have the effect of specifying that all names beginning with N refer to character string variables of length 20, and that the array *Names* consists of five such strings.

The following program will read the names of five persons and store them in the array *Names*. Then it will read an integer, and use this value as a subscript to select one of the persons. The name of the selected person will be printed.

```
* Example 1.
* Program to store five names, and then
* print a selected one of the names.
        CHARACTER*20 NAMES(5)
        DO 7, L = 1, 5
          READ *, NAMES(L)
  7       CONTINUE
        READ *, INTGR
        PRINT *, NAMES(INTGR)
        END
```

5.2.2 Substrings

It is often useful to be able to "extract" one or more of the characters from a string for further use in a program. Fortran contains a *substring* specification facility to permit this extraction operation. The name of a character variable or array element is written, followed by a parenthesized substring specification. For example, the first three character positions of the string named *Axe* would be designated as AXE(1:3), and the seventh through eleventh character positions of the fourth array element in the character array *Names* would be NAMES(4)(7:11).

```
* Example 2. Substring notation.
  CHARACTER*20 NAMES(5), AXE
  AXE = 'THE□QUICK□BROWN□FOX.'
  NAMES(4) = 'Carol□Logan-Forbes□□'
  PRINT *, NAMES(4)(7:11), AXE(1:3)
  END
```

Execution of this program will produce the output:

```
Logan     THE
```

The substring name consists of a variable name or an array element name, followed by a parenthesized substring designator that *must* include a colon. The integer expression to the left of the colon designates the first character position of the desired substring, and the integer expression to the right of the colon designates the last character position.

A special meaning is attached to a substring designator in which one or both of the expressions is omitted. Such substring designators are used to designate a substring consisting of all character positions *up to* a certain point or *starting from* a certain point. In the program of Example 2, NAMES(4)(:5) would designate the substring

```
Carol
```

while AXE(:3) would designate the same substring as AXE(1:3). Also, NAMES(4)(7:) designates all characters from the seventh to the end of the string NAMES(4), while AXE(17:) specifies the four-character substring

FOX.

Thus, a substring designator consists of parentheses enclosing a colon that separates two *optional* integer expressions. If the first of these is omitted, the default first character position is one, that is, the substring begins with the first character of the string. If the second expression is omitted, the substring ends with the last character of the string. Omitting both expressions has the effect of designating the entire string, just as if the entire parenthesized substring specification were omitted.

A single character position may be designated as a substring, by giving the same value to both substring designator expressions.

```
* Example 3. Substring notation for a single character.
      CHARACTER*8 AXE
      AXE = 'THE␣FOX.'
      DO 7, I = 1, 8
        PRINT *, AXE(I:I)
 7      CONTINUE
      END
```

Each execution of the PRINT statement will result in printing a single character item as a substring of *Axe;* thus, the result will appear as

```
T
H
E
␣
F
O
X
.
```

In a substring specification, designator expressions that are not omitted must have valid values. The first character position must be at least one, and the last character position must not be beyond the length of the string.

A substring of a character datum may be *replaced,* without altering characters in positions that are *not* part of the designated substring. When a substring name appears on the left side of an assignment statement, only the designated character positions are assigned new values.

```
* Example 4. Replacement of a substring.
      CHARACTER*20 AXE
      AXE = 'THE␣aaaaa␣BROWN␣FOX.'
      AXE(5:9) = 'QUICK'
      PRINT *, AXE
      END
```

In a character assignment statement, character positions to which new values are to be assigned must not be referenced in the character expression on the right side. For example, the following would not be acceptable, because character positions 2 and 3 are referenced on both sides:

```
AXE(1:3) = AXE(2:4)
```

However, the same character variable can be referenced on both the right and left sides provided that the references involve nonoverlapping substrings:

```
AXE(1:3) = AXE(17:19)
```

5.2.3   Joining Strings

A pair of strings may be joined into a single longer string. This operation is known as *concatenation*. It is specified by an operator, consisting of a pair of slashes, between a pair of character expressions. For example, `'ABC' // 'DEFG'` represents the concatenation of the three-character string ABC with the four-character string DEFG, to form the seven-character string ABCDEFG.

The character expressions that we have encountered so far are character constants, character variable names, character array element names, and substring names. We now see that a character expression can also be formed in another way, by concatenation of character expressions. Later on we shall encounter functions that produce values of character type; a reference to such a function is also a character expression. (Still another way to form a character expression is by enclosing a character expression in parentheses. However, there is little need to do this because there are no precedence problems with character expressions.)

Example

```
* Example 5. Concatenation of character expressions.
      CHARACTER*6 FIRST, SECOND
      CHARACTER*8 LONGER
      CHARACTER*2 SMALL
      CHARACTER*14 A, X
      FIRST = 'HELLO.'
      SMALL = '**'
      LONGER = FIRST // '[]Z'
      A = LONGER(1:7) // LONGER(1:7)
      SECOND = 'THERE.'
      X = SMALL // FIRST // SECOND
      PRINT *, LONGER, A, X
      END
```

Result:

```
HELLO.[]Z    HELLO.[]HELLO.[]    **HELLO.THERE.
```

Because of the prohibition against using character positions in the expression on the right that are also included in the string named on the left side of an assignment statement, such statements as the following would *not* be permitted:

```
X = 'ZZ' // X(3:14)
A = A(1:8) // FIRST
X = X( :7) // '▯' // X(9: )
```

Note that concatenation of more than two strings in a single expression is permitted. The three strings are joined from left to right, just as they appear in the expression.

Character expressions involving concatenation may be used directly in a PRINT statement. Adding the following statement to the program in Example 5

```
PRINT *, 'IT''S▯' // SECOND
```

would produce the printed result

```
IT'S▯THERE.
```

5.2.4 Mixed Length Assignment

Character assignment statements in the preceding examples have been uniformly constructed with an expression on the left of precisely the same length as the variable, array element, or substring on the right. However, Fortran permits assignments wherein the two sides are of different lengths, and provides rules to define the result of such assignments.

1. In a character assignment, if the expression on the right is *longer* than the datum (named on the left) to which it is assigned, the expression is *truncated* from the right before assignment takes place.

2. If the expression is *shorter* than the datum to which it is assigned, the expression is *extended* with blanks on the right before assignment takes place.

In the following examples, assume that *Datum* is a string of length six.

Assignment statement	*Result*
DATUM = 'ABCDEFGHI'	ABCDEF
DATUM = 'ABCD'	ABCD▯▯

The length of the character constant 'ABCDEFGHI' is nine, so the three rightmost characters are dropped and the first six characters are assigned to *Datum*. The length of the character constant 'ABCD' is only four, so two blanks are appended at the right.

Assignment to the character variable of length six *always* results in all six characters of *Datum* being replaced, regardless of whether the expression on the right is longer or shorter than six characters. If the expression is longer, the excess characters are in effect ignored. If it is shorter, extra blanks are inserted to complete the assignment, so that characters of the datum for which no specific characters are provided in the expression are replaced by blank characters.

If it is desired to leave characters of *Datum* unchanged during the assignment operation, then only a substring of *Datum* should be specified on the left. Suppose that *Datum* contains the characters ABCDEF, before the following sequence of three assignment statements is executed.

Assignment statement	Result
DATUM(3:4) = 'XY'	ABXYEF
DATUM(1:1) = 'LMN'	LBXYEF
DATUM(3:5) = 'H'	LBH☐☐F

The last two of these examples illustrate the fact that the rules for truncating or extending with blanks apply to a substring as well as to a character variable. When the substring on the left is of length one, for example, and the expression on the right is 'LMN', only the first character L is assigned, while the remaining characters of *Datum* remain unchanged. Also, assignment of 'H' to a substring of length three results in replacement of the *entire* substring, after extending the one-character expression with two added blanks; again, the characters of *Datum* that are not part of the specified substring remain unchanged.

The same rules also apply, of course, when the character expression on the right-hand side of an assignment statement includes variables, substrings, or concatenation. The rules also apply during input: The data value is truncated or extended on the right before being assigned to the character datum specified in the input list. The rules are not needed for list directed character output, because the number of characters transmitted is determined by the length of the character expression in the output list.

Now consider the following program example.

```
* Example 6. Concatenation with mixed length assignment.
      CHARACTER*10 LONG
      LONG = 'THE'
      PRINT*, LONG // 'BROWN☐FOX.'
      END
```

The assignment statement places THE in the first three character positions of *Long* and fills the remaining seven positions with blanks. The processor does not "remember" that these seven blanks were merely inserted to fulfill the requirements of mixed length assignment. Thus, the concatenation operation joins the second string to the *end* of the ten-character variable *Long*. The printed output will appear as follows:

```
THE☐☐☐☐☐☐☐BROWN☐FOX.
```

A more satisfactory result would be obtained by concatenating only a substring of *Long* with a constant string:

```
LONG( :3) // '⬚BROWN⬚FOX.'
```

The mixed length assignment rules apply only to *character* assignments with *length* incompatibilities. Mixed-*type* assignments are not permitted: If either side of an assignment involves character data, then the other side must also be of character type. However, relational expressions and functions may permit character strings to appear in a statement along with data of other types, as pointed out in the later sections of this chapter.

5.2.5   Comparing Character Expressions

A pair of character expressions may be compared by using a relational operator. The value of a character relational expression is either *true* or *false*.

Examples   Assume that each of the following statements is taken from a program containing the declaration IMPLICIT CHARACTER*6 (F − H).

```
IF (FIRST .GE. HAT) J = 1
IF (GOOD .NE. 'PRETTY') STOP
IF (H .EQ. F8(1:3) // 'XYZ') THEN
```

A character relational expression is a logical expression, and can be assigned as the value of a logical variable or used in the same way as any other logical expression. The expressions to be compared must *both* be of character type in a character relational expression.

The use of character relational expressions assumes the existence of a *collating sequence* among all Fortran and non-Fortran characters. The precise sequence will vary from one processor to another,† but four rules are required by Fortran:

1. All the uppercase (capital) letters are in order from A to Z; that is, A is considered less than B, which is less than C, etc.

2. The digits are in order from 0 to 9.

---

† Character relational expressions use the "native" collating sequence that is provided by the processor. Comparisons using the standard ASCII collating sequence are also possible, even on processors whose native collating sequence is not ASCII. The predefined functions LGE, LGT, LLE, and LLT have two arguments, each of which may be a character expression of any length. These functions return the logical value *true* or *false,* depending on a comparison of the two argument strings on the basis of the ASCII collating sequence. If the two argument strings are of unequal length, the effect is to extend the shorter string on the right with blanks for purposes of the comparison. These predefined functions produce logical expressions that can be used in exactly the same way as a character relational expression.

3. The uppercase letters and the digits do not overlap; that is, either the digits all *precede* the letters or the digits all *follow* the letters.

4. The blank character is less than any letter or number.

The ordering of punctuation and other symbols, and of non-Fortran characters (including lowercase letters), is left unspecified; thus it may vary among Fortran processors.

Ranking of strings of characters is implied in the obvious way by the ranking of individual characters: Given a pair of strings that are the same length, the initial characters of the two strings are first compared. Unless these are identical, the "larger" string is the one with the larger initial character. If the initial character is the same in both strings, the comparison proceeds with the second character of each string. Thus, the ranking of the strings is determined solely by the *first* character position at which the two strings *differ*. If there is no such position, then the two strings are equal. Thus, the assertion

```
'DOUGLAS□STEPHEN□□□' .LT. 'DOUGLASS□FREDERICK'
```

is *true*. We may ignore the first seven character positions, which contain the identical characters DOUGLAS in both strings, leaving □STEPHEN□□□ on the left and S□FREDERICK on the right. Since blank is less than S, the string on the left is considered less than the string on the right. Also *true* are the assertions

```
'APRIL□A' .LT. 'APRIL□B'
'APRIL□□' .LT. 'APRIL□1'
'APRIL□1986' .LT. 'APRIL□1987'
'APRIL□□□□□' .LT. 'APRIL□WOOD'
```

However, the result of a comparison between APRIL□1986 and APRIL□WOOD is processor dependent, because Fortran does not specify a standard comparison between the letters and the digits.

Character strings of unequal length can also be compared. Fortran provides that the shorter string is treated as if it were extended with blanks to the length of the longer string. Thus, the following assertions will be considered *true:*

```
'AS' .LT. 'ASTER'
'THE' .LT. 'THERE'
'A□BOOK' .LT. 'A□BOOKIE'
'XYZ' .EQ. 'XYZ□□'
```

Rules 1 and 4 guarantee that all processors will agree on the ranking of character strings consisting entirely of uppercase letters and blanks, such as might appear in a list of names or of cities. Ranking of more complicated strings, including those with lowercase letters, punctuation, or a mixture of letters and digits, will depend on the particular processor.

5.2.6 Exercises

1. Write a substring specification for designating:

    a) The characters OVER in the string

    THE␣QUICK␣BROWN␣FOX␣JUMPS␣␣OVER␣THE␣LAZY␣DOG.

    b) The characters GO in the character constant 'I␣CAN''T␣GO.

2. A program contains the declaration CHARACTER*44 FOXES and the assignment statement

    FOXES = 'THE␣QUICK␣BROWN␣FOX␣JUMPS␣␣OVER␣THE␣LAZY␣DOG.'

    Tell which characters are designated by the following substring specifications.

    a) FOXES(5:19)
    b) FOXES(:25)
    c) FOXES(27:)
    d) FOXES(13:18)

    With the declaration CHARACTER*6 MONTH and the assignment MONTH = 'MAY', which characters are designated by

    e) MONTH(3:5)
    f) MONTH(:)

3. Given the declarations

    CHARACTER*4 LIST(3)
    CHARACTER*12 LONGER

    write assignment statements to do the following:

    a) Assign to *Longer* a string of twelve characters obtained by concatenating together the three elements of the array *List*.
    b) Replace the eighth character of *Longer* by the letter A, leaving the remaining character positions unchanged.
    c) Replace the second array element of *List* by the sixth through ninth characters of *Longer*.

4. Write a program to read ten character strings, each up to twenty characters long, and arrange them alphabetically in an array (see Exercise 3 of Section 4.3.1).

5. Given a character array whose elements are strings that have been arranged in alphabetical order, write a program to find an array element string that matches a given input string (see Exercise 3 of Section 4.4.2).

6. Write a loop to move one character at a time from string *A* to string *B*, *reversing* the order of the characters in the string. That is, the characters from the first position in *A* should go to the last position in *B*, etc. Each string is 25 characters long.

7. *Removing leading blanks.* Write a program to find the first nonblank character in string *A*, and then assign the substring consisting of all of *A* except the blanks

that precede the first nonblank character to string *B*. The program might begin as follows:

```
CHARACTER*50 A, B
DO 7 NBC = 1, 50
   IF (A(NBC:NBC) .NE. '[]') GO TO 8
   . . .
```

If the exit to statement 8 does not occur within 50 traversals of the loop, what can you conclude about the string *A*?

5.3 PREDEFINED FUNCTIONS FOR CHARACTER MANIPULATION

5.3.1 Pattern Matching: The Index Function

Applications involving lines or paragraphs of text frequently require that a certain (usually short) pattern be located within a (longer) string. For example, we might wish to search the string THAT[]IS[]THE[]QUESTION. to find the location of the pattern THE. The predefined Fortran function *Index* provides a simple way to perform such a search or pattern matching operation. The function has two arguments of character type; the first identifies the longer string to be searched, while the second designates the pattern to be located within the longer string. The function value is an *integer* giving the beginning character position of the pattern as a substring of the longer string. For example, the value of

```
INDEX ('THAT[]IS[]THE[]QUESTION', 'THE')
```

would be 9, since THE is found as a substring beginning at the ninth character position in the string used as the first argument. To extend this example, let us consider the following program:

Example 1

```
CHARACTER*50 HAMLET(4)
HAMLET(1) = 'TO[]BE,[]OR[]NOT[]TO[]BE,[]-[]THAT[]IS[]THE[]QUESTION:[]-[][][][]'
HAMLET(2) = 'WHETHER[]''TIS[]NOBLER[]IN[]THE[]MIND[]TO[]SUFFER[][][][][][][][][][]'
HAMLET(3) = 'THE[]SLINGS[]AND[]ARROWS[]OF[]OUTRAGEOUS[]FORTUNE,[][][][][][]'
LOC1 = INDEX (HAMLET(1), 'THE')
LOC2 = INDEX (HAMLET(2), 'THE')
LOC3 = INDEX (HAMLET(3), 'THE')
PRINT *, LOC1, LOC2, LOC3
END
```

The printed results will be 32, 4, 1. The first occurrence of the pattern in the first array element is at positions 32 to 34, that is, in the phrase *that is the question.* The second result may be a bit unexpected—note that the pattern was found at the fourth character position, in the middle of the word *whether*. To find THE standing alone as a separate word, we would have to look for the pattern consisting of the five characters □THE□. The value of the expression

```
INDEX (HAMLET(2), '□THE□')
```

is 23, indicating the occurrence of the five-character pattern □THE□ in the phrase *nobler in the mind*. Remember that the double apostrophe counts as a single character.

Failure to match

It may happen, of course, that the pattern being searched for is not present anywhere in the string whose specification is given as the first argument of *Index*. The fourth line of the Hamlet soliloquy, for instance, does not contain the pattern THE.

```
HAMLET(4) = 'OR□TO□TAKE□ARMS□AGAINST□A□SEA□OF□TROUBLES,□□□□□□□□'
```

In these cases, the function returns the value zero; for instance, zero would be the value of

```
INDEX (HAMLET(4), 'THE')
```

The function value is also zero in case the length of the second argument string exceeds that of the first argument, as in the expression

```
INDEX ('□THE', '□THE□')
```

Multiple occurrences

We may wish to find *all* occurrences of a given pattern in a longer string, such as appearances of THE either as a separate word or as part of another word, within the second array element of *Hamlet*. Since the expression INDEX (HAMLET(2), 'THE') has the integer value 4, indicating the location of the first occurrence, the next appearance of the same string can be found by searching a string that does not contain the case already located. A satisfactory technique is to search the *substring* beginning just beyond the location at which the pattern was found:†

```
LOC5 = INDEX (HAMLET(2), 'THE')
LOC6 = INDEX (HAMLET(2)(LOC5 + 1: ), 'THE')
```

---

† In these examples, we search the substring beginning just beyond the *first* character of the pattern that has been located. A slightly superior technique would be to search beyond the *last* character of the pattern that has been located. For example, the substring specification could be changed from (LOC5 + 1:) to (LOC5 + 4:) because the pattern length is three.

```
* Example 2. Find all appearances of THE
* in the second line of Hamlet's soliloquy.
      CHARACTER*50 HAMLET(4)
      CHARACTER*3 TEXT
      HAMLET(2) = 'WHETHER□''TIS□NOBLER□IN□THE□MIND□TO□SUFFER□□□□□□□□□'
      TEXT = 'THE'
      LINE = 20
      LORIG = 0
      PRINT *, 'Soliloquy,□Line', LINE
      DO 7, LOOP = 1, 50
        LSUB = INDEX (HAMLET(LINE)(LORIG + 1: ), TEXT)
        IF (LSUB .EQ. 0) GO TO 8
        LORIG = LORIG + LSUB
        PRINT *, TEXT, '□appears□at□position', LORIG
7       CONTINUE
      STOP
8     CONTINUE
      PRINT *, 'End□of□appearances□in□this□line.'
      END
```
Figure 5.1

The value of *Loc6* will be the location of the pattern within the substring beginning at the fifth character of the array element, that is, within the substring

```
HER□'TIS□NOBLER□IN□THE□MIND□TO□SUFFER□□□□□□□□□
```

The location of THE in this substring is at position 20, since the pattern appears as characters 20 to 22 of this substring. Thus, *Loc6* will have the value 20 after these two statements are executed. The expression *Loc5* + *Loc6* then gives the location of the second occurrence of the pattern in the *original* string, that is, position 24.

We combine these ideas in the following program (Fig. 5.1). *Lorig* keeps track of the location in the original string, and *Lsub* is set each time to the result of the *Index* operation. The results will appear as follows:

```
Soliloquy,□Line    2
THE   □appears□at□position   4
THE   □appears□at□position   20
End□of□appearances□in□this□line.
```

5.3.2   Integer Value of a Character: The Functions *Char* and *Ichar*

It is often useful to be able to obtain an integer "code number" from a single character of text. The predefined Fortran function *Ichar* has an argument consisting of a single character (that is, a character expression of length one), and produces an integer value that can be used in numerical calculations to obtain a unique code value for each different character.

The set of specific integer values produced by *Ichar* is processor dependent. Fortran specifies that the values range from 0 up to $n - 1$, where n is the number of Fortran and non-Fortran characters recognized by the processor. The integer value corresponding to a given character is the position of that character in the collating sequence for the particular processor. The collating sequence is governed by the four rules listed in Section 5.2.5, but these are not sufficiently restrictive to require *Ichar* to produce the same integer result for a given character on different processors. (The rules do not even force the alphabet to occupy 26 consecutive positions in the collating sequence. Other symbols, though not digits, may be interspersed among the letters.)

The "inverse" function *Char* produces a single *character* given an integer in the proper range (between 0 and $n - 1$). That is, if J is an integer in the correct range, and if X is any character expression of length one, then

CHAR (ICHAR(X)) has the same value as X; and
ICHAR (CHAR(J)) has the same value as J.

Compact alphabets

A review of actual processors shows that many of them use collating sequences that include the 26 letters of the alphabet in *consecutive* positions, while others do not. (Of the two most widely used collating sequences, ASCII has such a "compact" alphabet, while EBCDIC intersperses symbols between letters of the alphabet.) A number of text processing applications can be programmed much more simply for a compact alphabet.

With a compact alphabet, it is possible to determine whether a character is a letter or not, simply by testing whether it lies between A and Z, inclusive:

```
IF ((NEXT .GE. 'A') .AND. (NEXT .LE. 'Z')) THEN
   ...
```

Other applications make use of *transformations* of the alphabet. For example, in a simple cryptographic application we might wish to move each character down the alphabet by one position, changing A to B, changing B to C, and so on, continuing by changing Y to Z:

```
KODE = ICHAR (NEXT)
KODE = KODE + 1
NEW = CHAR (KODE)
```

(Special provision must be made for changing Z back to A.) The three lines of code could be replaced by the single assignment

```
NEW = CHAR (ICHAR (NEXT) + 1)
```

5.3.3 Exercises

1. Write a program to read a string of up to 320 characters, and then count the number of words, the number of characters, and the number of occurrences of ⌷THE⌷. Use the following text as data.

   > Marley was dead, to begin with. There is no doubt whatever about that. The register of his burial was signed by the clergyman, the clerk, the undertaker, and the chief mourner. Scrooge signed it. And Scrooge's name was good upon 'Change for anything he chose to put his hand to. Old Marley was dead as a doornail.

2. Write a program to print text in lines of 50 characters or *less,* ending each line between words. Put as many words as possible on each line. Apply this program to the text given in Exercise 1.

3. Modify the program in Exercise 2 to *justify* the lines of text. That is, whenever a line will contain fewer than 50 characters, change blanks early in the line to pairs of blanks, so that each line will fill out the 50 character spaces (with a non-blank character in the last position). Do not justify the last line of text.

4. *Cryptogram* (for processors with compact alphabets). As an extension of the cryptogram example, each character might be moved down the alphabet by a fixed amount other than one. For example, moving the characters by five positions would change A through U into F through Z, and V through Z into A through E. Given a coded message, we suspect that it has been transformed in this manner, but we do not know the distance by which each letter was moved in the encoding transformation. We attempt to decode the message by printing each of the 25 possibilities, and trying to recognize English words from the printed results.

   Write a program to read the following cryptogram and print all 25 possible decoded messages. Tell which one you consider most likely to have been the original message. (Note that spaces have been deleted from the original message. Ignore the spaces that appear in the cryptogram.)

   > JURAL BHUNI RRYVZ VANGR QGURV ZCBFF VOYRJ UNGRI
   > REERZ NVAFU BJRIR EVZCE BONOY RZHFG ORGUR GEHGU

5. The sentence, "The quick brown fox jumps over the lazy dog," contains each of the letters of the alphabet at least once. Write a program to print the number of occurrences of each of the 26 letters. (Use uppercase letters only.)

CHAPTER 6

BASIC INPUT AND OUTPUT

As we have seen, Fortran input and output is a process whereby information is transmitted (in either direction) between the internal cells of a computer and various external devices. Much of this information transfer is intended to aid some human user, who wishes to furnish data to be used in a calculation or who wishes to obtain some results for further use. Up to this point we have restricted our attention to *list directed* input and output, which is easy to use and is mainly intended for communication between the computer and a human user. We have concentrated on the *internal* aspects of information transfer, largely ignoring those aspects of the process that concern the arrangement of information on external devices.

As we move beyond the simplest computer applications, however, we soon find it necessary to specify the *external* arrangement of data for many purposes. For example, an application may involve printing a report with a prespecified column arrangement—the printed characters may have to fit the columns of a preprinted form. Furthermore, we may encounter applications where the information to be transferred is not intended for communication directly with a human. An intermediate storage phase may be involved, where information produced by a computer is retained on a magnetic tape or storage disc and then furnished to the same computer or to a different computer later on. It is important for the later user to know how the information is arranged on the storage device, so that it can be interpreted correctly.

In this chapter we describe more completely the input and output features that are available in Fortran. We shall see how list directed input and output arises as a special case, but the major emphasis here will be on "explicitly formatted" input and output, that is, on the transmission of information when the external arrangement of the data is specified explicitly in the program.

6.1 INPUT AND OUTPUT CONCEPTS

6.1.1 Input and Output Statement Forms

The most general Fortran input and output statement forms are

> READ (*Clist*) *Input list*
> WRITE (*Clist*) *Output list*

The *Input list* in the READ statement specifies the variables (and other items such as array elements and substrings) whose values are to be read. The *Output list* in the WRITE statement specifies the expressions whose values are to be transmitted to the external device. The *Clist* is a *control list,* which specifies the external device to or from which the data is to be transferred, the format of the data on the external device, and optional information such as action to be taken when input data is exhausted.

For the vast majority of applications, most control information does not need to be stated explicitly. For example, output statements do not need to provide for the possibility that data will be exhausted. The external device specification can also be omitted in many cases, since *default* external devices for input and for output are selected automatically if the program does not specify them explicitly.

When the format is the only item of control information that needs to be specified, a simpler "short-form" input or output statement can be used:

> READ *Format*, *Input list*
> PRINT *Format*, *Output list*

We note the following details concerning these input and output statements.

1. Whereas the keywords READ and WRITE are used with the general input and output statement forms, the short form uses the keywords READ and PRINT.

2. The control list (including the format specification) is enclosed in parentheses; the format specification in the short form is not. The format specification is followed by a comma; the parenthesized control list is not.

3. The input or output list used for the short form is identical to that used for the long form.

The control list

A general discussion of control lists appears in Chapter 9. Most of the examples in this chapter use short-form READ and PRINT statements. However, the short-form READ statement cannot be used when we need to detect the end of data during input. In this case, we use a READ statement of the form

READ (*, *format*, IOSTAT = *Integer variable*) *Input list*

The asterisk in the control list of this statement is a *default* external device specification. The first position in a control list would ordinarily contain an indication of the external device from which the input data is to be obtained; an asterisk in this position indicates that the device to be used is the same default input device that is associated with the short form of the READ statement.

The external device

Fortran statements can be used to specify transmission of information to or from magnetic tapes, storage discs, or a wide variety of other devices. The default input and output devices that are automatically selected for the statement forms we use in this chapter will be assumed to be intended for communication with a human user. We shall call the default input device a *reader* and the default output device a *printer*.

In most cases, the reader will be either a card reader or an on-line terminal (typewriter-like console) into which the user types data for direct entry to the computer. The printer may be a line printer that produces a paper copy of the results, or it may be the same terminal operating as an output device.

Records

The information transmitted during any input or output operation is subdivided into *records*. Each record consists of characters—letters, digits, and special symbols. (These need not be limited to the characters of the Fortran character set, but may include any characters recognizable by the processor.) For each external device, the records have a definite maximum size (number of characters). In our examples, we assume that the reader can transmit records of up to 80 characters, and that the printer can accept records of up to 120 characters.

A special convention applies to records that are transmitted by a Fortran program to a printer. The first character of each output record is not printed but is used to control vertical spacing during the print operation; the remaining characters actually appear on the printer. Therefore, in our examples we will assume that at most 119 characters from a single output record actually appear on the printed line, and we will avoid placing a character that represents part of a data value in the first character position of an output record. (See also Section 6.2.7.)

The format specifier

A format specifier, in either the general form or the short form of an input or output statement, may have one of three representations.

1. It may be an asterisk, indicating that the arrangement of the external data depends only on the items in the input or output list.

2. It may be a character constant (in the input or output statement itself), or a reference to a character expression or to a character array that contains characters describing the external data format.

3. It may be a statement label reference to a FORMAT statement that contains the external data format description.

The first of these representations is, of course, the one that indicates the use of list directed formatting. This is adequate for almost all input, and for output where details of the appearance of results are not important. On the other hand, for formal reports and other kinds of output where the printed data must be arranged in columns or in some other precise form, list directed format control is inadequate.

The format description in either the second or the third representation consists of a parenthesized list of format codes. Each format code describes the details of transmission of one or more items of information, to or from the external device. The details of construction of this format description are explained in Section 6.2.

The second method, using a character constant in the input or output statement itself, is especially convenient in simple cases, as the following example indicates.

Example 1

```
READ '(3⌷G12.0,⌷2⌷I3)', A, B, C, J, K
```

Meaning: Read the five data items *A, B, C, J,* and *K,* using the format description

```
'(3⌷G12.0,⌷2⌷I3)'
```

Note that this is a READ statement of the short form. The parentheses enclosing the format description are *inside* the apostrophes that delimit the character constant; thus they should not be confused with the parentheses used in the general READ statement form to delimit the control list. A comma separates the format specification from the input list.

Instead of a character constant, the format specifier in an input or output statement may refer to a character array that contains the format description, or it may be a character expression. A format description constructed in this way may be useful when certain characters within it will need to be changed during execution of the program. Example 1 could be rewritten as follows:

```
CHARACTER*15 FMT
FMT = '(3□G12.0,□2□I3)'
READ FMT, A, B, C, J, K
```

The third form, using a separate FORMAT statement, is most useful when a long format specification is to be used several times in a program.

Example 2

```
        READ 14, A, B, C, J, K
14      FORMAT (3 G12.0, 2 I3)
```

A labeled FORMAT statement may be placed at any convenient point among the program statements; one good plan is to place it immediately after the first input or output statement that contains a reference to it. The FORMAT statement should not be repeated, even if there is more than one reference to it. The format statement label reference appears as a format specifier in either the short form or the general form of an input or output statement. In Example 2, the same format description used in Example 1 appears in a labeled FORMAT statement.

6.1.2 Input and Output Lists

The form of an input or output list does not depend on whether it appears in a short-form READ or PRINT statement or in a statement of the general form. Also, the form of the list does not depend on whether list directed or explicit format control is to be used. Each item in any input or output list may be:

1. A variable,
2. An array element name,
3. A substring name,
4. An implied DO loop, or
5. An array name.

In an output list, an item may also be:

6. An expression (including a constant).

If there are two or more list items, they must be separated by commas. (In the short-form statements, if there are no list items, the comma following the format specifier is omitted.)

The same list may contain items of integer, real, and character (as well as other) types. For example, a list could consist of all the following items:

```
A, B, D, P(14), J(I, K), J(25 * I - 4), A(K + 1), PAY, A(2 * L)
```

Each input list item designates a specific storage cell (or sequence of cells) for which values are to be assigned. Constants, and expressions in general, are prohibited as *input* list items because they are not associated with particular storage cells to which values could be assigned. However, *output* lists may include constants and expressions such as the following:

    A + B, −A, P(14) + 1.0, .TRUE., A .LT. B, 'Here' // '⎕it⎕is.'

The input or output list is scanned from left to right during data transmission. For example, the following list might appear in an input statement:

    A, B(I), I, C(I)

Assume that the value of *I* has been previously set to 10, and that the third data value encountered in the reader is 6. After the first two input data values have been read and assigned to *A* and to B_{10}, the value of *I* will be changed to 6 when the third data value is read. Thus, the fourth data value will be assigned to C_6 and not to C_{10}. This example illustrates the particular importance of relative list position when an integer variable appearing in the list is also used as a subscript in the same input list.

The use of substring names as list items introduces no special difficulty; some examples of such use appeared in Section 5.2.2.

Implied DO loops were discussed in Sections 4.1.3 and 4.2. As we indicated there, an implied DO loop has the form

    (*Sublist*, *Index* = *Initial value*, *Limit*, *Increment*)

Any item that can appear in an input or output list, including an inner implied DO loop, can also appear in the sublist of an implied DO loop. The index, initial value, limit, and increment are subject to the same rules that apply to DO loops, and are interpreted in an analogous manner. The increment, if omitted, is given the default value 1.

Array names as input or output list items

By special convention, an array name without a subscript represents the entire array when it appears as an input or output list item. For example, appearance of the array name *A* as a list item will cause transmission of all elements specified in the array declaration for *A*. The order in which the values will be transmitted is illustrated in Figs. 6.1, 6.2, and 6.3. (This is the same as the sequence of the array elements in storage, which is discussed further in Section 7.1.2.) The sequence for linear arrays is obvious: from lowest to highest subscript. For rectangular arrays (matrices), the sequence is by columns; that is, all the elements of the first column are transmitted, followed by the second column, and so forth. Arrays with three dimensions are subdivided into *planes,* and for each plane the third subscript has a fixed value. All the elements of the first plane are transmitted, followed by the second plane, and so on; within each plane the elements form a rectangular array whose elements are transmitted by columns, as before. A similar sequence is used for more than three dimensions. In general, the leftmost index varies most rapidly and the rightmost index least rapidly as we move through the sequence.

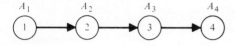

Fig. 6.1 Storage sequence for elements of a linear array. Arrows and circled numbers show implied order.

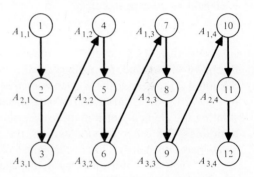

Fig. 6.2 Storage sequence for elements of a rectangular array. Arrows and circled numbers show implied order.

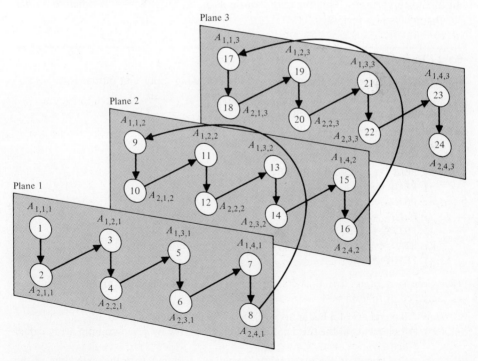

Fig. 6.3 Storage sequence for elements of an array with three dimensions. Arrows and circled numbers show implied order.

Example 3

```
REAL D(5, 7)
. . .
READ *, D
```

All 35 elements of D will be read. Incoming elements will be stored in order by columns: $D_{1,1}, D_{2,1}, D_{3,1}, D_{4,1}, D_{5,1}, D_{1,2}, D_{2,2}, D_{3,2}, D_{4,2}$, etc.

This "whole array" notation has two important advantages. Conceptually it is elegant to be able to consider an array as a single entity. Furthermore, the use of this form can considerably shorten an otherwise long and perhaps complicated list.

Nevertheless, there are two disadvantages as well. The first is the loss in flexibility (compared, for example, with the use of nested implied DO loops; see Section 4.2), because the sequence of transmission of the elements is controlled by the array declaration and is not specified within the list. In particular, for printing the elements of a matrix, the column sequence often turns out to be undesirable. The other disadvantage is the danger of inadvertently including an array name in a list. This occurs most often when a programmer uses a short symbol, such as A, for an array name, then forgets and uses the same name for an ordinary variable. This mistake can be avoided by choosing distinctive names for the arrays in a program.

6.1.3 Exercises

1. Find the Fortran language errors in the following input and output lists.

   a) PRINT *, A, B, C, (D(I) I = N, M)
   b) PRINT *, JOHN JACKSON, 14.35. X(1)
   c) READ *, L, JILL, JOHHNIE, JACOB(I), I = 1, N
   d) PRINT *, (A(I), I = 1, 1, 500, 1)
   e) READ *, 4, 16, 20
   f) READ *, ABLE, X, BAKER, (Y(2, J), J = 3.9)
   g) READ *,
   h) PRINT *, *
   i) PRINT *, −SQRT(C ** 2 + B ** 3) / 4,0
   j) PRINT *, (B(I), I = 1, K), C(3), I = 1, K), D, E
   k) READ *, N, B, B, (A(I), I = 1, N), 'A⌷='. A
   l) PRINT *, A

2. Construct *input lists* that assign values to the sequences of array elements described as follows.

   a) All elements of a linear array T having even subscripts up to 50.
   b) All elements in the third column of an eight-row by seven-column array called *Chek*.
   c) All elements in the first row, followed by all elements in the sixth row, of the same six-row by five-column array called R.

3. Construct short-form input or output statements, with list directed formatting, for each of the following.

  a) Read the elements A_1 through A_N inclusive, *preceded by* the value of N.

  b) Print all the elements of the fourth row of an M-row by N-column array called C.

  c) Print all elements of the Lth column of an N by N array named D.

  d) Read pairs of elements for the last two columns of an array called Q that has eight rows and nine columns.

  e) Print the 4 by 4 array called *Criss*; the elements are to be ordered by columns.

  f) Read pairs, each consisting of an element of the linear array A having an *odd* subscript $(1, 3, 5, \ldots, 2N - 1)$, followed by an element of the linear array B having an *even* subscript $(2, 4, 6, \ldots, 2N)$.

  g) Print the *odd* rows of an M-row by five-column array called *Crazy*.

4. Analyze the following pair of nested implied DO loops in detail, to determine the sequence of subscript values represented.

    ((MATRIX(I, J), I = J, 4), J = 1, 3)

You may wish to make a sketch of a 4 by 3 matrix (rectangular array).

5. Given a knight located at the point $K_{I,J}$ near the center of a chessboard, print the contents of all eight cells corresponding to locations to which the knight is permitted to move. (That is, the value of I may increase or decrease by 2, while the value of J increases by 1, or vice versa. See Fig. 6.4.)

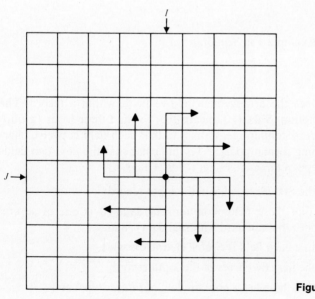

Figure 6.4

6.2 THE FORMAT DESCRIPTION

"Explicit" format control, in contrast to list directed formatting, permits the user to specify the arrangement of the characters in an input or output record on an external device. The format description consists of a parenthesized list of format codes (separated by commas), such as

(3 I10, I10, 4 F10.0, 5 G15.5)

The first two of these format codes include the letter I, indicating that the associated data is of integer type. The third code uses the letter F, and the fourth uses G; these are two of several codes that may correspond to data of real type.

Fields

Each record consists of a sequence of characters. Numerical data is represented externally by a string of decimal digits and other characters, while information of logical or character type is represented externally by a sequence of characters of some appropriate form.

We have seen that for list directed data processing, the string representing each data value may be positioned rather freely within the input or output record and is separated from the adjacent data representations by one or more blank spaces and possibly a comma. Under explicit format control, on the other hand, the record is more rigidly subdivided into groups of character positions called *fields;* each field holds the characters that represent a single numerical, logical, or character data value.

Example 1   (See also Example 1 in Section 6.1.1.)

(3 G12.0, 2 I3)

This specification describes the arrangement of five fields within a record. The first portion of the description, 3 G12.0, means that the first three fields (groups of characters) in the record contain real data, and that each field is twelve characters wide. The remaining format code, 2 I3, indicates that the next two fields contain data of integer type in three-character fields. Thus,

3	refers to the first *three fields* in the input record;
G	specifies that these fields contain *real* data (G is one of several format codes that are used with real data); and
12.0	specifies that each field is *twelve* characters wide.
2	refers to the next *two fields* of the input record;
I	specifies that these fields contain data of *integer* type; and
3	specifies that each field is *three* characters wide.

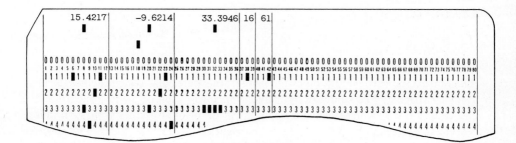

Figure 6.5

Figure 6.5 shows how data values might be prepared on an 80-column card, to be read with this format description. The data must be prepared in accordance with this description; that is, each of the first three groups of twelve columns must contain a real constant, and each of the next two three-column fields must contain an integer constant.

Format codes

As indicated in Example 1, each format code in a format description includes the following information.

1. A *count,* indicating the number of consecutive fields to which it corresponds. If there is no integer constant preceding the letter that indicates conversion mode, the count is 1 by default.

2. A *conversion mode,* indicated by a letter such as I, F, or G, which corresponds to the data type of the corresponding input or output list item, as well as to the form of the data item in the record.

3. A *field width;* that is, the number of characters in the record occupied by the field.

Some format codes also include a fourth item of information.

4. A *decimal position.* For output with real (or double precision) conversion modes, the field width is followed by a period and then by another integer constant that specifies the number of digits that will appear to the right of the decimal point. For real or double precision input, we use a zero in this position (except in certain cases that we will discuss later)—for example,

```
(F10.5, G14.6)
```

The first of these would specify a field of an output record that is ten characters wide, with five digits to the right of the decimal point. The second specifies a 14-character field, with six significant digits to the right of the decimal point.

Example 2

```
PRINT '(1X,□2□F10.5□/□1X,□F12.2)', SPOS, −SNEG, TOTAL
```

Meaning: Transmit to the printer the values of *Spos,* −*Sneg,* and *Total.* The code 1X controls the vertical motion of the printer; this particular code specifies normal (single) spacing. The values of *Spos* and −*Sneg* will each be printed according to the code F10.5, which means that they will be printed as real values, in fields ten characters wide, with five digits to the right of the decimal point. The slash **/** specifies the end of an output record. Since there is further information to be transmitted, a new record will be started. The 1X following the slash, as before, indicates single spacing for the printed line corresponding to the new output record. Then the value of *Total* is printed according to the format code F12.2— that is, in real form, in a field twelve columns wide, with two decimal digits to the right of the decimal point.

Example 3

```
READ '(I8)', N
```

Meaning: Transmit the value of *N* from the reader. The value of *N* will appear in integer form within the field consisting of the first eight characters of the record.

Example 4

```
READ '(F10.0)', A(I)
```

Meaning: Read the value of A_I. (The value of *I* must have been defined already.) The value of A_I will appear as a real constant, with a decimal point, in the first ten characters of the record.

Example 5

```
PRINT '(1X,□F15.3)', SUM
```

Meaning: Print the value of *Sum* in the first fifteen columns on the printer, printing three significant digits to the right of the decimal point.

Example 6 Sum the positive elements of a linear array *A* having *N* elements.

```
       READ '(I8)', N
       SUM = 0.0
       DO 50, I = 1, N
         READ '(F10.0)', A(I)
         IF (A(I) .GT. 0.0) SUM = SUM + A(I)
   50    CONTINUE
       PRINT '(1X,□F15.3)', SUM
       END
```

The first statement,

```
READ '(I8)', N
```

reads the numerical value of *N*. This value is the total number of elements of the array *A* that are to be read as data. The next input statement,

```
READ '(F10.0)', A(I)
```

is executed once each time the DO loop is traversed. Each time it is executed, this statement reads another record containing the value of the next element of the linear array *A*. The example also contains one output statement, namely,

```
PRINT '(1X,[]F15.3)', SUM
```

which prints the value of *Sum,* the result of the calculation.

Example 7   Sum separately the positive and the negative elements of the linear array *A ,* which has *N* elements.

```
          READ '(I8)', N
          SPOS = 0.0
          SNEG = 0.0
          DO 50, I = 1, N
            READ '(F10.0)', A(I)
            PRINT '(1X,[]F15.3)', A(I)
            IF (A(I) .GT. 0.0) THEN
                SPOS = SPOS + A(I)
              ELSE IF (A(I) .LT. 0.0) THEN
                SNEG = SNEG + A(I)
              END IF
   50     CONTINUE
          TOTAL = SPOS + SNEG
          PRINT '(1X,[]2[]F10.5[]/[]1X,[]F12.2)', SPOS, -SNEG, TOTAL
          END
```

The first statement inside the DO loop is a READ statement that is the same as in Example 6. It is immediately followed by a PRINT statement,

```
PRINT '(1X,[]F15.3)', A(I)
```

which prints the data just read in. This step, sometimes called an "echo print," is recommended, since it allows the user to verify that the proper data has been read. The last output statement, which prints the results of the calculation, is the same as in Example 2.

6.2.1 Integer Input and Output

Output

Figure 6.6 and Table 6.1 illustrate the use of the conversion mode Iw for printing data of integer type. We note the following points.

1. Integers are printed as far right as possible in the field, and unused space is filled with blank characters.†

2. If the value is negative, a minus sign is printed immediately to the left of the number. Positive integers (and zero) appear without plus signs (see also Chapter 9).

3. Integers are printed without decimal points.

If we fail to allot sufficient field width for printing an integer, the entire output field will be filled with asterisks. Programmers should follow the practice of liberally allocating columns for output to ensure that the field will be wide enough for the largest values of the output data that may be anticipated. Excess field width does no harm and improves readability.

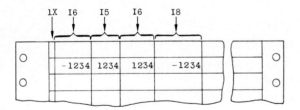

PRINT '(1X,␢I6,␢I5,␢I6,␢I8)', I, J, K, L

Fig. 6.6 Integer output.

Table 6.1 Integer output

Integer variable	Internal value	Format code	External appearance
I	−1234	I 6	␢−1234
J	+1234	I 5	␢1234
K	+1234	I 6	␢␢1234
L	−1234	I 8	␢␢␢−1234

† There is also a format code I$w.m$, which indicates that at least m digits are to appear in the output field, including leading zeros if necessary. Of course, m must not be larger than w. Also, by special convention, an entirely blank field will be printed for a zero data value when m is zero. This format code has no meaning for input.

Input

Some examples of integer input (using conversion mode I*w*) are shown in Fig. 6.7 and Table 6.2. We note the following points.

1. The data value, in the form of an integer constant (*without* a decimal point), may appear in the allotted group of character positions (field).

2. The constant need not fill the field, and may be preceded by blank columns. The exact position of the constant within its field is not important.† A field that is entirely blank represents a zero value. (Note that a blank field used with list directed input, on the other hand, does not represent zero but is treated as a "null" item. See Section 2.4.2.)

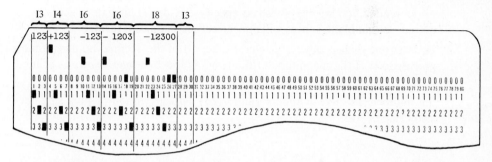

READ '(I3,⎵I4,⎵2⎵I6,⎵I8,⎵I3)', I, J, K, L, M, N

Fig. 6.7 Integer input.

Table 6.2 Integer input

External appearance	Field width	Format code	Internal value
123	3	I 3	+123
+123	4	I 4	+123
⎵⎵−123	6	I 6	−123
−⎵1203	6	I 6	−1203
⎵⎵−12300	8	I 8	−12300
⎵⎵⎵	3	I 3	0

† Fortran provides that a processor may establish either of two conventions for the handling of blank columns within a field on the "default" external input device: It may choose to ignore blank columns, or to replace them with zeros. Because previous versions of Fortran provided only the second of these options, a number of processors may be expected to continue to choose it for the sake of compatibility, if it is felt that a significant amount of the data to be processed will contain blank columns that are intended to be interpreted as zeros. For processors that make this choice, integer input data values must be positioned at the extreme right of their fields; the same applies to real data values that include an exponent.

3. A plus or minus sign may precede the integer, anywhere in the field to the left of the first digit. (Plus signs are ordinarily omitted.)

We have noted (see Section 2.1.4) that for each processor there is a limit to the size of integers that can be stored in a cell. Integer constants used as input data are subject to these same size limitations.

6.2.2   Real Input and Output

Output with the F conversion mode

The conversion mode F*w.d* is used for real output that is to appear in printed form *without* an exponent. Examples are shown in Fig. 6.8 and Table 6.3.

1. A number need not fill a field. It is printed as far right as possible. To improve readability, we may wish to specify a wider field than is actually required, so that blank spaces will appear between adjacent results.

2. At least one digit is always printed to the left of the decimal point (on most processors). If the magnitude of the result is less than one, a zero is printed.

3. If the value is negative, a minus sign is printed immediately to the left of the number. Positive numbers (and zero) appear without a plus sign (see also Chapter 9).

```
             PRINT 50, A, B, B, C, H
      50     FORMAT (1X, F10.3, F6.0, F8.2, F5.2, F6.3)
```

Fig. 6.8 Output of real data without exponents.

Table 6.3 Real output, F conversion mode

Real variable	Internal value	Format code	External appearance
A	−897.6577	F 10.3	⎕⎕−897.658
B	234.	F 6.0	⎕⎕234.
B	234.	F 8.2	⎕⎕234.00
C	−.12	F 5.2	−0.12
H	0.	F 6.3	⎕0.⎕⎕⎕

4. When a number is converted to external form, it is *rounded* to the least significant digit printed (that is, 0.5×10^{-d} is added to the absolute value of the number before the unwanted digits are dropped for printing). This rounding is illustrated on the first line of Table 6.3.

If we fail to allot sufficient field width to print a real number with F mode, the entire output field will be filled with asterisks. Even small numerical values require that w be at least 2 more than d to allow room for printing the decimal point and the digit that appears to its left (which may be zero); negative values require an additional space for the sign. Larger values require still wider fields. Even experienced programmers often have difficulty in estimating the sizes of the results that are to be printed. Division by an unexpectedly small number somewhere in the program, for example, may cause a variable to become far larger in magnitude than was anticipated. If there is any possibility that the field width will be insufficient, use of an E or G conversion mode is recommended.

Output with the E conversion mode

The conversion mode E$w.d$ is used for real output that is to appear in printed form *with* an exponent. Examples of output using this conversion are shown in Fig. 6.9 and Table 6.4.

```
       PRINT 70, A, A, B, C, D
70     FORMAT (1X, E15.8, E13.4, 2 E12.4, E10.2)
```

Fig. 6.9 Output of real data with exponents.

Table 6.4 Real output, E conversion mode

Real variable	Internal value	Format code	External appearance
A	-1.3496743	E 15.8	$-0.13496743E+01$
A	-1.3496743	E 13.4	☐☐$-0.1350E+01$
B	20.32×10^3	E 12.4	☐☐☐$0.2032E+05$
C	-20.32×10^{-3}	E 12.4	☐$-0.2032E-01$
D	6.023×10^{23}	E 10.2	☐☐☐$0.60E+24$

1. A number need not fill a field. It is printed at the right end of the field, with any extra blanks at the left providing improved readability.

2. The general form for printing results with E conversion is:

$\Box 0.xx \ldots xx\text{E}\pm ee$

where the x's represent the d significant digits, and the e's are the digits of the exponent. (If the exponent is less than 10, the first exponent digit is zero.) The significant digits and the exponent are each printed with a minus sign if negative. No sign is printed (see also Chapter 9) if the *value* printed is positive or zero; however, a positive or zero *exponent* is always printed with a plus sign.

3. The minimum field width for E mode should be kept clearly in mind. It takes at least seven print positions, besides the d significant digits, to print the complete form. The rule

$w \geq d + 7$

will guarantee enough space for:

- Four characters of the exponent (the letter E, the sign, and two numerical digits),
- The decimal point,
- The zero to the left of the decimal point, and
- The sign of the value.

An eighth extra column will guarantee a blank space separating adjacent fields. For display of results having eight significant digits, for example, the format code E16.8 is recommended.

4. As with the F mode, real numbers are rounded during conversion to the external form. Rounding is illustrated on the second and fifth lines of Table 6.4.

There is no danger that the field will be insufficient if we observe the rule $w \geq d + 7$, as explained above. However, if we fail to observe this rule, the entire output field may be filled with asterisks.

Output with the G conversion mode

The conversion mode G$w.d$ may be used for real output. Appearance of an exponent in the printed output will depend on the magnitude of the data value.

Comparing the F and E output modes, we see that the F mode is perhaps more straightforward to use, and the corresponding external field appearance is somewhat cleaner, because there are no exponents. However, the F mode cannot be used effectively for numerical values that are either very large or very small. In writing a program, if we know in advance that all data values will require the E output mode, we may as well use that mode from the beginning. But what shall we do if we suspect that most of our output values will be of "reasonable" size (neither astronomical nor microscopic), and yet we are afraid that a few exceptional cases may occur, which will cause trouble if we use the F mode exclusively? It was for precisely this situation that the G output mode was incorporated into Fortran. This mode is also especially useful in the related case, which occurs often during debugging, in which we are not sure how large or small our output values may be.

As a general rule, the G conversion mode works like F for values of "reasonable" size (neither very large nor very small), but it acts like E for numbers that would exceed the F field width, or where insignificant zeros would be printed to the right of the decimal point.

If the exponent would be between 0 and d, inclusive, the F mode is used, but with the value of w decreased by 4. (In other words, the number is printed in the first $w - 4$ columns of the output field, and it is followed by four blanks.) The total number of significant digits printed, both to the right and to the left of the decimal point, is always d.

On the other hand, if the exponent is negative or is larger than d, the output conversion is identical to E$w.d$.

Thus the G$w.d$ format can give the clean output appearance characteristic of the F output mode when the numbers printed are of "reasonable" size, while providing for the display of very large or small data values in the E style when necessary.

The E and G formats are compared in Table 6.5.

Table 6.5 Comparison of E and G output conversion modes

Internal value	External appearance	
	E 11.4 format code	G 11.4 format code
−8977.	−0.8977E+04	□−8977.□□□□
23.40	□0.2340E+02	□□23.40□□□□
−0.1200	−0.1200E+00	−0.1200□□□□
−1.395	−0.1395E+01	□−1.395□□□□
−20320.	−0.2032E+05	−0.2032E+05
0.02032	□0.2032E−01	□□0.2032E−01
−0.02032	−0.2032E−01	−0.2032E−01
0.00004999	□0.4999E−04	□□0.4999E−04

Input with the F, E, or G conversion modes

Input data to be converted with any of the three real modes, F$w.d$, E$w.d$, or G$w.d$, may appear in the input record in any valid real constant form. In particular, it is not necessary to include an exponent for E mode input conversion, or to omit the exponent when the F mode is used for input. Examples are shown in Figs. 6.10 and 6.11, and in Tables 6.6 and 6.7.

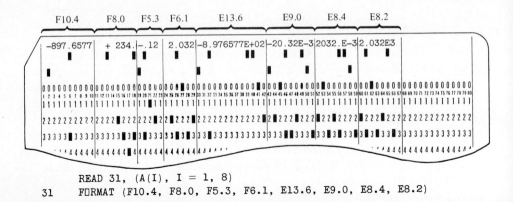

READ 31, (A(I), I = 1, 8)

31   FORMAT (F10.4, F8.0, F5.3, F6.1, E13.6, E9.0, E8.4, E8.2)

Fig. 6.10 Input of real data without exponents.

Table 6.6 Real input, explicit decimal point in external field

External appearance	Field width	Internal value
□−897.6577	10	−897.6577
□□+□234.	8	+234.
−.12□	5	−.12
□2.032	6	+2.032
−8.976577E+02	13	−897.6577
−20.32E−3	9	−.02032
2032.E−3	8	+2.032
2.032E3□	8	2.032×10^3

For any of the three input modes, F, E, or G, the following observations apply.

1. A plus or minus sign preceding the significant digits may appear anywhere in the field to the left of the first digit. Plus signs are ordinarily omitted.

2. The number need not fill the field. A field that is entirely blank represents a zero value. Note that when an exponent appears in the field, it will be treated as an integer. (Refer to the footnote on p. 207 concerning blanks within integer input.)

3. If a decimal point appears in the input field, the value of d in the format code is ignored, and the actual decimal point "overrides" the format specification.

4. If a decimal point does not appear explicitly, the value of d is used to determine the position of an "implied" decimal point, counting from the right end of the field (or from the first column to the left of the exponent, if there is one in the field).

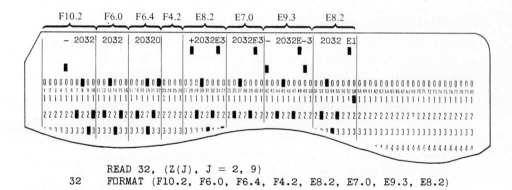

```
READ 32, (Z(J), J = 2, 9)
32      FORMAT (F10.2, F6.0, F6.4, F4.2, E8.2, E7.0, E9.3, E8.2)
```

Fig. 6.11 Input of real data with exponents.

Table 6.7 Real input, no explicit decimal point in external field

External appearance	Field width	Decimal position	Internal value
□□□□−□2032	10	2	−20.32
□2032□	6	0	+20320.
□20320	6	4	+2.032
□□□□	4	2	0.0
□+2032E3	8	2	+20320.
□2032E3	7	0	+2032000.
−□2032E−3	9	3	−0.002032
□20320E1	8	2	+2032.

5. An exponent may appear in the input record in any of several forms. The most complete form consists of the letter **E** followed by a plus or minus sign, followed by an integer constant. Either the **E** or the sign may be omitted but not both, since there must be some indication that an exponent is present. Table 6.8 shows several permissible forms for the characters in an input record representing the constant 0.2032×10^3, assuming a format code **E10.4**.

Table 6.8 Permissible forms for one input constant in E10.4 format

□□□□2032E3
□□□2032E+3
□□□2032E03
□□2032E□03
□□2032E+03
□□□.2032E3

Double precision input and output

Double precision data for input and output is handled in essentially the same way as real data. The E, F, and G conversion modes can be used for output of double precision data, or for input of data corresponding to a list item of double precision type.

The external form for input data of double precision type may be represented using the letter D or E to indicate the exponent; such data may be read with an E, F, or G conversion code. The format code D*w.d*, analogous to E*w.d*, is also available for use with data prepared with a D exponent; in fact, it will handle any of the external forms permitted for real input.

Double precision output data produced with the E conversion code will be printed with an E indicating the exponent; the G code may also produce output that contains the character E to indicate the exponent (depending on the magnitude of the data: see the description of G output conversion, above). For applications which require a printed D rather than an E to indicate the exponent, the format code D*w.d* may be used.

In short, all the D, E, F, and G conversion modes are interchangeable for input: Any of these codes may be used with list items of real or double precision types, and with input data prepared in any of the forms permitted for real input as well as any of those forms with a D replacing the E to indicate the exponent. For output, any of the codes D, E, F, or G may be used with a list item of real or double precision type. Only the appearance of the printed output will be affected by the choice among these codes. There is no difference between E*w.d* and D*w.d* output except for the printing of the letter E or D with the exponent.

Example

```
DOUBLE PRECISION FOX
FOX = 1.23456789012345 D 0
PRINT '(1X,⎵D22.15)', FOX
```

Complex input and output

Any of the real format specification codes may be used for input or output of data of complex type, but a pair of numeric fields and a pair of format codes correspond to a single complex variable (or expression) in the input or output list.

Example

```
COMPLEX RABBIT
RABBIT = (1.234567, 8.901234)
PRINT '(1X,⎵2⎵E14.7,⎵2⎵F8.2)', RABBIT, (1.234, 5.678)
```

Appearance of the output:

☐0.1234567E+01☐0.8901234E+01☐☐☐☐☐1.23☐☐☐☐5.68

The form of complex data prepared for input under explicit format control differs from the list directed form. For explicitly formatted input, the data is prepared in the form of two real fields (of any acceptable real form), whereas list directed input requires a form analogous to that of a complex constant, that is, two real numeric input values separated by a comma and enclosed in parentheses.

6.2.3 Logical Input and Output

The format code Lw is used for input or output of data corresponding to list items of logical type. The printed output appears as $w - 1$ blanks followed by a T or an F. For input, the external field may contain optional blanks and a T or F (optionally preceded and followed by a period).

6.2.4 Character Input and Output

The conversion modes A and Aw are used with character data. The second form, Aw, specifies a field width for the data in the external record. The first form omits the field width specification; the number of characters transmitted to or from the record is determined by the *length* of the character string that is referenced by the corresponding variable (or array element, substring, or expression) in the input or output list.

Output

We have seen how to annotate printed numerical results by printing words and phrases in the form of comments, titles, or headings. In the examples presented so far, the text was included as a character constant or referenced as a character expression in the output list of a list directed output statement. The A and Aw format codes provide this same facility, with additional control over the appearance of the output, when explicit formatting rather than list directed formatting is used. A different method, in which the text to be printed is incorporated into the format description, is covered in Section 6.2.7; that method is generally less flexible than that presented here, where the text is included in (or referenced from) the output list.

Example 8 Suppose that we wish to print two numbers, *Err* and *N,* and to properly identify each of them with certain alphanumerical information. Suppose that *Err* is the difference between a computed and an observed value of a function and may properly be called the error. Let us further suppose that *N* is the num-

ber of trials (observations) used in computing *Err*. Hence we wish to print a line
of the form

```
After xxx trials, error is yyyyy.yy
```

where *xxx* is the current value of the integer variable *N*, and *yyyyy.yy* is the current value of the real variable *Err*. Let us suppose that *N* is a three-digit integer,
and that *Err* is to be printed with a field specification F9.2. The output statement might read

```
PRINT 45, '⎕After', N, '⎕trials,⎕error⎕is', E
```

and the corresponding format statement would be

```
45 FORMAT (A6, I4, A17, F9.2)
```

The total width of the four fields printed by this statement is 36 characters. The
first six characters in the record transmitted to the printer will be ⎕After, the
next four will be the (three-digit integer) value of *N* preceded by a blank, the next
seventeen will be the characters ⎕trials,⎕error⎕is, and the last nine will be
the value of *Err* printed in F9.2 format.

In this example, the length of each character constant to be printed is the
same as the width of the corresponding A field. Therefore, the slightly simpler
format statement

```
45    FORMAT (A, I4, A, F9.2)
```

would produce the same output. This latter declaration also has some flexibility
in that it could be used with character constants of different lengths. For example,
another statement in the same program could use format statement 45 to print
the total of *N* data values:

```
PRINT 45, '⎕The⎕total⎕of', M, '⎕values⎕is', SUM
```

This flexibility of course imposes an additional burden if it is desired to *align* the
various items of output in some manner. It would be necessary to count the characters in each of the character constants, to determine the precise locations of
the numeric fields that would be printed.

On the other hand, use of the first format declaration (with field widths A6
and A17), along with character constants of lengths 13 and 10 respectively as in
the second PRINT statement, will result in *truncation* and *padding* of the character data to match the specified field widths. The data specified by the character
list item will be truncated from the right or padded with blanks on the left before
being transmitted to the output device. (Note that this is not the same as the

padding applied during character assignment; see Section 5.2.4.) The printed
result with

```
PRINT 45, '□The□total□of', M, '□values□is', SUM
45   FORMAT (A6, I4, A17, F9.2)
```

might appear as follows:

```
□The□t 107□□□□□□□□□values□is 43210.98
```

The character constant □The□total□of is truncated from thirteen to six characters, and the ten characters □values□is are padded with seven additional
blanks on the left.

Of course, character constants are not the only source of text for character
output. The following examples illustrate explicitly formatted input and output
of character variables and expressions as well as constants.

Example 9

```
      CHARACTER*7 FIRST, SECOND
      READ '(I3,□3□F8.0,□A7)', KODE, X, REALS, FLAG, FIRST
      SECOND = 'Payroll'
      PRINT 21, 179.3, X, SECOND, KODE, REALS
21    FORMAT (2 G15.8, A, I5, G15.8)
      PRINT 22, FLAG, X, REALS, 2.0, FIRST
22    FORMAT (4 G15.8, A)
      PRINT '(A14)', FIRST // SECOND
      END
```

Example 10

```
CHARACTER*50 HAMLET(6)
HAMLET(2) = 'Whether□''tis□nobler□in□the□mind□to□suffer'
LOC1 = INDEX (HAMLET(2), 'the')
PRINT '(I5,□A)', LOC1, HAMLET(2)(LOC1 + 1: )
END
```

Result:

```
□□□4her□'tis□nobler□in□the□mind□to□suffer□□□□□□□□□□
```

Input

The A and A*w* conversion modes are also used for character input.

Example 11　A chemist prepares data including the symbol for a chemical element and the number of atoms of the element in a certain complex molecule. A

program will read the data, look up the symbol in an internal table (using a linear search, for example, as described in Section 4.1.2), and use related data from the table to compute the molecular weight of the molecule. The input statement is written as

```
READ '(A2,☐I3)', NAME, NATOMS
```

The first two character positions of the input record contain the chemical element symbol, and the next three characters contain the number of atoms.

If the character variable *Name* is declared to be of length 2, this format could be replaced by (A,☐I3). For input of character data without a field width specification, the number of characters of the input record that will be used is determined by the character length specification for the input list item (variable, array element, or substring).

If a field width is specified, but is different from the actual character length of the input list item, the characters read will be padded on the right with blanks or truncated from the *left* to the length of the list item. Thus, if *Name* is of length 3, the statement

```
READ '(A2,☐I3)', NAME, NATOMS
```

along with the following characters in the input record

```
Cu107
```

will result in the characters Cu☐ being stored as the value of *Name*. However, if *Name* were of length 1, the field would be truncated from the left and only the character u would be stored.

Input data form

Character values for input with explicit format control are not enclosed in apostrophes. Unlike the list directed form, where the apostrophes are needed to establish the beginning and end of a character constant in the external record, the division of records into fields for this input form is sufficient to delimit character items. Apostrophes within an input data value are represented by only a single apostrophe in the input field (since there are no delimiting apostrophes).

Example 12   We wish to read from an input record the following information: (a) Name of a chemical element, *Name,* such as iron, cobalt, or zinc; (b) Heat capacity coefficients *A, B,* and *C.* Input data could be prepared on a card as shown in Fig. 6.12. An appropriate input statement is

```
READ '(A5,☐3☐G9.4)', NAME, A, B, C
```

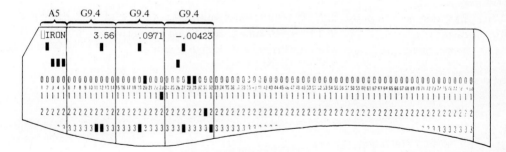

Figure 6.12

Example 13   We wish to read from a data card an arbitrary 80-column message to be printed out at a later time. A typical data card is shown in Fig. 6.13.

```
CHARACTER*80 SPOT(20)
READ '(A80)', SPOT(1)
```

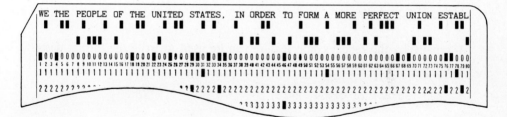

Figure 6.13

6.2.5 Format Code Repetition

When two or more adjacent fields of an input or output record are to have identical format codes, it is not necessary (as we have seen) to write out the code for each field separately if they can be combined by means of a *repeat count*. Thus,

```
G12.4, G12.4, G12.4
```

can also be written as

```
3 G12.4
```

Example 14   Suppose that we wish to read values for *A, B, C, J,* and *K* from a card, as shown in Fig. 6.14. *A, B,* and *C* are to be converted according to G mode, and *J* and *K* are to be converted according to I mode:

```
     READ 60, A, B, C, J, K
 60  FORMAT (G12.4, G12.4, G12.4, I3, I3)
```

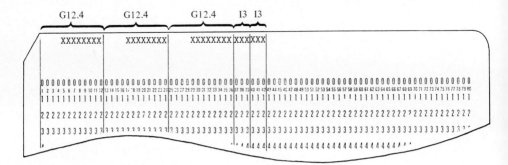

Figure 6.14

Alternatively, the repeat count feature can be used to write the format description in the simpler form

```
 60  FORMAT (3 G12.4, 2 I3)
```

(Compare Example 1 in Section 6.1.1.)

Repeated format code groups

A group of format codes can be enclosed in parentheses and preceded by a repeat count digit.

Example 15   The following two statements are equivalent.

```
READ '(G12.4,[]I3,[]G12.4,[]I3)', A, I, B, J
READ '(2[](G12.4,[]I3))', A, I, B, J
```

Example 16   If the list in Example 14 were rearranged, we might have

```
READ '(2[](G12.4,[]I3),[]G12.4)', A, J, B, K, C
```

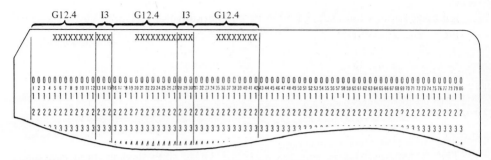

Figure 6.15

The associated data might appear on an input card as shown in Fig. 6.15.

Example 17   More complicated patterns of repeated code groups can easily be imagined. For example, we could have one repeated group of fields nested within another group. The following format descriptions are equivalent.

```
(2 (I5, I4, I3), F5.2, 2 (I5, I4, I3), F5.2, I6)
(2 (2 (I5, I4, I3), F5.2), I6)
```

6.2.6   Correspondence of List, Format, and Record

During execution of an input or output statement, a correspondence or matching occurs between the items of the input or output list, format codes in the format description, and fields of the input or output record on the external device. In this matching, repeated format codes are of course counted as matching the proper number of fields, and list items such as implied DO loops may correspond to multiple fields (and multiple format codes). The list, the format description, and the external record are all "scanned" *in parallel* during the input or output process, with repetitions as indicated by repeated format codes, implied DO loops, and so on. As we shall see (Section 6.2.7), there are also some format codes that are associated with a field of the record but do not correspond to a list item. When one of these codes is encountered, the scan of the input or output list is temporarily halted while the scanning process continues with the format description and the external record.

It may happen that there are exactly the same number of list items, format codes, and fields (taking into account the special cases just mentioned). When the last item of the list has been transmitted, the parallel scan will be completed and execution of the input or output statement comes to an end. Suppose, on the other hand, that there are more format codes than list items. In this case, when the list is exhausted and action has terminated, the remaining format codes are ignored. To illustrate, suppose that as an alternative to Example 16 we had used the format description

```
(3 (G12.4, I3))
```

with the list

```
A, J, B, K, C
```

This format description suggests a record whose sixth field is three characters wide and contains an integer. Since there are only five items in the list, however, the sixth format code will not be used, and the effect is identical to that of Example 16.

However, suppose that there are more list items than format codes in the format description. Since the end of the description signals the end of a record, the input or output process must continue to another record in order to complete the list. For instance, suppose that for Example 16 we had written the format

```
(G12.4, I3)
```

which specifies an input record containing only two fields. Since five data items must be read, the format must be *rescanned* to match the remaining items of the list. However, each rescanning corresponds to matching the list items with the fields of a new record. Thus, three records in all must be read before the list can be satisfied. The first record contains values for *A* and *J*, the second has values for *B* and *K*, and the third has the single value of *C*.

Extra characters of an input record will be ignored after the fields indicated in the format description have been transmitted. For instance, if only the two fields indicated by G12.4, I3 are to be read from a record, then any characters beyond character position 15 in the record are ignored: It is immaterial whether the record contains additional blanks or other characters, or whether the record contains only fifteen (or any larger number of) characters.

Rescanning the format description

In attempting to satisfy an input or output list by rescanning the format description, the processor does not necessarily return to the very beginning of the format. It returns to a *rescan point,* which is determined as follows:

Search backward from the right end of the format description until a right parenthesis (other than the terminal right parenthesis of the format) is encountered. Then find the matching left parenthesis. The rescan begins with this left parenthesis (or with the repeat count, if there is one, controlling this left parenthesis). If there are no parentheses inside the outermost pair that delimits the entire format description, the rescan includes the entire format. In the first of the following examples, the rescan point is near the middle of the format, whereas in the second the rescan point is at the beginning of the format.

```
FORMAT (2 (I5, I4, I3), F5.2, 2 (I5, I4, I3), F5.2, I6)
                                ↑
                          Rescan point
FORMAT (2 (2 (I5, I4, I3), F5.2), I6)
        ↑
  Rescan point
```

Once the rescan point is determined, the format description continues to be rescanned from this point as many times as necessary until the list is exhausted. Note that a new record is started each time the rescan occurs.

Example 18   Let us suppose that we wish to print the computed values of the variables *Fee, Fie,* and *Foe,* along with the first N elements of a linear array, *Fum.* Values for *Fee, Fie,* and *Foe* are to be printed on the first line, and the elements of *Fum* are to be arranged four per line. A suitable output statement and format description would be

```
        PRINT 60, FEE, FIE, FOE, (FUM(J), J = 1, N)
    60  FORMAT (1X, 3 G10.2 / (1X, 4 G10.4))
                                ↑
                          Rescan point
```

The first three data items, *Fee, Fie,* and *Foe,* will be printed according to the format code G10.2. The slash indicates the end of a record (that is, the end of a printed line). Only 31 characters of the first record have been specified, so the remainder of this record will be blank. The next record is described by the format description (1X, 4 G10.4), which will be used in printing the first four elements of the array *Fum.* Since this is the last parenthesized group in the format, the rescan point will be at the beginning of this group. Thus the format code (1X, 4 G10.4) will be used repeatedly until all of the first N elements of *Fum* have been printed, four per line. If N is not a multiple of 4, the list will be exhausted during the middle of a scan of this repeated format group; the output process will then terminate, ignoring the remaining format codes.

6.2.7   Format Codes Not Associated with a List Item

In addition to the format codes that are associated with list items, there are other "editing" codes that are used for such purposes as specifying the position of a field within the external record, or printing a fixed sequence of characters (independent of the output list). They do not correspond to any list item, and do not cause the values of any program variables to be transmitted.

Skipped fields

When one or more characters of an input record are to be ignored or skipped, or when one or more blank characters are to be inserted into an output record, we can designate this group of character positions as a field to be skipped, by incorporating in the format description the code wX, where w is the width of the field, that is, the number of character positions to be skipped. Of course, w must be an unsigned integer constant. Note that an X format code is *not* needed to cause the remainder of an input record (to the right of the last field of interest) to be skipped, nor to cause the remainder of a printed line (to the right of the last data value printed on the line) to be left blank.

In many instances, it is simpler to widen a numeric field than to introduce an extra skipped field. For example, if we wish to print five blank columns followed by a five-digit integer, we could use either the pair of format codes 5X, I5 or the single code I10. These two formats will have the same effect, except that the code I10 will avoid problems due to field overflow that could occur if the integer to be printed were unexpectedly larger than five digits.

Tabular format

Columns can also be skipped in a slightly different way, analogous to the use of the tabulation key on a typewriter. This feature is invoked by means of the format code Tw, which changes the sequence of processing of a record of input or output, such that the wth character of that record is the next one to be transmitted. This feature is especially attractive for use with columnar data output. A format such as

```
(T20, F7.3)
```

could be used with the format

```
(T20, 'HEADING')
```

for example, to guarantee that the characters printed by the two formats will be properly aligned vertically. This feature is particularly helpful for preparing columnar tables or graphs, especially in complicated cases.

Vertical spacing control

For each record to be printed, the program must specify the desired vertical line spacing. This spacing is controlled by a one-character code placed in the first character position of each record, which is transmitted to the printer but is *not* printed. Therefore, the format for each record to be printed must make provision for this first vertical positioning character. The lines on the printer can be advanced but cannot be rolled back.

The most common spacing mode is single line spacing. This means that the printer advances by one line position before the printing takes place. The character code used to indicate single line spacing is a blank (▯). We can force a blank in the first character position of any output record by making the first field a skipped field of any length, that is, by using any X format code, such as 1X or 5X, etc. Alternatively, we can widen the first output field to provide it with more than enough columns to print the required data and its sign. However, there is risk, especially with the I and F output modes, that the data may exceed the expected size and overflow into the vertical spacing control position.

The control characters listed in Table 6.9 are used in Fortran. At most computer installations, additional vertical positioning codes are available for more specialized uses such as triple spacing or skipping to the middle of a page.

Table 6.9 Vertical spacing control codes

Desired vertical spacing	Required character code
Single space	▯ (blank)
Double space	0 (zero)
Skip to top of next page	1
No space (overprint)	+

Multiple-record formats

We have seen that a format description may describe the fields of more than one record, either when a slash is included among the format codes or when rescan occurs. For either input or output, the slash indicates that transmission of the current record is to cease and a new record is to be started.

In connection with vertical spacing control for a printer, note that the first format code *after any slash* will correspond to the first field of a new record, and therefore provides vertical spacing information. When the format rescan point is other than the beginning of the format description, vertical spacing should be considered again at this point in the format, because the first format code *after the rescan point* will also correspond to the first field of a new record. In Example 18 in Section 6.2.6, we stated that the format

```
(1X, 3 G10.2 / (1X, 4 G10.4))
```

would be suitable. Note that we have included a one-column skipped field just after the rescan point (after the inner left parenthesis), as well as at the beginning of the format. Thus, each new record will begin with a one-column skipped field; that is, the first character of each record to be printed will be a blank. Since this first character is not printed but is used for vertical spacing control, the effect is to guarantee that single line spacing will occur just before each line is printed.

When consecutive slashes are used, as in the format

```
(1X, 3 G10.2 // (1X, 4 G10.4))
```

the first slash causes termination of the first output record. Since the format has not been exhausted, transmission of a second output record is initiated; however, the second slash immediately terminates this second record. The effect is to transmit the second record as an empty record, which will be printed as a blank line (including a blank vertical spacing control character).† Again, since the format has not been exhausted, transmission of a third output record is initiated, and this record is generated according to the format (1X, 4 G10.4), beginning with a one-column skipped field that provides a blank character for carriage control. If there are more than seven list items, the format will be rescanned and successive records will use the format (1X, 4 G10.4) again. Note that no list item corresponds to a skipped field, that is, to an X format code, so four list items will be transmitted each time the format is rescanned.

The format description as a source of text

Suppose that we have a number of output statements in a program, all with different lists of items to be printed, but with the same text to accompany the items in each of the different lists. For example, the program might contain the following statements. (Note the use of the $ in column 6 of a Fortran statement line, to indicate continuation of the statement from the previous line. Any other character except a zero or blank could have been used here as well.)

```
      PRINT 45, '□After□event□number', I1
     $  '□the□largest□element□is□at□location', L1,
     $  '□and□its□weight□is', W1
      ...
      PRINT 45, '□After□event□number', I2,
     $  '□the□largest□element□is□at□location', L2,
     $  '□and□its□weight□is', W2
      ...
      PRINT 45, '□After□event□number', LAST,
     $  '□the□largest□element□is□at□location', LOC
     $  '□and□its□weight□is', FINAL
```

---

† The number of records read by a formatted input statement can be determined from the following rule: A new record is always read at the beginning of execution of any input statement (even if the input list is empty), each time a slash is encountered in the format, and each time a format rescan occurs. The number of records written by a formatted output statement can be determined from the following rule: A record is written each time a slash is encountered in the format, each time a format rescan occurs, and at completion of execution of the statement (even if the output list is empty). Thus, for printed output the occurrence of n consecutive slashes results in $(n - 1)$ blank lines; the occurrence of n slashes at the beginning or end of a format description causes n blank lines to be printed. A complete format description consisting only of n slashes causes $(n + 1)$ blank lines to be printed (even if n is zero).

The repeated text may be removed from the individual output lists and placed in the format description, in the following manner.

```
45   FORMAT ('□After□event□number', I5,
     $   '□the□largest□element□is□at□location', I5,
     $   '□and□its□weight□is', E15.7)
```

The PRINT statements used with this format have the following simpler forms:

```
PRINT 45, I1, L1, W1
PRINT 45, I2, L2, W2
PRINT 45, LAST, LOC, FINAL
```

Execution of these statements with the revised format description has the same effect as before.

Text that appears within single quotes (apostrophes) in the format description is known as an "apostrophe format code." Such a code does not correspond to any item in the output list. Each time such a format specification is encountered during output processing, the prescribed text is copied to the output record directly from the format itself. The apostrophe format code must not be used for input.

This feature may also be used to provide the vertical spacing code that occupies the first character position of any record that is to be printed. Specifying vertical spacing in this way removes it from the output list, where it might prove distracting. For example (compare Example 18 in Section 6.2.6):

```
     PRINT 60, FEE, FIE, FOE, (FUM(J), J = 1, N)
60   FORMAT ('0', 3 G10.2 / ('0', 4 G10.4))
```

For variety, we have used here the vertical spacing control character zero, which will cause double spacing. Using the apostrophe format code '□' would have the same effect as the skipped field code 1X, that is, either of these format codes will cause one blank character to be transmitted to the output record.

Apostrophe format code in a character constant

We have illustrated the use of the apostrophe format code in a FORMAT statement that is referenced by a label in the output statement. When the format description appears as a character constant in the PRINT (or WRITE) statement, an extra precaution is necessary. An apostrophe format code within such a format description must have the enclosing apostrophes *doubled,* according to the convention for representing apostrophes within any character constant. Thus we would write

```
PRINT '(''0'',□3□G10.2)', FEE, FIE, FOE
```

to represent the format description

    ('0', 3 G10.2)

The apostrophes surrounding the zero are doubled in the PRINT statement because they appear within a character constant.

Even more awkward is the situation that occurs when an apostrophe format code includes an apostrophe to be printed. For example, we might wish to print the result

    ⎕⎕2⎕isn't⎕⎕3

specifying the integers 2 and 3 as numeric constants in the output list, but obtaining isn't from an apostrophe format code. The apostrophe format code will appear as follows:

    '⎕isn''t'

With the format description in a separate FORMAT statement, we would write

        PRINT 7, 2, 3
    7   FORMAT (1X, I3, '⎕isn''t', I3)

Incorporating the format description as a character constant in the PRINT statement leads to the following specimen of gross inelegance:

    PRINT '(1X,⎕I3,⎕''⎕isn''''t'',⎕I3)', 2, 3

Processing at the end of a list: Colon format code

While executing an input or output statement, the processor scans the list, the format description, and the record in parallel. If it arrives at the end of the input or output list when the format scan is at the *final right parenthesis,* or when the next format code is one *associated with a list item* (such as I, E, F, G, or A), execution of the input or output statement is terminated at that point. On the other hand, if the next format code is one (such as slash, X, T, or apostrophe) that *does not require a list item,* execution will continue *except* in the following two cases:

1. As we have just seen, processing continues through nonlist items only until the final right parenthesis of the format description is encountered—*no rescan* will occur after the list has been exhausted.

2. If a *colon format code* is encountered after the list has been exhausted, the scan terminates and execution of the input or output statement ceases. This

format code, consisting simply of a colon within the format description, therefore indicates that the nonlist format codes that follow are to be effective
only if the list is not exhausted.

Example 19

```
      PRINT 47, (I, A(I), I = 1, N)
  47  FORMAT (4(: '⌷I⌷ = ', I3, '⌷A(I)⌷ =', G16.8))
```

Careful study reveals that the repeated format group will be scanned four times
before the end of the format description is reached. Therefore, when N is not a
multiple of 4 the characters '⌷I =' would be printed after the last A_I value if
the colon were not included in the format. (See Exercise 7 in Section 6.2.8.)

If the list is empty initially, nonlist format codes will be processed in accordance with these same rules. Output statements with empty lists are often used
for printing messages, titles, and headings, or for skipping one or more lines,
without calling for the display of the values of any variables. The associated format description will not contain any of the codes that need to be associated with
a list item. Empty input lists are also used occasionally for positioning or other
editing of input records without data transmission—for example, to skip an input
record.

Example 20   An output statement with an empty list would have either of the
forms

```
  PRINT 𝒻ormat
  WRITE (𝒸list)
```

Note that there is no comma following the format specification in the short form
when there is no list.

Suppose we wish to print the three headings, Rate, Hours, and Pay, above
three columns of numbers. The columns will each be fifteen character positions
wide, with an extra five character positions to the left of the first column. We also
wish to skip two lines after printing the headings (see Fig. 6.16). Thus, the following are appropriate output statements and format descriptions.

```
      PRINT 100
  100 FORMAT (T17, 'Rate', T31, 'Hours', T48, 'Pay' //)
      . . .
      PRINT '(5X,⌷F15.2,⌷I15,⌷F15.2)', RATE, NHOURS, PAY
```

	Rate	Hours	Pay
	x.xx	*xx*	*xxx.xx*
	x.xx	*xx*	*xx.xx*
	x.xx	*xx*	*xxx.xx*
	x.xx	*xx*	*xxx.xx*
	. . .	. . .	. . .

Figure 6.16

Example 21 Suppose that at a certain point in the program we wish to print the message, Check data again.:

```
      PRINT 10
 10   FORMAT ('[]Check[]data[]again.')
```

Example 22 To print the title, The Automatic Change Maker at the top of the page and then skip four lines, we could use the following statements:

```
      PRINT 26
 26   FORMAT ('1', 26X, 'The[]Automatic[]Change[]Maker' ////)
```

6.2.8 Exercises

1. Write format descriptions appropriate to the following lists and record descriptions.

   a) Input list: A, B, C
      Each input record contains a single real number without an exponent, in a field ten columns wide, with an implied decimal point three places from the right hand. The field begins in column 21.

   b) Input list: A, B, C
      Each input record contains three real numbers without exponents, in fields ten columns wide, with decimal points included. The first field begins in column 1.

   c) Output list: A, B, C
      The numbers are to be printed, without exponents, in 20-column fields, with four digits to the right of the decimal point.

   d) Output list: A, B, C
      Numbers are to be printed with exponents and six significant digits. Choose an appropriate field width. Include vertical spacing control for normal (single) spacing.

   e) Output list: I, U, J, V, W, K, X, Y, Z

The numbers should be printed on three lines. The first line should contain one integer and one real number; the second line should contain one integer and two real numbers; and the third line should contain one integer and three real numbers. For each integer, the field width should be six; each real number should be printed in a 10-column field without an exponent and with two digits to the right of the decimal point.

f) Output list: I, J, A, B, C, D, E, F, G, H, X, Y
The first line should consist of two integers in 10-column fields. The remaining real numbers should be printed two per line. The first real number on each line should be printed in a 10-column field without an exponent, with one digit to the right of the decimal point; the second real number on each line should be printed in a 12-column field with an exponent and three significant digits.

g) No list. Print the message, Checker is off the board.

2. We wish to print a table of values, using the statements
   PRINT 16
   PRINT '(11X,⎕3⎕G15.6)', (ALPHA(I), BETA(I), AREA(I), I = 1, M)

   Construct a suitable FORMAT statement labeled 16, which will print labels above each of the three columns of output.

3. Write a format description for the list
   N, (A(I), I = 1, N)

   N is to be a three-digit integer printed on the first line. After skipping an extra blank line, we wish to print the elements of the array A in groups of six per line, single-spaced, in F mode, with two positions to the right of the decimal point; each F field is twelve columns wide. (Be sure to provide for vertical spacing control.)

4. Write a format description for the list
   ((K(I, J), J = 1, 8), I = 1, 8

   The array K represents a checkerboard. Display the contents of the cells of K, row by row, on the output page in a square arrangement, with elements spaced ten columns apart horizontally and six lines apart vertically. Allow a 20-column margin on the left side.

5. Modify Exercise 4 to print the title Checkerboard at the top of the page, centered above the display. Skip six vertical lines between the title and the display.

6. Modify Example 13 in Section 6.2.4 to read an 80-character string and print it at the top of a page with a 10-column left margin.

7. Study Example 19 in Section 6.2.7, considering each of the cases $N = 0, 1, 2, 3, 4,$ and 5. Describe the appearance of the printed output in each case. What would be the appearance of the printed output in each case if the colon format code were omitted?

8. Refer to the footnote on p. 207. Find out whether your processor ignores blank columns within a field, or replaces them with zeros.

CHAPTER 7

DECLARATION STATEMENTS

Besides executable statements such as assignment statements, input statements, and output statements, the Fortran language includes some nonexecutable, or *declarative,* statements. These statements, also known as declarations, furnish important information to the language processor. Type declarations and array declarations were introduced in Chapters 2 and 5, and FORMAT declarations were discussed in detail in Chapter 6. In this chapter we treat type declarations and array declarations in more detail, and we cover DATA, PARAMETER, and EQUIV-ALENCE declarations. Some other declarations, including COMMON declarations, are used mainly with subprograms; these will be discussed in Chapter 8.

Because declarations are not executable, they must never be referenced by a control statement such as a GO TO statement, and they must never be used to terminate a DO loop. It is best never to label any declarations except FORMAT declarations, to minimize the likelihood of unintended references to such statements.

Declarations are usually placed ahead of the executable statements in a program. Further information about the placement of declarations can be found in Section 7.4.

7.1 TYPE DECLARATIONS AND ARRAY DECLARATIONS

7.1.1 Type Declarations

The type of a varable is determined *implicitly* (depending on the first character of the symbolic name), or *explicitly* (by a declaration in which the entire name appears). Implicit typing may be *declared* or may be assumed by *default*. Thus we have the following categories.

1. Implicit type specification: This depends on the first character of the symbolic name.

   a) Default implicit type specification: In the absence of any declaration to the contrary, default rules are applied. If the first character of the name is one of the letters I, J, K, L, M, or N, the type is *integer*. If the first character is any other letter, the type is *real*. There is no default typing for any types other than integer and real.

   b) Declared implicit type specification: An IMPLICIT statement may be used to change the rules that are to be applied for determining the type from the first character of a name. For example, an IMPLICIT statement might declare that all names beginning with the letters N, O, or P refer to data of complex type.

2. Explicit type declaration: The default or declared implicit type specifications may be *superseded* for individual names. Thus explicit typing depends on the entire symbolic name, rather than on the first character alone.

The IMPLICIT declaration

In its most straightforward form, this statement consists of the word IMPLICIT followed by a list, each of whose items consists of a *Type* followed by a parenthesized sublist of initial letters, specifying that symbolic names having those initial letters are to be of that type. For example,

```
IMPLICIT INTEGER (A, B, C, D)
IMPLICIT REAL (M), COMPLEX (E, F, Z), CHARACTER*5 (Q)
```

Meaning: Variables and other symbolic names beginning with the letters A, B, C, or D refer to data of integer type. Those beginning with M are real. Names beginning with E, F, or Z refer to complex data. And finally, those beginning with Q refer to character strings of length five. For names beginning with letters that are not mentioned in the IMPLICIT statements, the default rules remain in effect. Thus, the letters I through L and N continue to imply integer type, and all other letters not explicitly mentioned will continue to imply real type.

A *range* of letters may also be specified. A pair of letters in alphabetical order, separated by a minus sign (regarded as a hyphen), is interpreted as including all letters between those mentioned. Thus, the following two statements are equivalent:

```
IMPLICIT COMPLEX (U, V, W, X, Y, Z)
IMPLICIT COMPLEX (U − Z)
```

Once a letter has appeared in an IMPLICIT statement, or has been included within a range of letters, it must not appear again in an implicit specification.

Explicit type declarations

The simple form of the explicit type declaration is

   Type List

All names in the *List* are thereby declared to be of the designated *Type*.

Examples

```
INTEGER A, B, I
REAL IRON, NAPER, KILOS, J, TAPE
LOGICAL SWITCH, KEGS, COUNT, LOW
DOUBLE PRECISION X, Y, Z
COMPLEX A, B, C
CHARACTER*5 ABLE, BAKER, ITEM
```

A program may have as many type declarations as are required. The same name must not be explicitly declared more than once (even if the same type is specified). An explicit type declaration may, of course, refer to a name that begins with one of the letters specified in an IMPLICIT declaration; the explicit typing supersedes the implicit typing in this case. It is permissible to declare a name to have the same type that would have been specified implicitly; for example, in the declarations illustrated above, the name *I* is already of default integer type and *Tape* is of default real type.

   Note that a one-letter name may be declared explicitly. For example, the following statements could appear in the same program:

```
IMPLICIT COMPLEX (M, Q − Z)
REAL L, M, Z
CHARACTER*5 P, Q, R
```

The first statement declares that all names *beginning with* the letter M, or with any letter of the alphabet between Q and Z inclusive, refer to data of complex type, *unless* a name beginning with one of those letters appears in an explicit type declaration. Because of this first statement, along with the default implicit type rules, variables beginning with the letters A through H are real, I through L designate integer type, M is complex, N is integer, P is real, and Q through Z designate complex; *except* for names declared explicitly. The REAL and CHARACTER explicit type declarations *do not* apply *in general* to all names beginning with certain letters, but *only* to the specific one-letter names given in the declaration. These explicit type declarations therefore do not modify the implicit rules—all names that begin with L, M, Z, P, Q, or R retain their implicit types, *except* for those individual one-letter names that are explicitly mentioned.

Character length

Every implicit or explicit declaration for names of character type includes *length* information—for example,

```
IMPLICIT CHARACTER*5 (Q, R), CHARACTER*8 (S - Z)
CHARACTER*7 TITLE
```

If the length information is not specified, 1 is used as the default length. In an explicit CHARACTER type declaration, names referring to strings of different lengths may be combined as follows.

```
CHARACTER ABLE*7, BAKER*8, CHARLY*3
```

7.1.2 Array Declarations

The processor must allocate sufficient storage space for every array mentioned in the program, so that the array element names will have proper meaning during execution of the program. Array declarations identify array names and tell the processor how much storage is to be allocated.

An array declaration may be included in an explicit type declaration, simply by including array size information along with the array name:

```
REAL MATRIX(20, 20), ABLE(17)
INTEGER ARRAY(4), CHEK(8, 8)
CHARACTER*50 HAMLET(8)
```

Array names may be combined with other names in a type statement:

```
REAL MATRIX(20, 20), LOOK, J, ABLE(17)
```

If the type for the array name is specified in another explicit type declaration, the array size information must be declared in a DIMENSION statement (to avoid multiple explicit typing for the same name), as follows.

```
REAL MATRIX
INTEGER ARRAY, CHEK
DIMENSION MATRIX(20, 20), ARRAY(4), CHEK(8, 8)
```

A DIMENSION statement may also be used where the array type is specified implicitly:

```
IMPLICIT CHARACTER*8 (A - D), COMPLEX Z
DIMENSION ABLE(17)
```

However, many programmers find it preferable to avoid the use of DIMENSION declarations whenever possible, and to include the array size information in an explicit type statement instead.

Most commonly, the array size information is specified as a list of constants enclosed in parentheses and separated by commas (if there is more than one). Each constant specifies an integer greater than zero. One constant appears for each array *dimension;* Fortran permits arrays of up to seven dimensions. The total number of cells in the array is determined by multiplying together the values of all of these listed constants—for example,

```
REAL W(4), MATRIX(20, 20), FIVES(3, 4, 5, 6, 2)
```

The total number of cells in the linear (one-dimensional) array W is 4; the rectangular (two-dimensional) array *Matrix* consists of 400 cells; and the five-dimensional array *Fives* contains 720 cells.

Storage sequence for array elements

A particular element of an array is designated by an array name along with a list of subscript expressions, one for each array dimension. The values of these expressions collectively specify the particular element of the array. For example, if the value of I is 3 and the value of J is 1, then the following array element names might be used with the above declaration:

```
W(I)
MATRIX(J + 15, I)
FIVES(I, J, 4, 2, J + 1)
```

The value of each subscript expression is at least one and is not greater than the declared bound for the corresponding dimension.

Elements of a linear array are stored in the obvious sequence, that is, in increasing subscript value order. Elements of an array of two or more dimensions are also stored in a sequence of consecutive cells. This sequence depends on the subscript values as follows: The leftmost subscript is varied first, then the next subscript, and so on. This sequence is illustrated for arrays of one, two, and three dimensions in Figs. 6.1–6.3. Figure 7.1 illustrates how a 3 by 3 array, with the declaration

```
REAL A(3, 3)
```

would be allocated to storage cells in the computer. The dotted lines in the figure show additional cells that would be allocated if the declaration were

```
REAL A(3, 4)
```

Cell sequence	1	2	3	4	5	6	7	8	9	10	11	12
	$A_{1,1}$	$A_{2,1}$	$A_{3,1}$	$A_{1,2}$	$A_{2,2}$	$A_{3,2}$	$A_{1,3}$	$A_{2,3}$	$A_{3,3}$			

Fig. 7.1 The elements of a 3 by 3 array are stored in a single sequence of cells.

An array of two or more dimensions is *equivalent,* in a certain sense, to a linear array having the same total number of cells. This "equivalent linear array" is invoked explicitly in certain `EQUIVALENCE` declarations (Section 7.3). For example, suppose that the array declaration is

Type Array name $(\mathcal{L}imit_1, \mathcal{L}imit_2, \mathcal{L}imit_3)$

Then a reference to

Array name $(\mathcal{S}ubscript_1, \mathcal{S}ubscript_2, \mathcal{S}ubscript_3)$

will designate the cell within the "equivalent linear array" whose subscript is

$$\mathcal{S}_1 + \mathcal{L}_1 \cdot (\mathcal{S}_2 - 1) + \mathcal{L}_1 \cdot \mathcal{L}_2 \cdot \mathcal{S}_3 - 1)$$

where $\mathcal{L}$ represents a limit value in the declaration, and $\mathcal{S}$ represents a subscript in the reference.

More general subscript ranges

Fortran permits the more general declaration

Type Array name $(\mathcal{J} : \mathcal{K})$

which specifies that subscript values are to be in the range between $\mathcal{J}$ and $\mathcal{K}$ inclusive. The number of cells in the array is then $\mathcal{K} - \mathcal{J} + 1$; for example,

```
REAL W(0 : 4), X(-3 : 9), M(1 : 4), TT1(6 : 9)
```

Here W has 5 cells, numbered from 0 to 4; X has 13 cells, numbered from -3 to 9; M has 4 cells, numbered from 1 to 4, just as if the declaration M(4) had been used; and *Tt1* has 4 cells, numbered from 6 to 9 inclusive.

Subscript ranges of this form may also be specified in DIMENSION declarations. The form may also be extended to arrays of more than one dimension:

```
DIMENSION X(-3 : 9)
INTEGER THREES(0 : 4, -1 : 3, 6 : 9)
REAL A(0 : 6), B(0 : 6, 0 : 6), C(7, 2 : 8)
```

Here, *Threes* is to be used with three subscripts; the first ranges from 0 to 4, the second from -1 to 3, and the third from 6 to 9. Also A is used with a single subscript that ranges from 0 to 6. B has two subscripts, each between 0 and 6 inclusive. C has 2 subscripts, the first between 1 and 7 and the second between 2 and 8.

The "equivalent linear array" formula for arrays with lower subscript bounds as well as upper bounds of course involves the bound values. Suppose that an array is declared with lower bounds $\mathcal{J}_1$, $\mathcal{J}_2$, $\mathcal{J}_3$, and upper bounds $\mathcal{K}_1$, $\mathcal{K}_2$, $\mathcal{K}_3$. An element is referenced with subscript values $\mathcal{S}_1$, $\mathcal{S}_2$, $\mathcal{S}_3$. The effective subscript value of this element in the equivalent linear array (whose lower subscript range bound is assumed to be 1) is given by the following formula:

$$1 + (\mathcal{S}_1 - \mathcal{J}_1) + (\mathcal{K}_1 - \mathcal{J}_1 + 1) \cdot (\mathcal{S}_2 - \mathcal{J}_2)$$
$$+ (\mathcal{K}_1 - \mathcal{J}_1 + 1) \cdot (\mathcal{K}_2 - \mathcal{J}_2 + 1) \cdot (\mathcal{S}_3 - \mathcal{J}_3).$$

This formula can be extended to more than three dimensions. It is indeed fortunate that the user does not need to work out this formula in order to reference an array. However, two important cases may be verified by reference to this formula.

1. The *first* element of the equivalent linear array, whose effective subscript value is 1, is obtained when each subscript $\mathcal{S}_i$ in the formula is equal in value to the corresponding lower subscript range bound $\mathcal{J}_i$. This element, which is associated with the first storage cell allocated to the array, is known as the *base element*. In certain situations (see Sections 7.3 and 8.3), a reference to the array name designates the base element.

2. The *last* element of the equivalent linear array, whose effective subscript value is equal to the number of elements, is obtained when each subscript $\mathcal{S}_i$ in the formula is equal in value to the corresponding upper subscript range bound $\mathcal{K}_i$.

Note that the upper subscript range bound for the *last* dimension does not appear in this formula; for certain uses in a subprogram (see Section 8.3.2) this last $\mathcal{K}$ value is never specified explicitly.

Role of the array declaration

From the foregoing discussion, we see that an array declaration performs three separate roles.

1. It informs the processor that the declared name is an array name and specifies the number of dimensions of the array. Thus, it "authorizes" use of the array name, along with the specified number of subscript expressions, to form an array element name.

2. It specifies the arrangement of the array elements in relation to the "equivalent linear array," and thus permits the processor to locate a particular array element within the sequence of storage cells occupied by the array.

3. It determines the total number of elements, and hence the total space allocation required, for the array.

7.1.3 Exercises

1. Write array declarations corresponding to each of the following array descriptions. (All lower bounds are 1 unless specified.)

   a) The checkerboard named *Chek* has 8 rows and 8 columns and is of integer type.

   b) The complex array *D* has 7 rows and 10 columns.

   c) *First* is a linear array of 17 character strings, each of length 8; *Second* is a linear array of 7 character strings, each of length 12.

   d) *X*, *Y*, and *Z* are real arrays of 13 elements each; *J* is an integer array of 39 elements.

   e) *Newton* is a linear array whose subscript values may range from 0 to 49, inclusive.

2. Write IMPLICIT statements to achieve the designated implicit typing. Use default implicit typing where possible.

   a) A through F are real; G through H are complex; I through N are integer; O through P are logical; Q through Z are character type of length 7.

   b) A through H are real; I through N are integer; O through Y are double precision; Z is complex.

   c) Default implicit typing, except that C indicates complex.

3. Write declarations as required, to specify that all names that begin with the letter N, except the variable name *N* itself, refer to data of logical type. The variable *N* is of complex type.

Correct any errors found in the declarations in Exercises 4–8. The purpose of each is described above it. Supply any declarations that appear to have been omitted.

4. Arrays *C* and *D* each contain 16 elements.

   ```
   DIMENSION C, D (16)
   ```

5. The array *Del* has 50 rows and 50 columns.

   `DIMENSION (2500, DEL)`

6. The array *Pel* has 50 columns and 50 rows.

   `DIMENSION REL(50, 50)`

7. The array *Kel* has 40 columns and 30 rows.

   `DIMENSION KEL(40, 30)`

8. The array *Kel* has 30 columns and 10 rows. *Rel* is the same size.

   `DIMENSION KEL(10, 30), REL`

9. *Use of subscripts for tallying.* A class of 40 students takes a test consisting of 100 "true-false" questions. After grading the test papers, the instructor assigns letter grades according to the number of questions answered correctly, as follows:

50 or below	F
51–55	D
56–60	C−
61–65	C
66–70	C+
71–75	B−
76–80	B
81–85	B+
86–90	A−
91–95	A
96–100	A+

   Write a program to read each student's name and score, and to print name, score, and letter grade. The program should also count the number of students achieving each of the 11 different letter grades and print a summary of the counts at the end.

10. *Pascal's triangle.* This exercise illustrates the fact that a two-dimensional pattern may often be generated and printed one line at a time, so that storage for only a *linear* array is enough.

    Pascal (1623–1662) showed how to find the number of possible combinations that can be formed when r objects are selected out of a group of n objects; he also showed that the same number is the coefficient of x^r in the binomial expansion of $(1 - x)^n$. The array of these numbers, denoted as $C[n, r]$, where n may be any nonnegative integer and r may be any integer between 0 and n inclusive, is called Pascal's triangle, or the table of binomial coefficients.

    Write a program to calculate all the elements of Pascal's triangle up to row M.

    a) The first row ($n = 0$) contains one entry. Each succeeding row contains one more entry than the preceding row.

    b) The first entry (at $r = 0$) and the last entry (at $r = n$) in each row are 1's.

    c) Each of the other entries in a row is obtained from the formula

    $$C[n, r] = C[n - 1, r] + C[n - 1, r - 1].$$

Thus the elements of row n can be stored, replacing the elements of row $n - 1$, provided that they are calculated in order of *decreasing* values of r. Since only enough storage for one row (at a time) is required, there is no need to provide a doubly subscripted array.

Run your program with 9 as the value of M.

11. A reasonably efficient procedure for calculating individual elements of Pascal's triangle is based on the mathematical definition

$$C[n, r] = \frac{n!}{r! \cdot (n - r)!}.$$

The expression $n!$ represents the factorial of n, that is, the product of all positive integers not exceeding n (see Example 12 in Section 4.1.1). A few examples illustrate the fact that many cancellations occur.

Write a program incorporating the following steps.

a) Read values for n and r (both of which are integers).

b) Assign to *Max* the smaller of r and $n - r$. Assign to *Cnr* the value 1.0.

c) For $i = 1$ to *Max*, assign to *Cnr* a new value obtained by multiplying its old value by the quotient

$(n + 1 - i)/i.$

(Convert the numerator and denominator of this quotient to real type before performing the division.)

d) Round the final value of *Cnr* to obtain *ICnr*; print the integer values n, r, and *ICnr*.

7.2 DATA AND PARAMETER DECLARATIONS

One difficulty with constants is that they are not always constant. It is often necessary to change some constants that are incorporated in the program text. Searching for all the appearances of a certain constant, among the statements of a long program, can be a laborious and error-prone task.

Fortran provides two *declarative* mechanisms for incorporating data values known prior to execution. Either of these can be used to establish a value that is used instead of a numerical constant in the program text. Specifying the value just once, in a declaration that appears ahead of the program body, makes it easier to locate and change later on.

Although DATA declarations and PARAMETER declarations can be used interchangeably for certain purposes, these two mechanisms actually operate quite differently. As we shall see, the DATA statement is especially useful for establishing the *initial* value of a variable that may change during program execution, while the PARAMETER declaration can specify the value of a constant in another *declaration*. Either mechanism may be preferable, depending on other circumstances, for setting a value that will be referenced in an executable statement but will not be changed during execution of the program.

7.2.1 DATA **Declarations**

A DATA declaration specifies data values that are to be assigned "initially," that is, stored in the associated cells *prior* to execution of the program. The general form is

DATA *List of items* / *List of constants* /

The list of items is similar to an input or output list, and the list of constants provides the corresponding values. These may be numerical constants, logical constants, or character constants.

Example 1

```
LOGICAL SW
CHARACTER*5 TITLE
DATA R, S(4), T(1, 3), MT / -9.25, 4.9E3, 5.9, 14 /
DATA SW, TITLE / .TRUE., 'Hello' /
```

The presence of this declaration is equivalent to the execution of the statements

```
R = -9.25
S(4) = 4.9E3
T(1, 3) = 5.9
MT = 14
SW = .TRUE.
TITLE = 'Hello'
```

prior to execution of any of the actual executable statements of the program. Note the one-to-one correspondence between the list of items and the list of constants.

The list of items may include array element names with integer constant expressions for subscripts. An array name may also appear in this list, with the same meaning as an array name in an input or output list (that is, the array name stands for all the elements of the array in storage sequence order: see Section 7.1.2). Substring names may also appear.

Implied DO loops in DATA *declarations*

An implied DO loop may be used in a DATA declaration in the same way as in an input or output list (see Sections 4.1.3 and 4.2).

Example 2

```
DATA (A(I), I = 1, 5) / 5.1, 6.2, 7.3, 8.4, 9.5 /
```

The list of items consists of a single implied DO loop that designates all the elements A_1 through A_5. The parameters (initial value, limit, and increment) must be integer constant expressions. Thus the implied DO loop

```
(A(I), I = J, M)
```

would be invalid even if values for J and M were specified in preceding DATA declarations.

Example 3 A repeat count notation is acceptable within the list of constants:

```
DATA R, (S(I), I = 1, 7), T / 4.4, 5 * 1.5, 2.5, 2 * 21.7 /
```

Five identical values of 1.5 are declared for S_1 through S_5; also both S_7 and T are given the value 21.7.

Example 4 Implied DO loops may be nested. The parameters of the outermost implied DO loop must be integer constant expressions. However, those of the inner loop may also involve integer variables that appear as parameters in the outer list of the same nest. In this example, the limit of the inner loop is I, which is the index variable for the outer loop.

```
DATA ((K(I, J), J = 1, I), I = 1, 8) / 36 * 1 /
```

The lower triangular portion of the array K is initialized with 1's (see Fig. 7.2).

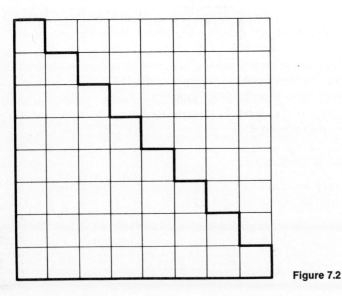

Figure 7.2

Mixed types in DATA declarations

The type of each name in the "list of items" must agree with the type of the corresponding constant when either is of type character or logical. A constant of any numeric type (integer, real, double precision, or complex) may correspond with a name of any numeric type; type conversion will occur automatically if necessary, in the same manner as for mixed-type assignment.

The length of a character list item need not match that of the corresponding character constant. The constant will be extended with blanks on the right or truncated from the right, if necessary (as for assignment), to match the length of the character variable.

7.2.2 PARAMETER Declarations

A PARAMETER declaration creates a "named constant," that is, a symbolic name (having the same appearance as a variable name) that can be used in a program in the same way as a constant. The use of named constants in executable statements should be considered as an alternative to using a variable whose value is set initially in a DATA statement.

Declarations, on the other hand, do not permit the inclusion of variables whose values are established during execution, or even just prior to execution in a DATA statement. A named constant, however, may be declared in a PARAMETER statement and then used in any declaration (except a FORMAT declaration) that follows it in the program text.

Example 5

```
PARAMETER (N = 100)
REAL MATRIX(N, N), W(N)
```

Here *Matrix* is declared as a 100 by 100 rectangular array, and *W* as a linear array of 100 cells. To change the size of *Matrix* to 50 by 50, while decreasing *W* to 50 cells as well, it is necessary merely to change the value of *N* specified in the PARAMETER statement to 50.

A PARAMETER declaration consists of the word PARAMETER, followed by a parenthesized list of pseudo-assignments. Each of these consists of a name (which is thereby declared to refer to a named constant), followed by an equals sign and an expression. The expression is composed of constants including previously declared named constants; it must not contain variables, array element references, or function references. The pseudo-assignment may involve mixed types in the same manner as an actual assignment statement; the type associated with the named constant is determined (implicitly or explicitly) by the declared name in the usual way.

Example 6

```
PARAMETER (LEN = 3)
IMPLICIT CHARACTER * (LEN) (A - C)
DIMENSION CABLE(10)
PARAMETER (ABLE = 'abc', J = 4, M = 7, NJM = 4)
DATA (CABLE(I), I = J, M) / NJM * '□□□' /
```

The first PARAMETER statement establishes the length for the character string declaration in the IMPLICIT statement. The fourth statement is another PA-RAMETER declaration that establishes the named character constant *Able* with the value `'abc'`, as well as setting up some values for use in the DATA declaration that follows.

When a named constant of character type is declared in a PARAMETER statement, it is not necessary to explicitly declare its length. An explicit type declaration, designating the name to be of character type, may include an *indefinite* length specification when the name is to refer to a constant—for example,

```
CHARACTER*(*) WORD
PARAMETER (WORD = 'Supercalifragilisticexpialidocious')
```

An asterisk replaces the length specification in the type declaration; the actual length of the named constant *Word* is taken from the length of the string appearing in the PARAMETER declaration. Note that such an indefinite length can only be declared *explicitly;* an implicit type declaration must include a definite length for character strings that begin with designated letters.

7.2.3   Exercises

1. The program of Example 7 in Section 4.1.1 (and Fig. 4.6) may be used to compute the terms of the classical Fibonacci sequence. Modify the program of Section 4.1.1 as follows.

   a) Read the value of M, but initialize Fi and Fj to 1 by means of a DATA declaration.

   b) The ratio of successive Fibonacci numbers approaches the constant

   $$\alpha = \frac{1 + \sqrt{5}}{2},$$

   which has been admired since classical Greek times as the "golden ratio" or "golden section"; it is the ratio of the sides a and b of a rectangle such that $(a/b) = ((a + b)/a)$. At the end of each traversal of the loop, insert a statement to print the value of the ratio Fj/Fi. When the value of K reaches the input value, *M,* print the "theoretical" value of this ratio, which may be computed as

```
0.5 + SQRT (1.25)
```

2. Write three short programs, each of which will print a character string containing your name. In the first program, include your name as a character constant in a PRINT statement. In the second, replace the constant by a character variable and preassign your name to the variable in a DATA declaration. In the third, the output list will include a named constant (having the same form as the variable in the second program) whose value is specified in a PARAMETER statement.

7.3 THE EQUIVALENCE DECLARATION

It is frequently desirable to have two or more names referring to the same storage cells. The motivation for such space sharing may vary. In these examples we shall see how the EQUIVALENCE declaration is used for this purpose.

Example 1 We may wish to inform the processor that certain groups of names are to be considered synonymous: *N* and *Number;* B_1 and *Bone;* and *Hrs, Hours,* and *Time.* The following declarations will achieve these objectives.

```
EQUIVALENCE (N, NUMBER)
EQUIVALENCE (B(1), BONE)
EQUIVALENCE (HRS, HOURS, TIME)
```

We may also combine the declarations above into one.

```
EQUIVALENCE (N, NUMBER), (B(1), BONE), (HRS, HOURS, TIME)
```

All the names enclosed in a given set of parentheses form an *equivalence class.* Any number of such equivalence classes can be declared in a single declaration. Within one equivalence class the order is immaterial.

The names in each equivalence class may be array element names, but the subscripts must be integer constant expressions. Thus, in the second example, B(I) could not have been used (unless *I* were a named constant).

An array name (without a subscript) may appear in an equivalence class. The effect is to specify the *base element* of the array (see Section 7.1.2), that is, the element specified by the lowest subscript value in the declared range for each dimension, which is the first element in the equivalent linear array.

Example 2 Another frequent reason for forming equivalence classes is to conserve storage by allowing values for variables that may be used at quite different times during execution of the program to reside in the same cells. Thus, the linear array elements $B_1, B_2, \ldots, B_{10}$ and $C_1, C_2, \ldots, C_{10}$ may be allowed to share the same cells, if we declare

```
EQUIVALENCE (B(1), C(1))
```

Note that the relationship thus established for elements B_1 and C_1 is sufficient to establish automatically the relationship between B_2 and C_2, between B_3 and C_3, and so on. Since it is the base elements of the two arrays that are specified in the foregoing declaration, we can alternatively write simply

```
EQUIVALENCE (B, C)
```

In general, when an element of one array appears in an equivalence class with an element of another array, the remaining elements of both arrays are automatically made equivalent through a positional correspondence, as illustrated in Figs. 7.3 through 7.6.

The motive of storage conservation is even more important with large arrays. For example, suppose that early in the execution of a program we need a 24 by 60 array, and then later in the program, after we are finished with that one, we

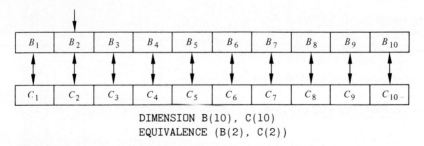

```
DIMENSION B(10), C(10)
EQUIVALENCE (B(2), C(2))
```

Fig. 7.3 Full overlap of two linear arrays.

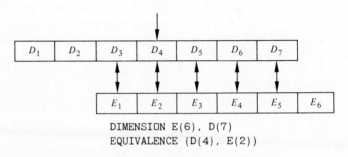

```
DIMENSION E(6), D(7)
EQUIVALENCE (D(4), E(2))
```

Fig. 7.4 Partial overlap of two linear arrays.

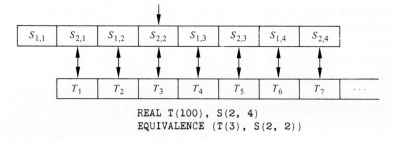

REAL T(100), S(2, 4)
EQUIVALENCE (T(3), S(2, 2))

Fig. 7.5 Partial overlap of a linear array and a rectangular array.

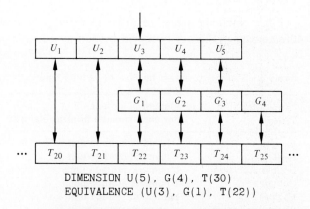

DIMENSION U(5), G(4), T(30)
EQUIVALENCE (U(3), G(1), T(22))

Fig. 7.6 Partial overlap of three linear arrays.

need a 90 by 16 array. Since each array occupies 1440 cells, we can save storage by declaring the two arrays to be equivalent. We could not use the same name for both arrays since there is no element subscripted (90, 16), for example, in the first array. The use here of an equivalence declaration is a reasonable way to conserve space.

Example 3   Sometimes we wish to refer to an element of an array of two or more dimensions, alternatively in the same program, with a single subscript denoting the linear position of the element in the equivalent linear array (discussed in Section 7.1.2). For example, suppose that we have declared P to be a 3 by 3 array. Then in subsequent statements, the name P must be used with two subscripts. If we wish to refer to the sixth element, $P_{3,2}$, with the single subscript 6, we can call the array by a new name, say Q, and refer to the element as Q_6. Appropriate declarations would be

REAL P(3, 3), Q(9)
EQUIVALENCE (P, Q)

Example 4 If proper care is exercised, the EQUIVALENCE declaration may be used so that variables of different types may occupy the same cells. Suppose that we wish to store integers in column 8 of a real array named *Harry.* We can do so if an array of type integer, say *Jerry,* is declared to be equivalent to a portion of the array *Harry.* We can then use the array name *Jerry* when we wish to manipulate elements of column 8, but we will use the array name *Harry* when manipulating elements in any of the other columns. If *Harry* is a 5 by 18 array, then suitable declarations might be

```
DIMENSION HARRY(5, 18), JERRY(5)
EQUIVALENCE (HARRY(1, 8), JERRY)
```

In combining arrays of different types, it is necessary to take into account the amount of storage occupied by data of each type, as displayed in Table 7.1.

Table 7.1 Storage occupied by data of various types

Type	Amount of storage (for each variable or array element)
Integer	1 numeric storage unit
Real	1 numeric storage unit
Double precision	2 numeric storage units
Complex	2 numeric storage units
Logical	1 numeric storage unit
Character (length n)	n character storage units

Any numeric type (integer, real, double precision, or complex) can be combined with any other numeric type or with logical type. When combining integer, real, or logical with double precision or complex, it is important to allocate sufficient space for the complex or double precision data.

Character data is not permitted to share storage with numeric or logical data, since the space correspondence between numeric and character storage units depends on the processor. However, several arrays or variables of character type may be declared equivalent to each other.

7.3.1 Partial Equivalence

Figures 7.5, 7.6, and 7.7 illustrate partial overlap of arrays. It may be noted that array elements with subscript values *smaller* than that mentioned in the EQUIVALENCE declaration are also made equivalent.

Each element of a complex array consists of two real data items, the first of which is the real part and the second of which is the imaginary part of the complex element. Partial equivalence may be used to relate two complex arrays in

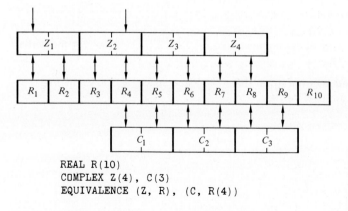

```
REAL R(10)
COMPLEX Z(4), C(3)
EQUIVALENCE (Z, R), (C, R(4))
```

Fig. 7.7 Partial equivalence of complex arrays.

such a way that an element of one is associated with parts of two elements of the other, as shown in Fig. 7.7. A real array may also be included in the same equivalence class.

Character arrays

All the elements of a character array are combined into a single storage sequence. Thus the total number of character storage units occupied by a character array is found by multiplying the length of each element by the number of elements.

Figure 7.8 illustrates several overlapping character variables and arrays. Note that substring names may appear in an equivalence class; they specify the position within a string that will determine the equivalence relations among the variables and array elements of character type. The specified character storage position is the *first* character of the designated substring.

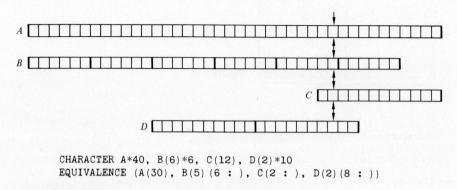

```
CHARACTER A*40, B(6)*6, C(12), D(2)*10
EQUIVALENCE (A(30), B(5)(6 : ), C(2 : ), D(2)(8 : ))
```

Fig. 7.8 Equivalence of strings and arrays of character type.

7.3.2 Exercises

Write the appropriate array declarations and EQUIVALENCE declarations for the verbal statements in Exercises 1–5.

1. Two arrays, A and B, overlap or share the same space, as shown in Fig. 7.9. Array A is 8 by 8 and B is 8 by 6.

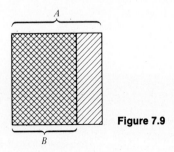

Figure 7.9

2. The array A described in the preceding exercise must occasionally be referred to in executable steps of the program with a single subscript. How can this be done?

3. An array called *Deck* has 13 rows and 4 columns. Each column of this array is also to be referred to by a different name. The alternative name for the first column is *Spades*, for the second *Hearts*, for the third *Diamds*, and for the fourth *Clubs*.

4. A region of storage totaling 200 consecutive cells is to be used as shown in Fig. 7.10. The rectangular array A is 10 by 15 and begins at the first cell. The rectangular array B is 10 by 10 and begins in cell 101. (This cell is also called $A_{11,1}$.) The linear array C also begins at the first cell and contains 200 elements.

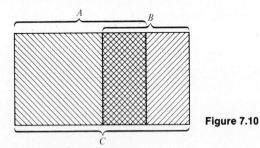

Figure 7.10

5. Store both real and integer values in the same space, a 3 by 5 array. Denote the real array by RA and the integer array by IA.

Correct errors or supply missing declarations in Exercises 6–8.

6. The array F has 3 rows and 4 columns; G_8 occupies the same cell as $F_{2,2}$.

```
REAL F(34), G(44)
EQUIVALENCE (F(22), G(8))
```

7. The array *Cube* is 3 by 3 by 3 and lies totally within the linear array *Kube,* with $Cube_{2,2,2}$ occupying the same cell as $Kube_{20}$.

   ```
   REAL CUBE(27), KUBE(25)
   EQUIVALENCE (CUBE(4), KUBE(21))
   ```

8. The array *Dice* is 2 by 2 by 2, and $Dice_{2,2,1}$ occupies the same cell as $Kube_{20}$.

   ```
   REAL DICE(2, 2, 2), KUBE(25)
   EQUIVALENCE (DICE(1), KUBE(17)
   ```

7.4 PLACEMENT OF PROGRAM STATEMENTS

In general, all declarations except FORMAT statements must precede the executable statements of a program. Fortran also has some detailed rules concerning the placement of various kinds of declarations. Rather than discuss these rules in detail, we present here a suggested sequence of placement of statements that will satisfy the requirements of Fortran in most cases. For completeness, we include in this list some statements that have not yet been mentioned in the text; these are introduced in Chapter 8.

1. PROGRAM, SUBROUTINE, FUNCTION, or BLOCK DATA statement (see Chapter 8)
2. IMPLICIT declarations, explicit type declarations, and PARAMETER declarations (see note below)
3. Array declarations, including DIMENSION declarations
4. COMMON declarations (see Chapter 8)
5. EQUIVALENCE declarations
6. EXTERNAL declarations (see Chapter 8)
7. DATA declarations
8. Statement function definitions (see Chapter 8)
9. Executable statements, ENTRY statements (see Chapter 8), and FORMAT statements
10. END statement

Note: An IMPLICIT declaration or an explicit type declaration for character type may include a named constant for the length specification. Also, an explicit type declaration may include named constants as array bounds. Such declarations would necessarily follow the PARAMETER statements that define those named constants used in the declarations. Otherwise, type declarations should precede PARAMETER statements because the constant name need not be of default implicit type. Example 6, Section 7.2.2, illustrates these points.

CHAPTER 8
DEFINING AND USING SUBPROGRAMS

8.1 INTRODUCTION

In Section 2.3 we learned to use predefined functions such as ABS and SQRT. We often find that a function or special procedure that would be particularly suitable for the program we are writing is not included among the predefined functions. It is then up to us to define the procedure. In this chapter we see how to define procedures using the Fortran language. When supplied to the computer along with our main program, a procedure can be referred to in much the same way as a predefined function.

Motivation for using procedures

During the course of developing a computer program for some task, we may notice that the same sequence of steps appears at more than one point in the program. Of course, it is possible to repeat the same sequence of program statements at each of these points. On the other hand, this chapter shows how we might write the special sequence of statements just once, and refer to it from various points.

There are at least two reasons why this latter approach might be desirable. First, it avoids the (often error-prone) task of writing the same statements repeatedly and it shortens the program. More important, it increases the comprehensibility of the program. We can analyze and develop the special statement sequence independently, and we can understand references to it (from the main sequence) at a higher and less detailed level of refinement (as discussed in Section 1.4).

Example 1

To illustrate these ideas, we consider the following program, which was explained in Section 3.1.4 (Example 20), to arrange three data values into ascending order.

```
READ *, A, B, C
IF (A .GT. B) THEN
    AUX = A
    A = B
    B = AUX
  END IF
IF (B .GT. C) THEN
    AUX = B
    B = C
    C = AUX
    IF (A .GT. B) THEN
        AUX = A
        A = B
        B = AUX
      END IF
  END IF
PRINT *, A, B, C
END
```

We now suggest that the statements for interchanging a pair of data values be written as a separate *procedure,* which can then be referred to as needed (see also Fig. 8.1).

```
* Program to arrange three data values in ascending order
      PROGRAM ASCEND
      READ *, A, B, C
      IF (A .GT. B) CALL SWAP (A, B)
      IF (B .GT. C) THEN
          CALL SWAP (B, C)
          IF (A .GT. B) CALL SWAP (A, B)
        END IF
      PRINT *, A, B, C
      END
* Procedure to interchange a pair of data values
      SUBROUTINE SWAP (X, Y)
      AUX = X
      X = Y
      Y = AUX
      RETURN
      END
```

(The **PROGRAM** statement will be discussed in Section 8.1.1.)

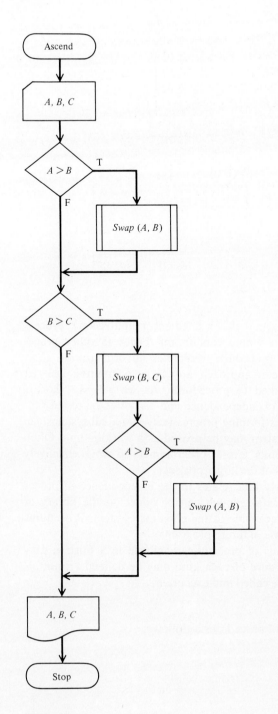

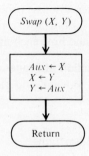

Figure 8.1

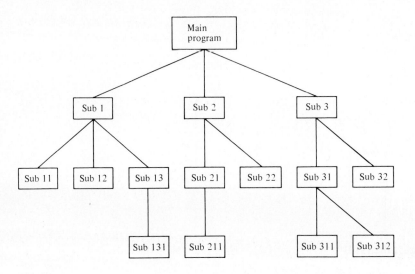

Figure 8.2

Sometimes it is desirable to carry this refinement (subdivision) process even further, so that one procedure may contain references to other procedures. The resulting hierarchy of procedures resembles an organization chart (see Fig. 8.2). If we wish, we can approach any large computing task by viewing it as a main program linked to procedures. As we will see shortly, each procedure possesses a degree of independence and can often be tested separately. Groups of tested procedures forming progressively larger subsystems can be tested, until finally the entire system may be proved as a working unit. Often the independence of the parts permits several programmers to work effectively under one supervisor on subsections of the larger project.

There is another useful property that relates to the independence of procedures. A procedure that proves useful enough can be added to the library of "predefined" procedures that are accessible to the computer system. Procedures in the library become available for use in future programs.

This chapter discusses the kinds of procedures available to a Fortran programmer. It describes how a procedure of each kind may be defined (if not already defined) and how each may be called into execution.

8.1.1 Classification of Procedures

We may classify the different kinds of procedures as follows:

Subroutines
Functions
    External functions
    Statement functions
    Predefined functions

There are some differences in the ways in which these procedures are defined and referenced.

Subroutines

A subroutine is defined by an independent block of statements prepared by the programmer, and is referenced *explicitly* by means of a CALL statement.

Functions

A function is not referenced explicitly by a separate CALL statement; rather it is referenced *implicitly,* merely by the appearance of the function name as part of an expression.

External functions. An external function is defined by an independent block of statements prepared by the programmer. Thus it differs from a subroutine mainly in the way in which it is referenced.

Statement functions. Whereas a subroutine or external function is defined independently, a statement function is defined by a single statement that appears within the main program (or subroutine or external function) that references it. Section 8.6 describes the way in which statement functions are defined, and the special rules that apply when they are referenced.

Predefined functions. Predefined functions are referenced in the same way as external functions. The only difference is that the programmer may use a predefined function without being concerned about defining it.

Program units

The block of statements that defines a subroutine or an external function is called a *subprogram.* Subprograms and main programs are *program units.* Each program unit consists of a collection of Fortran statement lines and comment lines, beginning with a distinctive statement and ending with an END line. A subroutine begins with a SUBROUTINE statement; an external function begins with a FUNCTION statement; a main program may begin with a PROGRAM statement (or this statement may be omitted). Another form of subprogram, the *block data subprogram,* which cannot be referenced as a procedure, is described in Section 8.5.2. A block data subprogram begins with a BLOCK DATA statement.

A complete program consists of one main program and all the subprograms (if any) that it references. If these subprograms reference other subprograms in turn, they must be included as well. In order for a main program to be executed, all the subprograms must be made available to the processor. Predefined functions are automatically made available without any action being needed to supply them.

8.1.2 Procedure Reference

A subroutine or external function may be referenced more than once from the same program unit, just as the predefined functions SQRT, ABS, and so on, may be used more than once. Whenever a procedure reference is executed, the effect is much the same as if all the statements of the subprogram were copied into the referencing program unit at the point where the reference appears.

Subroutine reference

A subroutine must be referenced explicitly, by means of a special statement of the form

    CALL *Name* (*Argument list*)

Execution of a CALL statement suspends execution of the program unit containing the call; execution proceeds with the statements of the subprogram that defines the subroutine, beginning with the first executable statement in the subroutine.

Example   The statement

    CALL SWAP (A, B)

calls explicitly for the execution of a subroutine named *Swap,* which requires two arguments.

Subroutine calls may require no arguments, one argument, or many arguments. If there is more than one, the arguments inside the parentheses are set apart by commas. If there are no arguments, the parentheses may be omitted and the following simpler form may be used:

    CALL *Name*

Function reference

Functions (including external functions, predefined functions, and statement functions) are referenced implicitly by the appearance of the function name as part of an expression. Execution of a function reference results in the calculation of a single *function value* or result that is substituted in the expression at the point where the function name appears. For example, in the statement

    Y = A + B * SQRT (X)

a numerical value is defined to replace SQRT (X) in the expression on the right, thus permitting calculation of a single numerical value that can be assigned to *Y*. The function reference, SQRT (X), may therefore be said to "have a value" that is *returned* to the expression and replaces the function name, at the point where the reference appears.

A function reference may require no arguments, one argument, or many arguments. If there are two or more arguments inside the parentheses in a function reference, they are separated by commas. In the statement

```
Y = A + AREA (X, R) * C
```

the value of a function, *Area,* whose arguments are X and R, is returned. (This value is multiplied by the value of C, and the value of A is added to obtain the expression value that will be assigned to Y.)

If there are no arguments, the function name must be followed by an empty pair of parentheses:

```
Y = A + FUN ( ) * C
```

Unlike the subroutine reference in a CALL statement, a function reference without the parentheses is prohibited. (Without the parentheses, the processor would assume that *Fun* is a variable.)

Type of a function reference

Since a *value* is associated with the execution of a function reference, a specific *type* must be considered to apply to the reference. For an external function or a statement function, the type is determined from the function name in the usual way, by default implicit typing, declared implicit typing, or explicit typing.

In the simplest case, the value returned by an external function or statement function is of real or integer type, as determined by applying the default implicit typing rules to the function name.

On the other hand, an external function definition may include statements that declare a different type for the function name. In this case, the program unit that references the external function must also include an implicit or explicit type declaration that applies to the function name.

The type of the result from a predefined function reference is not determined from the form of the function name. Default implicit typing does not apply to predefined function names, and implicit or explicit type declarations have no effect. Table 8.1 contains a list of predefined function names, along with the acceptable argument types and corresponding result types for each of these functions.

It may be noted that many of these functions accept arguments of more than one type, and they return a result whose type may depend on the type of the argument. In effect, the name of such a function is a *generic* name for a family of related functions. The functions in a given family perform similar operations, but they differ with regard to the types of arguments and results, while sharing

Table 8.1 Predefined function names

Operation	Function name	Number of arguments	Type of arguments†	Type of result
Type conversion with truncation	INT	1	Integer, real, double, complex	Integer
Type conversion with rounding	NINT	1	Real, double	Integer
Type conversion	REAL	1	Integer, real, double, complex	Real
Type conversion	DBLE	1	Integer, real, double, complex	Double
Type conversion	CMPLX	1 or 2	Integer, real, double, complex	Complex
Type conversion	ICHAR	1	Character	Integer
Type conversion	CHAR	1	Integer	Character
Truncation	AINT	1	Real, double	Same as argument
Rounding	ANINT	1	Real, double	Same as argument
Absolute value	ABS	1	Complex	Real
		1	Integer, real, double	Same as argument
Remainder	MOD	2	Integer, real, double	Same as argument
Sign transfer	SIGN	2	Integer, real, double	Same as argument
Excess	DIM	2	Integer, real, double	Same as argument
Double product	DPROD	2	Real	Double
Largest value	MAX	2 or more	Integer, real, double	Same as argument
Smallest value	MIN	2 or more	Integer, real, double	Same as argument
Character length	LEN	1	Character	Integer
Pattern match location	INDEX	2	Character	Integer

† All arguments in a given reference must be of the same type.

the same generic name. Therefore, it is not always possible to determine the type of a predefined function reference from the name alone, without also taking into account the type of the arguments used in the reference.

For example, it was pointed out in Section 2.3.1 that the function *Abs* will produce a result of real type when its argument is a real expression, but the re-

Table 8.1 (cont.)

Operation	Function name	Number of arguments	Type of arguments†	Type of result
Imaginary part	AIMAG	1	Complex	Real
Complex conjugate	CONJG	1	Complex	Complex
Square root	SQRT	1	Real, double, complex	Same as argument
Exponential	EXP	1	Real, double, complex	Same as argument
Natural logarithm	LOG	1	Real, double, complex	Same as argument
Common logarithm	LOG10	1	Real, double	Same as argument
Sine	SIN	1	Real, double, complex	Same as argument
Cosine	COS	1	Real, double, complex	Same as argument
Tangent	TAN	1	Real, double	Same as argument
Arcsine	ASIN	1	Real, double	Same as argument
Arccosine	ACOS	1	Real, double	Same as argument
Arctangent	ATAN ATAN2	1 2	Real, double	Same as argument
Hyperbolic sine	SINH	1	Real, double	Same as argument
Hyperbolic cosine	COSH	1	Real, double	Same as argument
Hyperbolic tangent	TANH	1	Real, double	Same as argument
ASCII compare	LGE	2	Character	Logical
ASCII compare	LGT	2	Character	Logical
ASCII compare	LLE	2	Character	Logical
ASCII compare	LLT	2	Character	Logical

† All arguments in a given reference must be of the same type.

sult is of integer type when its argument is an integer expression. Similarly, predefined mathematical functions such as *Sqrt, Log, Exp, Sin,* and *Cos* can be used with real, double precision, or complex arguments to produce a result of the corresponding type. (Note that when a predefined function name is used with two or more arguments, all must be of the same type at a given reference.)

8.2 DEFINING A SUBROUTINE OR EXTERNAL FUNCTION

A subroutine or an external function is defined by means of a subprogram, which consists of a collection of Fortran statement lines and comment lines. The first statement in a subroutine definition is a SUBROUTINE statement, and the first statement in an external function definition is a FUNCTION statement. (Either of these may be preceded by one or more comment lines.) The last line in the subprogram must be an END line (see Section 3.3).

The SUBROUTINE or FUNCTION statement gives the name of the procedure that is being defined, and lists its *dummy arguments,* if any. Thus, the processor is able to determine that the collection of statements is a subprogram rather than a main program.

One or more RETURN statements may appear in a subprogram to terminate execution of the sequence of statements in the subprogram, thus causing execution of the referencing program unit to resume and to proceed from the point where the reference appeared. Execution of an END statement in a subprogram has the same effect as a RETURN statement.

Subprogram patterns

The pattern of Fortran statements for a subprogram can be represented in skeleton form. The pattern for a subroutine subprogram is

```
SUBROUTINE Name (List of dummy arguments)
    .
    .
    .
RETURN
    .
    .
    .
END
```

while the pattern for an (external) function subprogram is

```
FUNCTION Name (List of dummy arguments)
    .
    .
    .
Name = Expression
    .
    .
    .
RETURN
    .
    .
    .
END
```

Examples of SUBROUTINE **and** FUNCTION **statements**

```
SUBROUTINE SWAP (X, Y)
SUBROUTINE FIND (A, N, X, LOC)
SUBROUTINE REVERS (A, N)
SUBROUTINE SWAPIT (INT1, STR1, INT2, STR2)
FUNCTION IFACT (K)
FUNCTION SIGNAL (X)
FUNCTION SCAPR (X, Y, N)
FUNCTION STRING (A, B)
```

A subprogram name is formed in the same way as a variable or an array name: It consists of between one and six letters and digits, the first of which must be a letter. Since a function name will acquire a value, the proper type must be associated with the name (see Section 8.2.2). Subroutine names, on the other hand, have no type associated with them.

When a subprogram is referenced, the first step executed will be the first executable statement appearing in the subprogram. The last step executed before resuming execution of the referencing program unit will be a RETURN (or END) statement. There may be several RETURN statements in a subprogram, and a RETURN statement is permitted as the dependent statement of a logical IF statement. Thus the RETURN statement in a subprogram plays a role exactly analogous to that of the STOP statement in a main program (see Section 3.3). A STOP statement may also be used in a subprogram to terminate execution of the entire program. Note, however, that execution of an END statement in a subprogram has the same effect as a RETURN statement, whereas in a main program it acts as a STOP.

We see that a RETURN (or END) statement in a subprogram specifies that the sequence of execution of the statements of the subprogram is to be discontinued, and that execution is to resume and proceed from the point of the reference in the program unit which made reference to the subprogram.

Some basic rules for defining and referencing procedures

Before illustrating in detail the statements used to define and to refer to subroutine and function subprograms, we will state some simple basic rules. Additional rules will be mentioned later.

1. *Dummy arguments* (which appear in the first statement of the subroutine or function subprogram) may be variables or array names of any type. (They *must not* be constants, array element names, or other expressions.)

2. The *actual arguments* used in the reference to the subprogram may be constants, variable names, array names, array element names, or expressions. The type of each actual argument must match that of the corresponding dummy argument.

3. The actual arguments in the reference should agree in *number, order, type,* and *array size* with the dummy arguments.

4. A subprogram may have no arguments, one argument, or more than one argument. If there are no arguments, a FUNCTION statement must include an empty pair of parentheses, but in a SUBROUTINE statement the empty parentheses are optional. Thus the first statement of a subprogram may have any of the following forms:

```
SUBROUTINE Name (List of dummy arguments)
SUBROUTINE Name ( )
SUBROUTINE Name
FUNCTION Name (List of dummy arguments)
FUNCTION Name ( )
```

5. To designate the value to be returned, in a *function* subprogram it is necessary to use the *function name* as though it were a variable. The value that is to be returned must be assigned to this name. Assignment can be achieved in any valid manner; the most common way is with an assignment statement of the form

$$Name = Expression$$

where the expression can have any legitimate form. The value returned by the function is the value of this expression, and its type is that of the function name. (There are other ways to give a value to the function name, such as including it in an input list.) A value is not given to the subroutine name in a subroutine subprogram.

6. The statements in a subprogram must not reference, directly or indirectly, the procedure being defined by the subprogram. In other words, a subroutine must not call itself, and a function subprogram must not contain a reference to its own name (as a procedure name) in an expression. Furthermore, execution of a procedure must not cause activation of another procedure that in turn activates the first procedure (either directly, or indirectly via a further chain of procedure references).

8.2.1 Defining a Subroutine

In this section, we present a number of examples showing how subroutines may be defined. In each case we also show a simple main program that might be used to reference the subroutine.

Example 1   Most of the elements of a given array are zeros. We wish to locate the nonzero elements and move them to a smaller array; we also wish to keep a

record of the position (within the original array) at which each of the nonzero
elements was found. The subroutine *Find* (see Figs. 8.3 and 8.4) locates the

```
* Subroutine to locate the next nonzero element, at
* position N or beyond, in an array A containing 100
* elements. X will be set to the value of the element
* found, and Loc will be set to the position in A at
* which it was found. If there are no nonzero elements in
* A at position N or beyond, X will be set to zero and Loc
* will be set to 101.
        SUBROUTINE FIND (A, N, X, LOC)
        REAL A(100)
        DO 7, LOC = N, 100
          IF (A(LOC) .NE. 0.0) THEN
              X = A(LOC)
              GO TO 8
          END IF
7       CONTINUE
        X = 0.0
8       CONTINUE
        RETURN
        END
```

Figure 8.3

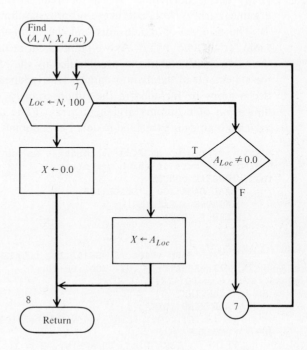

Figure 8.4

next nonzero element in the array A (beyond a specified position), and returns the element value and the position at which it was found. The main program in Figs. 8.5 and 8.6 uses *Find* to construct the condensed array.

The subprogram *Find* has four dummy arguments. These are

1. The array, A, to be searched;
2. The beginning search position, N;
3. The resulting nonzero element value, X; and
4. The location, *Loc,* where the nonzero element was found in A.

The main program specifies that the array named *Data* is to be searched, beginning at position J. The third and fourth actual arguments, in the CALL statement, name the cells in which the nonzero element value and its location are to be stored.

We note the following points.

1. The subroutine definition corresponds to the pattern shown above.
2. In the main program, actual arguments in each reference to the subroutine agree in number, order, type, and array size with the corresponding dummy arguments in the subprogram.
3. Array declarations must appear both in the main program for the actual argument array, *Data,* and in the subprogram for the dummy argument array, A. The number of dimensions and the number of elements should be the same for the two arrays. As we pointed out at the beginning of this chapter, the subprogram statements are handled by the processor independently from the statements of the main program. This independence requires that separate declarations be included in the subprogram to specify the bounds for each dimension of a dummy argument array. (The use of array arguments with variable bounds is explained in detail in Section 8.3.2.)

```
* Main program using Find to condense an array of 100
* elements, most of which are zeros.
      PROGRAM CONDNS
      REAL DATA(100), SMALL(100)
      INTEGER LOCATE(10)
      READ *, DATA
      J = 1
      DO 50, I = 1, 10
        CALL FIND (DATA, J, SMALL(I), LOCATE(I))
        IF (LOCATE(I) .GT. 100) GO TO 60
        J = LOCATE(I) + 1
50      CONTINUE
      CALL FIND (DATA, J, R, K)
      IF (K .GT. 100) PRINT *, 'More⎵than⎵10⎵nonzero⎵elements.'
60    CONTINUE
      PRINT *, (SMALL(M), LOCATE(M), M = 1, I − 1)
      END
```

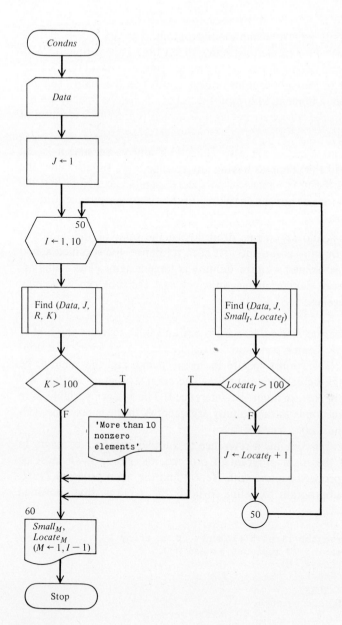

Figure 8.6

 Figure 8.5

4. Two CALL statements appear in the main program. The first of these is inside a loop, so it will be executed as many as ten times. Each time a CALL statement is executed, control passes to the subroutine. Execution of the RETURN statement in the subprogram returns control to the main program, continuing with the statement following the CALL. Note the special *predefined process* box in the flowchart in Fig. 8.6, which represents execution of the entire subroutine.

5. The subroutine name *Find* is not associated with any value, and it is not meaningful to regard this name as having any specific type. In particular, the initial letter of a subroutine name has no special significance. Note that the subroutine name does not appear anywhere in the subprogram except in the beginning statement.

6. The names of the actual arguments need not be the same as the names of the corresponding dummy arguments. At each reference, the specified actual argument value is associated with the dummy argument name. The actual arguments may be array element names, in which case the subscript value may change at each reference.

Example 2 The subroutine *Revers* (see Figs. 8.7 and 8.8) reverses the first N elements of the array A (which can hold 200 elements). A program unit containing a reference to *Revers* must specify the array name, and the value to be associated with N, in the actual argument list. The simple program in Figs. 8.9 and 8.10 illustrates how *Revers* might be referenced. The integer variable L in this main program corresponds to the dummy argument N in the subroutine. (Of course, the value of L must not exceed 200.)

The subroutine *Revers* contains a reference to another subroutine, *Swap*. In order for execution of the main program to procced, therefore, *Swap* must be made available to the processor along with *Revers* and the main program *Test1*. We assume that the subprogram to define *Swap* is the same as that shown in Example 1 in Section 8.1.

```
* Subroutine to reverse the first N elements of an array A
* containing 200 elements. (N must not exceed 200.)
      SUBROUTINE REVERS (A, N)
      REAL A(200)
      IF (N .GT. 200) THEN
         PRINT *, 'N is too large.'
         STOP
       END IF
      MIDDLE = N / 2
      DO 10, I = 1, MIDDLE
         CALL SWAP (A(I), A(N + 1 - I))
 10      CONTINUE
      RETURN
      END
```

Figure 8.7

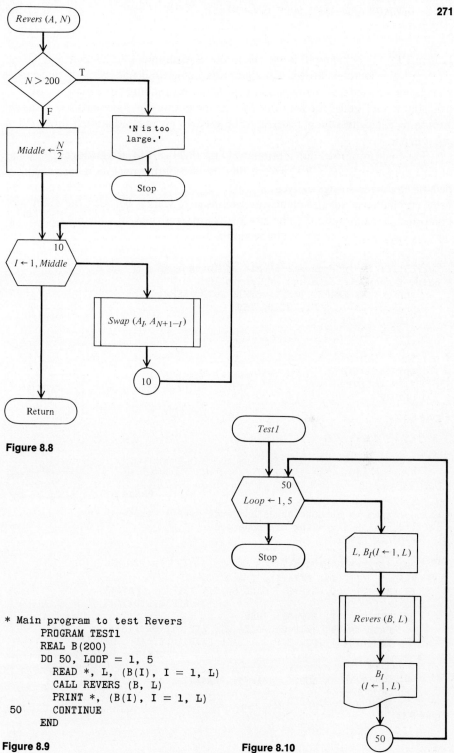

Figure 8.8

Figure 8.9

```
* Main program to test Revers
      PROGRAM TEST1
      REAL B(200)
      DO 50, LOOP = 1, 5
         READ *, L, (B(I), I = 1, L)
         CALL REVERS (B, L)
         PRINT *, (B(I), I = 1, L)
50       CONTINUE
      END
```

Figure 8.10

Example 3 This example is an extension of Example 1 in Section 8.1. Given an array of character strings containing the names and addresses of three individuals, and an integer array containing the corresponding zip codes, we wish to print the names and addresses in order of increasing zip codes. This is a simple *sorting* problem, in which a *key* is to be used to arrange additional information in sequence.

The main program and subroutine (Figs. 8.11–8.14) are analogous to those of Example 1 in Section 8.1, except that the subroutine must now interchange a pair of character strings as well as a pair of integer values. Note the agreement between character string lengths, as well as array sizes, between the main program and the subroutine. (The use of character strings of indefinite length as dummy arguments is explained in Section 8.3.3.)

```
* Subroutine to interchange a pair of integer values and a
* pair of character strings of length 100.
      SUBROUTINE SWAPIT (INT1, STR1, INT2, STR2)
      CHARACTER*100 STR1, STR2, TEMP
      ITEMP = INT1
      TEMP = STR1
      INT1 = INT2
      STR1 = STR2
      INT2 = ITEMP
      STR2 = TEMP
      RETURN
```
Figure 8.11

```
Swapit
(Int1, Str1,
Int2, Str2)
```

```
Itemp ← Int1
Temp ← Str1
Int1 ← Int2
Str1 ← Str2
Int2 ← Itemp
Str2 ← Temp
```

```
Return
```
Figure 8.12

```
* Main program to arrange names and addresses of three
* individuals in ascending zip code order
      PROGRAM ZIPPY
      INTEGER ZIP(3)
      CHARACTER*100 DATA(3)
      READ *, (ZIP(I), DATA(I), I = 1, 3)
      IF (ZIP(1) .GT. ZIP(2)) CALL SWAPIT (ZIP(1), DATA(1),
     $                                     ZIP(2), DATA(2))
      IF (ZIP(2) .GT. ZIP(3)) THEN
         CALL SWAPIT (ZIP(2), DATA(2), ZIP(3), DATA(3))
         IF (ZIP(1) .GT. ZIP(2)) CALL SWAPIT (ZIP(1), DATA(1),
     $                                        ZIP(2), DATA(2))
      END IF
      PRINT '(I 10, A 100)', (ZIP(I), DATA(I), I = 1, 3)
      END
```
Figure 8.13

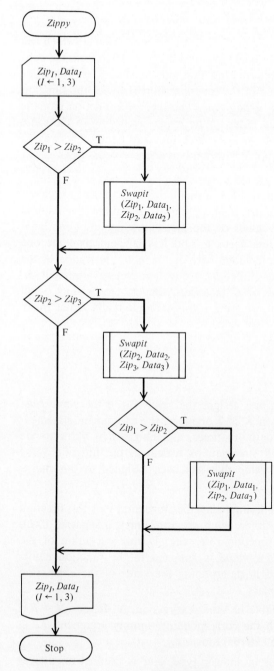

Figure 8.14

8.2.2 Defining an External Function

When a function is referenced (during evaluation of an expression in which the function name appears), the function name acquires a *value*. Therefore, the subprogram statements that define an external function must include steps that associate the desired value with the name of the function. Furthermore, the function name must be considered to have a certain *type*. The type of a function name is normally determined from the initial letter of the name, according to the same default implicit type rules that apply to a variable or array name. The way to define functions whose names do not correspond to these default rules is explained later in this section.

Example 4   In Exercise 11 in Section 7.1.3, a method was presented for calculating elements of Pascal's triangle of binomial coefficients. An alternative method requires the computation of three values of the *factorial* function. (For large parameter values, this method is less accurate and less efficient than the one presented earlier; nevertheless, it is included here as a simple illustration of the process of defining and using external functions.) Given an integer argument, K, the function *Ifact* returns the value of K factorial—that is, the product of all positive integers up to K. The main program in this example reads values for N and R, and prints the binomial coefficient value

$$C[N, R] = \frac{N!}{R! \cdot (N - R)!}.$$

(See Figs. 8.15–8.18.)

The subprogram defining *Ifact* first assigns the value 1.0 to the name *Ifact* as though it were a variable. Next, if K is 2 or more, the assignment statement in the loop will be executed one or more times, assigning a new value to the function name. When the RETURN statement is executed, the function value that will be returned is the latest value that has been assigned to this name. Note the following points.

1. The function *Ifact* is referenced simply by the appearance of the function name in an expression (in the referencing program unit); a separate CALL statement is not used for a function reference. During execution of the external function subprogram, a value is assigned to the function name; this value is subsequently used in determining the value of the expression in which the function name appears.

2. The actual argument is a variable or other expression, N, R, or $(N - R)$, which must agree in type with the corresponding dummy argument, K, in the subprogram that defines the external function.

3. The returned function value is of integer type, and is used in an integer expression in the referencing program unit. In the subprogram, an integer value is assigned to the function name in each of the two assignment statements.

```
* Function to compute the factorial of a given integer.
      FUNCTION IFACT (K)
      IFACT = 1
      DO 93, I = 2, K
        IFACT = IFACT * I
   93   CONTINUE
      RETURN
      END
```

Figure 8.15

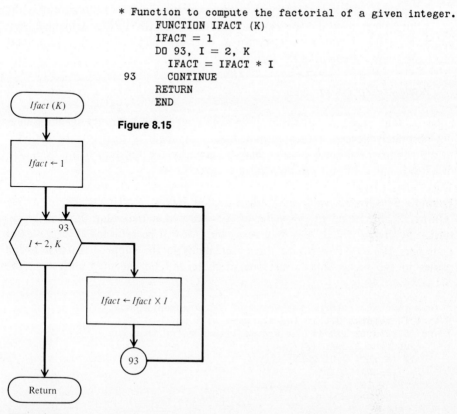

Figure 8.16

```
* Main program using Ifact to compute binomial coefficients
      PROGRAM BINOM
      INTEGER R
      READ *, N, R
      PRINT *, N, R, IFACT (N) / (IFACT(R) * IFACT (N − R))
      END
```

Figure 8.17

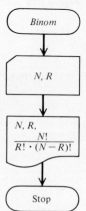

Figure 8.18

In general, the value returned by an external function subprogram is the last value assigned to the function name before the RETURN statement is executed. Note that in the pattern shown at the beginning of Section 8.2, at least one assignment statement of the form

$Name = Expression$

appears. (In Example 4 there are two such statements.) Strictly speaking, it is not absolutely necessary that an assignment statement *in this form* be included in the subprogram, since a value may be given to the function name by means of a READ statement, for example, or in some other way.

Example 5 Given a value of X, the function *Signal* (see Figs. 8.19 and 8.20) returns a value equal to the value of X, except that the value 0.0 will be returned by *Signal* if X is less than zero, and 1.0 will be returned if X is greater than one. Note that there are three statements in the subprogram that assign values to the name *Signal*; just one of these will be executed each time the

```
* This function returns the value of its argument, except
* that it returns 0.0 if the argument is less than zero,
* and it returns 1.0 if the argument is greater than one.
      FUNCTION SIGNAL (X)
      IF (X .LT. 0.0) THEN
          SIGNAL = 0.0
      ELSE IF (X .GT. 1.0) THEN
          SIGNAL = 1.0
      ELSE
          SIGNAL = X
      END IF
      RETURN
```

Figure 8.19

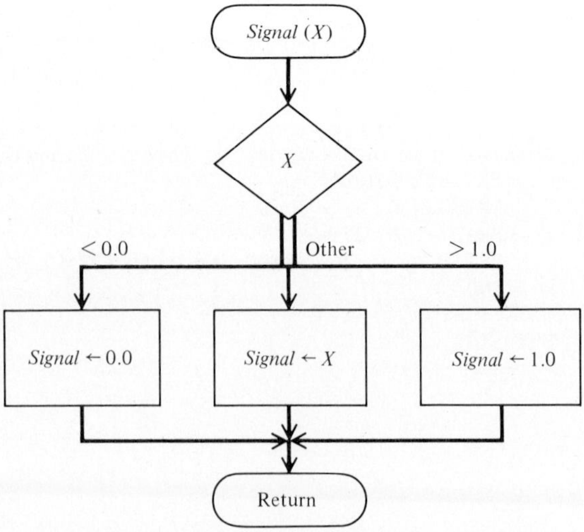

Figure 8.20

function is referenced. Figures 8.21 and 8.22 illustrate how such a function might be used. The main program reads values of *A*, *B*, and *C*, and uses the smaller of *A* and *B* as the argument for *Signal*. The result is multiplied by *C* to obtain *Z*. Finally, the values of *A*, *B*, *C*, and *Z* are printed.

```
* Main program to test Signal
      PROGRAM SGTEST
      READ '(3□F□10.5)', A, B, C
      IF (A .GT. B) THEN
         Z = C * SIGNAL (B)
        ELSE
         Z = C * SIGNAL (A)
        END IF
      PRINT '(1X,□4□G16.8)', A, B, C, Z
      END
```

Figure 8.21

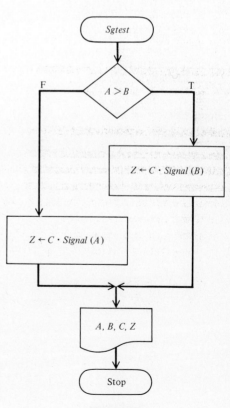

Figure 8.22

Example 6 The dummy arguments of the function *Scapr* (see Figs. 8.23 and 8.24) are two vectors, *X* and *Y*, and an integer, *N*. The function computes the *scalar product,* or sum of products of corresponding elements, of the two vectors, up to the element whose subscript value is *N*. Array declarations are needed in the subprogram for the dummy argument arrays, as well as in the main program for the actual argument arrays.

The sum (which is assigned to the name *Scapr,* as though it were a variable) is first set to zero, and is then augmented as each product is added to it. The final value is returned to the main program.

A simple main program that would reference *Scapr* is shown in Figs. 8.25 and 8.26. Values for the number of elements, *Len,* and for the element values in three arrays *A*, *B*, and *C*, are read. The scalar product of each pair of arrays is printed. We wish to note the following points.

```
* Function to compute the scalar product of two vectors,
* X and Y, up to element N
      FUNCTION SCAPR (X, Y, N)
      REAL X(40), Y(40)
      SCAPR = 0.0
      DO 806, I = 1, N
         SCAPR = SCAPR + X(I) * Y(I)
 806     CONTINUE
      RETURN
      END
```

Figure 8.23

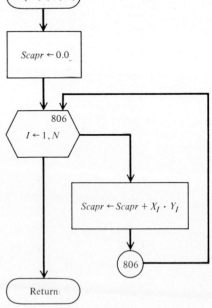

Figure 8.24

1. In each reference to *Scapr,* the actual arguments agree in number (three), in type, and in array size with the corresponding dummy arguments in the subprogram.

2. The dummy arguments X and Y, as well as the actual arguments A, B, and C, are declared to be arrays of up to 40 elements.

3. The scalar product returned by the function is of real type.

```
* Main program to test Scapr
        PROGRAM VECTORS
        REAL A(40), B(40), C(40)
        READ *, LEN
        IF (LEN .GT. 40) STOP
        READ *, (A(I), I = 1, LEN)
        READ *, (B(I), I = 1, LEN)
        READ *, (C(I), I = 1, LEN)
        PRINT *, SCAPR (A, B, LEN), SCAPR (A, C, LEN),
     $  SCAPR (B, C, LEN)
        END
```

Figure 8.25

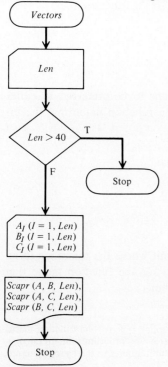

Figure 8.26

Type specification for external function subprogram names

In the absence of any declaration to the contrary, the type for an external function subprogram name is determined from the first character of the name, according to the rules of implicit type specification (see Section 7.1). The default implicit rules may be changed by an IMPLICIT declaration in the subprogram, or the function name may be included in an explicit type declaration. Both forms of type declaration in an external function subprogram apply to the function name as well as to variables and array names.

For example, *Dscapr* might be the name of a function that computes the double precision scalar product of two vectors of real type. Since there is no default implicit type specification for double precision, an IMPLICIT statement in the subprogram could be used to declare all names that begin with D, including the function name *Dscapr,* to be of double precision type:

```
FUNCTION DSCAPR (X, Y, N)
IMPLICIT DOUBLE PRECISION (D)
 . . .
```

Perhaps better would be an explicit type declaration for the function name:

```
FUNCTION DSCAPR (X, Y, N)
DOUBLE PRECISION DSCAPR
 . . .
```

A third form is also permitted, which is perhaps to be preferred to either of the other two. An explicit type declaration for a function name may be included in the FUNCTION statement:

```
DOUBLE PRECISION FUNCTION DSCAPR (X, Y, N)
```

Generally, a FUNCTION statement may have the form

    Type FUNCTION *Name* (*List of dummy arguments*)

As we pointed out in Section 8.1.2, the program unit where the reference to an external function appears must also specify a type for the function name that agrees with the specification in the defining subprogram.†

---

† When an external function definition retains the *default* implicit type for the function name, care must be taken *not* to declare a different type in the referencing program unit. In particular, if an IMPLICIT declaration in the referencing program unit applies to the function name, it may have to be superseded by an explicit type declaration.

A function of character type also requires a length specification. This appears along with the type specification for the function name, in any of its forms:

```
FUNCTION STRING (A, B)
CHARACTER*20 A, B, STRING
 . . .
```

or

```
FUNCTION STRING (A, B)
IMPLICIT CHARACTER*20 (A - Z)
 . . .
```

or

```
CHARACTER*20 FUNCTION STRING (A, B)
```

8.2.3 Exercises

1. Study the subroutine *Find* in Example 1 in Section 8.2.1, and the main program *Condns* (Figs. 8.3–8.6). Suppose that this program is provided with data consisting of all zeros, except that the thirty-first data item is 36.70, the forty-eighth item is 17.24, and the ninety-second item is 831.16. Tell what results will be printed.

2. Study the subroutine *Revers* and the program *Test1* in Example 2 in Section 8.2.1 (Figs. 8.7–8.10). Suppose that this program is provided with each of the following data cases:

	L	B_I ($I = 1$ to L)					
Case 1.	6	1.0	2.0	3.0	4.0	5.0	6.0
Case 2.	4	1.0	2.0	3.0	4.0		
Case 3.	5	9.8	7.6	5.4	3.2	1.0	

   In each case, tell:
   a) What values A_I and A_{N+1-I} will have, after the reference to *Swap* has been executed, when the value of *I* equals *Middle*.
   b) What results will be printed.

3. Prepare some data for Example 3 in Section 8.2.1, based on the names and addresses of yourself and two friends. Submit the three sets of data to the computer in "random" order. Check to see that the results are ordered correctly.

4. Write a main program that will read an array *A* of ten real values, and then will read a pair of integers *I* and *J* and call *Swap* to exchange A_I and A_J.

5. Write a subroutine *Sort* that arranges the elements of an array in ascending order using the method suggested in Exercise 3 in Section 4.3.1. Assume that the array does not contain more than 100 elements.

6. Study the function *Signal* and the main program *Sgtest* in Example 5 in Section 8.2.2. Tell what results will be printed if the main program and subprogram are executed with each of the following sets of input data:

	A	B	C
Case 1.	−2.0	0.5	2.0
Case 2.	0.5	−2.0	2.0
Case 3.	0.3	0.8	3.0

7. Study the function *Scapr* and the main program *Vectors* in Example 6 in Section 8.2.2. Tell what results will be printed if the main program and subprogram are executed with the following data:

Len: 6

A_I ($I = 1$ to 6): 1.0000   0.5000   0.3333   0.2500   0.2000   0.1667
B_I ($I = 1$ to 6): 0.3333   0.2500   0.2000   0.1667   0.1429   0.1250
C_I ($I = 1$ to 6): 0.1667   0.1429   0.1250   0.1111   0.1000   0.0909

8. Prepare a double precision scalar product function similar to *Scapr*. Use the predefined function *Dprod* to compute the product of two real array elements, and add them to the double precision sum. Test this program using data similar to that in Exercise 7, that is generated internally rather than read from an external source: Let $A_I = 1/I$; $B_I = 1/(I + 2)$; $C_I = 1/(I + 5)$. Compare the results with those obtained from Exercise 7.

9. *Cube root*. Write a function to compute the cube root of a real argument, by Newton's method: Starting with $Q = 1.0$, evaluate the expression

   (2.0 * Q + R / (Q * Q)) / 3.0

   where R is the given real argument. If this expression has almost the same value as Q, return this value as the cube root of R. Otherwise, assign this expression value as the next value of Q, and repeat the calculation. (*Problem:* What is meant by "almost the same value"?)

   Draw a flowchart and write a *function* subprogram appropriate to each of the descriptions in Exercises 10–14.

10. Given a value of X, *Flag* returns the absolute value of X if that value does not exceed 1.0; if the absolute value of X is greater than 1.0, however, the value of *Flag* is 1.0.

11. Given a value of X and a value of Y, *Iquad* returns the integer value 1, 2, 3, or 4 according to the quadrant in which the point (X, Y) lies:

    1 if X is positive or zero and Y is positive or zero;
    2 if X is negative and Y is positive or zero;
    3 if X is negative and Y is negative;
    4 if X is positive or zero and Y is negative.

12. *Large* returns the largest value in *List* (a linear array of n elements) that does not exceed the given value k. If every element of the linear array exceeds k, *Large*

returns the value of k itself. Assume that n does not exceed 100. For example, if $List_1$ through $List_4$ contain the values (12, 78, 14, -9) and the value of k is 39, then the value of LARGE (LIST, 4, K) will be 14. However, if the $List$ values are (42, 59, 108, 72) and k is 39, the same expression will have the value 39.

13. *TriSum* returns the sum of values of array elements $Chek_{i,j}$ above the main diagonal (that is, the sum of all those elements for which $i < j$).

14. *Euclid's algorithm.* The following algorithm for finding the greatest common divisor of a pair of integers, $I1$ and $I2$, is attributed to the Greek mathematician Euclid (c. 300 B.C.).

    Step 1. Divide $I1$ by $I2$, ignoring the quotient and saving the remainder. (*Hint:* Use the MOD function.)

    Step 2. If the remainder is zero, then $I2$ is the greatest common divisor.

    Step 3. Otherwise, return to Step 1 to divide $I2$ by this remainder. (To keep the notation straight, assign $I2$ to $I1$ and the remainder to $I2$, before returning to Step 1.)

    a) Write a function with two integer parameters, $I1$ and $I2$, whose value is the greatest common divisor of $I1$ and $I2$.
    b) Write a main program to read two integers, find their greatest common divisor (using the function just written), and print the result.

15. Section 3.4.2 includes an example illustrating "rational arithmetic," which involves fractions represented by pairs of integers. Complete the program in Fig. 3.21 by dividing $Num3$ and $Iden3$ by their greatest common divisor to reduce the fraction represented by ($Num3$, $Iden3$) to lowest terms before printing the result. Run the program, using the data given in Section 3.4.2.

8.3 ASSOCIATION BETWEEN ACTUAL AND DUMMY ARGUMENTS

A description of actual and dummy arguments and rules for their use have been given in Section 8.2. That discussion is adequate for reasonably simple problems. In more advanced cases, however, it is important to understand how the association between arguments takes place, when a subroutine or an external function is referenced.

The information that becomes directly available to the procedure is not the *values* of the arguments but rather their *cell names* (or *addresses*). (We assume that each cell of computer storage has a numeric address in machine code, which gives its location among all the storage cells.) This information acts as a *pointer* to the cell where the actual value is stored.

For a dummy argument that is a variable, the information transmitted to the procedure is simply the pointer to (that is, the address of) the cell where the value is stored. In the procedure this information is interpreted to locate the cell where the value can be found.

For an array, the address of the *base element,* which is the first cell in the equivalent linear array (see Section 7.1.2), is transmitted. (This is the cell referenced by the lowest subscript value in the declared range for each dimension.) The procedure uses this information as a pointer to the base element, or modifies it appropriately to locate other elements of the array.

8.3.1 Variables as Dummy Arguments

For each variable in a subroutine or external function subprogram, the processor checks whether it appears as a dummy argument in the SUBROUTINE or FUNCTION statement at the head of the subprogram. If so, the processor interprets the information that has been communicated from the calling program as a pointer (address) rather than as an argument value. The processor must take further steps in order to use this pointer to obtain the value itself; therefore, we say that reference to a variable that appears as a dummy argument is *indirect.* On the other hand, a reference in the subprogram to a variable that does *not* appear as a dummy argument is *direct.*

Corresponding to a dummy argument that is a variable, the matching actual argument in the referencing program unit may be a *variable,* an *array element name,* a *constant,* or an *expression* of some other form. If the subprogram assigns a new value to this dummy argument variable, the pointer that has been furnished will be used to locate the cell where the value is to be stored. When the actual argument is a variable or an array element name, this will produce the desired result. However, when the actual argument in the referencing program unit is an *expression* that needs to be evaluated, the referencing program unit evaluates it, stores the value in a cell that is *inaccessible* to the Fortran programmer, and gives the procedure a pointer to this inaccessible cell. The subprogram will use the pointer to assign a new value to the inaccessible cell, but this will have no effect on the referencing program unit. Even worse, when the actual argument is a *constant,* an assignment to the corresponding dummy argument may change the value of the constant (!), which can cause severe difficulty later on.

Therefore, the rules of Fortran require that a dummy argument that receives a new value during execution of a subroutine or external procedure (by assignment, input, or otherwise) must correspond to an actual argument that is a variable or an array element name. A constant, or an expression that requires evaluation, *must not* be used as an actual argument corresponding to a dummy argument that is given a new value during subprogram execution.

When the actual argument is an array element name, the subscript expression is evaluated when the procedure is referenced, and the information transmitted is the address of the specified element of the array. This address is used as a pointer to reference the actual array element from within the procedure. The pointer value is not changed during execution of the subroutine or external function procedure, even if the procedure assigns a new value to some variable appearing in the subscript expression. The subscript will not be evaluated again until the *next* time the procedure is referenced.

For example, the following subroutine *Find* compares a value X with each element A_K until it finds $A_K < X$, and it returns the value of K thus determined.

Example 1

```
* Subroutine to find the first element of A
* that is smaller than X
        SUBROUTINE FIND (X, A, K)
        DO 17, K = 1, 20
          IF (A(K) .LT. X) RETURN
17      CONTINUE
*       . . The value of K is 21 at this point
        RETURN
        END
```

We can call *Find* with the statement

```
CALL FIND (B(I), C, I)
```

Although the variable K in the subroutine corresponds to the actual argument variable I, the identity of the argument variable B_I does *not* change when the value of K changes. The pointer to the array element B_I, corresponding to the dummy argument X, is established on the basis of the value of I at the time of execution of the CALL statement.

8.3.2 Arrays as Arguments

We have noted that the statements of each program unit are handled independently by the processor, so that it is necessary for each subprogram to include array declarations for its dummy argument arrays, even though array declarations for the actual arguments must also appear in the referencing program unit.

Using a portion of an array

There is, of course, no requirement that all elements of a dummy argument array be used during execution of a subroutine or external function procedure. The function *Scapr* in Example 6 in Section 8.2.2 has two dummy argument arrays of length 40, but uses only the first N elements of each (where N is a dummy argument whose value is assumed to be less than or equal to 40). The following example illustrates the same point with regard to a rectangular array.

Example 2   The following subroutine transposes the first N elements in the first N columns of a 40 by 40 matrix.

```
      SUBROUTINE TRANSP (A, N)
      REAL A(40, 40)
      DO 9, I = 1, N
        DO 8, J = 1, I
          CALL SWAP (A(I, J), A(J, I))
8         CONTINUE
9       CONTINUE
      RETURN
      END
```

(The subroutine *Swap,* referenced by *Transp,* is again assumed to be the same subroutine discussed in Example 1 in Section 8.1.)

If the subroutine *Transp* is referenced by the call statement

```
CALL TRANSP (WIG, 4)
```

where *Wig* is a 40 by 40 matrix, the procedure will be used to transpose the upper left-hand 4 by 4 submatrix (leaving the remainder of *Wig* undisturbed).

In applications requiring the use of arrays of different sizes in a single overall calculation, it is possible to declare an array that is large enough to cover all cases, and then use only a portion of it each time as required. For example, with the foregoing subroutine *Transp,* we could read an array of arbitrary size (not exceeding 40 by 40), transpose it, and print the results:

```
READ *, N, ((WIG(I, J), J = 1, N), I = 1, N)
CALL TRANSP (WIG, N)
PRINT *, ((WIG(I, J), J = 1, N), I = 1, N)
```

The main program could include the declaration REAL WIG (40, 40).

Up to this point, we have suggested that actual and dummy argument arrays be declared with precisely matching dimensions. We continue to recommend this practice as a general rule. It is possible with Fortran to achieve certain effects that are needed in advanced applications by relaxing this rule. The remainder of Section 8.3.2 deals with these effects, which require considerable care and a detailed knowledge of the way in which actual and dummy argument arrays are associated.

Those readers who have no immediate interest in these special effects, and who plan to continue following the rule of precisely matching declarations for actual and dummy arguments, may skip to the beginning of Section 8.3.3.

Storage space for dummy argument arrays

The first point to keep in mind is that the processor does not set aside any separate storage space to hold the elements of a dummy argument array. The storage cells must be provided by the actual argument array. The actual array elements are not moved to the subprogram; rather, pointers and other information (such as array bounds) are transmitted. This information is used by the subprogram to locate the elements of the actual array.

Reconfiguring an array

The number of dimensions, and the bounds for each dimension, need not agree between the actual argument array and the dummy argument array, so long as the actual array provides sufficient space for all elements of the dummy array. For example, the subprogram might contain the declaration

```
REAL A(12, 12)
```

while the referencing program unit declares

```
REAL WIG(16, 9)
```

Thus each array consists of 144 elements. It must be emphasized that the subscript sequence for a dummy argument array and for an actual argument array are determined *independently:* In effect, the "equivalent linear array" formula discussed in Section 7.1.2 is applied separately in the subprogram and in the referencing program unit. Thus, in the main program the array element named WIG(1, 2) is the seventeenth element in the storage sequence for the array, but the same cell would be called A(5, 2) in the subprogram since the dummy argument array *A* has only twelve elements in each column.

The same array, *Wig,* could also be used as an actual argument for some other subprogram, to correspond to a dummy array declared as

```
REAL VECTOR(144)
```

or as

```
REAL BLOCK(3, 6, 8)
```

The seventeenth element of *Vector* would be named simply VECTOR(17), but the correspondence between elements of *Wig* and those of *Block* is more difficult to determine. (The seventeenth element of *Block* is called BLOCK(2, 6, 1).)

As a special case of array reconfiguration, an *array element name* may be used as an actual argument when the dummy argument is an array name. For example, suppose that the subroutine *Fixit* contains a linear array declared as

```
INTEGER LIST(100)
```

and the main program has an array named *Kode* with more than 100 elements:

```
INTEGER KODE(120)
```

We may now call *Fixit* from the main program, using $Kode_{17}$ as an actual argument. In effect, the argument array as seen from the subroutine will then consist of the elements $Kode_{17}$, $Kode_{18}$, . . . , $Kode_{116}$ —that is, the 100 elements of the array *Kode* beginning with the element specified as the actual argument. Any element from $Kode_1$ through $Kode_{21}$ could be properly used as the actual argument, because there are at least 100 elements in the actual array sequence that begins with any of these elements.

As another example, suppose that *Work* is a 5 by 7 rectangular array (matrix). We have a subroutine, *Calc,* which requires a vector as its argument, and we want to apply *Calc* to the third column of *Work.* Since the elements of a column of *Work* occupy consecutive cells in the storage sequence for the array, the five elements in a column of the array can be treated by *Calc* as though they formed a five-element vector. We may call *Calc,* using as the actual argument the *first* element of the desired column of *Work:*

```
CALL CALC (WORK(1, 3))
```

Because of the way in which an array storage sequence is defined, we can use a column (but not a row) of a matrix as an actual argument to a subprogram that expects a vector.

Now suppose that there is another subroutine, *Grind,* which requires an argument that is a 5 by 5 square matrix. Again, the main program contains the 5 by 7 matrix *Work.* We can pass the last five columns of *Work* to the subroutine by specifying WORK(1, 3) as the actual argument.

More complicated is the fact that we can, in effect, form a 5 by 5 square matrix from *any 25 consecutively stored elements* of *Work.* The actual argument specifies the first of these elements; the subroutine *Grind* will assume that they form a 5 by 5 matrix (because of the declaration in the subroutine) stored in conventional order, beginning with the specified element. Still more complicated is a situation related to Example 2, in which only a portion of the actual argument array is processed by the subprogram. If we call the subroutine in Example 2 with

```
CALL TRANSP (WIG(7, 3), 4)
```

a certain set of elements of *Wig* will be rearranged. These elements can be identified by carefully applying the "equivalent linear array" formula to the declarations in the subroutine, using the actual argument array element to determine the starting point for the dummy array.

Other examples are possible involving arrays with specified lower subscript bounds other than 1.

When an array name appears as a dummy argument in a procedure, the corresponding actual argument must be an array name or an array element name. A reference to the procedure transmits a pointer to the base element of the actual argument array or to the designated array element. The procedure uses this pointer to refer to the base element of the dummy argument array.

Array reconfiguration should be avoided except where it is absolutely necessary, since in most cases it leads to programs that are difficult to understand and to modify. Nevertheless, it introduces no great difficulty for the *processor,* which merely applies the array declaration to the dummy argument in the subprogram where it appears, independently of any declaration for a corresponding array in a different program unit. The array declaration in the subprogram "authorizes" use of the dummy array name along with the designated number of subscript expressions. The subscript range bounds that appear in this declaration are used to establish the arrangement of the elements of the dummy array, on the basis of the "equivalent linear array" formula in Section 7.1.2. The Fortran rule, that the value of each subscript expression must lie within the declared subscript range bounds, applies only with regard to the declaration for an array name within the same program unit.

A dummy argument array may be smaller, but must not be larger, than the actual argument array. For example, corresponding to the actual array *Wig* with 144 elements, the dummy array *A* could be declared in the subprogram as

```
REAL A(12, 10)
```

but not as

```
REAL A(12, 16)
```

Strictly speaking, this restriction applies not to the *declaration* in the subprogram but to the statements that actually refer to elements of the dummy array. Thus, the dummy array could be declared as REAL A(12, 16) with no ill effects, so long as only the first twelve columns (that is, the first 144 elements) of *A* are used by the subprogram. However, some processors will provide assistance in ensuring array size conformance, if the dummy array bounds are kept within the bounds of the actual array.

Nonconstant array bounds

The technique that we have described for using a portion of an array may often result in wasted storage space; this may be important for an application that uses several large arrays. For instance, in Example 2 we assumed that a 40 by 40 matrix (1600 storage cells) would be declared even when we wish to transpose a matrix as small as 4 by 4 elements (16 cells).

Fortran permits array declarations in a subprogram with *variable* subscript limits, provided that the following rules are observed:

1. All *variables* that appear in a subscript bound expression must appear in the subprogram as dummy arguments or in a COMMON statement (see Section 8.5). The values of such variables must be defined before the subprogram is referenced.

2. The name of each *array* for which variable subscript bounds are given must appear as a dummy argument of the same subprogram.

3. Each subscript bound expression must be composed of integer constants and integer variables. (No procedure references or array element names are permitted.)

An actual array, with constant array bounds, must appear as the corresponding actual argument. (In a hierarchy of procedures such as that illustrated in Fig. 8.2, the actual argument array may have variable bounds but it must correspond in turn to an array with constant bounds at *some* higher level.)

Example 3

```
        SUBROUTINE TRANSP (A, N)
        REAL A(N, N)
        DO 9, I = 1, N
          DO 8, J = 1, N
            CALL SWAP (A(I, J), A(J, I))
8           CONTINUE
9         CONTINUE
        RETURN
        END
```

This subroutine could be used with the following main program statements:

```
        PROGRAM TRACK
        REAL FIG(4, 4), WIG(36, 36)
*       . . Statements to read data into Fig and Wig
         .
         .
         .
        CALL TRANSP (FIG, 4)
        CALL TRANSP (WIG, 36)
         . . .
```

The first time it is referenced, *Transp* will assume that the dummy argument array A is 4 by 4; the second time, A will be assumed to be 36 by 36. The current value of N is used for locating the specific elements of A that are needed in each case.

Care must be taken to ensure that the actual array provides enough space for all the elements of the dummy argument array. However, it is not necessary that the sizes of the dummy and actual arrays agree exactly. All the usual precautions that apply to array reconfiguration must be observed, with the additional complication that the reconfiguration parameter values are not known in advance.

Assumed array bounds

An array declaration in a subprogram performs two of the three roles that were discussed in Section 7.1.2: It "authorizes" use of the array name with the proper number of subscripts, and it establishes the arrangement of the elements of the array. However, it is not always necessary for a subprogram to specify the total number of elements in a dummy argument array. The external function subprogram for *Scapr* in Example 6 in Section 8.2.2 does not actually make any use of the fact that the vectors X and Y each contain 40 elements. The array declarations for X and Y are needed only to establish that these are array names.

Fortran permits a declaration for a dummy argument vector with an unspecified number of elements. The declaration in the subprogram *Scapr* can be replaced by

```
REAL X(*), Y(*)
```

Generally, we can leave unspecified the upper subscript range bound for the last dimension in any dummy argument array declaration, by writing an asterisk in place of the subscript bound expression. Since this bound has no effect on the arrangement of the array elements, it is not needed except when the subprogram must specify the total number of elements in the array.

Example 4   The following function computes the double precision scalar product of row I of the M-rowed matrix A, and column J of the N-rowed matrix B. The function does not need to know the number of columns of A or of B.

```
      DOUBLE PRECISION FUNCTION SCAPR (A, B, M, N, I, J)
      REAL A(M, *), B(N, *)
      SCAPR = 0.0D0
      DO 7, K = 1, N
        SCAPR = SCAPR + DPROD  (A(I, K), B(K, J))
  7     CONTINUE
      RETURN
      END
```

The argument N is used both for dimension information and for loop control. The argument M is needed only to specify the storage sequence of the elements of the array A—in particular, the spacing between consecutive elements of a row of A.

Unspecified ("assumed") array bounds cannot be used in subprograms that need array size information. For example, when the name of a dummy argument array appears in an input or output list (in the subprogram), indicating that the entire array is to be transmitted (see Section 6.1.2), data transmission is controlled by the array declaration in the subprogram and requires knowledge of all subscript range bounds. The processor would be unable to interpret correctly the statement

```
PRINT *, B
```

if it were added to the program in Example 4, unless the declaration for B is modified to provide a definite upper bound for the second dimension.

8.3.3 Arguments of Character Type

A dummy argument in a subprogram may be a variable or an array name of character type.

For a dummy argument that is a *variable,* the corresponding actual argument may be a constant, a variable, a substring name, an array element name, or an expression of character type. The length of the dummy argument must not exceed that of the actual argument.

An asterisk may be used in place of the length specifier for a dummy argument of character type. The effect will be that the character dummy argument assumes the length of the corresponding actual argument. For example, the declaration

```
CHARACTER*(*) STRING
```

may appear in a subprogram when *String* is a dummy argument. The length of the dummy argument will then be determined by the length of the actual argument used in the reference to the subprogram. A restriction on the use of a character dummy argument with "assumed" length must be noted, however. Such a variable must not be used *as an operand for concatenation* except in the expression on the right-hand side of an assignment statement.

For a dummy argument that is a character *array,* the actual argument may be a character array, array element, or array element substring. All the characters in all the elements of an argument array form a single *storage sequence:* The last character in an array element is immediately followed by the first character of the following array element. The lengths of dummy and actual array elements need not agree, but the storage sequence implied by the declaration for the dummy argument character array must not extend beyond the end of the actual array.

8.3.4 Procedure Names as Arguments

A dummy argument in a subprogram may be a procedure name. The corresponding actual argument must then also be a procedure name. Wherever the dummy argument appears, it represents the procedure whose name appears as the actual argument. If the dummy argument is used as the subroutine name in a CALL statement, the actual argument must be a subroutine name; and if the dummy argument is used as a function name in an expression, the actual argument must be a function name. The referencing program unit (which uses the procedure name as an actual argument) must also list the procedure name in an EXTERNAL statement.

Example 5   Exercise 4 in Section 4.4.2 describes a method for finding a "root" of the function *Fun*, that is, a value of X such that $Fun(X)$ is close to zero. A pair of argument values A and B are given, such that $Fun(A)$ and $Fun(B)$ have opposite signs. The values of A and B are replaced by a pair of values that are closer together, so that $Fun(A)$ and $Fun(B)$ still have opposite signs. This step is repeated, decreasing the distance between A and B each time, until A and B differ by no more than a specified tolerance (say, 0.001); at this point the average of the values of A and B is returned as an approximate root of *Fun*.

We may wish to develop this method as a subprogram for general use, to find an approximate root of any function whose *name* is given as an argument. The subprogram will also require as arguments the initial values of A and B, and the tolerance value to be used for accepting the approximate root.

```
* Subprogram for finding an approximate root
* of any function of one argument.
      FUNCTION ROOT (FUN, A, B, TOL)
      FA = FUN (A)
      FB = FUN (B)
*     . . Check for error in initial values of A and B.
      IF (FA * FB .GT. 0.0) THEN
          PRINT *, 'Improper[]A[]and[]B[]values.'
          STOP
      END IF
*     . . Subdivide the (A, B) interval as many as 20 times.
      DO 7, LOOP = 1, 20
        C = 0.5 * (A + B)
        FC = FUN (C)
        IF (ABS (A - B) .LE. TOL) THEN
            ROOT = C
            RETURN
        END IF
        IF (FC * FA .GT. 0.0) THEN
            A = C
        ELSE
            B = C
        END IF
7       CONTINUE
      END
```

The first dummy argument of *Root* represents the function whose approximate root is to be found. The corresponding actual argument in any reference to *Root* must be the name of a procedure for which an external function subprogram is available to the processor.

To use *Root,* we first define one or more external functions whose roots are to be found. Each such function must be capable of being matched to the dummy function *Fun* in *Root.* Thus, it must have a single argument of real type, and must return a value of real type, so that a proper reference will be made, upon substitution of the actual function for the dummy *Fun,* when statements such as

```
FA = FUN (A)
```

are executed. For example, we might be interested in two different polynomials, which we define as follows.

```
* First test polynomial for Root
      FUNCTION POLYA (Z)
      POLYA = 17.3 + Z * (23.4 + Z * (137.0 + Z * (64.2 - Z)))
      RETURN
      END
* Second test polynomial for Root
      FUNCTION POLYB (Z)
      POLYB = -102.4 + Z * (51.2 + Z * (25.6 + Z))
      RETURN
      END
```

We may then use a main program that calls *Root* to find a root of either of these functions. In the main program, we must include EXTERNAL declarations for the two polynomial functions used as actual arguments, so that the processor can recognize that *Polya* and *Polyb* are external function names.

```
* Program to find roots of Polya and Polyb
      PROGRAM GEORGE
      EXTERNAL POLYA, POLYB
      RTA = ROOT (POLYA, 0.0, 100.0, .001)
      RTB = ROOT (POLYB, 0.0, 100.0, .001)
      PRINT *, RTA, RTB
      END
```

The function *Root* and the two polynomial functions *Polya* and *Polyb* must be furnished to the processor along with this main program. The first reference to *Root* requests that a root of *Polya* be found between 0 and 100, within a tolerance of 0.001. The second reference to *Root* specifies similar conditions for finding a root of *Polyb*. The PRINT statement in the main program then displays the approximate roots.

The EXTERNAL *declaration*

When interpreting an actual argument list containing a subprogram name, as illustrated in the foregoing example, the processor needs to be informed that the name is that of a subprogram and not of a variable or an array. In general, this information cannot be determined from the context, since the processor is operating on the main program separately from the subprograms. Therefore, the programmer must include an EXTERNAL declaration whenever a subprogram name is to be used as an argument in a calling program. This declaration has the form

    EXTERNAL *list*

For example, see the declaration

    EXTERNAL POLYA, POLYB

in the main program of the foregoing example.

Note that a function *value* may appear as an *expression* in an argument list, corresponding to a parameter that is a *variable*. This situation should not be confused with that in which the function *name* argument appears, corresponding to a parameter that is a subprogram *name*.

8.3.5 Statement Labels as Arguments

Exception handling

In many of the subprograms illustrated so far, we have tacitly assumed that the input arguments have "proper" values, that is, values which fall in ranges for which the task to be performed makes sense. For example, in Section 8.2.1, the subroutine *Find* assumes that *N* does not exceed 100; and in Section 8.3.2, the subroutine *Transp* assumes that the actual argument array *A* is 40 by 40. It is presumed that if there is any doubt, the main program will test for improper variable values before using them as actual arguments: See Example 6 in Section 8.2.2 (Figs. 8.25 and 8.26). If such tests are not made, the results produced by the subprogram may be nonsensical, and may lead to further errors later on.

Other examples arise in the use of common mathematical functions. Predefined procedures may test to see if the argument values are in the proper range: For example, *Sqrt* may require that its argument value be greater than or equal to zero. The particular action taken when such an error occurs may depend on the processor; in some cases, execution of the program is abruptly terminated.

It would be helpful if either the procedure or the referencing program unit would assume responsibility for checking parameter values and taking appropriate corrective action. In practice, since activation of a function occurs implicitly (in the middle of the evaluation of an expression), it is awkward for the calling program to detect an error that occurs during execution of the function, to take corrective action, and then to resume evaluation of the expression. Alternatives are to check the argument values before executing the statement containing the function reference, to rearrange the entire program to use a subroutine instead of a function, or to attempt corrective action after completing execution of the statement containing the function reference. The third alternative may be particularly awkward if the expression is part of the assertion controlling execution of an IF statement.

For subroutine subprograms, we have a bit more flexibility. The most straightforward approach is to add an extra argument for error detection purposes. The subroutine assigns one of several values to this argument as a result of tests made in the subroutine. Thus, for each of several distinct conditions, the "test" parameter may be assigned a different value. Upon return to the calling program, a control statement can be executed to direct control to the desired location, where alternative action can be taken.

Example 6   The program in Fig. 3.12 (Section 3.1.2) can be used as the basis for a subroutine to find all roots of a quadratic equation. See Figs. 8.27 and 8.28. The main program reads coefficients *C1*, *C2*, and *C3* corresponding to the dummy arguments *A*, *B*, and *C* in the subroutine *Quad*. The subroutine sets values of the argument variables *R1* and *R2*, and an "indicator" variable, *Indic*. The subroutine sets this integer dummy variable to one of three values:

1. *A* is zero. The given coefficients do not specify a quadratic equation. The values of *R1* and *R2* are set to zero.
2. *A* is not zero; the discriminant is negative. There are two complex roots. *R1* is set to the real part, and *R2* to the imaginary part.
3. *A* is not zero; the discriminant is nonnegative. There are two real roots (which may be equal). *R1* and *R2* are set to the values of these real roots.

Upon return from the subroutine, the main program takes the appropriate action, based on the value of *Indic*.

Using alternate returns

A second approach involves the use of a statement label as an actual argument. (This use of statement labels, like those described in Section 3.4, can interfere with program comprehension.) The special "alternate return" form provides that one or more of the dummy arguments of a subroutine (not a function) may consist of merely an asterisk. The corresponding actual argument must be a statement label in the referencing program unit. Within the subroutine, the statement

RETURN 1

```
* Subroutine to find all roots of a quadratic equation,
* given the coefficients A, B, and C. Sets Indic to 1
* if A, B, and C do not specify a quadratic equation;
* to 2 if the equation has 2 complex roots; to 3 if the
* equation has 2 real roots (which may be equal).
      SUBROUTINE QUAD (A, B, C, R1, R2, INDIC)
      IF (A .EQ. 0.0) THEN
          R1 = 0.0
          R2 = 0.0
          INDIC = 1
          RETURN
      ELSE
*          .. A is not zero. Find discriminant.
          PART1 = −B / (2.0 * A)
          DISC = B ** 2 − 4.0 * A * C
          PART2 = SQRT (ABS (DISC)) / (2.0 * A)
          IF (DISC .LT. 0.0) THEN
*              .. Discriminant is negative. Roots are complex.
              R1 = PART1
              R2 = PART2
              INDIC = 2
              RETURN
          ELSE
*              .. For maximum accuracy, force signs to agree.
              PART2 = SIGN (PART2, PART1)
              R1 = PART1 + PART2
              IF (R1 .NE. 0.0) THEN
                  R2 = C / (A * R1)
              ELSE
                  R2 = PART1 − PART2
              END IF
              INDIC = 3
              RETURN
          END IF
      END IF
      END
```

Figure 8.27

```
* Main program using Quad to find roots of quadratic
* equation with coefficients C1, C2, C3.
      PROGRAM USEME
      READ *, C1, C2, C3
      PRINT *, 'Coefficients are', C1, C2, C3
      CALL QUAD (C1, C2, C3, R1, R2, INDIC)
      GO TO (10, 20, 30), INDIC
10    CONTINUE
      PRINT *, 'Not a quadratic.'
      STOP
20    CONTINUE
      PRINT *, 'Complex roots', PART1, '+ or − i', PART2
      STOP
30    CONTINUE
      PRINT *, 'Real roots', R1, R2
      END
```

Figure 8.28

causes a return to the statement label corresponding to the *first* asterisk that appears among the dummy arguments. Similarly, RETURN 2 causes a return to the statement label corresponding to the *second* asterisk among the dummy arguments, and so on.

Each actual argument, in the CALL statement that references the subroutine, must appear as a statement label preceded by an asterisk.

For example, in the subroutine *Quad* let us replace the statements

```
INDIC = 1
RETURN
```

by the statement

```
RETURN 1
```

and similarly delete the other statements that assign values to *Indic,* changing the following RETURN statements to RETURN 2 and RETURN 3, respectively. Also we rewrite the dummy argument list as

```
(A, B, C, R1, R2, *, *, *)
```

Now, in the main program, we replace the CALL statement by

```
CALL QUAD (C1, C2, C3, R1, R2, *10, *20, *30)
```

and delete the computed GO TO statement that follows the CALL.

Execution of one of the RETURN statements will select the actual statement label 10, 20, or 30, corresponding to the designated one of the asterisks in the dummy argument list. The designated statement will be executed immediately upon return from the subroutine. Thus execution of a CALL statement with statement label arguments has the effect of a multiway branch.

8.3.6 Exercises

1. Show what changes you might make in the definition of *Revers* (Figs. 8.7 and 8.8) that would make it applicable to arrays of arbitrary length. Write a statement to call *Revers* to reverse the first 300 elements of an array of length 500.

2. Define a subroutine *Norm* that computes the square root of the sum of the squares of all the elements in a linear array, *V*. The subroutine returns this result as the value of a dummy argument named *Sum,* and sets the value of the logical dummy argument *Flag* to .FALSE. if *Sum* is smaller than 10^{-5}; *Flag* is set to .TRUE. otherwise.

3. *Scalar products and matrix multiplication.*
   a) Use the function *Scapr,* defined in Fig. 8.29, to compute the product of two matrices. The element in the *I*th row and *J*th column of the *product matrix* is the scalar product of the *I*th row of the first matrix and the *J*th column of the second matrix.
   b) Write a complete program to read the elements of two matrices, compute their product, and print the elements of the product matrix.

Data:

First matrix | | | Second matrix | |
--- | --- | --- | --- | --- | ---
Case 1. | 1.0 | 2.0 | 3.0 | −11.0 | 18.0 | −13.0
| 5.0 | 7.0 | 4.0 | 9.0 | −15.0 | 11.0
| 6.0 | 8.0 | 3.0 | −2.0 | 4.0 | −3.0

First matrix | | | Second matrix | |
--- | --- | --- | --- | --- | ---
Case 2. | 1.0 | 2.0 | 3.0 | 4.0 | 5.0 | 1.0 | 7.3
| 1.6 | 4.1 | 8.2 | 3.1 | 1.8 | 1.0 | 2.4
| 1.0 | −1.0 | 1.0 | −1.0 | 1.0 | 1.0 | 1.6
| | | | | | 1.0 | 0.8
| | | | | | 1.0 | 9.7

```
* Function to compute the scalar product of row I of the
* M by N matrix A, and column J of the N-rowed matrix B.
      FUNCTION SCAPR (A, B, M, N, I, J)
      DOUBLE PRECISION SUM
      REAL A(M, N), B(N, *)
      SUM = 0.0D0
      DO 7, K = 1, N
        SUM = SUM + DPROD (A(I, K), B(K, J))
7       CONTINUE
      SCAPR = REAL (SUM)
      RETURN
      END
```

Figure 8.29

8.4 ALTERNATIVE ENTRY POINTS FOR SUBPROGRAMS

It is sometimes desirable to construct a subprogram with more than one starting point. This can be done by providing secondary entries through the use of the ENTRY statement, whose general form is

ENTRY *Name* (*List of dummy arguments*)

For example, a subroutine has been prepared that reads data into an array, sorts it into a predetermined sequence, and prints the resulting sorted array values.

However, for some purposes it is desirable to use the same subroutine with data that has already been read into the array. We define the subroutine *Insort* for sorting with input, and we provide a secondary entry named *Arsort* for sorting data that is already in an array.

```
* Subroutine with two entry names.
* Call Insort to read an array and sort it.
      SUBROUTINE INSORT (ARRAY, NMAX, N)
      REAL ARRAY (0: NMAX − 1)
      DO 7, N = 0, NMAX − 1
        READ (*, '(F10.0)', END = 8) ARRAY(N)
7       CONTINUE
8     CONTINUE
      PRINT *, N, 'values␣have␣been␣read␣into␣Array.'
*     .. Call Arsort to sort data already in the array.
      ENTRY ARSORT (ARRAY, N)
      ...

         (Sort procedure)

      ...
      PRINT '(8 G15.6)', (ARRAY(I), I = 1, N)
      RETURN
      END
```

When the subroutine is called using the name *Insort,* execution begins at the first executable statement of the subroutine. After statement 8 is executed, the ENTRY statement is ignored (since ENTRY statements are nonexecutable statements) and execution continues at the point beyond the ENTRY statement. When *Arsort* is called, execution begins at the first executable statement that follows the ENTRY statement.

Note that the two entry points may have different argument lists. The call to either name must provide actual arguments corresponding to the particular list for the entry point that is used. For example, *Arsort* does not use *Nmax,* so this argument is not included in calls to *Arsort.*

An ENTRY statement may appear anywhere in a subprogram except within an IF block or a DO loop.

8.4.1 Function Subprogram Entry

Execution of an external function may be caused by reference (in an expression) to any of the names that appear in ENTRY statements, as well as by reference to the function name itself. If (as would be usual) all entry names in a function subprogram are of the same type as that of the function name, then any of these names may be used in an assignment statement (or other statement) that designates the function value to be returned. Giving a value to any of the entry names of the same type will have the same effect as giving a value to the function name.

Entry names may be of a different type from the function name, provided that the following restrictions are observed.

1. If the function name is of character type, then all entry names must also be of character type, and all must have the same length. If the function name is not of character type, then none of the entry names in the function subprogram may be of character type.

2. When the function name, and one or more entry names in the same subprogram, do not all have the same type, it is necessary to ensure that at each reference one of these names having the *same type as the currently referenced name* is given a value in order to designate the function value to be returned.

8.5   THE COMMON DECLARATION

As we noted at the beginning of Section 8.3.1, references occurring within a subprogram to a name appearing in the argument list result in *indirect* access to the referenced data. During either the translation phase or the execution phase, the processor must expend some extra effort to accomplish these indirect references. Although the details of this process vary somewhat, we may think of an indirect reference as being approximately twice as expensive as a direct reference. The computer must first examine the pointer to a data element, and then use that pointer in referring to the data itself.

When the amount of information transfer between the various program units is relatively small, we usually prefer to incur this extra effort to gain the conceptual simplicity of the argument approach. However, as the system of subprograms becomes more complex (for example, as complicated as the system indicated in Fig. 8.2), or as the number of arguments required by the individual subprograms increases, it may become more attractive to use the alternative approach described in this section. This approach depends on the establishment of certain *Common* regions of storage that can be referenced (that is, shared) *directly* by two or more independent program units, as suggested in Fig. 8.30.

Two or more independent program units may each include a statement of the form

COMMON *£ist*

where the list consists of variables and array names. The cells of the *Common* region will be allocated to the variables and array names *in the order of their appearance within the list*.

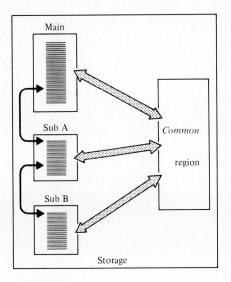

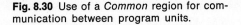

Fig. 8.30 Use of a *Common* region for communication between program units.

Example 1

```
REAL B(10, 5)
COMMON A, B, C, D
```

The array declaration specifies that B is an array of 50 cells. The COMMON declaration specifies that the first 53 cells of the *Common* region are to be allocated by the processor in the following pattern. The first cell is allocated to A, the second through fifty-first cells are allocated to $B_{1,1}$ through $B_{10,5}$, and the fifty-second and fifty-third cells are allocated to C and to D.

It is also possible to combine the array declaration with the COMMON declaration.

Example 2

```
COMMON A, B(10, 5), C, D
```

This single declaration would have exactly the same effect as the pair of declarations in Example 1, so long as B is of implicit real type.

As with arguments, the names used in the various program units need not be the same.

Example 3 The following example (see Fig 8.31) shows how we might redefine the subroutine *Revers* and the associated main program *Test1* (Example 2 in Section 8.2.1) to use COMMON declarations and eliminate the arguments. Note

```
* Subroutine to reverse the first N elements of an array A
        SUBROUTINE REVERS
        COMMON N, A(200)
        IF (N .GT. 200) THEN
            PRINT *, 'N is too large.'
            STOP
        END IF
        MIDDLE = N / 2
        DO 10, I = 1, MIDDLE
            CALL SWAP (A(I), A(N + 1 - I))
  10    CONTINUE
        RETURN
        END
* Main program to test Revers
        PROGRAM TEST1
        COMMON L, B(200)
        DO 50, LOOP = 1, 5
            READ *, L, (B(I), I = 1, L)
            CALL REVERS
            PRINT *, (B(I), I = 1, L)
  50    CONTINUE
        END
```

Figure 8.31

that the COMMON declarations are required both in *Revers* and in the main program. Although the names listed in the two declarations are not the same, their
positional correspondence in relation to the sequence of cells in the *Common* region achieves the desired matching. This positional correspondence is illustrated
in Fig. 8.32.

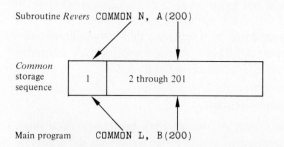

Fig. 8.32 Communication through
positional correspondence in the
Common region.

It is still important that the names in the COMMON declarations agree in *type,*
even though the names themselves may differ. For instance, the first cell of the
Common region in this example contains a number stored in the integer internal
representation, while the next 200 are stored in the real representation.

All cells in the *Common* region form a single storage sequence. The COMMON
declaration in each program unit establishes the allocation of this storage se-

quence into arrays of different sizes, along with individual variables. Thus, a subprogram could declare

    COMMON X(20), TRIAL(3, 3), ABLE, CROW(4), ITEMS(6), KODE

and this subprogram could be used with a main program containing the declarations

    COMMON ARRAY(34), LIST(2, 2), I, J, K

In each case, the *Common* storage sequence consists of 34 cells allocated to real data, followed by 7 cells of integer type. The reconfiguration of the arrays is specified for each program unit independently. Of course, complicated rearrangements such as the one illustrated here can lead to programs that are difficult to understand, and should usually be avoided.

The *Common* region must consist entirely of data of character type, or it must consist entirely of data of other types (integer, real, double precision, complex, and logical). If character data is used, the *Common* region consists of a single character storage sequence, which is allocated to character variables and character arrays as specified in the COMMON declarations in each of the program units.

A restriction

Although an *actual argument* in the calling program may be a name that refers to data in the *Common* region, it is illegal for a *dummy argument* name in a subprogram to appear also in a COMMON declaration in the same subprogram. The reason is that the processor would not know in such circumstances whether to find the designated data by direct reference, according to the position of the variable in the list of the COMMON declaration, or whether to find it by indirect reference via the dummy argument pointer. This restriction applies even when the direct and indirect references would lead to the same data.

8.5.1 Named and Unnamed Common Regions

In some programs the *Common* region of storage may be treated as a single block, whereas in others the programmer may wish to subdivide the *Common* region into smaller blocks, giving each block a separate name. One reason for doing this relates to the fact that a single *Common* block cannot contain both character and noncharacter data: Thus it may be desirable to specify one block for all *Common* storage of character type and another for noncharacter storage. Another reason appears when there are several program units, a few of which have a need to share data that is of no concern to the others. Figure 8.33 illustrates this point. *Common* block *S,* for example, is not declared in subroutine *B,*

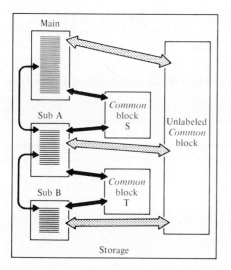

Main

Common block S

Sub A

Unlabeled Common block

Common block T

Sub B

Storage

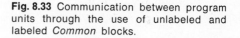

Fig. 8.33 Communication between program units through the use of unlabeled and labeled *Common* blocks.

so this subroutine need not be cluttered with references to it, and furthermore, the programmer can be sure that no statements in subroutine *B* can affect *Common* block *S*.

A *Common* block is given a name in a COMMON declaration of the following general form.

    COMMON / *Block name* / *List*

The block name is formed in the same way as a variable or array name; there is no type associated with a *Common* block name. In all program units using the same named *Common* block, the same block size must be maintained; that is, each of the lists associated with a given block must agree with regard to the total number of cells in the storage sequence that it establishes.

Example 4

    COMMON / S67 / A, B, C, K1

Variables *A, B, C,* and *K1* are assigned, in the order listed, to the cells in a *Common* block named *S67*. Let us imagine that this declaration appears in a subprogram called *Sub6,* which communicates with another called *Sub7*. The corresponding variables in the latter subprogram are named *Ta, Tb, Tc,* and *Ind*. The declaration needed in *Sub7* is therefore

    COMMON / S67 / TA, TB, TC, IND

It should be obvious that the same *Common* block name is used to refer to a given block in the declarations of two (or more) program units from which that block is to be referenced. The names of the individual variables and arrays in the block may be different (for example, the cell referred to as *A* in the subprogram *Sub6* is called *Ta* in *Sub7*), but the block name and the total number of cells in the block must agree.

Example 5   Consider the program units suggested in Fig. 8.33 and in Tables 8.2 through 8.4, and suppose that the following are the only variables assigned to the *Common* regions.

For the main program:

Unnamed *Common* region: A, B, and $X_1, \ldots, X_{50}$;
Common region S: $P_1, \ldots, P_{100}$.

Table 8.2

Position in unnamed *Common* region	Name		
	In main program	In subprogram A	In subprogram B
1	A	AA	A
2	B	BB	$B3$
3	X_1	XX_1	
4	X_2	XX_2	
.			
.			
.			
21	X_{19}	XX_{19}	
22	X_{20}	XX_{20}	
.			
.			
.			
30	X_{28}		
31	X_{29}		
32	X_{30}		
33	X_{31}		$Tim_{1,1}$
34	X_{32}		$Tim_{2,1}$
.			
.			
.			
50	X_{48}		$Tim_{3,4}$
51	X_{49}		$Tim_{4,4}$
52	X_{50}		$Tim_{5,4}$

For subprogram *A:*

> Unnamed *Common* region: AA, BB, and $XX_1, \ldots, XX_{20}$;
> *Common* region S: $R_{1,1}, \ldots, R_{10,10}$;
> *Common* region T: F, G, and $H_1, \ldots, H_{10}$.

For subprogram *B:*

> Unnamed *Common* region: A, *B3*, and $Tim_{1,1}, \ldots, Tim_{5,4}$ where $Tim_{1,1}$ occupies the same cell as X_{31} in the main program;
> *Common* region T: $Q_{1,1}, \ldots, Q_{4,3}$.

Table 8.3

Position in *Common* block S	Name	
	In main program	In subprogram *A*
1	P_1	$R_{1,1}$
2	P_2	$R_{2,1}$
.		
.		
.		
10	P_{10}	$R_{10,1}$
11	P_{11}	$R_{1,2}$
.		
.		
.		
99	P_{99}	$R_{9,10}$
100	P_{100}	$R_{10,10}$

Table 8.4

Position in *Common* block T	Name	
	In subprogram *A*	In subprogram *B*
1	F	$Q_{1,1}$
2	G	$Q_{2,1}$
3	H_1	$Q_{3,1}$
4	H_2	$Q_{4,1}$
5	H_3	$Q_{1,2}$
.		
.		
.		
10	H_8	$Q_{2,3}$
11	H_9	$Q_{3,3}$
12	H_{10}	$Q_{4,3}$

Note that *unnamed Common* regions in all the subprograms do not need to be of the same length: The unnamed *Common* region in subprogram *A* is considerably shorter than that in the main program.

In order to achieve the desired match between the elements of *Tim* in subprogram *B* and *X* in the main program, a "dummy" array may be inserted in the COMMON declaration in the subprogram to occupy the 30 cells that are not referred to in the subroutine. Thus, the following COMMON declarations might appear.

In the main program:

```
COMMON A, B, X(50)
COMMON / S / P(100)
```

In subprogram *A:*

```
COMMON AA, BB, XX(20)
COMMON / S / R(10, 10)
COMMON / T / F, G, H(910)
```

In subprogram *B:*

```
COMMON A, B3, DUMMY(30), TIM(5, 4)
COMMON / T / Q(4, 3)
```

8.5.2 Preassigned Data in Named Common Regions

Occasionally we may wish to predefine, by means of a DATA declaration, values for certain variables that are listed in a COMMON declaration. Our first inclination might be to construct and insert the required DATA declaration in the appropriate program unit, wherever it appears most meaningful to insert it. However, two restrictions must be observed. First, DATA declarations can be used to preassign values for variables (and array elements) in *named Common* regions, but not in *unnamed Common* regions. Second, preassignment of data to a *Common* region must take place in a *separate* program unit of a special kind, called a *block data* subprogram. This subprogram contains only *declarations* (no executable statements may be included). It may be recognized by its opening declaration, which is simply

```
BLOCK DATA
```

or

```
BLOCK DATA Name
```

To illustrate, suppose that in the foregoing Example 5 we wish to preassign values for P_1, P_3, and P_{10} in named *Common* block *S*, and for *F* and H_8 in block *T*. A suitable block data subprogram might be:

```
BLOCK DATA
COMMON / S / P(100)
COMMON / T / F, G, H(10)
LOGICAL F, G, H
DATA P(1), P(3), P(10) / 2.0, 3.0, 4.0 /
DATA F, H(8) / .TRUE., .FALSE. /
END
```

We note that any names for which values are to be preassigned must appear in named COMMON declarations. Furthermore, the size of each *Common* region listed in the block data subprogram must agree with its size in the other program units that mention this named *Common* region.

8.5.3 Interaction of COMMON and EQUIVALENCE Declarations

It is permissible for a variable or an array name to appear both in a COMMON and in an EQUIVALENCE declaration in the same program. However, there are some restrictions that must be observed in order to avoid difficulties when the EQUIVALENCE causes an implied lengthening of the *Common* region.

1. An *unnamed Common* region may be lengthened only in the direction of increasing positional value. For example, suppose that variables *A, B,* and *C* are allocated to the first three cells of the unnamed *Common* region by the declaration

COMMON A, B, C

Now, further suppose that D_1, the base element of a linear array of three cells, is declared equivalent to *B*. Figure 8.34 suggests how the *Common*

```
DIMENSION D(3)
COMMON A, B, C
EQUIVALENCE (D(1),B)
```

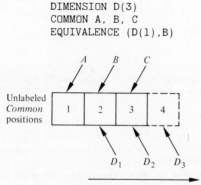

Unlabeled *Common* positions

Valid direction for extension

Fig. 8.34 Extending the unlabeled *Common* region in a valid manner by declaring equivalence to an element in a *Common* region.

region is extended implicitly in a valid manner. In contrast, to declare D_3 equivalent to B would imply extension of the *Common* region in an *invalid* direction, as suggested in Fig. 8.35.

```
DIMENSION D(3)
COMMON A, B, C
EQUIVALENCE (D(3),B)
```

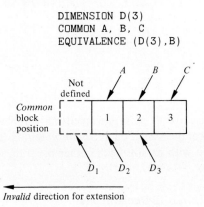

Fig. 8.35 Extending a *Common* block in an invalid manner by declaring equivalence to an element in a *Common* region.

2. Concerning *named Common* regions, remember that identically named blocks in two or more program units that are to be used together must be of the *same* length. Hence extension of such a region is permissible only if corresponding adjustments are made in all named COMMON declarations specifying the same name in other program units.

3. Within a given program unit, no two variables or array names may be declared equivalent if *both* names also appear in COMMON declarations (for the same region or different regions). Such a practice would imply a contradictory relationship, as suggested in Fig. 8.36.

```
COMMON A, B, C
EQUIVALENCE (A,C)
```

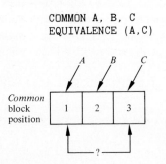

Fig. 8.36 Examples of an illegal equivalence class, where both elements belong to a *Common* region.

8.5.4 Exercises

1. Study Fig. 8.31. Answer the following questions.

   a) Consider "position 4" as allocated within the *Common* region. By what name would this cell be referred to in the subroutine *Revers?* Within the main program?

b) Using the input data for Exercise 2 in Section 8.2.3, what value would be read into this cell, in each case, during execution of the main program in Example 3 of this section?

2. Redefine the subroutine *Find* in Example 1 in Section 8.2.1, so that the array A and the variable N are in the *Common* region. Show the changes in the subprogram and in the calling program, in each of the following cases.

a) X and *Loc* remain as arguments.

b) X and *Loc* are variables in the *Common* region. The main program must now transfer the data from these cells to the arrays *Small* and *Locate* after each call to the subroutine.

3. Consider the function *Signal* in Example 5 in Section 8.2.2. Can the use of a *Common* region significantly simplify communication between this subprogram and a calling program? Explain.

8.6 STATEMENT FUNCTIONS

A statement function is a function that can be defined by a single statement embedded within a Fortran program unit. A statement function produces a single value (associated with the function name) and is referenced implicitly (by appearance of the function name, with an argument list, in an expression) in the same way as an external function. Thus, a statement function is analogous to an external function subprogram consisting of a single assignment statement. The form is

$$\textit{Name (List of dummy arguments)} = \textit{Expression}$$

Although it has the form of an executable statement, such a statement is actually a *declaration* that defines the function. The type associated with the value produced by a statement function is determined implicitly from the initial letter of the name, or explicitly from a type declaration in which the function name appears.

Certain restrictions must be observed in defining and referencing statement functions.

1. The form can be used only when the function is simple enough to be defined in a single statement.

2. A statement function declaration should not be given a label.

3. A statement function is known only within the program unit in which it is defined. Thus it cannot be referenced from another program unit (although, of course, an identical statement function definition can appear within another program unit). A statement function name must not be passed as a subprogram name argument, and must not appear in an EXTERNAL statement.

4. The dummy arguments must be variables. The corresponding actual arguments may be variables, constants, or other expressions of matching type, and must have defined values when the statement function is referenced.

5. Variables in the defining expression that do not appear in the dummy argument list are treated as ordinary variables at the time the expression is evaluated. That is, the current values of those variables, in the program unit that contains the statement function definition, are used in computing the function value.

6. The defining expression may involve predefined functions, external functions, or other statement functions; however, if other statement functions are used, they must be defined earlier in the program unit. That is, a statement function must precede other statement function definitions that refer to it.

Example

```
      SUMSQ (X, Y, Z) = X ** 2 + Y ** 2 + Z ** 2 - T ** 2
      READ *, N, T
      DO 20, I = 1, N
        READ *, A, B, C
        IF (SUMSQ (A, B, C) .GE. 0.0) THEN
            R = SQRT (SUMSQ (A, B, C))
            PRINT *, A, B, C, T, R
        ELSE
            PRINT *, A, B, C, T
        END IF
 20     CONTINUE
      END
```

The processor recognizes the first line as a statement function definition, because it consists of a name followed by parentheses, and the name does not appear in an array declaration. The first READ statement assigns values to N and T. The value of N specifies how many data cases follow, and the value of T is used in the function *Sumsq*. If the function value is positive, its square root is printed; if it is negative, the square root is not calculated.

8.6.1 Exercises

Find the errors, if any, in the statement function definitions (and in some cases their calling statements) following their verbal descriptions in Exercises 1–4. Assume implicit types.

1. *Able* returns the product of I, J, and IP. I and IP are the parameters.

   ```
   ABLE(I, IP) = I * J IP
   ```

2. *Simple* returns the value of $A/X + \sqrt{2}$, where A and X are parameters.

   ```
   SIMPLE (A, X) = A / X + 2
   ```

3. *Alta* returns the value of the expression

    $C + D \cdot \sqrt{Fun(X^2)};$

    Fun returns the absolute value of the fifth root of its (positive) parameter; *C* and *X* are the parameters of *Alta*.

    ```
    FUN (Y) = ABS (Y ** 0.2)
    ALTA (C, X) = C + D * SQRT (FUN (X * X))
    READ (5, 6) A, D, G
    Z = ALTA (A, D) + ALTA (A, G)
    WRITE (6, 9) Z
    ```

4. *C123F* returns $A^i + B^j + C^k$, where *i*, *j*, and *k* are parameters.

    ```
    C123F (I, J, K) = (A + B + C) ** (I + J + K)
    READ (5, 20) X, Y, Z, A, B, C
    ZZ = C123F (X, Y, Z)
    WRITE (6, 21) ZZ
    ```

Write statement function definitions for the descriptions in Exercises 5–8.

5. *XXL* returns the product of *I, J,* and *LL. J* is the parameter.

6. *Grief* returns the value of the expression

    ```
    A + B / COS (X + 2.0 * Y)
    ```

    X and *Y* are the parameters.

7. *Putt* returns the value of *Zeff* $(X)/Y$, with *Y* the parameter of *Putt*. *Zeff* returns the value of $A \cdot XX + B$, with *XX* the parameter of *Zeff*.

8. *Tiff* returns the result of *Grief* evaluated by means of the two parameters, $\sqrt{F}$ and $0.5 \cdot \log_e(G)$, corresponding respectively to *X* and *Y* in Exercise 6. *F* and *G* are the parameters of *Tiff*.

In Exercises 9–11, the statement function definitions, calling statements, and current values of the parameters and variables are given. Compute the values returned by the functions in the calling statements.

9.  ```
    FRST (X) = A * X + B
    Z = FRST (G + 6.0)
    ```
    $A = 3.0; B = 6.0; G = 7.0.$

10. ```
    TRST (B, X) = A * X + B
    Z = TRST (H / 4.0, SQRT (TT))
    ```
    $A = 2.0; H = 10.0; TT = 16.0.$

11. ```
    SCND (X) = A * X + B
    THRD (D) = SCND (E) / D
    Z = THRD (P)
    ```
    $P = 4.0; A = 3.0; B = 6.0; E = 5.0.$
    ```

CHAPTER 9

ADVANCED INPUT AND OUTPUT

Most ordinary computer applications that require the reading of data and the printing of results can be programmed using the basic input and output features described in Chapter 6. For some purposes, however, more complex manipulations of the data are required. The Fortran language provides a number of additional input and output features that are useful for such applications. These are covered in some detail in this chapter.

9.1 THE CONTROL LIST

We noted in Section 6.1.1 that other information, in addition to the format specifier and the input or output list, may be included in an input or output statement of the general forms

```
READ (Clist) List
WRITE (Clist) List
```

The keyword WRITE is used in this form instead of PRINT. The control list, *Clist,* is enclosed in parentheses and is not separated by a comma from the input or output list.

9.1.1   Direct Access and Unformatted Input and Output

An external device, at the time it is made available for transfer of data to or from a Fortran program (see Section 9.4), is designated as giving either *sequential access* or *direct access,* and as containing *formatted* or *unformatted* information. In all our examples so far, we have been describing *formatted sequential* data transfer.

Sequential access means that records are normally written consecutively, and must normally be read in the same sequence, while direct access means that records may be accessed in an arbitrary sequence. Thus, an input or output statement for direct access must include a *record number*. Another difference is that sequentially accessed records may be followed by an indication of the *end* of the record sequence, so that the program that reads the records can determine when the data has been exhausted.

Formatted records are those, such as the ones we have been describing, that are composed of *characters* representing the data values. Each formatted record corresponds exactly to a punched card or a printed line. An input or output statement for formatted data transfer must include a format specifier (see Section 6.1.1). This may be an asterisk, designating list directed formatting, or it may have any of the representations that are permitted for explicit reference to a format description. Thus, formatted data transfer includes both list directed formatting and explicit formatting. However, list directed input or output is permitted only with sequential access, while explicitly formatted input or output is possible either with sequential access or with direct access.

Unformatted records, on the other hand, contain information in a processor dependent form that is obtained by transferring data to or from internal storage without any editing or other transformation. The external representation of the data corresponds exactly to its internal representation. Thus, unformatted data transfer is more efficient, because the data is merely copied between the external device and the internal storage of the computer. A disadvantage of unformatted records is that they are unsuitable for communication with humans, unless further processing is applied to convert between the internal representation and a form readable by humans. An input or output statement for unformatted data transfer does not include a format specifier. Unformatted input and output are permitted with either sequential access or direct access.

From the viewpoint of a Fortran program, the structure (length and arrangement) of a record on the external medium is established at the time the record is written. In preparing a program to write records and then read those same records, a programmer needs very little understanding of their structure. However, the records may be read or written by a different program, by a COBOL or PL/I program, or even on a different computer. The designer of a Fortran program to use these records must understand their structure in detail, so that the input or output list and the format specification can be prepared properly.

9.1.2 Device Codes

A control list includes a device code, which is either an integer expression with a zero or positive value, or an asterisk. An asterisk specifies that the external device to be used is the same as the default device (reader or printer) that would be used if no control list were provided. A given integer value identifies the same device throughout all the program units of a complete program.

9.1.3 Control Information

The following information may be included in the control list of an input or output statement:

- Unit specifier,
- Format specifier,
- Record number specifier,
- Status specifier,
- Error specifier,
- End specifier.

The unit specifier must always be present. It has either of the forms

UNIT = *Device*

or simply

Device

If the keyword UNIT = is omitted, the unit specifier must be the first item in the control list. The device code may be an integer expression or an asterisk (see Section 6.1.1).

The format specifier must be present for formatted input or output. It has either of the forms

FMT = *Format*

or simply

Format

The keyword FMT = may be omitted only if the keyword in the unit specifier is also omitted, and in this case the format specifier must be the second item in the control list. The format code may have any of several forms, as described in Section 6.1.1.

The record number specifier must be present for direct access. It has the form

REC = *Record number*

The keyword must not be omitted. The record number is an integer expression with a positive value, designating a record to or from which information is to be transferred.

The status specifier, error specifier, and end specifier are optional. Their forms are

IOSTAT = *Status variable*
ERR = *Label*
END = *Label*

When these specifiers are used, the keywords must not be omitted. The status variable is an integer variable or array element to which a status code will be assigned on completion of the input or output operation. This code will be zero if the operation was completed normally, positive if an error has occurred, and negative if the operation was a sequential input operation and no error has occurred but the end indicator was detected during the operation, meaning that the transfer of data specified by the list was not completed because of exhaustion of the record sequence. The labels given in the error and end specifiers must reference executable statements in the same program unit. Control will be transferred to the designated label if the corresponding condition is detected.

Example 1   Suppose that the unit specified by device code 3 contains direct access unformatted data. We wish to write some information at record 176 on this device.

```
DOUBLE PRECISION DPVAR
CHARACTER*10 STR
IMPLICIT COMPLEX (A — C)
READ *, I, KODE, STR, BUGLE, DPVAR
WRITE (UNIT = 3, REC = 176) I, KODE, STR, BUGLE, DPVAR
END
```

In this example there are two statements that are used for input or output. The READ statement appears without a control list; therefore, the information is to be found on the *default* input unit. (This unit, and the default output unit, are designated by Fortran as containing data in *formatted sequential* form.) No unit specifier is required, and the format specifier consists of an asterisk to designate list directed input (see Section 2.4.2). This statement does not include a record number specifier (which would be permitted only for direct access), nor any of the other three optional specifiers. These four specifiers can appear only in a READ statement with a control list.

The WRITE statement designates device number 3. Since there is no format specifier, it must be assumed that data on this device is *unformatted*. Presence of a record number specifier indicates that access to device number 3 is *direct* rather than sequential. Again, no status or error specifiers are included. An end specifier is not permitted in a WRITE statement.

Example 2   In Section 6.1.1, we mentioned use of the form

READ (*, *format*, IOSTAT = *status variable*) *list*

for input from the *default unit* with error or end control. Section 4.4.1 (see Fig. 4.17) includes some examples using this form with an asterisk format specifier (indicating list directed formatting).

Here are some further examples of READ and WRITE statements with control lists.

```
READ (*, *) I, KODE, STR, BUGLE, DPVAR
WRITE (3, REC = 176) I, KODE, STR, BUGLE, DPVAR
READ (*, *, END = 8, ERR = 8) RATE, HOURS
READ (UNIT = *, FMT = *) I, KODE, STR, BUGLE, DPVAR
READ (*, FMT = *) I, KODE, STR, BUGLE, DPVAR
READ (UNIT = 7, FMT = 57, REC = 176) X, Y, A(2), A(4)
WRITE (7, '(4 G15.6)', REC = 176) X, Y, A(2), A(4)
```

The first two of these statements correspond exactly to the two input and output statements in Example 1. The third example corresponds to the input statement in Fig. 4.17. The fourth and fifth are further alternatives to the input statement in Example 1. The last two statements among these examples would be used with a formatted direct access device, designated as unit 7.

9.2   FORMATTED INTERNAL DATA TRANSFER

Formatted data transfer includes two separate processes: the change in *representation* of data between its internal form and its external form, and the *transmission* of the data to or from the external device. For formatted input, data in the form of a string of characters is transmitted from the external device to a "buffer" that is inside the computer but is inaccessible to the Fortran program; it is then converted from character string form to the form required by the internal representation (integer, real, logical, character, and so on), and is thus made available for further processing. Formatted output reverses these steps: Internally represented data is converted to a character string in an internal buffer, and then transmitted to the external device.

We see that a Fortran processor, since it is capable of formatted input and output, includes a very powerful facility—namely, the ability to convert data under format control between an internal representation and a character string that humans can read. It would seem useful to separate this facility from the process of transmitting data (without any conversion) between the buffer and the external device. Actually, all that is needed is a way to make a *buffer* accessible to the Fortran program.

Accordingly, the Fortran input and output statements for formatted data transfer are extended to permit specification of an internal buffer or character storage area, instead of an external device. Rather than an integer expression or asterisk in the *Unit specifier* position of the control list, a character variable (or array element, array, or substring) designates the character storage area containing a buffer or "internal file." The characters in the buffer are treated as a single *record* (see Section 6.1.1), except that if the buffer is designated as a character array, the array elements are treated as a sequence of records.

In most respects, the buffer is used for purposes of internal data transfer as if it were a formatted sequential external device. However, note that a statement that calls for internal data transfer must not specify list directed formatting. *External* data transfer with respect to the same buffer is possible: Such data transfer may be unformatted or list directed, or may have any other properties that are appropriate for the external device to or from which the data is to be transferred. Assignment statements or other statements may also refer to the character data in the buffer.

Example 1 An unformatted direct access device (unit 23) contains 100 records, numbered from 1 to 100. Each record contains 80 characters. The first character is either a blank or a C. If it is a blank, the second through seventy-ninth characters consist of thirteen six-digit *real* fields (and the eightieth character is blank). If the first character is a C, the remaining 79 character positions contain arbitrary Fortran or non-Fortran characters that are to be printed as a comment.

```
          CHARACTER*80 BUFFER
          REAL Z(13)
          DO 219, LOOP = 1, 100
            READ (23, REC = LOOP) BUFFER
            IF (BUFFER(1 : 1) .EQ. 'C') THEN
                PRINT *, BUFFER(2 : )
              ELSE
                READ (UNIT = BUFFER, FMT = '(1X, 13 F6.2)') Z
                CALL CALC (Z, RESULT)
                PRINT *, RESULT
            END IF
      219   CONTINUE
          END
```

The first READ calls for unformatted data transfer, from the record whose number is equal to the *Loop* index, to the *Buffer* character variable. If the first character position of this variable contains C, the remaining characters are printed—that is, they are transmitted to the default output device (because the PRINT statement is used) with list directed formatting (because the format specifier is an asterisk). If the first character of *Buffer* is not a C, *formatted internal data transfer* takes place. Data from the *Buffer* is converted to real internal representation as specified by the format (1X, 13 F6.2) and stored in the thirteen cells of the array *Z*. This array is passed as an actual argument to the subroutine *Calc,* which uses it in some manner to obtain the desired *Result* value. This value is then printed with list directed formatting. Finally, the iteration continues with the next record number, until all 100 records have been read and processed.

9.3 ADDITIONAL FORMAT CODES

There are some format codes whose use is infrequent enough, or complicated enough, to justify their omission from the discussion in Chapter 6. These codes, S, SP, SS, *k*P, BN, and BZ, are covered in this section.

9.3.1 Optional Sign Control

An output field produced by I, F, E, D, or G editing includes an optional sign in the position immediately to the left of the numeric digits representing the value. The sign must appear if the numeric value is negative, but the processor has some leeway in case it is positive. For example, the processor may choose to suppress the sign of a positive value that would otherwise be too large for the designated field width, while printing plus signs on smaller positive numbers.

At the beginning of execution of each Fortran output statement, the printing of these plus signs is entirely subject to the option of the processor. However, an S, SP, or SS format code may appear anywhere in the format description to control sign printing. The control specified by such a format code remains effective until another S, SP, or SS code is encountered in the format scan.

An SP format code specifies that "optional" plus signs are to be *printed,* and an SS code specifies that they are to be *suppressed.* The S code restores the processor option.

These codes do not have any effect if they are encountered in a format description being used for input.

9.3.2 Scale Factor Control

The *k*P format code specifies a scale factor, *k,* which is an optionally signed integer constant. The value of the scale factor in effect at the beginning of execution of an input or output statement is zero. The effective value of the scale factor changes only when a *k*P format code is encountered during the format scan.

Input

During input editing, the scale factor affects only fields *without* an explicit exponent, during F, E, D, or G conversion. An input field for one of these conversion modes is converted as though it were followed by the exponent $-k$. For example, with a 2P scale factor in effect, a three-column input data field containing the characters 123 would represent the value 1.23 internally. An input scale factor can be used with a data field that is too narrow to hold an explicit decimal point.

Output

During output editing, the scale factor affects all F, E, and D conversions, as well as those G conversions that actually use E mode.

For F output editing, the scale factor is added to the exponent of the internal data value. For example, with 2P, F6.2 editing, the internal value 2.3402 is printed as 234.02. This feature might be useful for conversion of units, as when a length measured in meters is to be printed in centimeters.

For E or D output editing, the scale factor must be greater than $-d$ and must not exceed $d + 1$ (where d is the decimal position specified in the format code). If $-d < k \leq 0$, there will be exactly $|k|$ leading zeros and $d - |k|$ significant digits after the decimal point. If $0 < k \leq d + 1$, there will be exactly k significant digits to the left of the decimal point and $d - k + 1$ significant digits to the right of the decimal point (thus a total of $d + 1$ significant digits in the output field). The output exponent is adjusted to produce a correct representation of the magnitude of the output data value. For example, the value 23.402 with format code E11.4 would be printed as ⸏0.2340E+02, but with scale factor 1P it would print as ⸏2.3402E+01.

For G editing, the effect of the scale factor depends on whether the F mode or the E mode is actually used for output: This choice is made *before* considering the scale factor. If the exponent would be between 0 and d inclusive, the F mode is used and the scale factor is ignored. If the exponent (before considering the scale factor) would be negative or larger than d, the E mode is used, and the scale factor is applied to determine the number of leading zeros after the decimal point.

Table 9.1 presents some examples of E and G output conversion, with various scale factor values. (Compare Table 6.5.) This table demonstrates that the scale factor has no effect on G editing when the exponent (before considering the scale factor) would be in the range for which F conversion is used. It also illustrates the fact that when E mode is used for G editing, the effect is the same (for any scale factor value) as if the corresponding E format code had been specified originally.

One other interesting observation can be made from Table 9.1. An E format code, or a G format code that is applied as an E conversion mode, causes output

Table 9.1 Use of scale factor with E and G output conversion modes

Internal value	External appearance					
Format code	E11.4 or 0P, E11.4	1P, E11.4	G11.4 or 0P, G11.4	-1P, G11.4	1P, G11.4	5P, G11.4
-8977.1	-0.8977E+04	-8.9771E+03	□-8977.□0000	□-8977.□0000	□-8977.□0000	□-8977.□0000
23.402	□0.2340E+02	□2.3402E+01	□□23.400□□	□□23.400□□	□□23.400□□	□□23.400□□
-0.12003	-0.1200E+00	-1.2003E-01	-0.1200□□□	-0.1200□□□	-0.1200□□□	-0.1200□□□
-1.3954	-0.1395E+01	-1.3954E+00	□-1.395□□□	□-1.395□□□	□-1.395□□□	□-1.395□□□
-20320	-0.2032E+05	-2.0320E+04	-0.2032E+05	-0.0203E+06	-2.0320E+04	-20320.E+00
0.020320	□0.2032E-01	□2.0320E-02	□0.2032E-01	□0.0203E+00	□2.0320E-02	□20320.E-06
-0.020321	-0.2032E-01	-2.0321E-02	-0.2032E-01	-0.0203E+00	-2.0321E-02	-20321.E-06
0.000049991	□0.4999E-04	□4.9991E-05	□0.4999E-04	□0.0500E-03	□4.9991E-05	□49991.E-09

of *one more significant digit* when the scale factor has a positive value (up to the limit, $d + 1$), as compared to a zero scale factor. Also, the number of significant digits is *decreased* when a negative scale factor is used. In particular, a scale factor value of 1 produces output in the "classical" scientific notation, with exactly one significant figure to the left of the decimal point and d significant figures to the right.

9.3.3 Blank Character Positions within Input Fields

A traditional rule in Fortran has been that any blank character position ("blank column") within an input field will be treated as a zero during formatted input conversion. In particular, this rule requires care to ensure that integer data (and integer exponents appearing at the right on real input data) is positioned at the extreme right of its input field. The BN format code makes it possible to override this convention, and to specify that any blanks appearing within a field on formatted input are ignored ("treated as *null* characters"). The BZ format code restores the traditional interpretation (so that blanks are "treated as *zeros*"). For example, with the traditional or BZ editing, an integer field containing the characters 12300 is interpreted as 12300, and a real input data field containing 1.23E+20 is interpreted as 1.23×10^{20}. With BN editing, the resulting values are 123 and 1.23×10^2, respectively.

At the time an external device is made available for *input* of data to a Fortran program, a "blank significance" property is established if the device is designated as containing data in the *formatted* representation. The blank significance property is either *zero* or *null*.

At the beginning of execution of each formatted input statement in the Fortran program, the blank significance property that was originally established for the device is in effect. The effective blank significance property can change only when a BN or BZ format code is encountered during format scan.

The blank significance property, and the BN and BZ format codes, have no effect on output.

9.4 FILES

Processors that execute Fortran programs vary widely in their ability to perform complicated input and output operations, especially those that involve a number of different external devices. The Fortran language includes a nucleus, or core, of capabilities that can be adapted to the requirements of many different processors. Central to these capabilities in the Fortran language is the concept of a *file*.

A file is an external source from which data may be obtained, or an external destination to which it may be sent.

Data cannot be transferred to or from a file until the file is *connected* to the program. The principal purpose of file connection is to designate a *unit number* to be used by the program in referring to the file, and to establish certain *prop-*

erties that affect the ways in which data can be transferred to or from the file. A file may be *preconnected* (before execution of the program begins), or it may become connected as a result of the execution of an OPEN statement (see Section 9.4.1).

There are two special files that are always preconnected to a program.† These are a default input file and a default output file. The default input file is automatically designated for a READ statement without a control list, or for a READ statement with a control list that includes an asterisk as the unit specifier. The default output file is automatically designated for a PRINT statement, or for a WRITE statement that includes an asterisk as the unit specifier. Both of these are formatted sequential files.

A file may *preexist* (that is, it may be known to the processor before execution begins), or it may be *created* by the program during execution. A file may be created by execution of an OPEN statement; a preconnected file may also be created by execution of the first statement that transfers data to the file. A preexisting file must either have a *name* or be preconnected.

9.4.1 Connection Properties

At the time a unit becomes connected to a file (either by preconnection or by execution of an OPEN statement), the following properties may be established.

1. An *access* method, which is *sequential* or *direct,* is always established.

2. A form, which is *formatted* or *unformatted,* is established for a connection to a preexisting file or to a file that is created at the time it becomes connected. Execution of an OPEN statement may establish, by default, that a sequential access file is formatted or that a direct access file is unformatted. For a preconnected, preexisting file, the form is established by the preconnection. For a preconnected file that is not preexisting, the form may be established either by the preconnection or by the statement that creates the file.

3. A record length may be established. If the access method is direct, the connection establishes a record length, which is the length of each record of the file. If the access method is sequential, this property does not apply.

4. A blank significance property, which is *zero* or *null* (see Section 9.3.3), is established for a connection if the form is *formatted.* This property has no effect on input. For a connection that results from execution of an OPEN statement, the blank significance property is *null* by default if no blank significance property is specified. For a preconnected file, the property is established by the preconnection.

---

† The processor does not need to preconnect a reader or a printer to a program, if it can determine in advance that the program will not actually use them.

The OPEN *statement*

This statement designates the unit number and establishes the connection properties for a file that is not preconnected. The statement consists of the keyword OPEN, followed by a list of specifiers enclosed in parentheses. The list must include a unit specifier (see Section 9.1.3), which must not be an asterisk or an internal file designator. The following specifiers may also be included in the list, in addition to the unit specifier.

ACCESS = *Acess,* where *Acess* is 'SEQUENTIAL' or 'DIRECT'. If this specifier is omitted, the default access method is *sequential.*

FORM = *Form,* where *Form* is 'FORMATTED' or 'UNFORMATTED'. If this specifier is omitted, the default form is *formatted* if the access method is *sequential,* or *unformatted* if the access method is *direct.*

RECL = *Record length,* where *Record length* is an integer expression whose value is positive. This specifier must appear only if the access method is *direct.*

BLANK = *Blank,* where *Blank* is 'NULL' or 'ZERO'. If this specifier is omitted, the default blank significance property is *null.*

Examples of OPEN *statements*

```
OPEN (UNIT = 6, ACCESS = 'SEQUENTIAL', BLANK = 'ZERO')
OPEN (UNIT = J)
OPEN (UNIT = 31, ACCESS = 'DIRECT', RECL = 720)
```

9.5 FILE POSITIONING

9.5.1 Direct Access

Each record of a file connected for direct access has a unique record number, which is established when the record is written and does not change. Records may be written in any order. There is no way to delete a record, but a record may be rewritten.

A file connected for direct access is implicitly positioned during execution of a READ or WRITE statement. Prior to data transfer, the file is positioned at the beginning of the record specified in the control list, and data transfer takes place to or from this record.

More than one record may be read or written during formatted data transfer (if a slash format code is encountered, or if rescan occurs). The record numbers of the additional records follow consecutively after the number specified in the control list.

9.5.2 Sequential Access

A file connected for sequential access consists of a sequence of (zero or more) records, which may be followed by an *endfile* indicator.

Let us suppose that a file designated by device code 7 has been connected for sequential access. The file contains several records and an *endfile* indicator, and is to be used for input.

First we wish to position the file at its *initial point,* that is, at the beginning of the first record of the file. This is accomplished by means of the statement

```
REWIND (7)
```

designating the unit number of our file as the device to be rewound. We then give a sequence of READ statements to be executed. If the file is unformatted, each READ will advance the file by one record; if it is formatted, each READ will advance the file by one record plus additional records that are read when a slash is encountered or when rescan occurs. At the end of execution of each READ statement, the file is positioned at the end of the record just read. Eventually, the *endfile* indicator is encountered during an input operation. The file is then positioned following the *endfile* indicator. At this point, no further data transfer is possible until the file has been repositioned (for example, by another REWIND).

Now let us consider a file that is to be used for sequential output. Suppose this file is referenced by device code 13; it contains no records and no *endfile* indicator. Again we begin by positioning the file at its initial point by means of the statement

```
REWIND (13)
```

We now give a sequence of WRITE statements. If the file is unformatted, each WRITE will add one record to the file; if it is formatted, at least one record will be added, plus additional records if a slash is encountered or rescan occurs. At the end of execution of each WRITE statement, the file is positioned at the end of the record just written. After the desired data has been transmitted to the file, an

```
ENDFILE (13)
```

statement may be executed to append an *endfile* indicator following the last record written. When this statement has been executed, the file is positioned after the *endfile* indicator and no further data transfer is permitted until the file has been repositioned.

We see that file positioning occurs implicitly during execution of a READ, WRITE, PRINT, or ENDFILE statement, and explicitly by execution of a REWIND statement. Another statement is available for explicit positioning. When the file is positioned *after* a record or after the *endfile* indicator, execution of a BACK-SPACE statement—for example

```
BACKSPACE (7)
BACKSPACE (13)
```

—will reposition it *before* the same record (or *endfile* indicator). (If the file is already at its initial point, this statement has no effect.)

A sequential file may be used for both input and output. READ statements may be executed to position the file at the end of a particular record. WRITE statements may then be used to add new data to the file beyond that point. It should be noted that the last record written on a sequential file becomes the *last* record of the file: Any records that were previously present on the file *beyond* that point are lost.

The *endfile* indicator is written on the file by execution of an ENDFILE statement. A READ operation that moves the file position past this indicator must include an IOSTAT specifier or END specifier; the status variable will then be set, or the indicated control transfer will take place (or both), as described in Section 9.1.3.

We have noted that data transfer is prohibited while a file is positioned beyond the *endfile* indicator (as a result of a READ or ENDFILE operation). A REWIND may be executed to reposition the file at its initial point, or a BACKSPACE may be executed to reposition the file ahead of the *endfile* indicator, after which further input and output operations may take place. A likely example would be the process of appending a set of records on the end of a preexisting file, as illustrated in the following example. The file is read until the *endfile* indicator is encountered. Then the END = 9 specifier causes a transfer to statement 9. The following statements backspace the file and write additional records, beyond those that were formerly present on the file.

```
* Example. Appending records to an existing file.
      OPEN (2)
*      . . Access is sequential, and Form is formatted,
*         by default.
      DO 8, LOOP = 1, 4000
        READ (2, '([])', END = 9)
  8     CONTINUE
*      . . Stop if the file contains more than 4000 records.
      STOP
  9   CONTINUE
      BACKSPACE (2)
      WRITE (2, . . .
      . . .
```

Record length for sequential files

We have seen that all records of a direct access file have the same length, which is established at the time the file is connected. In contrast, the length of each record of a sequential file is established when the record is written. Record lengths for an *unformatted* file are processor-dependent, since the amount of space required on the external device depends on the representation of data by the processor. *List directed formatting* also produces records whose lengths are somewhat unpredictable. *Explicitly formatted* records, however, consist of a sequence of characters whose length is completely specified by the rules of Fortran. For example, the Tw format code changes positioning within a record, but does not actually increase the record length until another data item is transmitted.

The length of a formatted record may be zero: for example, a record produced by a list directed or explicitly formatted WRITE statement with an empty list, or a record written when the format scan encounters two consecutive slashes.

A formatted record may have been prepared by some other means than execution of a Fortran program, but in any case it consists of some fixed number of characters.

Formatted input must respect these established record lengths. It is impossible to read from a record more characters than have been written there. (For example, a record of zero length can be read only by a statement with no list, or by a format containing two consecutive slashes, or by some other means that does not require any transmission of data from the record.) It is legitimate, however, to read fewer characters than the record contains. Unfortunately, Fortran does not provide a means for reading an "indefinite" amount of data from a record (with a subsequent inquiry to ascertain the amount actually read). Therefore, a program can successfully read the records of a file only if it has information available to it concerning the lengths of the records of the file—or at least a lower bound for the length of each record.

PART 3
FORTRAN APPLICATIONS

CHAPTER 10

FORTRAN APPLICATIONS

In this chapter we consider six different areas of application of computers:

Simulation,
Sorting and merging,
Payroll,
Printer plots,
The calendar,
Trees and graphs.

This list, of course, does not exhaust the areas in which computers can be used, but the applications are chosen to demonstrate what can be accomplished with a Fortran program of reasonable complexity (typically, between 30 and 100 statements).

The six application areas are mutually independent. For example, it is possible to understand the payroll application without first studying the description of sorting and merging.

Each section of the chapter concentrates on one of these six areas. In a book of this size it is impossible to cover all aspects within such an area, but we present a few programs of increasing length, and with most of them we include complete flowcharts, typical data, and corresponding results. Toward the end of each section, we propose one or more projects for the student to attempt. Some of the projects simply require minor modifications of the programs that have been presented, but others are significantly challenging.

10.1 SIMULATION

10.1.1 Random Number Generators

For simulating any sort of process subject to "unknown" effects, the ability to obtain "random" numbers is indispensable. The idea of generating random numbers by an algorithmic process may seem self-contradictory; nevertheless, programs can be written to produce sequences that behave, for many purposes, in the desired "random" manner. A very complete discussion of the philosophical and algorithmic aspects of this question is given by D. E. Knuth in *The Art of Computer Programming: Seminumerical Algorithms,* Volume 2, Chapter 3 (Addison-Wesley, 1969).

The requirement for random numbers usually appears in one of two forms. The numbers generated are required to be *uniform* on some interval, or they are required to have a *normal* or Gaussian distribution with specified mean and variance. We shall first consider the problem of obtaining uniformly distributed random numbers. The term "uniformly distributed" means that if we divide the interval into subintervals of equal size, the number of terms of the generated sequence in each subinterval will tend *in the long run* to be approximately the same.

The simplest procedure, and the first one to be considered when it is available, is to generate a uniform sequence by means of the random number generator included with the system subprogram library at most computer installations. Usually such programs are carefully designed and thoroughly tested, and they are fast and easy to use as well. There is no standard name or argument convention for such a function, so relevant information will have to be obtained from the local computer center. Furthermore, expressions involving this function may have to be modified to make them work at different computer installations. If such a subprogram is not available at your computer center for some reason, you may have to use a method you prepare for yourself.

Once you have a source of uniform random numbers, it is not too hard to generate numbers having any other specified distribution, such as the Gaussian distribution which arises in many simulation problems involving experimental measurements. An easy way to generate a fairly accurate approximation to a Gaussian distribution is to find the *sum* of 12 *uniformly* distributed random numbers. The number 12 is convenient because, when the uniform numbers come from the interval $(0.0, 1.0)$, their sum approximates a Gaussian distribution that happens to have standard deviation 1.0 (and mean 6.0).

Details of a Fortran program for generating random numbers

Those readers who are not interested in the inner workings of random number generators may prefer to skip the following paragraphs and to go on reading from the beginning of Section 10.1.2, where we continue our discussion of simulation and related applications. We present these details, nevertheless, not only to provide a behind-the-scenes look at how a random number generator might work, but also to define a "random" sequence that can be used as a specific test case in further examples and projects.

The method most commonly used for generating a sequence of uniform random numbers is the *congruential* method, which starts with a value IX between 0 and $(M - 1)$ and calculates the next value of IX by the expression

```
MOD (J * IX + K, M)
```

for suitable choice of J, K, and M. It is usually possible to choose J, K, and M so that the sequence of values of IX will progress "at random" through *all* of the M different integers between 0 and $(M - 1)$, before the sequence repeats (as it eventually must).

For rapidly generating a great many uniform random numbers, a subprogram written in Fortran is necessarily inefficient. Furthermore (since J must not be too small, as can be shown on theoretical grounds), the intermediate value $J * IX + K$ will assume values much larger than M, and therefore there is no way, staying within the Fortran language, to use a value of M anywhere near as large as the maximum integer that can be stored on a given computer.†

Although the following subroutine is inefficient for the reasons just mentioned, it may be used to generate a sequence of length 566927; here M is 566927, J is 3612, and K is 5701.

```
SUBROUTINE RAND (X)
DATA K, J, M, RM / 5701, 3612, 566927, 566927.0 /
IX = INT (X * RM)
IRAND = MOD (J * IX + K, M)
X = (REAL (IRAND) + 0.5) / RM
RETURN
END
```

† Special techniques suggested by Schrage (*ACM Transactions on Mathematical Software* 5(2): June 1979, p. 132–138) result in reasonable efficiency while maintaining compatibility with almost all Fortran processors.

Before this subroutine is used the first time, the main program should assign to X a value between 0.0 and 1.0. The precise value is unimportant; in our examples we will use $X = 0.5$ as the starting value. Table 10.1 lists the first 100 numbers generated from the subroutine. These are listed across the page, by rows; that is, the first 5 numbers in the sequence are shown on the top line.

Table 10.1 A listing of the first 100 numbers generated by the subroutine *Rand*, with $M = 566927$, $J = 3612$, and $K = 5701$, starting from $X = 0.5$

0.00687	0.82584	0.95692	0.40010	0.15538
0.22276	0.60224	0.29382	0.29751	0.61330
0.24119	0.18118	0.43328	0.99747	0.87377
0.06217	0.56267	0.37527	0.49998	0.93679
0.68570	0.74671	0.11982	0.80504	0.80235
0.11177	0.73329	0.66692	0.91264	0.47047
0.34040	0.52243	0.01656	0.82279	0.94113
0.37157	0.11411	0.16875	0.53549	0.21434
0.20529	0.50834	0.12349	0.05074	0.29010
0.84156	0.70511	0.88078	0.36854	0.16840
0.28037	0.70444	0.44061	0.48888	0.84926
0.52173	0.50631	0.80299	0.41177	0.33266
0.56564	0.11073	0.96792	0.13721	0.61861
0.41210	0.51770	0.93540	0.66520	0.70710
0.06111	0.72721	0.70542	0.99573	0.59815
0.51266	0.73928	0.27800	0.12882	0.29174
0.76676	0.55389	0.65312	0.06445	0.78788
0.82341	0.17105	0.83079	0.80262	0.08657
0.68261	0.59075	0.81100	0.34335	0.18780
0.34435	0.81301	0.59377	0.68662	0.09158

This subroutine, if called 566927 times, will produce exactly once each of the following values—$(0.5/RM)$, $(1.5/RM)$, $(2.5/RM)$, ..., $((RM - 1.5)/RM)$, $((RM - 0.5)/RM)$—but of course not in this sequence. If called 566928 or more times, it will begin to repeat the previous sequence of values.

Note that we have divided the terms of the sequence by RM, which has the same numerical value as the modulus M. Thus the values in the sequence lie in the interval between 0.0 and 1.0; this pattern conforms to the convention used in many system library procedures. However, some of them use $(-1.0, 1.0)$ or some other interval. It is easy to scale the result to obtain numbers uniformly distributed in some other interval: First multiply by a constant to obtain the desired interval width, and then add another constant to shift one end of the interval to the correct point, as required.

Since *IX* is an integer between 0 and $(M - 1)$, the second assignment statement of the foregoing subroutine generates intermediate results as large as

$$J \cdot (M - 1) + K.$$

The parameters have been chosen so that the value of this expression will never exceed 2^{31}. However, some small computers cannot handle integers this large and will require a different choice of values for *J*, *K*, and *M*. The book by D. E. Knuth cited in the first paragraph of this section explains in a rather theoretical way the criteria that must be applied in choosing appropriate values. Values whose size is desirable from the point of view of a Fortran program and that satisfy Knuth's criteria may be obtained by the following procedure.

1. Choose a small prime number, *IP1* (between 13 and 47, for example).
2. Let *L* be the largest integer that the computer can handle. Choose a prime number, *IP2*, slightly smaller than the cube root of $L/(IP1^2)$.
3. Use $(IP1 \cdot IP2 + 1)$ as the value of *J*, and use $(IP1 \cdot IP2^2)$ as the value of *M*. For *K*, choose a prime near the square root of *L*. Check to see that

$$J \cdot (M - 1) + K$$

does not exceed *L*; choose a smaller prime as *IP2* if necessary.

We have used $IP1 = 23$, $IP2 = 157$. Our subroutine may be varied to produce a different sequence by choosing a value of *K* different from 5701. Choosing too large a value of *IP1* will reduce *M* (which is the period of the sequence of random numbers); too small a value of *IP1* seems to give a sequence with other undesirable properties.

For many purposes, a period as short as 566927 is inadequate. A method of extending the period of any "fairly random" sequence is implemented in the subroutine called *Extend,* which is represented in Figs. 10.1 and 10.2.

The idea is to maintain a table of 100 random numbers and to choose elements at random from this table. The value of *IFlag* will be zero the first time *Extend* is called and 1 thereafter. When *IFlag* is zero, 100 values are obtained from *Rand* and stored in *Table*. Then, each time *Extend* is called, two more values are obtained from *Rand;* one of them is used to choose an element from the table, and the second is stored in place of the chosen element.

The first 100 numbers generated by the program in Fig. 10.2 are listed as results in Fig. 10.3.

```
      REAL RESULT(100)
      DO 388, I = 1, 100
        CALL EXTEND (Y)
        RESULT(I) = Y
388   CONTINUE
      PRINT 688, RESULT
688 FORMAT (1H0, 10 F8.5)
      END

      SUBROUTINE EXTEND (Y)
      REAL TABLE(100)
      DATA IFLAG / 0 /
      IF (IFLAG .LE. 0) THEN
          X = 0.5
          DO 9, I = 1, 100
            CALL RAND (X)
            TABLE(I) = X
9         CONTINUE
          IFLAG = 1
      END IF
      CALL RAND (X)
      J = INT (100.0 * X) + 1
      Y = TABLE(J)
      CALL RAND (X)
      TABLE(J) = X
      RETURN
      END
```

Fig. 10.1 Program for extending the period of a random number generator.

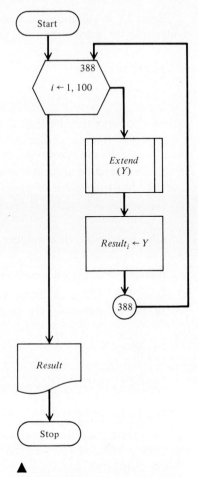

Fig. 10.2 Flowchart for extending the period of a random number generator. ▶

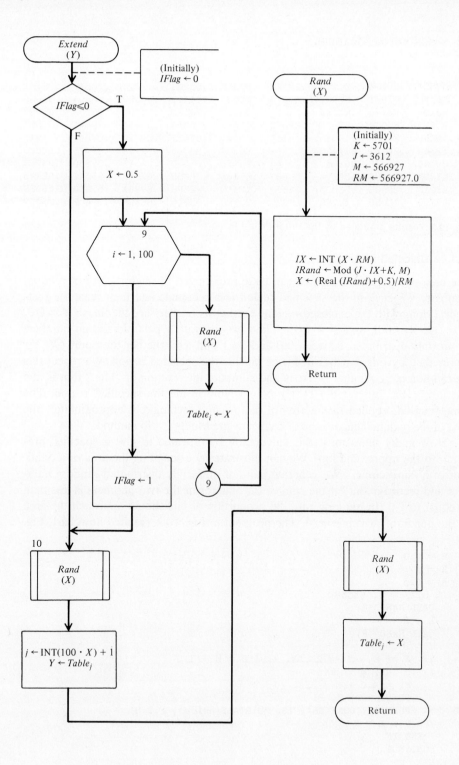

.76676	.37527	.29174	.51770	.12882	.87377	.51266	.11073	.70542	.29751
.70710	.84926	.61861	.00687	.33266	.29010	.44121	.80262	.36854	.01656
.50834	.53173	.94113	.83244	.11177	.36779	.56153	.14385	.29382	.20529
.59377	.83781	.83079	.93679	.89073	.80299	.16833	.34435	.70444	.21357
.53549	.96250	.80235	.15538	.24119	.53571	.07877	.59815	.07549	.73219
.96792	.12349	.84156	.11428	.91264	.60224	.59535	.38114	.59075	.66520
.72721	.09158	.26448	.01940	.34040	.45256	.61330	.82341	.87630	.99747
.14146	.51992	.74983	.56694	.56267	.81100	.76659	.43078	.93540	.92795
.75786	.41210	.29506	.53003	.34555	.18118	.22596	.69861	.52243	.56088
.82584	.85916	.75030	.18780	.37670	.23190	.08510	.66398	.78408	.28037

Fig. 10.3 Results produced by the program in Fig. 10.1.

10.1.2   Calculating Areas

The area of a region of a plane can be approximated through the use of random numbers. We enclose the specified region in a rectangle and then scale the rectangle (along with the enclosed region) so that its borders are the lines ($X = 0.0$, $X = 1.0$, $Y = 0.0$, and $Y = 1.0$). Then we generate a pair of random numbers (uniformly distributed between 0.0 and 1.0) and test whether the point (X, Y) represented by this pair lies inside or outside the specified region. We repeat this operation a large number of times and compute the *fraction* of "hits," that is, the fraction of the generated (X, Y) points lying inside the specified region. The same fraction, applied to the area of the original rectangle, is approximately the area of the region. This process is known as the Monte Carlo method.

How many times must this calculation be repeated to give a specified precision to the approximation? We can illustrate by calculating the area of a quadrant of a "unit circle." We generate pairs of uniformly distributed random numbers and record a "hit" if the sum of the squares of the two numbers is less than or equal to 1.0. In the long run, the proportion of hits should approach the area of the quadrant, which is $\pi/4$. The program in Fig. 10.4 (related flowchart, Fig.

```
      H = 0.0
      K = 1
      R = 0.5
      DO 5, J = 1, 65536
        CALL RAND (R)
        X = R
        CALL RAND (R)
        Y = R
        IF (X ** 2 + Y ** 2 .LE. 1.0) H = H + 1.0
        IF (J .GE. K) THEN
          PI = 4.0 * H / REAL (J)
          PRINT 905, J, PI
905       FORMAT ('0␣AFTER', I6, '␣TRIALS,␣PI␣=', F11.8)
          K = 2 * K
        END IF
5     CONTINUE
      END
```

Fig. 10.4 Program for calculating area by simulation.

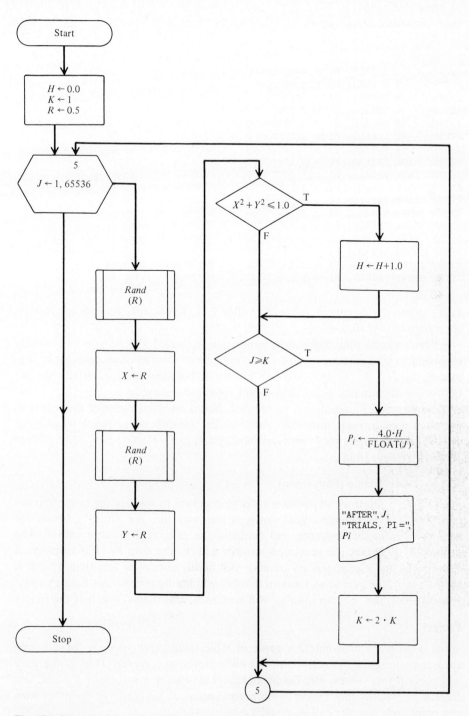

Fig. 10.5 Flowchart for calculating area by simulation.

```
AFTER      1 TRIALS, PI = 4.00000000
AFTER      2 TRIALS, PI = 2.00000000
AFTER      4 TRIALS, PI = 3.00000000
AFTER      8 TRIALS, PI = 3.00000000
AFTER     16 TRIALS, PI = 2.75000000
AFTER     32 TRIALS, PI = 3.12500000
AFTER     64 TRIALS, PI = 3.12500000
AFTER    128 TRIALS, PI = 3.12500000
AFTER    256 TRIALS, PI = 3.09375000
AFTER    512 TRIALS, PI = 3.11718750
AFTER   1024 TRIALS, PI = 3.16015625
AFTER   2048 TRIALS, PI = 3.15429688
AFTER   4096 TRIALS, PI = 3.15527344
AFTER   8192 TRIALS, PI = 3.14941406
AFTER  16384 TRIALS, PI = 3.14038086
AFTER  32768 TRIALS, PI = 3.14355469
AFTER  65536 TRIALS, PI = 3.14276123
```

Fig. 10.6 Results from the program in Fig. 10.4.

10.5) prints the estimated value of π after 2, 4, 8, 16, . . . , repetitions. Results are shown in Fig. 10.6.

We conclude that this simple simulation approach should not be seriously considered as a practical way of calculating areas to more than one or two significant figures. A reasonable rough answer is obtained after 32 trials, but the improvement from that point on does not appear to justify the further effort. However, more efficient simulation techniques, based on refinements of this method, are often used to solve practical problems that are difficult to attack by analytic means. (For example, see J. M. Hammersley and D. C. Handscomb, *Monte Carlo Methods*, Wiley, 1964.)

10.1.3 Table Tennis (Ping-Pong)

We can use a sequence of uniform random numbers to simulate an event that occurs with a given probability, P, between zero and one. We simply generate the next number in the sequence and compare the generated number with P. The probability is P that the generated number will be less than P. (For instance, if P is nearly one, the generated number will nearly always be less than P; if P is close to zero, the generated random number will hardly ever be less than P; and if P is one-half, the random number will tend to be less than P one-half the time.)

Project

Write a program to simulate a game of table tennis (ping-pong). Read a data card containing the "effectiveness" of each player as a server. That is, the card will contain two values: $P1$, the probability that Player 1 will make a point; and $P2$, the probability that Player 2 will make a point. (One player or the other wins one point each time the ball is served.)

For each serve, we generate a random number and compare it with $P1$ or $P2$ (depending on which player is serving). The server wins the point if the random number is less than the "effectiveness" value; otherwise, the player who is not serving wins.

Let us assume that Player 1 serves first. The serve changes after every five serves. The game ends when either player has 21 points if the other player has 19 or less. If the score (20, 20) is reached, the players alternate service from that point on until one of the players is 2 points ahead of the other.

Data:

	P1	*P2*
Case 1.	0.46	0.43
Case 2.	0.39	0.47
Case 3.	0.63	0.71

10.2   TABLE SORTING, INDIRECT SORTING, AND MERGING

10.2.1   The Basic Insertion Sort Algorithm

A fairly simple sorting algorithm that is reasonably efficient for small amounts of data is the Insertion sort. This is one of several methods that are called "bubble sorting" (W. A. Martin, "Sorting," *Computing Surveys,* vol. 3, pp. 147–174, December 1971), and it may be described by analogy to the way a person might arrange a hand of bridge cards. (See also Exercise 3 in Section 4.3.1.)

At first, let us assume that we have an array, L, in storage large enough to hold all the items to be sorted, and that the items (each consisting of a single integer) are available on data cards, one item per card. To make the explanation slightly simpler, we assume that all the items have *different* values.

We begin by reading the first item into L_1. However, instead of reading the next item into L_2, we read it into an auxiliary cell *Next,* because we want to store the first two items in the desired ascending order. We compare the new item with L_1. If the new item is larger, we simply store it at L_2; otherwise, we move L_1 to L_2 and store the new item at L_1. In either case, the first two elements of the linear array L are now in correct ascending order, and we read the third data item.

Again we read the new item into *Next.* We do not want to store it in the linear array L until we find out where to put it. We first want to be sure that the largest of the three items read so far will go into L_3.

Since we have guaranteed that the larger of the two previous items is in L_2, we know that the largest of the three is either in L_2 or in *Next.* Therefore we compare these two items, and if *Next* is larger, we store it in L_3.

However, if L_2 is larger than *Next,* we move L_2 to L_3, thus guaranteeing that the largest of the three items is stored in L_3. In this case, then, the new item remains in *Next,* and the cell L_2 is now available. We know that *Next* is smaller than the number now in L_3, but we do not yet know its rank relative to L_1. Thus we are in the same position as when we had just read the second item. We compare *Next* with L_1. If the new item is larger, we store it in L_2; otherwise, we move L_1 to L_2 and store the new item at L_1. We now have the first three items in correct ascending order, and we read the fourth item into *Next*.

Each time we read a new item, we store it temporarily at *Next,* and then we compare it with the items already stored in the linear array, beginning with the largest and working backward toward the beginning of the linear array. Each time we come to a previously stored item that is larger than the new item, we move it to the next higher position in the linear array, thus making its former position available. As soon as we come to an item in the linear array that is smaller than the new item, we store the new item in the available position of the linear array and proceed to read another new item.

The flowchart in Fig. 4.13 shows how this algorithm would be applied to the task of sorting N items into ascending order. Figure 10.7 is a slight modification of that flowchart, which works when the items are already in the linear array L, rather than on data cards. Each item in turn is moved to *Next,* and the remaining steps proceed as before. Note that in either of these flowcharts it is not actually necessary to assume that the items all have different values; the test is made such that when *Next* is equal to L_i the effect is the same as when *Next* is *larger*. Thus the extra move of L_i to L_{i+1} is avoided except when *Next* is actually smaller than L_i. Furthermore, in order to sort items into *decreasing* sequence, we need only change the relation in the assertion (where *Next* is compared with L_i) from $\geq$ to $\leq$.

A simple measure of the efficiency of various sorting methods is the *number of comparisons* required for sorting an array of n items. For the insertion method, the expected, or "average," number of comparisons (when n is large) is approximately one-fourth of n^2. If the data is already in order, only n comparisons are needed to establish that fact, but if it is in exactly the wrong order, approximately one-half n^2 comparisons will be needed. Various other simple sorting algorithms require from two to four times as many comparisons. (The advantage of the insertion method stems from the exit from the inner loop when the proper position for the new item has been located.) Some more complicated methods are faster for long arrays, such as the Shell and Quicksort algorithms (see Martin, *loc. cit.*), for which the number of comparisons is a small multiple of $n \log_e n$.

10.2.2   Direct Sorting of Long Items

It often happens that the items to be sorted do not consist of a single number each, in contrast to our assumption of that form heretofore. Very little additional complication is required with longer items, however. It is merely necessary to expand each "move" operation to include the entire item.

For example, let us assume that the items to be sorted are the rows of the rectangular array A. Suppose that there are 40 rows (items) to be sorted, and

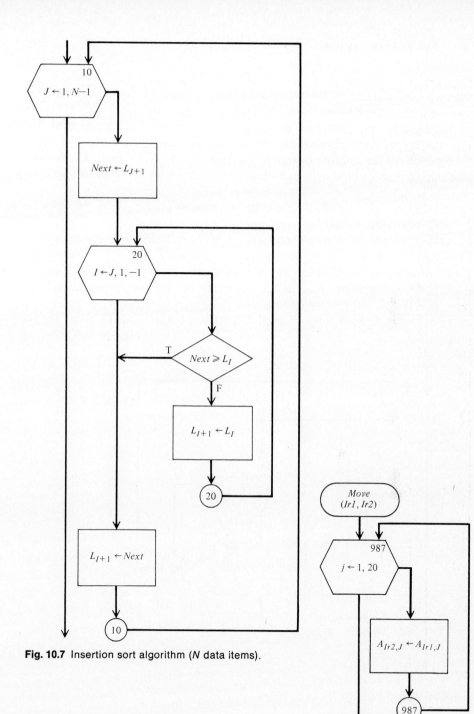

Fig. 10.7 Insertion sort algorithm (*N* data items).

▶
Fig. 10.8 Flowchart for subroutine *Move*.

that each item is stored in 20 cells (thus A has 20 columns). We add a forty-first row to play the role of *Next*.

Let the *key*—the portion of the item to be used as the basis for ranking the items during the sorting procedure—be the first element in each row. We write a subroutine for the "move" operation (see the flowchart in Fig. 10.8). We replace the three assignment steps by calls to *Move:*

`CALL MOVE (J + 1, 41)`	replaces	$Next \leftarrow L_{I+1}$
`CALL MOVE (I, I + 1)`	replaces	$L_{I+1} \leftarrow L_I$
`CALL MOVE (41, I + 1)`	replaces	$L_{I+1} \leftarrow Next$

Expansion to a multiple-cell key is only slightly more complicated. For example, if the key consists of the first five elements in each row, we might replace

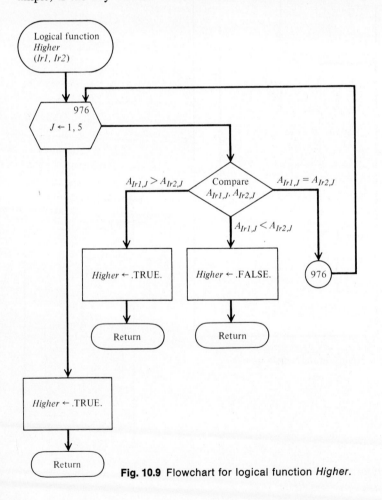

Fig. 10.9 Flowchart for logical function *Higher*.

the assertion *Next* $\geq L_I$ in Fig. 10.7 by an assertion involving the logical function *Higher,* whose flowchart appears in Fig. 10.9.

```
          LOGICAL FUNCTION HIGHER (IR1, IR2)
          COMMON A(41, 20)
          DO 976, J = 1, 5
            IF (A(IR1, J) .GT. A(IR2, J)) THEN
                HIGHER = .TRUE.
                RETURN
              ELSE IF (A(IR1, J) .LT. A(IR2, J)) THEN
                HIGHER = .FALSE.
                RETURN
              END IF
    976     CONTINUE
    *       . . Rows Ir1 and Ir2 are equal
          HIGHER = .TRUE.
          RETURN
          END
```

As soon as an element of row *Ir1* is found that is not equal to the corresponding element of row *Ir2*, the function value is set and a RETURN is executed. However, so long as corresponding elements of the two rows are equal, the loop continues. If all five elements agree, the loop terminates. We want to treat this case the same as we would if *Ir1* were larger than *Ir2*, so we set the function value to .TRUE..

The program in Fig. 10.10 shows how *Move* and *Higher* may be used to sort an array of 40 items, each occupying 20 cells, with the first five cells containing the key. As before, we add a forty-first row for auxiliary storage. The flowchart is shown in Fig. 10.11, and sample data and results are displayed in Fig. 10.12.

```
* Program to sort long items with long key
* using subprograms Move and Higher
        LOGICAL HIGHER
        COMMON A(41, 20)
        READ *, ((A(J, L), L = 1, 20), J = 1, 40)
        DO 10, J = 1, 39
          CALL MOVE (J + 1, 41)
          DO 20, I = J, 1, -1
            IF (HIGHER (41, I)) GO TO 9
            CALL MOVE (I, I + 1)
    20      CONTINUE
    9     CALL MOVE (41, I + 1)
    10    CONTINUE
        PRINT *, ((A(J, L), L = 1, 20), J = 1, 40)
        END
```

Fig. 10.10 Main program, which uses subprograms *Move* and *Higher* for sorting long items with long key.

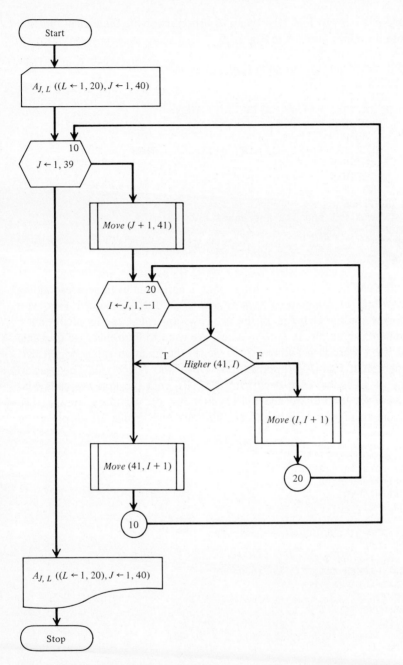

Fig. 10.11 Flowchart showing use of subprograms *Move* and *Higher* to sort long items with long key.

Data (first 5 items)

20.0000	19.1908	18.0000	17.0000	16.0000	15.0000	14.3252	13.2099
12.4715	11.0000	10.0000	9.0000	8.1506	7.0000	6.1352	5.0000
4.0000	3.4224	2.0000	1.0000				
20.0325	19.1908	18.4334	17.0000	16.0000	15.0000	14.0000	13.2099
12.4715	11.0000	10.2110	9.0000	8.1506	7.0000	6.0000	5.0000
4.0000	3.0000	2.3771	1.0087				
20.0325	19.0000	18.0000	17.0000	16.3879	15.4193	14.0000	13.0000
12.4715	11.2471	10.0000	9.0000	8.1506	7.0000	6.1352	5.1285
4.0597	3.4224	2.3771	1.0000				
20.0000	19.1908	18.0000	17.0000	16.0000	15.4193	14.3252	13.0000
12.0000	11.0000	10.2110	9.3800	8.1506	7.3591	6.0000	5.1285
4.0597	3.0000	2.0000	1.0000				
20.0000	19.1908	18.0000	17.0000	16.0000	15.0000	14.3252	13.2099
12.4715	11.0000	10.0000	9.3800	8.1506	7.0000	6.1352	5.0000
4.0000	3.4224	2.3771	1.0043				

Results

```
20.0000 19.1908 18.0000 17.0000 16.0000 15.0000 14.3252 13.2099 12.4715 11.0000
10.0000  9.0000  8.1506  7.0000  6.1352  5.0000  4.0000  3.4224  2.0000  1.0000
20.0000 19.1908 18.0000 17.0000 16.0000 15.4193 14.3252 13.0000 12.0000 11.0000
10.2110  9.3800  8.1506  7.3591  6.0000  5.1285  4.0597  3.0000  2.0000  1.0000
20.0000 19.1908 18.0000 17.0000 16.0000 15.0000 14.3252 13.2099 12.4715 11.0000
10.0000  9.3800  8.1506  7.0000  6.1352  5.0000  4.0000  3.4224  2.3771  1.0043
20.0325 19.0000 18.0000 17.0000 16.3879 15.4193 14.0000 13.0000 12.4715 11.2471
10.0000  9.0000  8.1506  7.0000  6.1352  5.1285  4.0597  3.4224  2.3771  1.0000
20.0325 19.1908 18.4334 17.0000 16.0000 15.0000 14.0000 13.2099 12.4715 11.0000
10.2110  9.0000  8.1506  7.0000  6.0000  5.0000  4.0000  3.0000  2.3771  1.0087
```

Fig. 10.12 Sample data and results for program in Fig. 10.10.

10.2.3 Indirect Sorting

We have noted that the efficiency of sorting algorithms is often estimated by counting the number of comparisons required to sort n items. However, if each item is as long as 20 cells, considerable additional time may be required to *move* the items that are found to be out of order. For long items, then, it may be advantageous to determine the rank of each item, without actually moving the items into sorted sequence.

Such *ranking,* or *indirect sorting,* algorithms typically require an additional array of integers, one integer for each complete data item. In our example, there would be 40 such integers or *pointers.* These integers are called pointers because they are used as subscripts to designate ("point" to) data items, that is, row numbers within the array A.

We assume that the linear array *IPtr* initially contains the consecutive integer values from 1 to 40; that is, $IPtr_J$ is initialized to the integer value J. The purpose of indirect sorting is to rearrange the elements of this linear array so that $IPtr_1$

will be the subscript of that row of the data array A corresponding to the smallest key, $IPtr_2$ will be the row subscript of the second smallest key in A, etc. Thus the rows of A can be accessed in ascending order *indirectly,* via the linear array *IPtr.* Figures 10.13–10.16 show how this is accomplished. The algorithm is quite similar to the preceding one, except that when an item is found to be out of order, only the *pointer* to it is moved, while the data itself remains in its original location in storage. The indirect sorting algorithm is written as a subroutine; the main program initializes *IPtr,* reads the input data, calls *Sort,* and prints the results. (The data is the same as in Fig. 10.12.) Note that the *Common* region does not have an extra row.

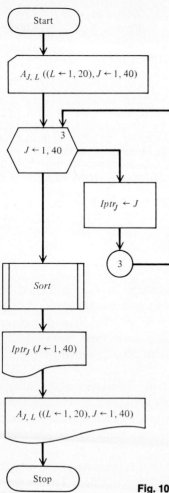

Fig. 10.13 Flowchart showing use of indirect sorting algorithm.

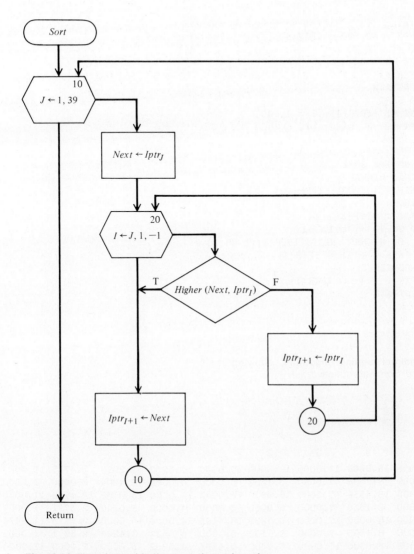

Fig. 10.14 Flowchart of indirect sorting subroutine.

```
* Main program for indirect sorting
      COMMON A(40, 20), IPTR(40)
      READ *, ((A(J, L), L = 1, 20), J = 1, 40)
      DO 30, J = 1, 40
        IPTR(J) = J
   3    CONTINUE
      CALL SORT
      PRINT *, (IPTR(J), J = 1, 40)
      PRINT *, (J, (A(J, L), L = 1, 20), J = 1, 40)
      END

      SUBROUTINE SORT
      LOGICAL HIGHER
      COMMON A(40, 20), IPTR(40)
      DO 10, J = 1, 39
        NEXT = IPTR(J + 1)
        DO 20, I = J, 1, -1
          IF (HIGHER (NEXT, IPTR(I))) GO TO 9
          IPTR(I + 1) = IPTR(I)
  20      CONTINUE
   9      IPTR(I + 1) = IPTR(I)
  10      CONTINUE
      RETURN
      END
```

Fig. 10.15 Indirect sorting algorithm, showing main program and *Sort* subroutine.

	1	4	5	3	2					
1	20.0000	19.1908	18.0000	17.0000	16.0000	15.0000	14.3252	13.2099	12.4715	11.0000
	10.0000	9.0000	8.1506	7.0000	6.1352	5.0000	4.0000	3.4224	2.0000	1.0000
2	20.0325	19.1908	18.4334	17.0000	16.0000	15.0000	14.0000	13.2099	12.4715	11.0000
	10.2110	9.0000	8.1506	7.0000	6.0000	5.0000	4.0000	3.0000	2.3771	1.0087
3	20.0325	19.0000	18.0000	17.0000	16.3879	15.4193	14.0000	13.0000	12.4715	11.2471
	10.0000	9.0000	8.1506	7.0000	6.1352	5.1005	4.0597	3.4224	2.3771	1.0000
4	20.0000	19.1908	18.0000	17.0000	16.0000	15.4193	14.3252	13.0000	12.0000	11.0000
	10.2110	9.3800	8.1506	7.3591	6.0000	5.1285	4.0597	3.0000	2.0000	1.0000
5	20.0000	19.1908	18.0000	17.0000	16.0000	15.0000	14.3252	13.2099	12.4715	11.0000
	10.0000	9.3800	8.1506	7.0000	6.1352	5.0000	4.0000	3.4224	2.3771	1.0043

Fig. 10.16 Results for indirect sorting algorithm.

10.2.4 Alphabetic Sorting

Project

Adapt the program in Fig. 10.7 to sort 40 strings, each consisting of 20 characters. Use the data listed in Table 10.2.

Table 10.2 Data for alphabetic sorting project

Hill, Lister	Fong, Hiram L.
Sparkman, John J.	Inouye, Daniel K.
Bartlett, E. L.	Church, Frank
Gruening, Ernest	Jordan, Len B.
Fannin, Paul J.	Douglas, Paul H.
Hayden, Carl	Dirksen, Everett M.
Fullbright, J. W.	Bayh, Birch
McClellan, John L.	Hartke, Vance
Kuchel, Thomas H.	Hickenlooper, Bourke
Murphy, George	Miller, Jack
Allott, Gordon	Carlson, Frank
Dominick, Peter H.	Pearson, James B.
Dodd, Thomas J.	Cooper, John Sherman
Ribicoff, Abraham A.	Morton, Thruston
Boggs, J. Caleb	Ellender, Allen J.
Williams, John J.	Long, Russell B.
Holland, Spessard L.	Muskie, Edmund S.
Smathers, George A.	Smith, Margaret C.
Russell, Richard B.	Brewster, Daniel B.
Talmadge, Herman E.	Tydings, Joseph D.

10.2.5 Merging

A problem closely related to that of sorting a group of items into a desired (e.g., ascending) order is the problem of *merging* into a single ordered sequence two (or more) groups of items that have already been sorted separately. An algorithm for merging proceeds along the following lines.

Let the previously sorted items be stored in linear arrays A and B of 40 items each, and let linear array C of 80 items be set aside to receive the merged items. Use three counters: KA and KB to keep track of scans through arrays A and B, respectively; and KC to designate the next available position in array C. (Assume that the 80 items to be merged all have *different* values; in the absence of this assumption the problem would not be essentially more difficult, but the algorithm would be slightly harder to explain.)

1. Set all three counters, KA, KB, and KC, initially to 1.

2. Compare the items designated by the counters KA and KB. If A_{KA} is smaller than B_{KB}, then move A_{KA} to C_{KC} and increase KA and KC each by 1. If B_{KB} is smaller than A_{KA}, then move B_{KB} to C_{KC} and increase KB and KC each by 1.

3. When either KA or KB is increased beyond the maximum value of 40, steps must be taken to ensure that all the remaining items will be taken from the opposite list.

4. After all the items have been transferred to array C, print the merged array and stop.

Projects

1. Construct a flowchart and program for this algorithm. Run the program, using the data listed in Table 10.3.

Table 10.3 Data for merging project

Group *A*

2	3	5	7	11	13	17	19	23	29	31	37	41	43	47
53	59	61	67	71	73	79	83	89	97	101	103	107	109	113
127	131	137	139	149	151	157	163	167	173					

Group *B*

4	8	12	16	20	24	28	32	36	40	44	48	52	56	60
64	68	72	76	80	84	88	92	96	100	104	108	112	116	120
124	128	132	136	140	144	148	152	156	160					

2. Suppose that the items in linear arrays *A* and *B* are arranged in order, as before, and that no item appears more than once in the same array. However, assume now that the same item may appear in both arrays. Construct a flowchart and a program for a merging algorithm that will eliminate duplicates, so that an item that appears both in array *A* and in array *B* will appear only once in *C*. Note that *C* will have fewer than 80 items if duplicates occur. Use the same data as before, except in *A* change 53 to 48 and 131 to 128; and in *B* change 28 to 29, 96 to 97, and 160 to 157.

10.3 PAYROLL CALCULATION

A computer application that affects almost everyone—at least, all those who work for a company or an institution with more than a handful of employees—is the calculation of payrolls. Although to the uninitiated it might seem that a "universal" payroll program could be developed for everyone to use, this idea has proved to be impractical. Each employer has a different set of deductions for retirement, employee investment plan, insurance, and so on; and each employer has differing requirements for preserving and using data generated during the payroll calculation.

In this section we consider some typical basic payroll applications. We present two examples worked out in detail, with sample data and results, and then we describe some projects that can be programmed as extensions of the ideas presented.

10.3.1 Basic Weekly Payroll

Let us see how we might write a program to take care of three important features of a payroll calculation: gross pay, including overtime; social security (FICA) deduction; and income tax withheld.

The first step for each employee is to compute gross pay by multiplying the basic hourly rate by the number of hours worked during the week. As is customary, employees who work more than 40 hours in a week are paid an overtime premium for the excess hours. We have seen (Figs. 3.2 and 4.17; see also Section 2.3.3) how to write Fortran statements to accomplish this part of the calculation. The data required for this step consists of the *Rate* and the number of *Hours* worked; the result is the employees' *Gross* pay.

The social security (FICA) deduction is computed according to a formula prescribed by the federal government. The formula involves two parameters that are changed from time to time: the rate to be applied, and the maximum annual amount of wages to which it is to be applied. We shall assume a 6% rate and a maximum of $10,000.00. The deduction involves three categories, depending on the relation of the employee's total annual wages to the prescribed maximum.

1. If the employee's total wages prior to the current week have already exceeded the maximum, the deduction is zero.

2. If the employee's total wages including those of the current week are less than the maximum, the deduction is 6% of the gross pay for the current week.

3. Otherwise, the deduction is 6% of the amount needed to bring the annual total up to the prescribed maximum; that is, it is 6% of the amount obtained by subtracting from $10,000.00 the employee's total annual wages prior to the current week.

In order to compute this deduction, then, it is necessary to know the amount of the employee's total annual wages prior to the current week.

To compute income tax withholding, it is also necessary to know the number of "withholding exemptions" claimed by the employee. For each such exemption, $14.40 is subtracted from the employee's weekly gross pay before the withholding deduction is calculated. The remainder is then looked up in a table to determine the amount of the deduction. As a first approximation, we will compute the deduction according to the formula

$$x \cdot (0.14 + 2.2 \cdot 10^{-4} \cdot x),$$

where $x = Gross - 14.4 \cdot Exemp - 11.0$. Note that these formulas seem to produce a negative withholding deduction for an employee whose gross pay, minus the allowance for exemptions, is less than $11.00. However, the Fortran program uses the function *Max* to give x the value zero in this case, so that nothing is withheld. The deduction rate begins at 14% and increases as x becomes larger. The withholding deduction computed from this formula is based on the rates in effect at the time this material was prepared, but they may of course be changed from time to time.

Figures 10.17–10.19 provide a flowchart and program, along with data and results, for the payroll of a group of employees. For each employee a card contains the following input data:

Identification number (social security number),
Name,
Number of withholding exemptions claimed,
Basic hourly wage rate,
Total annual wages prior to the current week,
Number of hours worked during the current week.

The result of the payroll calculation is transmitted to the printer (Device 6), and an updated version of the input data is also transmitted to Device 7, which we assume to be a card punch. The card punched as output from this program is almost ready for use as an input card the following week; only the number of hours worked that week will need to be punched into it.

10.3.2 Payroll with a Data File (See Fig. 10.20.)

In most payroll applications, it is desirable to maintain a *file* of data concerning each employee on an auxiliary storage medium, such as a magnetic tape. Fixed data (such as social security number, name, number of withholding exemptions, and basic hourly wage rate) remains on the file from week to week, and other information (such as total annual wages to date) is updated, that is, changed and rewritten, each week. Besides the data concerning the employees, the file can also contain totals for later use, such as total overtime premium pay, total social security deductions, and total income tax withheld from employees' pay.

Let us assume that data from the previous week's payroll is on Device 3, which is connected to the program at the beginning of the payroll calculation. The updated payroll data is written to Device 4 as the program is executed. Let us further assume that the payroll data file contains data concerning 100 employees (arranged in order according to social security number), as well as certain overall totals that are to be updated for later use.

The data read from Device 5 consists of a heading card that contains the date and the number of holidays that occurred during the week, followed by one card for each employee containing social security number and the number of hours worked during the week. These employee data cards need not be arranged in any particular sequence. Each time a card is read, a binary search (see Exercise 3 in Section 4.4.2) is made to locate the corresponding item in the file.

The payroll file includes for each employee the vacation time balance, which is the total number of hours of vacation time earned but not used. The file also includes an integer variable that serves as a flag indicating whether or not the

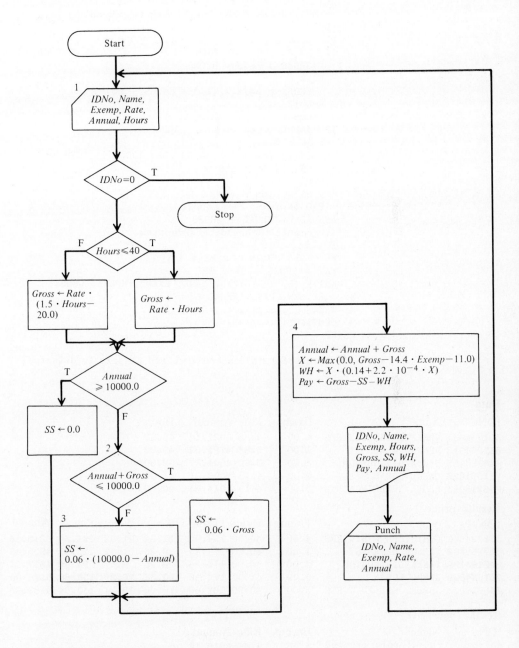

Fig. 10.17 Flowchart for basic weekly payroll.

Fig. 10.18
Program for
basic weekly
payroll.

▶

```
* Program for basic weekly payroll
      CHARACTER*28 NAME
      PARAMETER (NEMP = 300)
      DO 9, LOOP = 1, NEMP
         READ (UNIT = 5, FMT = 101, END = 19)
     $      IDNO, NAME, EXEMP, RATE, ANNUAL, HOURS
101      FORMAT (1X, I9, IX, A28, 1X, 7 F8.2)
*        .. Compute gross pay including overtime
         IF (HOURS .LE. 40) THEN
            GROSS = RATE * HOURS
          ELSE
            GROSS = RATE * (1.5 * HOURS - 20.0)
          END IF
*        .. Compute social security deduction
         IF (ANNUAL .GE. 10000.0) THEN
            SS = 0.0
          ELSE IF (ANNUAL + GROSS .LE. 10000.0) THEN
            SS = 0.06 * GROSS
          ELSE
            SS = 0.06 * (10000.0 - ANNUAL)
          END IF
         ANNUAL = ANNUAL + GROSS
*        .. Compute withholding deduction
         X = MAX (0.0, GROSS - 14.4 * EXEMP - 11.0)
         WH = X * (0.14 + 2.2E-4 * X)
         PAY = GROSS - SS - WH
         WRITE (6, 101) IDNO, NAME, EXEMP, HOURS, GROSS,
     $      SS, MH, PAY, ANNUAL
         WRITE (7, 101) IDNO, NAME, EXEMP, RATE, ANNUAL
9        CONTINUE
      STOP
19    CONTINUE
*        .. This point is reached when end of data is detected
      STOP
      END
```

Data

IDNo	Name	Exemp	Rate	Annual	Hours
301724601	CHRISTOPHER WINTERS	4.00	4.85	6021.14	40.00
517260912	VERNON DEMEREST	1.00	3.86	4751.02	40.00
645183155	TANYA LIVINGSTON	3.00	3.62	4501.27	32.00
731064826	CAROL LOGAN	0.00	4.15	5006.81	41.00
746218093	ROGER CHILLINGWORTH	3.00	4.19	5014.63	40.00

Results (printed)

IDNo	Name	Exemp	Hours	Gross	SS	WH	Pay	Annual
301724601	CHRISTOPHER WINTERS	4.00	40.00	194.00	11.64	21.02	161.34	6215.14
517260912	VERNON DEMEREST	1.00	40.00	154.40	9.26	21.72	123.41	4905.42
645183155	TANYA LIVINGSTON	3.00	32.00	115.84	6.95	9.47	99.42	4617.11
731064826	CAROL LOGAN	0.00	41.00	172.22	10.33	28.29	133.60	5179.03
746218093	ROGER CHILLINGWORTH	3.00	40.00	167.60	10.06	18.71	138.84	5182.23

Results (punched)

IDNo	Name	Exemp	Rate	Annual
301724601	CHRISTOPHER WINTERS	4.00	4.85	6215.14
517260912	VERNON DEMEREST	1.00	3.86	4905.42
645183155	TANYA LIVINGSTON	3.00	3.62	4617.11
731064826	CAROL LOGAN	0.00	4.15	5179.03
746218093	ROGER CHILLINGWORTH	3.00	4.19	5182.23

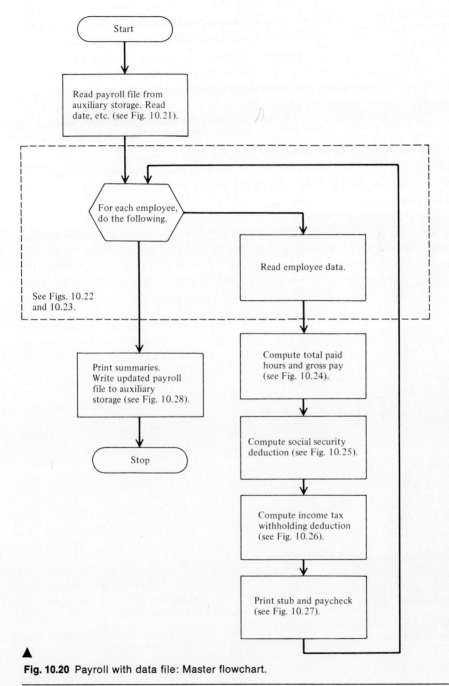

▲
Fig. 10.20 Payroll with data file: Master flowchart.

Fig. 10.19 Sample data and results for basic weekly payroll.

employee is considered a full-time employee. (If not, the employee does not accrue any vacation time and is not eligible for overtime pay.)

Execution of the payroll program begins with the reading of the payroll file from auxiliary storage (Device 3) into the computer. The heading card is read from Device 5, and the current date is printed on Device 6 (along with the previous date, which serves to identify the incoming payroll file). The number of holidays, which is included on the heading card, is next converted to *hours*. This initial portion of the program corresponds to the flowchart in Fig. 10.21.

The next section of the program (see Fig. 10.22) is executed once for each employee data card that is read from Device 5. If the *endfile* indicator (see Section 9.5.2) is not detected, the subroutine *Search* (see Fig. 10.23) is used to locate the employee data in the file.

After the employee data is extracted from the file, the next step is to compute the total paid hours and gross pay (Fig. 10.24). First the actual number of hours the employee worked is increased by eight for each holiday. If the flag indicates that the employee does not work full time, the gross pay is computed simply by multiplying hours (including holiday hours) by pay rate. However, if

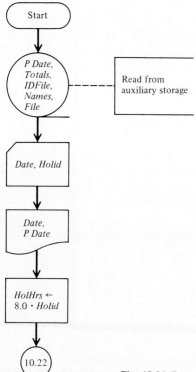

Fig. 10.21 Payroll with data file: Flowchart for initialization section.

the employee works full time, vacation and overtime must be taken into account. First the vacation balance is increased by three hours for all full-time employees. Then, if the employee has worked fewer than 40 hours during the week, vacation time is charged for the difference, up to the balance of vacation time that has been accrued. If the number of hours worked is 40 or more, the gross pay calculation is modified to include overtime.

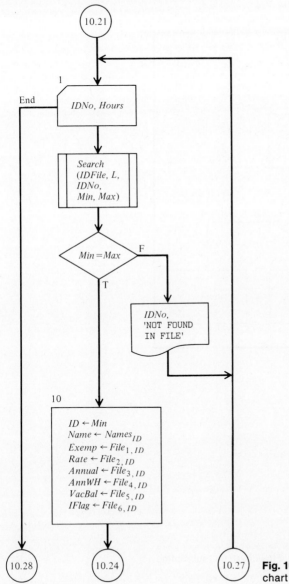

Fig. 10.22 Payroll with data file: Flowchart for employee data input section.

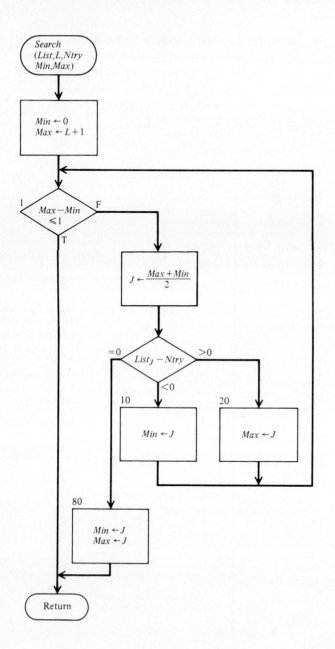

Fig. 10.23 Payroll with data file: Flowchart for subroutine to search for employee file.

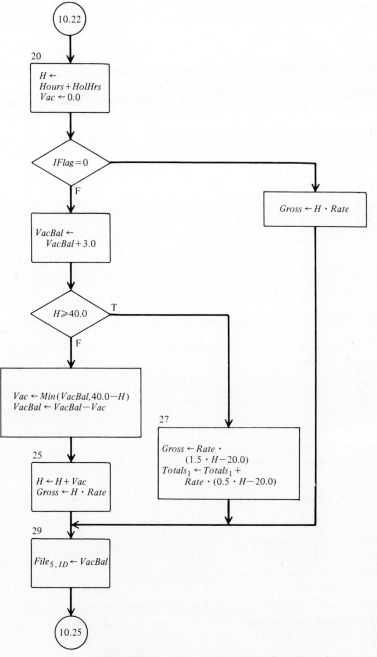

Fig. 10.24 Payroll with data file: Flowchart for gross pay calculation.

The social security and income tax withholding deductions (Figs. 10.25 and 10.26) are calculated exactly as in the previous program (Section 10.3.1).

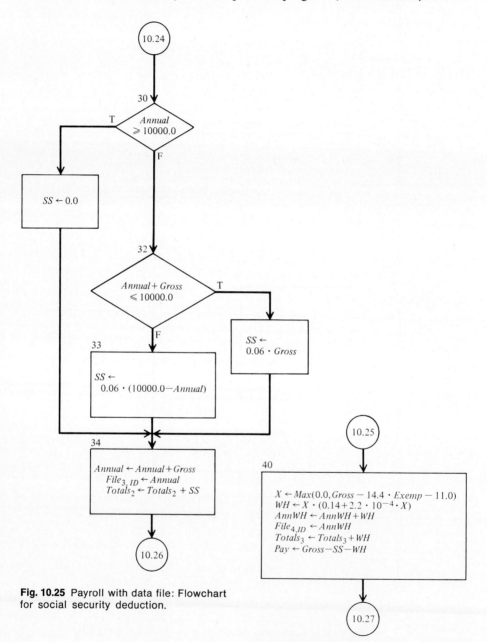

Fig. 10.25 Payroll with data file: Flowchart for social security deduction.

Fig. 10.26 Payroll with data file: Flowchart for income tax withholding deduction.

Information is printed on Device 6 in the form of a stub and a paycheck. The printer will be provided with a form 44 lines (7⅓ inches) high, the top half of which is the stub form, the bottom half the paycheck form. The printer skips to the top of the stub form and prints six double-spaced lines containing date, social security number; name, number of exemptions; hours worked, holiday hours, vacation hours used, total paid hours; gross pay, social security deduction, income tax withholding deduction, net pay; total annual wages to date, total income tax withheld to date; and vacation time balance. It then prints five double-spaced blank lines to reach the bottom of the stub form. It prints another double-spaced blank line, followed by two lines (printed near the top of the paycheck form) containing date, name, and net pay (see Fig. 10.27).

Eventually the end of the data will be encountered. At this point, summaries are printed, and the updated payroll file is written back to auxiliary storage Device 4 (see Fig. 10.28). Figure 10.29 shows the program (including the binary

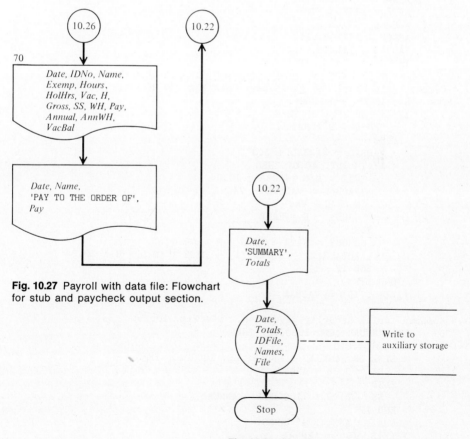

Fig. 10.27 Payroll with data file: Flowchart for stub and paycheck output section.

Fig. 10.28 Payroll with data file: Flowchart for summary section.

```
* Initialization Section.  See Fig. 10.21.
      CHARACTER PDATE*10, NAME*20, NAMES(100)*20, DATE*10
      DIMENSION TOTALS(3), IDFILE(100), FILE(6,100)
      PARAMETER (L = 100, NEMP = 300)
      READ (UNIT = 3) PDATE, (TOTALS(I), I = 1, 3),
     $ (IDFILE(I), NAMES(I), (FILE(J, I), J = 1, 6), I = 1, L)
      READ (5, *) DATE, HOLID
      WRITE (6, 102) DATE, PDATE
 102  FORMAT ('1' / '0', A10 / '0Previous date ', A10)
      HOLHRS = 8.0 * HOLID


* Employee Data Input Section.  See Fig. 10.22.
      DO 9, LOOP = 1, NEMP
         READ (UNIT = 5, FMT = *, END = 90) IDNO, HOURS
*        .. Extract employee data from file.
         CALL SEARCH (IDFILE, L, IDNO, MIN, MAX)
         IF (MIN .EQ. MAX) GO TO 10
*        .. Print error message.
         WRITE (6, *) IDNO, ' ID not found in file'
         GO TO 9
 10      ID = MIN
         NAME = NAMES(ID)
         EXEMP = FILE(1, ID)
         RATE = FILE(2, ID)
         ANNUAL = FILE(3, ID)
         ANNWH = FILE(4, ID)
         VACBAL = FILE(5, ID)
         IFLAG = FILE(6, ID)


* Compute paid hours and gross pay.  See Fig. 10.24.
 20      H = HOURS + HOLHRS
         IF (IFLAG .EQ. 0) THEN
             GROSS = H * RATE
           ELSE
             VACBAL = VACBAL + 3.0
             IF (H .LT. 40.0) THEN
                 VAC = MIN (VACBAL, 40.0 - H)
                 VACBAL = VACBAL - VAC
                 H = H + VAC
                 GROSS = H * RATE
               ELSE
                 GROSS = RATE * (1.5 * H - 20.0)
                 TOTALS(1) = TOTALS(1) + RATE * (0.5 * H - 20.0)
               END IF
           END IF
         FILE(5, ID) = VACBAL


* Compute social security deduction.  See Fig. 10.25.
 30      IF (ANNUAL .GE. 10000.0) THEN
             SS = 0.0
           ELSE IF (ANNUAL + GROSS .LE. 10000.0) THEN
             SS = 0.06 * GROSS
           ELSE
             SS = 0.06 * (10000.0 - ANNUAL)
           END IF
         ANNUAL = ANNUAL + GROSS
         FILE(3, ID) = ANNUAL
         TOTALS(2) = TOTALS(2) + SS
```

```
* Compute income tax withholding deduction.  See Fig. 10.26.
  40      X = MAX (0.0, GROSS - 14.4 * EXEMP - 11.0)
          WH = X * (0.14 + 2.2E-4 * X)
          ANNWH = ANNWH + WH
          FILE(4, ID) = ANNWH
          TOTALS(3) = TOTALS(3) + WH
          PAY = GROSS - SS - WH

* Print stub and paycheck.  See Fig. 10.27.
  70      WRITE (6, 104) DATE, IDNO, NAME, EXEMP
  104     FORMAT ('1' / '0', A10, I10 / '0', A20, F10.0)
          WRITE (6, 105) HOURS, HOLHRS, VAC, H, GROSS, SS, WH, PAY
  105     FORMAT '0', 4 F10.2
          WRITE (6, 106) ANNUAL, ANNWH, VACBAL
  106     FORMAT ('0', 2 F10.2 / '0', F10.2 / 4 '0' /))
  *
          WRITE (6, 107) DATE, NAME, PAY
  107     FORMAT ('0' / A10 / '0Pay□to□the□order□of□', A20, F18.2)
  *
  9     CONTINUE

* Print summaries and write file to device 4.  See Fig. 10.28.
  90    WRITE (6, 109) DATE, (TOTALS(I), I = 1, 3)
  109   FORMAT ('1' / '0', A10 / '0Summary' / '0', 3 F10.2 / '1')
        WRITE (UNIT = 4) DATE, (TOTALS(I), I = 1, 3),
     $    (IDFILE(I), NAMES(I), (FILE(J, I), J = 1, 6), I = 1, L)
        END

* Binary search subroutine. See Fig. 10.23.
        SUBROUTINE SEARCH (LIST, L, NTRY, MIN, MAX)
        INTEGER LIST(L)
        MIN = 0
        MAX = L + 1
  1     CONTINUE
        IF (MAX - MIN .LE. 1) GO TO 90
  5     J = (MAX + MIN) / 2
        IF (LIST(J) - NTRY) 10, 80, 20
  10    MIN = J
        GO TO 1
  20    MAX = J
        GO TO 1
  80    MAX = J
        MIN = J
  90    RETURN
        END
```

◀ ▲

Fig. 10.29 Payroll with data file: Program with *Search* subroutine.

search subroutine). Partial data are shown in Fig. 10.30, and results are illustrated in Fig. 10.31.

Data   (input file)
PDate   Totals(1) (2)   (3)
08/03/1999 3046.21 37220.41 50261.36
IDNo   Name   Exemp   Rate Annual   AnnWH   VacBal   IFlag
301724601 CHRISTOPHER WINTERS   4.00   4.85 6021.14   646.06 21.00   1.00

Data   (card reader)
Date   Holid
08/10/1999 0
IDNo   Hours
301724601 40.0

Results (printed)
08/10/1999
PREVIOUS DATE 08/03/1999

Fig. 10.30 Sample data for program in Fig. 10.29.

```
DATE          SS NO.
08/10/1999 301724601
NAME                      EXEMPTIONS
CHRISTOPHER WINTERS         4
     HRS WORKED  HOLIDAY HRS  VACATION HRS  TOTAL PAID HRS
       40.00       0.00         0.00          40.00
     GROSS PAY    SS DED       WH DED        NET PAY
      194.00      11.64        21.02         161.34
     GROSS Y/D   WH Y/D
      6215.14    667.08
     VACATION BAL
       24.00

    - - - - - - - - - - - - - - - - - - - - - - - - - -

 8/10/1999
 PAY TO THE ORDER OF CHRISTOPHER WINTERS    161.34
```

08/10/1999
SUMMARY
   3046.21 37232.05 50282.38

Results (output file)
08/10/1999 3046.21 37232.05 50282.38
301724601 CHRISTOPHER WINTERS   4.00   4.85 6215.14 667.08 24.00   1.00

Fig. 10.31 Results for program in Fig. 10.29.

10.3.3 Monthly Payroll

A similar program can be written for monthly payroll processing. In a typical situation, there would be the following differences.

1. Input data for each employee consists of percentage of time employed, rather than hours worked. No special provision is made for holidays, and no over-time is paid.

2. Vacation accrual is 0.1 month per month, rather than 3 hours per week. All employees accrue vacation time.

3. For computing income tax withholding, the appropriate formula for a monthly payroll is

$$x \cdot (0.14 + 5.0 \cdot 10^{-5} \cdot x),$$

where $x = Gross - 62.5 \cdot Exemp - 46.0$ but x must not be negative. There is no difference between weekly and monthly social security deductions. The flowchart is almost the same as the flowchart for the weekly payroll (Fig. 10.17).

Project

Modify the program shown in Fig. 10.29 to obtain a program for monthly pay-roll processing.

10.3.4 Employee Investment Plan

Employees who work 20 hours or more during a week (based on the number of hours from which their gross pay is calculated; see the variable H at statement 20, Fig. 10.29) may participate in an employee investment plan. Five percent of their gross pay is set aside and used to purchase shares in the company. The heading card in Device 5 includes the price per share to be paid by each em-ployee, which is the current market price less 15%. The payroll file for each employee includes the balance of funds that have been deducted but have not yet been used to purchase shares. One-tenth percent (per week) interest is added to this balance, and the investment-plan payroll deduction for the current week (if any) is added; then as many whole shares as possible are purchased. Each em-ployee's social security number and name and the number of shares purchased are transmitted to Device 7 (the card punch); the cards thus produced will be used to issue a stock certificate to the employee. The balance of funds insufficient to purchase another share is recorded on the payroll file, to be updated the fol-lowing week.

Individuals who are paid monthly are eligible for participation in the invest-ment plan if they are employed at 50% time or more (including vacation; see the

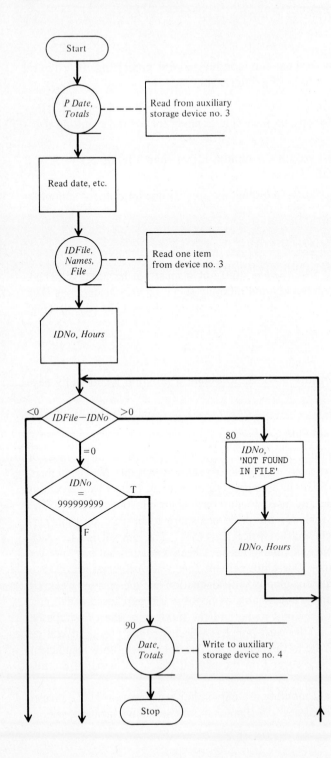

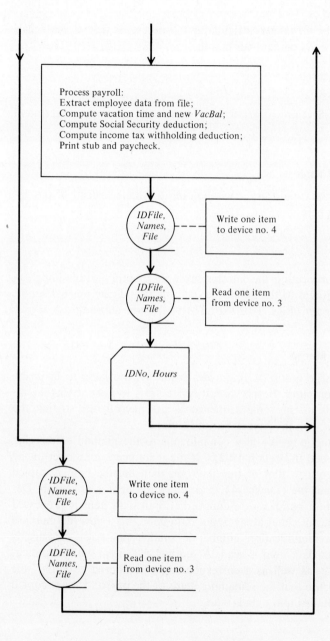

Process payroll:
Extract employee data from file;
Compute vacation time and new *VacBal*;
Compute Social Security deduction;
Compute income tax withholding deduction;
Print stub and paycheck.

IDFile, Names, File

Write one item to device no. 4

IDFile, Names, File

Read one item from device no. 3

IDNo, Hours

IDFile, Names, File

Write one item to device no. 4

IDFile, Names, File

Read one item from device no. 3

◄ Fig. 10.32 Flowchart for payroll with file merge.

variable *Time* used in the *Gross* pay calculation). Interest on partial share balances is paid at the rate of $\frac{1}{10}$ percent per month.

Project

Modify the program of Section 10.3.2 to incorporate the employee investment plan.

10.3.5 Withholding Tax Table

An actual payroll program would use a withholding tax table instead of the approximate formula given here.

Project

Write a subroutine incorporating the latest weekly or monthly withholding tax tables available. Add an item to the employee data file to indicate marital status. Modify the payroll program (Figs. 10.29–10.31) to use this subroutine.

10.3.6 Payroll with File Merge

The payroll file for a large group of employees would be too large to fit in the internal storage of the computer. In this case, it is necessary to assume that the input data on Device 5 is in the same sequence as the payroll file, so that the input data can be *merged* with the payroll file on Device 3.

The basic idea of merging two files is analogous to the method of merging two linear arrays, discussed in Section 10.2.5. If the identification number of the input data item is larger than that of the file item, then the file item is copied from the file to the output file (Device 4), and a new file item is read from Device 3. If the identification numbers are equal, the input data item is processed and written on the output file, and a new input data item and a new file item are read. If the input data identification number is smaller, an error message is printed, and a new input data item is read. A sentinel data item with identification number 999999999, as well as a correspondingly numbered "dummy" file item, may be used to ensure that the remaining items of the payroll file are copied to the output file after all the input data is read.

Project

Modify the payroll program of Fig. 10.29 to use a file merge operation rather than store the entire payroll file internally in the computer. An outline of the flowchart is shown in Fig. 10.32.

10.4 PLOTTING WITH THE LINE PRINTER

10.4.1 Function Values

Pictures, curves, and bar graphs can be generated by a computer to give a dramatic view of the results of a calculation. However, at most computer centers such graphic results are expensive to produce and require considerable time for processing. Thus an attractive alternative in some cases is to produce graphic output by using a line printer as if it were a plotter.

As a plotter, the line printer attached to a computer suffers a number of serious disadvantages. The most serious is lack of resolution, since only about ten characters per inch can be placed across a line. Also awkward is the fact that points cannot be plotted with equal spacing in the horizontal and vertical directions, because most line printers space ten characters per inch horizontally and six lines per inch vertically.

Nevertheless, the line printer is very useful for giving a quick, rough picture of the results of a calculation, since most computer centers are equipped to return line printer results to the user much sooner than any other form of graphical results. For most purposes, then, it is best with line printer plots to avoid elaborate detail, to keep labeling to a minimum, etc., and to concentrate on producing a simple, rough, quick picture of the results.

The most straightforward use of line printers for graphical output is for plotting function values. The independent variable is plotted in the *vertical* direction, so that the plotted values can be computed and printed one at a time with a minimum requirement for storage of results. The general idea follows.

1. The independent variable is set initially to its minimum value.
2. A value of the dependent variable is calculated from the given function.
3. The result is *scaled* and rounded to an integer between 0 and 100.
4. A line is printed, consisting mostly of blank characters, but with a symbol in the character position corresponding to the function value (dependent variable). The value of the independent variable may also be printed at the left end of the line.
5. The independent variable is advanced to the next value, and the process is repeated until enough values of the independent variable have been plotted.

The calculation is nearly trivial; the only part requiring much thought is the *scaling,* that is, the choice of maximum and minimum values for the independent and dependent variables, and of an interval size for the independent variable. These values must be large enough to provide a broad view of the function, yet small enough to give adequate detail. In some cases it may be necessary to make several computer runs with the same function, increasing or decreasing the scale factors until an appropriate range is found. Or the plot may be subdivided into several sections, using a different scale factor (if appropriate) for each section.

The following program will produce a printer plot of the trigonometric sine function. It is discussed below.

```
* Printer plot of Sine function
      CHARACTER*101 LINE
*     . . Statement function for scaling
      JSCALE (Z) = NINT (50.0 * (Z + 1.0)) + 1
*
      DO 66, X = 0.0, 6.28318, 0.1256637
        LINE = '[]'
        IS = JSCALE (SIN (X))
        LINE(IS : IS) = 'S'
        WRITE (*, 77) X, LINE
   77   FORMAT (1X, F10.5, 8X, A101)
   66   CONTINUE
      END
```

Note the use of a statement function, JSCALE, to perform the scaling of the dependent variable values. This function is intended for argument values between −1.0 and 1.0, such as are produced by the sine function. This scaling function first adds 1.0 to eliminate negative values; after this step, the values lie between 0.0 and 2.0. Multiplying by 50.0 gives values between 0.0 and 100.0; these values are then rounded to the nearest integer. Adding 1, we obtain integer values between 1 and 101, suitable for use as subscripts for the array *Line*.

The DO 66 loop is traversed once for each value of the independent variable. Each time, the array *Line* is reinitialized to a string of blank characters. Next the sine function is evaluated, and the function value is scaled to obtain an integer between 1 and 101.

The statement LINE(IS : IS) = 'S' is the heart of the algorithm. It is this step which stores the plotting symbol in the appropriate position in the string *Line*, replacing one of the blank characters in that string. The WRITE statement then prints this string of characters, along with the numerical value of the independent variable at the left side of the page.

Of course, the particular scaling function used here will work only for functions whose values lie between −1.0 and 1.0; for other functions the constants in the scaling function would be different. For the sine function, we know that values outside this range will never occur. For other less well-known functions, we could "clamp" the scaled values to guarantee that they lie between 1 and 101, inclusive.

```
IS = MIN (101, MAX (1, JSCALE (FFF)))
```

We often need to compare the values of two or more functions. It is not much harder to do so, once the problem of scaling is solved. If we use the simplest plotting method, only one symbol will be printed at a given spot on the paper. For rough work this is usually acceptable.

The program in Fig. 10.33 produces a printer plot, as shown in Fig. 10.34, of the trigonometric sine and cosine functions.

```
* Printer plot of Sine and Cosine functions
      CHARACTER*101 LINE
*     .. Statement function for scaling
      JSCALE (Z) = NINT (50.0 * (Z + 1.0)) + 1
*
      DO 66, X = 0.0, 6.28318, 0.1256637
        LINE = '0'
        LINE(1 : 1) = '-'
        LINE (51 : 51) = '0'
        LINE (101 : 101) = '+'
        IS = JSCALE (SIN (X))
        LINE(IS : IS) = 'S'
        IC = JSCALE (COS (X))
        LINE(IC : IC) = 'C'
        WRITE (*, 77) X, LINE
77      FORMAT (1X, F10.5, 8X, A101)
66      CONTINUE
      END
```

Fig. 10.33 Sine and cosine printer plot program.

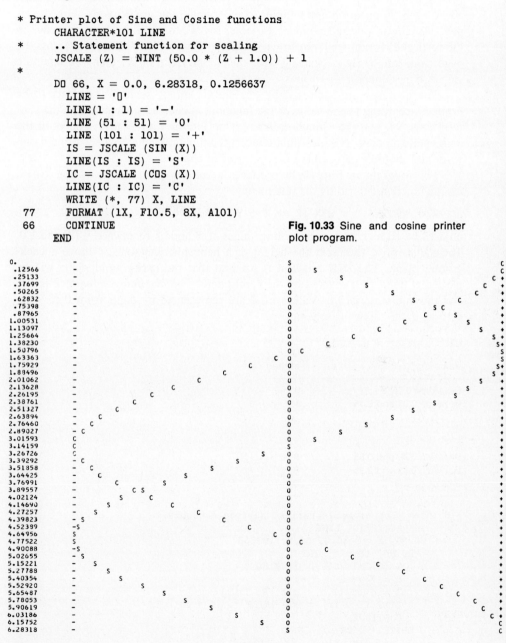

Fig. 10.34 Printer plot of sine and cosine functions.

10.4.2 Contour Plots

Printer plots are also useful for preliminary explorations of functions of two variables, such as occur in topographic contour-mapping applications. For such a plot, we choose one independent variable, say X, to increase down the page in the vertical direction while the other independent variable, Y, increases across the page from left to right. Starting with the initial value of X, then, we compute values of the function for various values of Y.

The contours are indicated by our choice among several characters to be printed, according to the value of the function, at each (X, Y) point. In the simplest case, we scale the function value as an integer from 0 to 9, and print the corresponding digit. (Or we could convert the function value to a substring designator and choose a plot symbol from a string of characters.)

The program in Fig. 10.35 produces a contour plot, shown in Fig. 10.36, for the function defined by the statement

```
Z = SQRT (1.0 - MIN (X ** 2 + Y ** 2, 1.0))
```

on a 10 by 10 inch grid, representing values of X and of Y between -1.0 and 1.0. The values of Z represent the height of a hemispherical surface above a background plane. The MIN function is used so that the background plane will be plotted at points not covered by the hemisphere. The maximum value of Z is 1.0, and the minimum is 0.0. Values of Z are represented by digits from 0 to 9 according to the following scheme.

Value of Z	Digit plotted
Less than 0.05	0
Between 0.05 and 0.15	1
.	.
.	.
Between 0.75 and 0.85	8
Between 0.85 and 0.95	9
0.95 or greater	0

```
* Printer plot of hemispherical surface contours
      CHARACTER*101 LINE
      DO 66, X = -30.0, 30.0, .03333
         DO 55, IY = 1, 101
            Y = REAL (IY - 51) / 50.0
            R = X ** 2 + Y ** 2
            Z = SQRT (1.0 - MIN (R, 1.0))
            LINE(IY : IY) = MOD (NINT (10.0 * Z), 10)
55          CONTINUE
         WRITE (*, 77) X, LINE
77       FORMAT (1X, F10.5, 8X, A101)
66       CONTINUE
      END
```

Fig. 10.35 Contour plot program: Hemispherical surface.

```
-1.00000    000000000000000000000000000000000000000000000000000000000000000000000000000000000000000000000000000000000
 -.96667    00000000000000000000000000000000000000111222222223333332222222210000000000000000000000000000000000000000000
 -.93333    00000000000000000000000000000000000012223333333333334444444433333333332221000000000000000000000000000000000
 -.90000    00000000000000000000000000000000001222333334444444444444444444444333332221C0000C0000000000000000000000000000
 -.86667    00000000000000000000000000000001223334444444555555555555555554444444333322210000C000000000000000000000000000
 -.83333    00000000000000000000000000122334444455555555555555556666665555555555544444433332210000C000000000000000000000
 -.80000    00000000000000000000002233444445555556666666666666666666666666666555555544443332200000000C00000000000000000
 -.76667    000000000000000000122333444455555566666666666666666666666666666666555555444433322100000000000000000000C00C
 -.73333    00000000000000223344444555556666666677777777777777777777666666666555555444433322000000000000000000000000000
 -.70000    0000000000000012334444455556666666777777777777777777777777776666666555554444332100000000000000000000000000
 -.66667    00000000000000123344455556666666677777777777777777777777777776666666555554444332100000000C0000000000000000
 -.63333    000000000000012334445555566666667777777778888888888888887777777777666666555554443321000CC000000000000000000
 -.60000    00000000000022334455566666667777777788888888888888888888887777777766666655554443321000000CC00000000000000
 -.56667    0000000000123344455556666677777777788888888888888888888888887777777766666555544433210C0000000000000000000
 -.53333    00000001233444555566666777777788888888888888888888888888887777777766666655554443321000000000000000000000
 -.50000    0000001233444555666677777778888888888889999999999999998888888888887777776666655554433210000000000000000
 -.46667    0000012334445555666667777778888888889999999999999999998888888888887777776666655554433210000000000000000
 -.43333    000002334455556666777777788888888999999999999999999999998888888887777776666655554433200000000000000000
 -.40000    000023344555566667777778888888999999999999999999999999998888888887777776666655554433200000000000000000
 -.36667    0000123444555666677777888888889999999999999999999999999999988888888887777766665555443210000000000000000
 -.33333    00012334455566677777788888888899999999999999999999999999999998888888887777766665555443320000000000000000
 -.30000    00023344555566667777888888889999999999999000000000999999999998888888877777666655554433200000000000000000
 -.26667    0012334455566677777888888399999999999999000000000000999999999999988888887777766665555443320C000000000000
 -.23333    0022334455566667777788888899999999999990000000000000009999999999998888888777776666655554443220C0000000000
 -.20000    0023344555666677777788888899999999999900000000000000000999999999998888888777776666655554443210000000000
 -.16667    01234455566677778888889999999999999000000000000000000009999999999998888888877776665555443210000000000
 -.13333    0123445556667777788888889999999999990000000000C0000000000000099999999999888888877776665555443210000000
 -.10000    0234455566677777888888999999999990000000000000000000000000000099999999998888888777766665555443320000000
 -.06667    02334455566677778888899999999999990C0000000000000000000000000009999999998888888777776665555443320000
 -.03333    02334455566677778883888999999999990000000000000000000000000000099999999999888888877776665555443320000
 0.         0233445556667777788883889999999999990C00000000000000000000000009999999999998888888777766655554433200
  .03333    0233445556667777788888899999999999990C0000000000000000000000000999999999998888888877776665555443320
  .06667    02334455566677778888889999999999999000000000000000000000000000099999999998888888877776665555443320
  .10000    0233445556667777788888899999999999990C000000000000000000000000009999999999888888877776665555443320
  .13333    0234455566677778888899999999999900C000000000000000000000000009999999998888888777766655554433200
  .16667    01234455566677778888899999999999900000000000000000000000000099999999998888888877776665555443210
  .20000    0023344555666777778888889999999999000000000000000000000000999999999998888888877776665555443200
  .23333    0022334455666777788888899999999990000000000000000000000099999999998888888777776666655554433210
  .26667    00123344555666777788888899999999990000000000000000000009999999999988888887777766665555443321000
  .30000    00023344555566677777888888999999999999999990000000999999999999998888888877776665555443321000C
  .33333    0001233445556667777788888889999999999999999999999999999998888888887777766665555443321000C
  .36667    000012344555666777778888888899999999999999999999999999999988888888887777766665555443210000
  .40000    000002334455566667777778888889999999999999999999999999998888888877777666655554433200000
  .43333    000000233445555666677777778888888999999999999999999998888888887777766665555443320000000
  .46667    000000123445555666677777788888888899999999999999998888888888877777666655554433210000000
  .50000    00000012334445555666666777777788888888888999999999988888888888877777666655554433210000000
  .53333    0000000123344455556666677777778888888888888888888888888888877777776666655554433210C0000000
  .56667    000000001234455555666666777777778888888888888888888888888877777776666655554433220000000000
  .60000    0300000000223344555556666666777777777888388488888888888888887777777776666655554433220000000000
  .63333    000000000001234455555566666666677777777788888888888888888877777777777666665555443321000000000000
  .66667    0000000000001234455556666666777777777888888888888888887777777777776666665555444332100000000000
  .70000    0000000000001233444555566666666777777777777777777777777776666666555554433210000000000000000000
  .73333    0000000000000000223344455556666666677777777777777777777666666666555555444332200000000000000000
  .76667    00000000000000000001223334445555556666666666666666666666666555555544444332210000000000000000000
  .80000    0000000000000000000022333444455555556666666666666666666665555555544444333220000C0000000000000000
  .83333    00000000000000000000000122334445555555555555566666665555555555544444333221000000C00000000000000
  .86667    00000000000000000000000000012233344444445555555555555555544444433333221000000C0000000000000000
  .90000    0000000000000000000000000000011222333333334444444444444443333333333222100000000000000000000000000
  .93333    00000000000000000000000000000000001222233333333334444333333333222210000000000000000000000000000
  .96667    000000000000000000000000000000000000011222222223333332222222211000000000000000000000000000000000
1.00000     00000000000000000000000000000000000000000000000000000000000000000000000000000000000000000000000000
```

Fig. 10.36 Results for contour plot program: Hemispherical surface.

The program in Fig. 10.37 produces the plot in Fig. 10.38 of the function

$$Z = 0.1 * (X + SIN (3.141592 * X) + Y ** 2)$$

for 126 values of X, starting at 0.0 and increasing in steps of 0.04 to 5.0; and for 101 values of Y, starting at -1.0 and increasing in steps of 0.02 to 1.0. Values of Z lie between 0.0 and 1.0, and they are scaled the same as before.

```
* Printer plot of undulating surface contours
      CHARACTER*101 LINE
      DO 66, X = 0.0, 5.0, 0.04
        DO 55, IY = 1, 101
          Y = 0.4 * REAL (IY - 51)
          Z = 0.1 * (X + SIN (3.141592 * X) + Y ** 2)
          LINE(IY : IY) = MOD (NINT (10.0 * Z), 10)
55        CONTINUE
      WRITE (*, 77) X, LINE
77    FORMAT (1X, F10.5, 8X, A101)
66    CONTINUE
      END
```

Fig. 10.37 Contour plot program: Undulating surface.

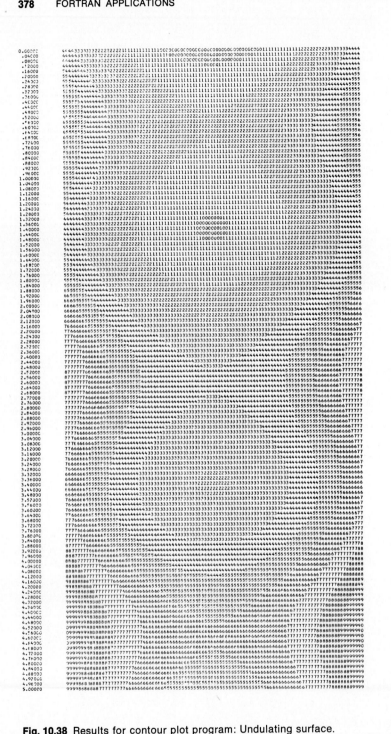

Fig. 10.38 Results for contour plot program: Undulating surface.

10.4.3   Random Halftones

When a photograph is printed in a newspaper, it appears to be shaded with a full range of levels of gray, from white to black. However, a close examination discloses that each spot on the paper is actually either white or black. Darker regions are simply those where black dots are printed more densely.

We can achieve somewhat the same effect in rough form on the line printer by choosing at each print position whether or not to plot a symbol. (We shall use a fixed symbol throughout, such as an asterisk. Finer gradations can be obtained if we can choose among several symbols.) At a given print position, we plot the symbol with a *probability* proportional to the desired intensity of the picture at that point. (Compare the simulation of table tennis in the project in Section 10.1.3.) We scale the desired intensity so that it lies between 0.0 (white) and 1.0 (black), and then we generate a random number between 0.0 and 1.0. The probability that the random number is *less than* the scaled intensity value will be equal to the intensity.† Therefore we plot a symbol if and only if we find that the random number is less than the scaled value of the desired intensity at that point.

Project

Plot the function defined by the expression

```
Z = SQRT (1.0 - MIN (X ** 2 + Y ** 2, 1.0))
```

as in Fig. 10.36 but plot it in the form of a random halftone. The function values range from 0.0 to 1.0. For each print position, generate a random number (see Section 10.1), and store either a blank or an asterisk at LINE(IY), depending on whether the function value is greater or less than the random number.

10.5   THE CALENDAR

Calendar dates follow a sequence that is very familiar. Nevertheless, the sequence is complicated by certain irregularities, such as the differing number of days in various months, and the extra day that is added to each leap year. A computer program dealing with calendar dates usually contains a few statements to process the regular parts of the sequence, along with a larger number of statements to handle the irregularities.

Several programs for handling particular problems connected with calendar dates are presented in this section.

† For example, suppose that there is a region of ten points where the desired intensity is 0.9. We can expect that nine out of ten random numbers (uniformly distributed between 0.0 and 1.0) will be less than 0.9. Thus approximately nine of the ten points in the region will contain a printed symbol—the region will be fairly densely covered. On the other hand, in a region where the intensity value is 0.1, the random numbers will only rarely be less than 0.1 and the symbols will be printed rather sparsely.

10.5.1 Elapsed Days

Computer programs to determine the number of days between two dates are required in many fields of application. Astronomers need to find the periods of variable stars or of comets, for example, and bankers need to calculate elapsed days in order to compute interest.

Rather than attempting to calculate the number of Februarys or the number of extra leap-year days *between* two dates, we adopt an approach based on relating each of two given dates to a common origin or base date. January 1, 1901 is a convenient base for dates in the twentieth century. To determine the number of days that have elapsed since this base date, we proceed in two steps. First we find the number of days from the base date up to the *beginning* of the specified year. Then we find the number of days that have elapsed *within* the given year.

Days to beginning of year

Ordinary years have 365 days, but leap years have 366 days. So we first compute the number of years since 1901, and multiply by 365; then we add an extra day for each leap year that has occurred.

How many extra days need to be added to account for leap years? This number is shown in Table 10.4. We note that the number of extra days changes when the year number is *one greater* than a multiple of four. If this seems strange, recall that the extra day in 1904, for example, did not occur until the end of February, and so had no effect on January 1.

Table 10.4 Number of extra days, due to leap years, between January 1, 1901, and January 1 of specified year.

Year	Extra days	Year	Extra days
1901	0	1976	18
1902	0	1977	19
1903	0	1978	19
1904	0	1979	19
1905	1	1980	19
1906	1	1981	20
1907	1	1982	20
1908	1	1983	20
1909	2	1984	20
1910	2	1985	21
1911	2	1986	21
1912	2	1987	21
1913	3	1988	21
1914	3	1989	22
1915	3	1990	22
...	...	...	...

How can we use Fortran statements to describe the calculation of the numbers in the second and fourth columns of Table 10.4? Something about the cyclic nature of leap years suggests the cyclic number systems that were mentioned in Section 2.3.3. A little experimentation with the predefined functions *Mod* and *Int* results in the formula

```
INT ((IYR − 1901) / 4)
```

for the numbers in the second and fourth columns of the table.

Days within current year

In effect, we must write Fortran statements that are the equivalent of "Thirty days hath September, April, June, and November." We can then determine the number of days from January 1 up to the beginning of the specified month. Adding the day of the month will complete the calculation.

Rather than put the actual lengths of the months into the program, we can simply give it the *cumulative* total number of days for the year up to the beginning of each month. Table 10.5 gives these cumulative totals for "ordinary" years and for leap years. We can insert these numbers into a Fortran program by means of a DATA declaration:

```
INTEGER NDTBOM(12)
DATA (NDTBOM(I), I = 1, 12) / 0, 31, 59, 90, 120, 151,
$                             181, 212, 243, 273, 304, 334 /
```

Table 10.5 Cumulative total number of days in year up to beginning of month.

Month	Month number	Days	
		Ordinary year	Leap year
January	1	0	0
February	2	31	31
March	3	59	60
April	4	90	91
May	5	120	121
June	6	151	152
July	7	181	182
August	8	212	213
September	9	243	244
October	10	273	274
November	11	304	305
December	12	334	335

For leap years, the number of days to the beginning of each month, except for January and February, is greater by one than the above figures. We could store another table for leap years, or (perhaps better) test and add 1 if the month number is 3 or greater.

Putting this all together, we have the following external function subprogram for calculating the number of elapsed days from January 1, 1901, to any date in the twentieth century.

```
* Elapsed days from January 1, 1901, to any given date
* in the twentieth century.
      FUNCTION KOUNT (IYR, MON, IDAY)
      INTEGER NDTBOM(12)
*     .. Table of number of days to beginning of each month.
      DATA (NDTBOM(I), I = 1, 12) / 0, 31, 59, 90, 120, 151,
$                                 181, 212, 243, 273, 304, 334 /
      K1 = 365 * (IYR - 1901) + INT ((IYR - 1901) / 4)
      K2 = NDTBOM(MON)
      IF ((MOD (IYR, 4) .EQ. 0) .AND. (MON .GE. 3)) K2 = K2 + 1
      KOUNT = K1 + K2 + IDAY
      RETURN
      END
```

Projects

1. Write a program to read the year, month, and day numbers for a date in the twentieth century, and to determine the number of elapsed days since January 1, 1901, by a reference to the function *Kount*.

2. Write a program to read the year, month, and day numbers for each of two different dates in the twentieth century, and compute the number of elapsed days between the two dates, using two references to *Kount*. *Options:* (a) Check the input data for validity. For example, the year number must be greater than 1900 but not greater than 2000, and the month number must not exceed 12. (b) Store a table of *month names* (or three-letter abbreviations) and print the results in a form similar to the following:

```
16127 days between Nov 24 1928 and Jan 19 1973
```

10.5.2   Julian Date and Day of the Week

The year contains (very nearly) 365.2422 days. In 45 B.C., Julius Caesar introduced the "Julian calendar" based on a year of 365.25 days. By the sixteenth century, the accumulation of 0.0078 day per year was having a noticeable effect on the calculation of religious seasons and astronomical events. An adjustment was made in Catholic Europe under Pope Gregory XIII in 1582, but in England the change was delayed until 1752, and in some countries until even later. Thus, in computing dates earlier than about 1800, it is necessary to take into account the difference between the Gregorian or New Style calendar and the Julian or Old Style dates.

The adjustment to the Gregorian calendar was made by completely eliminating a certain number of days (that is, the extra days that had accumulated up until the date of the adjustment), and the adjustment was maintained by modifying the leap year rule: Three out of four "century" years (those not divisible by 400, such as 1700, 1800, and 1900) are *not* leap years in the Gregorian calendar. This modification results in an average year length of 364.2425 days. Further corrections will ultimately be required to eliminate three leap years every 10,000 years.

Astronomers use an "elapsed-days" calendar similar to that implemented in the function *Kount* in Section 10.5.1. However, they use January 1, 4713 B.C., as the base date. This origin was chosen by the sixteenth-century astronomer Joseph Scaliger because it is the first day of a 7980-year period related to the coincidence of several long astronomical cycles. The number of days from the beginning of that period to any given date is called the Julian day number for that date, or the Julian date. (The name does not honor Julius Caesar, but rather Scaliger's father.) The Julian date for January 1, 1901, was 2,415,386; therefore we can determine the Julian date for any specified day in the twentieth century by adding this number to the elapsed days since January 1, 1901, as obtained from the function *Kount* in Section 10.5.1.

For other centuries, we merely need to make the required adjustment for leap years, and take into account the Gregorian calendar reform. A more general

```
* Julian date, i.e., number of elapsed days since
* January 1, 4713 B.C. Includes correction to
* Gregorian (New Style) calendar for dates after
* September 2, 1752 (Julian date 2361221).
        FUNCTION JULIAN (IYR, MON, IDAY)
*       .. First calculate Julian date for old style.
        KYR = IYR + 4712
        K1 = 365 * KYR + INT (KYR / 4)
        IF (MON .LT. 3) THEN
            K2 = INT (30.6 * MON - 30.6)
        ELSE IF (MOD (KYR, 4) .EQ. 0) THEN
            K2 = INT (30.6 * MON - 31.8)
        ELSE
            K2 = INT (30.6 * MON - 32.8)
        END IF
        JULIAN = K1 + K2 + IDAY
        IF (JULIAN .GT. 2361221) THEN
*           .. Adjust to new style.
            KYR = IYR - 300
            IF (MON .LT. 3) KYR = KYR - 1
            ICENT = INT (KYR / 100)
            JULIAN = JULIAN - INT ((ICENT * 3) / 4) - 1
        END IF
        RETURN
        END
```

Fig. 10.39 Function *Julian*, which converts calendar date to Julian day number.

Data

01	01	1974
12	31	1899
01	01	1900
02	28	1900
03	01	1900
09	02	1752
09	14	1752
01	01	0300
01	01	0000
01	01	−4712
01	−1	0000

Fig. 10.40 Sample data and results for the function *Julian*.

Results

```
01 01 1974
  TUE JAN  1 1974 2442049
12 31 1899
  SUN DEC 31 1899 2415020
01 01 1900
  MON JAN  1 1900 2415021
02 28 1900
  WED FEB 28 1900 2415079
03 01 1900
  THU MAR  1 1900 2415080
09 02 1752
  WED SEP  2 1752 2361221
09 14 1752
  THU SEP 14 1752 2361222
01 01 0300
  MON JAN  1  300 1830633
01 01 0000
  THU JAN  1    0 1721058
01 01-4712
  MON JAN  1-4712      0
```

subprogram is shown in Fig. 10.39, with data and results in Fig. 10.40. The function *Julian* first calculates the number of days since January 1, 4713 B.C., on the basis of the 365.25-day year of the Old Style calendar. The value of K1 is the Julian date for January 1 of the specified year, and the days within a year are treated the same as in the subprogram *Kount* (Section 10.5.1). This preliminary calculation gives the correct Julian day number for dates prior to the calendar reform, but for later dates a further adjustment is required.

In Great Britain and the American colonies, the New Style calendar was adopted on September 2, 1752 (Julian date 2,361,221). For days after that date, we must subtract a correction term. The Old Style and New Style calendars would have agreed on January 1, A.D. 300, and then diverged by three days every four centuries from that point on. For other countries, the same correction formula is valid, but the date of adoption of the New Style calendar is different. In Italy and most other Roman Catholic countries, the New Style calendar was adopted on October 15, 1582 (Julian date 2,229,161). The constant can easily be changed to conform to that date.

Once we have the correct Julian day number, it is a simple matter to determine the day of the week. Julian dates that leave a remainder of zero when divided by 7 correspond to Mondays. A remainder of 1 indicates Tuesday, a remainder of 6 designates a Sunday, and so on.

We have chosen some interesting dates among the test cases for Fig. 10.40. We have checked that the program proceeds smoothly from December 31, 1899, to January 1, 1900, that it recognizes 1900 as a nonleap year, and that it correctly omits the 11 dates in September 1752 that were dropped in the change from

Old Style to New Style. We have also tested January 1 of several years, including 1974, 300, zero (the astronomers' designation for 1 B.C.), and −4712 (or 4713 B.C.).

Project

Write a program to read Julian date and print month, day, and year.

10.5.3 Printing a Calendar

Using a procedure such as that in Fig. 10.39 to find the day of the week for any given date, we can easily produce a listing of the days of any specified month.

Projects

1. Write a program to produce a list of the days of any specified month. The program should read two integers representing the year and the month. It should determine the name of the month and the number of days in the month (from a table, for example). It should then print one line for each day of the month, giving

   a) the day of the week, printed alphabetically,
   b) the name of the month, also printed alphabetically,
   c) the date within the month, and
   d) the year.

2. Write a program to print a more elegant calendar for the entire current year on one page, with four months in each of three columns. The months and the days of the week should be appropriately labeled. To make the calendar more interesting, you may wish to print an extra page ahead of the calendar listing, which could contain a design or picture of some sort. The year (perhaps in block letters) could also appear on this extra page. If you are not so ambitious, simply print the year numerically at the top of the calendar page itself.

   The main calendar page begins with the year number. Next is a line with headings for January, February, and March, followed by a line with the names of the days of the week (printed once for each of the three months). As many as six lines may be required for the dates in these three months. The arrangement is then repeated for the second, third, and fourth quarters.

   Since there will be 21 dates across each row, each date should be given 3, 4, or 5 character spaces. The two main complications are the need to print dates alphabetically (because the blanks at each end of a month cannot be printed with numeric format), and the need to print parts of three different months on each line. A suggested method follows.

   a) Store the names of the months in a 3 by 4 array. (Use a DATA statement or a PARAMETER statement, or read them from an input source.)

b) Read the number of the specified year. Print the year (with or without an additional design).

c) Using the function *Julian,* compute and store (in a linear array of 13 elements) the Julian date for the first day of each month of the specified year and for the first day of January of the following year.

d) For each of the 12 months of the year, generate a six-line (42-element) *numerical* calendar image. From the array of Julian dates, determine where in the image the first day of the month belongs; store zeros in all cells ahead of that one. Also use the Julian date for the beginning of the *following* month to locate the last day of the month; store zeros in all cells beyond that one.

e) Using a nest of four DO loops, print the calendar. The first loop is traversed once for each *quarter* of the year; it begins by printing the headings (including the names of the three months, and the labels for the days of the week). The second loop is traversed once for each of the six *lines* of the calendar image. The third loop is traversed once for each of the three *months* in the quarter, and the fourth loop is traversed once for each of the seven *days* of the week. Inside the fourth loop, an element of the numerical calendar image is converted to alphabetic form (applying the predefined function *Char* to each digit, and changing leading zero digits to blanks) and stored in the proper character position of a 21-character (or longer) alphabetic line image. The line is printed just ahead of the end of the second DO loop.

10.6 TREES AND GRAPHS

Many computer applications involve a quantity of data that possesses an inherently more complex structure than that of a linear or rectangular array. Fortran programs for such applications must use the simple storage techniques that are available, but it is possible to associate with the basic data additional (explicit or implicit) information concerning the relationships among the various items in storage.

A *graph* is a set of data items, called *nodes,* along with a set of *edges* interconnecting some of the nodes. A *tree* is a certain kind of graph without loops. In this section we consider two different applications involving graphs.

In the first example, the nodes are the 64 squares of a chessboard, and the edges connect any pair of nodes separated by a single knight's move (see Fig. 10.41). The interconnections are never entered into the computer, but they are implicit in the program. The problem is to find a path that visits each node exactly once.

In the second example, the edges are the corridors of an arbitrary labyrinth, and the nodes are the junctions of the corridors (see Figs. 10.54 and 10.55).

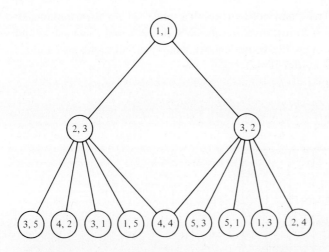

Fig. 10.41 Graph showing possible moves of a knight on a chessboard, starting from square (1, 1). Only the first two moves are shown.

The connections are represented explicitly with a matrix. The problem is to exhaustively explore all the corridors, visiting each junction as many times as necessary, until a certain predetermined junction is encountered.

10.6.1　The Knight's Delight or Knight's Tour Problem

In the game of chess, a knight is authorized to move in a special, but restricted, manner. If he is on the square in row I and column J, his move is restricted to one of the eight shown in Table 10.6.

Table 10.6　The eight moves that can be made by a knight at row I and column J near the center of the chessboard

Change in I	Change in J
1	2
2	1
2	−1
1	−2
−1	−2
−2	−1
−2	1
−1	2

Of course, the new row and column number must lie on the chessboard; that is, *I* plus the change in *I* must give an integer between 1 and 8 inclusive, and similarly for *J*. A knight near the center of the board has all eight possibilities open to him, as illustrated in Fig. 10.42.

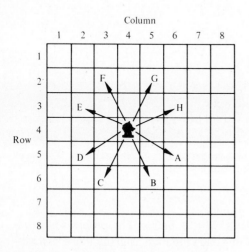

Fig. 10.42 A knight near the center of the chessboard can move to any one of the eight squares labeled A through H.

Starting from a particular square, a certain number of moves may be made. For example, from the square at row 1 and column 1 (the upper left corner of the board), two moves are possible: to row 2, column 3; or to row 3, column 2. From each resulting position, further moves are possible; thus there is a network of possible moves from any starting point. Figure 10.41, which is a graph of such a network, shows the possibilities for the first two moves, starting from square (1, 1). These moves are further expanded in Table 10.7, which includes all possibilities for the first three moves from this same starting point, excluding those sequences that would take the knight to the same square more than once. Although the two possible first moves, 11 possible second moves, and 50 possible third moves, along with the original square (1, 1), apparently total 64 squares reachable within three moves, Fig. 10.43 shows that, because of duplications, only half of the squares are in fact reachable. (A similar explanation refutes the assertion that, since a person has two parents, four grandparents, eight great-grandparents, etc., the entire population of the world a few hundred years ago would not be sufficient to include one person's ancestors.)

Table 10.7

```
1, 1                 1, 1 (cont.)              1, 1 (cont.)
   2, 3                 2, 3 (cont.)              3, 2 (cont.)
      3, 5                 4, 4                      5, 3 (cont.)
         4, 7                 5, 6                      4, 1
         5, 6                 6, 5                      3, 4
         5, 4                 6, 3                      4, 5
         4, 3                 5, 2                   5, 1
         1, 4                 3, 2                      6, 3
         1, 6                 2, 5                      7, 2
         2, 7                 3, 6                      4, 3
      4, 2              3, 2                         1, 3
         5, 4                 4, 4                      2, 5
         6, 3                 5, 6                      3, 4
         6, 1                 6, 5                      2, 1
         2, 1                 6, 3                   2, 4
         3, 4                 5, 2                      3, 6
      3, 1                    2, 3                      4, 5
         4, 3                 2, 5                      4, 3
         5, 2                 3, 6                      1, 2
         1, 2              5, 3                         1, 6
      1, 5                    6, 5
         2, 7                 7, 4
         3, 6                 7, 2
         3, 4                 6, 1
```

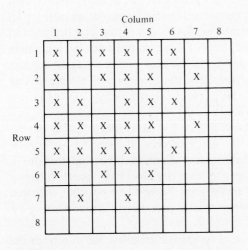

Fig. 10.43 The squares of the chessboard marked X can be reached by a knight within three moves from square (1, 1).

The knight's tour

Is it possible for a knight to make a sequence of 63 moves so as to land on each square of the chessboard exactly once, including the initial starting square? The great mathematician Euler (1707–1783) demonstrated this possibility. (It is of course assumed that the chessboard contains no other pieces, so that the knight's movement is unhampered.)

Try your hand at this puzzle. Unless you use great care, you will find that after a certain number of moves the knight will be in a position such that all valid moves would take him to squares already visited, although there are still some unreachable squares that have not been visited. We will define a "knight's tour" as a sequence of valid moves of the knight such that he never goes to a square on which he has landed previously. The *length* of the tour is the total number of squares visited (including the starting square), and a complete, successful knight's tour touches all 64 squares of the chessboard.

We will consider some strategies for making the knight's tours as long as possible, using a computer. We will always start the tour from square (1, 1), but you may wish to make some computer runs to study the effect of starting at a different square.

Systematic strategies

As our simplest strategy, we will make each move from the current square in direction A, as indicated in Fig. 10.42, if possible. If this move would take the knight beyond the edge of the board or to a square that has already been visited, we will try to move in direction B. If this move cannot be made, we will try C, D, etc., up to H, in clockwise order, until we find a move that can be made in accordance with the rules of the knight's tour. (If we do not find any legitimate move, we are stuck, and the tour is ended.) For the next move, we again attempt direction A first, then B, and so on. Note that the sequence of attempts is in accordance with the list of moves in Table 10.6. As shown in Fig. 10.44(a) this tour ends after 36 squares have been visited.

We next try using the same clockwise search for an available move, but we start the search at a different point on the list. However, at each step we consistently start the clockwise search with the same direction. We find that for a tour beginning at square (1, 1) it is best to start the clockwise search for each move with direction F. That is, we will make move F whenever possible, followed by G, H, then A, B, etc. Such a strategy results in a knight's tour visiting 44 squares, as shown in Fig. 10.44(b).

Summarizing, we find that if we use a systematic strategy, starting from the upper left corner square, making each move in a predetermined direction whenever possible, and searching among the other seven directions in clockwise order

1	0	0	0	0	0	0	0
0	0	2	0	0	0	0	0
0	32	0	0	3	0	0	0
34	0	0	27	0	0	4	0
31	10	33	0	0	26	23	0
18	35	28	11	24	21	14	5
9	30	19	16	7	12	25	22
36	17	8	29	20	15	6	13

(a)

1	22	39	20	3	18	9	16
0	37	2	23	8	15	4	13
35	40	21	38	19	12	17	10
0	0	36	41	24	7	14	5
0	34	0	32	0	28	11	26
0	0	0	0	42	25	6	29
0	0	33	0	31	0	27	44
0	0	0	0	0	43	30	0

(b)

Fig. 10.44 Knight's tours produced by systematic strategy: (a) Starting direction A, tour length 36; (b) starting direction F, tour length 44.

until we find a valid move, we obtain knight's tours of lengths between 32 and 44 squares (see Table 10.8).

Table 10.8

Starting direction for clockwise search (see Fig. 10.42)	Length of resulting knight's tour
A	36
B	36
C	42
D	33
E	32
F	44
G	42
H	35

The program implementing this strategy is shown in Fig. 10.45 (related flow-chart, Fig. 10.46). At the beginning of the program, we initialize the 64 squares of the board with zero values. When the knight visits a square at move N, we store the value of N in the corresponding cell of the array. A valid move is defined as one which does not take the knight beyond the edge of the board or to a square that has already been visited.

```
* Knight's tour by systematic strategy
      LOGICAL MOVE
      INTEGER BOARD
      COMMON BOARD(8, 8), KO
*     KO is starting direction for each move.
      DO 19, KO = 1, 8
*        .. Set BOARD array to zeros.
*        .. Set IT and JT to one.
         CALL RESET (BOARD, IT, JT)
         DO 15, N = 0, 63
*           ..Record current board position.
            I = IT
            J = JT
            BOARD(I, J) = N + 1
*           ..Try all 8 directions, starting with KO.
            DO 11, K = 1, 8
               IF (MOVE (I, J, K, IT, JT)) GO TO 15
 11         CONTINUE
*           .. Can't move from square (I, J).
            PRINT *, 'Stuck□at□square', I, J, '□after', N, '□moves.'
            GO TO 17
*           .. Successful move to square (IT, JT).
 15         CONTINUE
*        .. 64 successful moves. Tour is complete.
         PRINT *, 'Success□with□starting□direction', KO
 17      CONTINUE
         PRINT *, N
         PRINT '('' ''0'', 8 I3)', ((BOARD(I, J), J = 1, 8), I = 1, 8)
 19      CONTINUE
      END


* Attempts move from (I, J) in direction (K + KO),
* arriving at (IT, JT). If (IT, JT) is on board
* and is unoccupied, return with Move = .TRUE.
      LOGICAL FUNCTION MOVE (I, J, K, IT, JT)
      INTEGER BOARD
      COMMON BOARD(8, 8), KO
      INTEGER IM(8), JM(8)
      DATA (IM(L), L = 1, 8) / 1, 2, 2, 1, −1, −2, −2, −1 /
      DATA (JM(L), L = 1, 8) / 2, 1, −1, −2, −2, −1, 1, 2 /
*
      K1 = MOD (K + KO − 2, 8) + 1
      IT = I + IM(K1)
      JT = J + JM(K1)
      IF (      ((IT .GE. 1) .AND. (IT .LE. 8))
     $   .AND. ((JT .GE. 1) .AND. (JT .LE. 8))
     $   .AND. (BOARD(IT, JT) .EQ. 0)) THEN
         MOVE = .TRUE.
      ELSE
         MOVE = .FALSE.
      END IF
      RETURN
      END
```

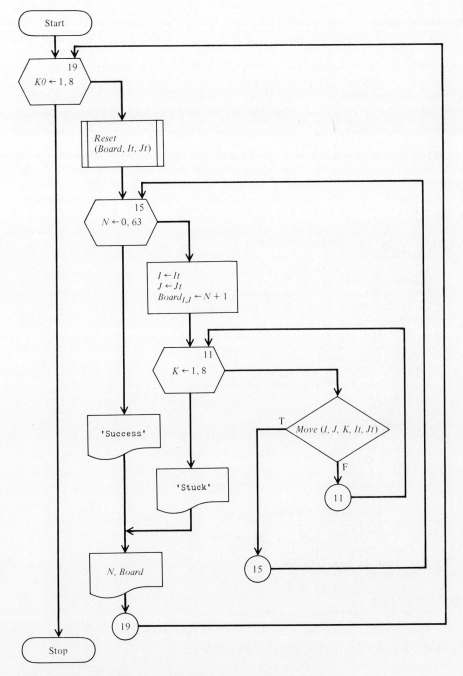

▲ **Fig. 10.46** Flowchart for knight's tour by systematic strategy.

◀ **Fig. 10.45** Program using systematic strategy for knight's tour.

Random strategy

Why should we restrict ourselves to the systematic strategy of starting the clockwise search for a valid move always in the same direction? Many variations on this systematic strategy are possible; you may wish to try a strategy of your own invention. In the program of Fig. 10.47 (flowchart, Fig. 10.48) we again make a clockwise search for a valid move, but at each step we choose a *random* starting direction. The formula

    KO = INT (8.0 * X) + 1

converts the random real number X between 0.0 and 1.0 into an integer between 1 and 8, which is used to select the starting direction from the eight possibilities, A through H.

```
* Knight's tour by random strategy.
      LOGICAL MOVE
      INTEGER BOARD, HIST(64)
      COMMON BOARD(8, 8), KO
      DATA (HIST(L), L = 1, 64) / 64 * 0 /
*         .. Initialize random number generator.
      X = 0.5
*         .. Make 100 tests
      DO 19, LOOP = 1, 100
        CALL RESET (BOARD, IT, JT)
        DO 15, N = 0, 63
*           .. Record current board position.
          I = IT
          J = JT
          BOARD(I, J) = N + 1
*           .. Generate random starting direction for next move.
          CALL RAND (X)
          KO = INT (8.0 * X) + 1
          DO 11, K = 1, 8
            IF (MOVE (I, J, K, IT, JT)) GO TO 15
 11       CONTINUE
*           .. Stuck after N moves.
          GO TO 17
*           .. Successful move to square (IT, JT).
 15       CONTINUE
*         .. Tour is complete. N is 64.
 17     CONTINUE
        HIST(N) = HIST(N) + 1
 19   CONTINUE
      PRINT *, (I, HIST(I), I = 1, 64)
      END
```

Fig. 10.47 Program using random strategy for knight's tour.

Fig. 10.48 Flowchart for knight's tour by random strategy. ▶

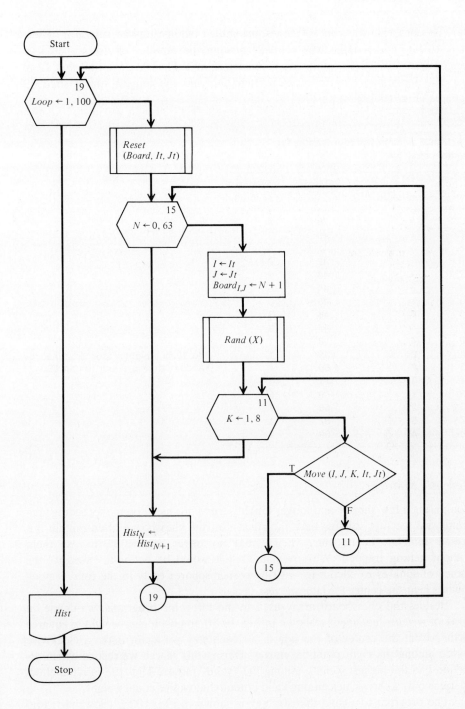

This program was run 100 times, using the random number generator of Section 10.1.1, and a table was printed showing the number of times each tour length occurred. These results are summarized in Table 10.9. We find that 12 of the 100 tours had lengths of more than 50, and the longest tour visited 59 squares (Fig. 10.49).

Table 10.9 Summary of tour lengths for random strategy

Length	Number of tours	Length	Number of tours
12	1	39	4
16	1	40	1
18	1	41	3
20	1	42	8
22	3	43	3
24	6	44	6
25	1	45	9
26	1	46	3
27	4	47	3
30	4	48	1
32	2	49	1
33	2	50	4
34	3	51	4
35	1	52	5
36	2	56	1
37	5	57	1
38	4	59	1

Fig. 10.49 Knight's tour produced by random strategy; tour length 59.

Heuristic strategy

Comparing a few shorter and longer knight's tours produced by the foregoing programs, we see that squares near the corners of the chessboard often remain unvisited until late in the tour, when it may no longer be possible to visit them without getting trapped. We speculate that it would be better to "weight" the choice of squares to encourage visiting corner squares early in the tour, leaving squares near the center for later moves.

Besides the chessboard array used in the foregoing programs, we define an array of *weights,* assigned as shown in Fig. 10.50, to give higher weight to squares farther from the center of the board. At each step we again make a clockwise search among the eight potential moves. During this search we record which direction had the highest weight, among the "valid" moves. Thus the random effect operates only to break ties among valid potential moves of equal weight.

The program for using this strategy is shown in Fig. 10.51 (flowchart, Fig. 10.52). After 100 trials with this program, we find eight "successful" full-length

7	6	5	4	4	5	6	7
6	5	4	3	3	4	5	6
5	4	3	2	2	3	4	5
4	3	2	1	1	2	3	4
4	3	2	1	1	2	3	4
5	4	3	2	2	3	4	5
6	5	4	3	3	4	5	6
7	6	5	4	4	5	6	7

Fig. 10.50 Weights for heuristic strategy, increasing with distance from center of board.

```
* Knight's tour by heuristic strategy.
      LOGICAL MOVE
      INTEGER BOARD, HIST(64), W(8, 8)
      COMMON BOARD (8, 8), KO
      DATA (HIST(L), L = 1, 64) / 64 * 0 /
*     .. Initialize random number generator and table of weights.
      X = 0.5
      DO 9, I = 1, 8
        DO 8, J = 1, 8
          W(I, J) = (ABS (2 * I - 9) + ABS (2 * J - 9)) / 2
8       CONTINUE
9     CONTINUE
*     .. Make 100 tests.
      DO 19, LOOP = 1, 100
        CALL RESET (BOARD, IT, JT)
        DO 15, N = 0, 63
*         .. Record current board position.
          I = IT
          J = JT
          BOARD(I, J) = N + 1
*         .. Generate random starting direction for next move.
          CALL RAND (X)
          KO = INT (8.0 * X) + 1
*         Find maximum weight among legal moves.
          MW = 0
          DO 11, K = 1, 8
            IF (MOVE (I, J, K, IT, JT)
             .AND. (W(IT, JT) .GE. MW) THEN
                MW = W(IT, JT)
                IMW = IT
                JMW = JT
              END IF
11        CONTINUE
          IF (MW .EQ. 0) GO TO 17
          IT = IMW
          JT = JMW
15      CONTINUE
*       .. Tour is complete. N is 64.
        PRINT *, N
        PRINT '(''0'', 8 I3)', ((BOARD(I, J), J = 1, 8), I = 1, 8)
17      CONTINUE
        HIST(N) = HIST(N) + 1
19    CONTINUE
      PRINT *, (I, HIST(I), I = 1, 64)
      END
```

Fig. 10.51 Program for knight's tour by heuristic strategy.

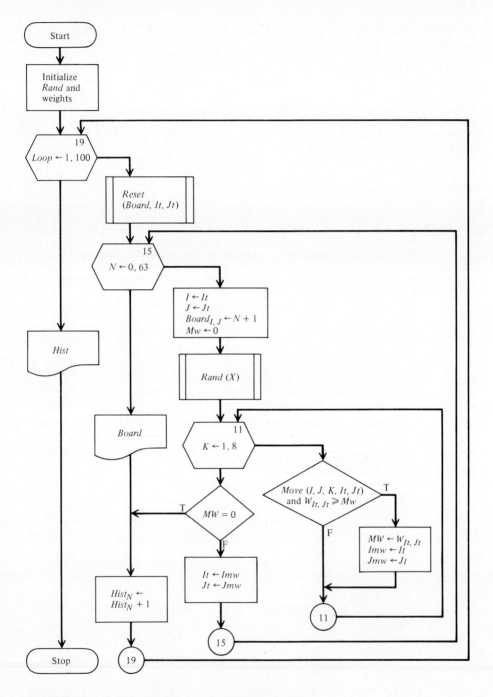

Fig. 10.52 Flowchart for knight's tour by heuristic strategy.

tours and 34 tours of length 63 (see Table 10.10). Upon closer examination, however, we find that two of the eight full-length tours are identical. Thus our program has "discovered" seven different knight's tours. One of these is displayed in Fig. 10.53.

Table 10.10 Summary of tour lengths for heuristic strategy

Length	Number of tours	Length	Number of tours
36	1	56	3
44	6	57	4
47	2	58	5
50	6	59	2
51	3	60	1
52	2	61	14
53	1	62	4
54	1	63	34
55	3	64	8

1	38	3	18	35	40	13	16
4	19	36	39	14	17	34	41
37	2	57	54	59	42	15	12
20	5	62	43	56	53	60	33
49	44	55	58	61	64	11	26
6	21	48	63	52	27	32	29
45	50	23	8	47	30	25	10
22	7	46	51	24	9	28	31

Fig. 10.53 Successful knight's tour produced by heuristic strategy; tour length 64.

"Look-ahead" strategy

In another strategy, when a valid "next" move is found, instead of making the move immediately, we determine whether it can be followed by another valid move. This strategy can be used alone or in combination with the heuristic strategy to improve the probability of finding a successful full-length knight's tour. The "look-ahead" strategy, when used alone, will have little effect near the beginning of the tour, but it will result in improvement by avoiding one-move "traps" from which there is no escape. (For example, see the two tours in Figs. 10.44, a and b.) Such traps could of course be avoided easily by a human analyst. A further modification would be to look ahead two or more moves.

Backtracking strategy

The look-ahead strategy can be extended still further. In principle, it is possible to perform a look-ahead all the way from the beginning of a knight's tour to detect potential traps. The data storage requirements for such a strategy are quite different from those discussed above, however. In this approach, known as *backtracking,* it is necessary to keep a record of unsuccessful moves taken from each point on the path, and to back up and try a new move from an earlier point when a particular sequence runs into a block.

A backtracking algorithm can, in principle, discover *all* possible complete knight's tours. (However, the time required to do this would be prohibitive.)

You may wish to devise a backtracking algorithm for the *last* few moves of a knight's tour. After a certain number of moves have been taken by one of the simpler methods, search among the remaining possibilities until a complete knight's tour is found.

The data that needs to be stored for such an algorithm may be more clearly understood after a study of the following labyrinth example.

10.6.2   Computer Solution of a Labyrinth

In Greek mythology, we read of the hero Theseus, who killed a monster called a Minotaur in order to win the hand of the maiden Ariadne. Ariadne helped him to find his way to the Minotaur, which was kept in a labyrinth; she gave him a ball of thread to unwind as he searched through the corridors of the labyrinth, while she held one end of the thread firmly in her hand. After killing the monster, Theseus returned to claim the maiden by rewinding the thread.

We can represent the predicament of Theseus on the computer and solve his problem by finding the Minotaur, if it is accessible, and then returning to Ariadne.

First we must have a means of representing the labyrinth. We may use a "connection matrix," which is simply a doubly subscripted array of dimension n by n, where n is the number of junctions (intersections of corridors) in the labyrinth. Let the array be called C. The connections are indicated by setting $C_{i,j} = 1$ and $C_{j,i} = 1$ if the ith and jth junctions are connected by a corridor; otherwise we set the elements of C to zero. (See Figs. 10.54 and 10.55.)

We also need two integer variables, *Maid* and *Mino,* whose values represent the number of the junction at which Ariadne and the Minotaur, respectively, are located.

We use a linear array, *IPath,* to record the current path of the thread in the labyrinth. Since the algorithm described below is clever enough never to go through the same junction twice, except temporarily, the length of this linear array need not exceed $n + 1$.

Two more integer variables are needed: *Jc*, the number of the junction at which Theseus is currently located; and *Lp*, the current path length, or number of junctions through which the thread currently passes.

The first step in the program is to read values for the elements of the connection matrix, C, as well as the junction numbers for *Maid* and *Mino.* Then, starting from the junction where the maiden is located, use the following strategy.

1. Add the current junction to the path.
2. Determine whether the Minotaur is at the current junction; if so, begin the "return path" phase described in step 6 below.
3. Determine whether the current junction is already on the path. (This condition corresponds to Theseus's arriving at a junction and finding that the string

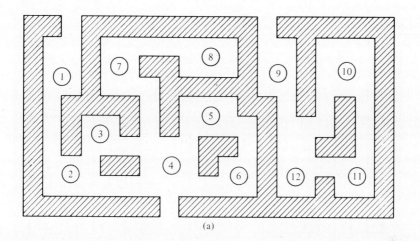

(a)

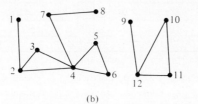

(b)

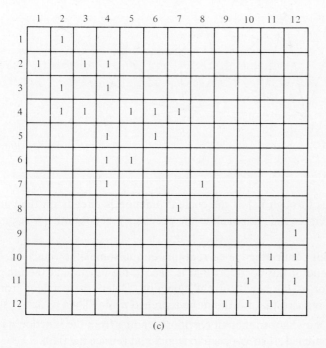

(c)

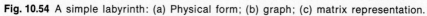

Fig. 10.54 A simple labyrinth: (a) Physical form; (b) graph; (c) matrix representation.

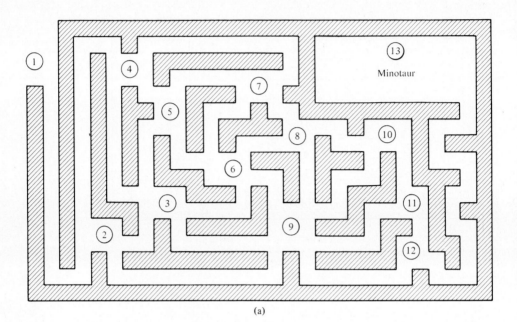

(a)

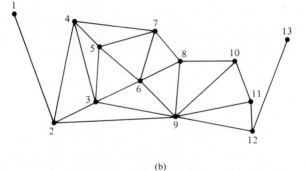

(b)

already passes through it.) If the current junction is already on the path, go
to step 5 to retrace the path back to the previous junction; otherwise proceed
to step 4.

4. Find a corridor connecting the current junction to some other junction. Move
to the other end of this corridor; that is, record the junction at the other end
of the corridor as the new "current" junction. Delete the corridor from the
connection matrix so that it will not be searched again. Then return to step 1.

Note: It may happen that all corridors leading from the junction have already been searched. If so, proceed to step 5 and retrace the path.

◀ **Fig. 10.55** A more complex labyrinth: (a) Physical form; (b) graph; (c) matrix representation.

▼

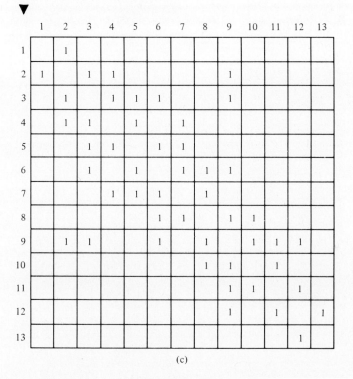

	1	2	3	4	5	6	7	8	9	10	11	12	13
1		1											
2	1		1	1					1				
3		1		1	1	1			1				
4		1	1		1		1						
5			1	1		1	1						
6		1		1		1	1	1					
7			1	1	1		1						
8						1	1		1	1			
9		1	1			1			1	1	1		
10									1	1		1	
11									1	1		1	
12									1		1		1
13												1	

(c)

5. Back up by rewinding the string. That is, move to the previous junction as recorded in the array *IPath*. Then continue the search from step 1 without modifying the connection matrix.

     Before backing up, however, test whether the path has been retraced all the way to Ariadne. If so, all accessible corridors have been searched, so the Minotaur must be in a part of the labyrinth that is not connected to Ariadne's junction.

6. When the Minotaur is located, rewind the string all the way, thus returning to Ariadne in triumph.

Project

Write a program, as outlined above. The program should print a statement giving the beginning junction number, and then, as the search proceeds, it should print one line at each step giving the current junction number. If the Minotaur is located, that fact should be reported and the return path should be printed, step by step. An appropriate comment should be printed at the end.

Use the labyrinth graph shown in Fig. 10.54 with any of the following initial junction numbers. (In case 2, the Minotaur is inaccessible; see Fig. 10.54.)

	Ariadne	*Minotaur*
Case 1.	1	5
Case 2.	8	9
Case 3.	1	8
Case 4.	9	11
Case 5.	4	8

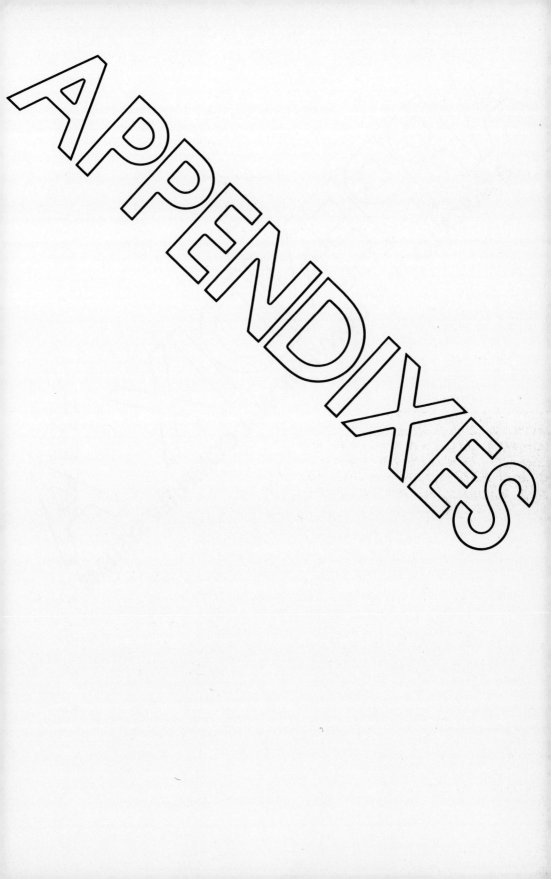
APPENDIXES

APPENDIX A

A QUICK LOOK AT CONVENTIONAL COMPUTER SYSTEMS

A.1 COMPONENTS OF A COMPUTER

The principal components of the computer are: (1) one or more *input devices,* such as keyboard, punched card, magnetic tape, and paper-tape readers; (2) *storage,* wherein are placed the coded instructions and values pertinent to the problem being executed; (3) one or more *output devices,* such as card and paper-tape punches, typewriter and line printers, magnetic tape writers, and television picture display; (4) a *processing unit* capable of addition, subtraction, multiplication, and division, as well as of sensing either a negative or a zero value, comparing two values, and so on; and finally (5) a *control mechanism* whose function is to control the sequence of events within the computer by interpreting and causing the execution of the coded instructions received from storage.

A.2 ORGANIZATION OF A COMPUTER SYSTEM

The relationships among the five principal computer components can best be understood by examining the system diagram shown in Fig. A.1.

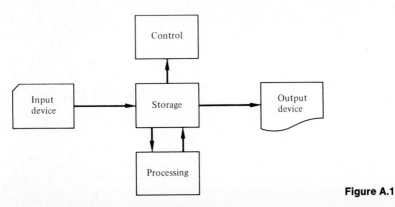

Figure A.1

The silhouettes used for input and output suggest a punch-card reader for input and a line printer or typewriter for output, connected *directly* to the computer. Many computer systems have precisely such an arrangement. On the other hand, the input and output devices of a system may be numerous and diverse, as suggested in Fig. A.2.

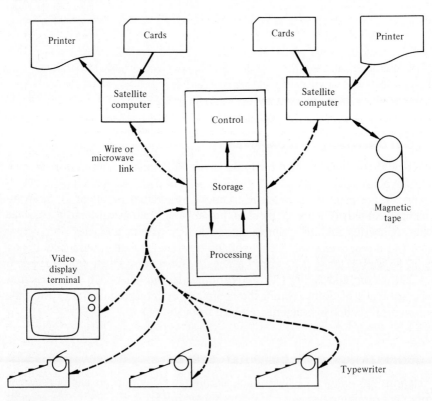

Figure A.2

Systems may receive input information from and send output information to stations that are remote from the main computer. Communication is accomplished by wire or microwave channel, often over long distances.

These remote stations, often called *satellites,* or *remote consoles,* may be video display terminals, typewriters, card readers, line printers, or even other computers that are themselves connected in network fashion to input and output devices.

A.3 LOCATION-ADDRESSED STORAGE

Information storage devices, often referred to as *memories,* are subdivided into individual units, or cells, each capable of storing a certain amount of information. (These units correspond to the windowed containers of the ideal computer.) In some computers the unit of storage capacity is a single character, like the letter Q, the digit 6, or the dollar symbol, $. In other computers the unit of storage is large enough to hold a ten-digit decimal number. In any case, each unit, often called a *word,* is *individually addressable;* that is, in the course of executing a given instruction, the computer is capable of retrieving from or storing information in any word. Addresses are usually numbered from 0, in increments of 1, to an upper limit representing the last word in storage. For example, a computer might have a storage capacity of 32,768 words, with addresses that run from 00000 consecutively up to 32767.

A characteristic property of storage is *destructive read-in* and *nondestructive read-out;* that is, each time information is stored in a given word, the contents of that word are erased as the new information is "read in." When information is "read out" of a given word of storage, the contents of the storage location itself are undisturbed. Hence information may be "read out" of a given storage location as many times as needed without destroying the contents of the word itself.

These properties of storage are mirrored exactly by the ideal computer. The assignment of a value to a windowed container involves first "dumping out" the old value before inserting the new one. The value of a container may be read (through the window) and copied onto a fresh slip of paper as often as needed without disturbing the value *in* the container.

The primary storage units of a computer may be extended in capacity by the use of various technologies, of which the most popular one of late is called "virtual" storage. Virtual storage employs a group of separate actual storage units, all attached to the same computer system. These units, which may have different physical characteristics of speed (time to fetch or store), capacity, and cost, together serve as if they were a single unit of sequentially addressed storage cells, each of which is directly "addressable" by the processing and control units of the computer system. With virtual-storage technology it is possible to economically increase the storage capacity of the computer system several orders of magnitude (by attaching devices of ever larger capacity and lower speed and cost) without decreasing in a significant way the average speed of the storage system as a whole.

Some computers have special-purpose ROM (read-only memory) storage, whose contents cannot be modified while the computer is in operation. Such storage is reserved for control information, and is not available to the user for storing programs or data.

A.4 BASIC OPERATION AND USE OF THE COMPUTER

We can gain some insight into the question of how to use a computer if we examine the process that occurs within the machine during its actual operation. The key to the operation is the component referred to above as the "control unit." This device is capable of retrieving the contents of words in storage, one after the other, in an orderly way. Each time such information is brought to the control unit, it is interpreted as an *instruction* and is then executed. The act of executing an instruction involves calling into action one or more of the other main computer components. Thus, if the instruction is an order to perform some arithmetic calculation, the processing unit, as well as some of the cells of the storage, may be involved. If it is an input instruction, the input device—keyboard, card reader, or whatever—is activated, and information is channeled from that device to certain locations in storage that receive it. An output instruction, by analogy, involves copying information from certain cells of the storage unit and channeling it to some activated output device.

Naturally, this brief description of the operation is an oversimplification. Nonetheless, we can surmise the following without additional detail. The use of a computer involves a process that somehow places in storage a sequence of instructions in the order in which they will be fetched, interpreted, and executed. The computer program is a string of instructions so arranged that execution accomplishes the desired objective.

A.5 THE NATURE OF COMPUTER INSTRUCTIONS

The instructions themselves are numerical or alphabetic codes which, while in their storage cells, *are indistinguishable* from any other kind of information stored there. These codes are recognized and interpreted as instructions only after being copied into the control unit. If brought to the control unit via the arithmetic unit, such codes can actually be changed into other instructions in transit. The possibility that some instructions of a program can be given a different interpretation each time they are executed suggests that a digital computer possesses an inherent power beyond its sheer speed. This capability for multiple interpretation has the effect that most programs require a much smaller total number of instructions than would otherwise be expected. Many programs, even complicated ones, can be stored entirely within a computer's primary storage unit.

Each type of computer is distinguished by its own repertoire or list of instructions that the control unit is capable of interpreting and executing. The repertoire is generally fixed and is furnished as built-in circuitry by the computer designer or is stored in read-only memory. In some machines there are several hundred different instructions available in the repertoire.

A.6 DESIGN OF A MINIATURE COMPUTER

The principles developed in the foregoing sections can be better understood if we digress here to design a very small, simple computer and see how it might be operated to solve one or two simple problems. By "design" we mean that we will specify the main characteristics of the computer's key components.

The storage unit

First we shall design a small storage unit, as shown in Fig. A.3, which consists of 25 cells numbered from 01 to 25. Each cell will be able to hold a number represented by three decimal digits and a sign.

For simplicity we will assume that our computer will deal with integers that are limited to the range -999 to $+999$, so that any such number may be contained in a single word of storage. Similarly, we will assume that each instruction is represented by a three-digit code. An instruction can also be stored in a single word. The sign position of an instruction will always be plus.

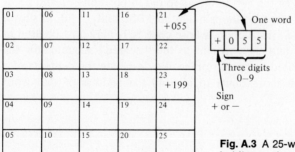
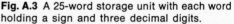

Fig. A.3 A 25-word storage unit with each word holding a sign and three decimal digits.

The order list

If we agree that the computer has an order list of no more than ten instructions, we can assign a one-digit code, 0 through 9, for each instruction. A possible set of simple orders is given in Table A.1. The order list will be better understood when we explain how the processing, control, and input-output units are to function.

Table A.1 A simple order list for a miniature computer

	Action	Symbolic abbreviation	Machine code
1. Arithmetic	Clear and add	CLA	1
	Add	ADD	2
	Subtract	SUB	3
	Store	STO	4
	Multiply	MPY	5
	Divide	DIV	6
2. Input-	Read	RDS	7
output	Print	PRT	8
3. Control	Transfer unconditionally	TRA	9
	Transfer on minus	TMI	0

The processing unit

At the heart of the processing unit is a device for holding the results of individual additions, subtractions, multiplications, or divisions. We call this device the *accumulator*. In our machine, the accumulator, often abbreviated as ACC, holds a sign and six digits. To see how the accumulator might be used, let us imagine that we wish to find the sum of the two numbers found in positions 21 and 23 of storage. The values found in these locations might be +055 and +199, as shown in Fig. A.3. The *clear and add* instruction, whose code is 1, may now be used to make the accumulator zero and then to add to the "cleared" accumulator the number found in any designated word of storage. To designate the contents of a particular word requires two more digits to identify the address of that word uniquely. For example,

     1 21

might be made to mean: *clear* the accumulator to zero *and add* (to the accumulator) the contents of word 21. Then

     2 23

might mean: *add* (to the accumulator) the *contents* of word 23.

In this way we have a concept of what an instruction for our computer should be. In our example, after the 1 21 instruction is executed, the ACC would contain +000055. Then, after the execution of the 2 23 instruction, the ACC would contain +000254. We are now ready to formalize this concept.

Instructions

The instruction code is represented as a three-digit number. The first digit is a code for the particular *operation,* or action, that we wish the computer to take; the last two digits form the *address* of a number that is to be involved in the action.

We continue with our example. Having formed the sum of the two numbers in the accumulator, we now wish to place it in some word of storage, say at address 25. In our example the accumulator now contains +000254. The code

    4 25

means: *store* the sign and the three lowest-order (rightmost) digits of the accumulator† at address 25. If properly interpreted and executed, this instruction would accomplish our objective. In short, the sequence of instructions

    1 21
    2 23
    4 25

can be thought of as a "program" to form the sum of two numbers found at addresses 21 and 23 and to store this sum at address 25.

Machine codes and a symbolic equivalent

These three-digit instructions are often called *machine codes* because they are the codes understood by the machine we are designing.

Our problem might have been initially stated as: "Form c as the sum $a + b$" or "Let $c = a + b$" or even more simply, "$c \leftarrow a + b$."

Let us imagine that we want the computer to perform this task. As a first step we might choose to describe the desired computer action in an "intermediate" language, say,

    CLA A
    ADD B
    STO C

---

† A sum or product that extended beyond the third digit could not be stored in its entirety, using the *store* instruction. However, another type of store instruction might be added to the order list of Table A.1, which when executed would copy and store the three highest-order digits. Without this extension the computer, as we now describe it, is admittedly limited rather severely. Note that, although for practical purposes, no final arithmetic result can exceed three digits in size and be stored, an *intermediate* result of a computation might exceed three digits. Consider the computation $50 \times 50 - 45 \times 55 = 2500 - 2475 = 25$. The intermediate products have four digits, but the final result has only two digits.

These "symbolic" codes can then be transformed to the numerical machine codes, provided we are willing to identify certain storage addresses with particular variables. Thus, if we agree that A, B, and C are to correspond respectively, say, to addresses 21, 23, and 25, we can transform the intermediate symbolic code to machine code in a straightforward one-to-one correspondence. (Recall that there was a corresponding idea in the ideal computer. It involved choosing a container and labeling it.) Figure A.4 displays the process of translation from problem statement to machine code. Professional programmers are often forced to write instruction sequences in a symbolic equivalent of machine code. The translation to machine code is then accomplished automatically by the computer with the aid of specially written programs called *assembly programs*. Of course, our own miniature computer is probably not capable of performing this translation.

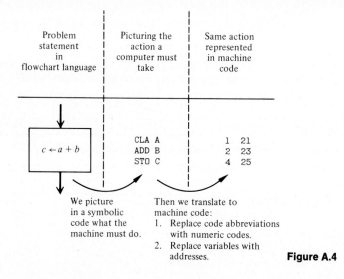

Figure A.4

The control unit

The control unit will have two registers, for interpreting and executing the desired sequence of instructions. Registers are much like storage cells in that they will each hold one number. However, they tend to be much more specialized in function and faster in operation as well. One of the control registers, called the instruction register (IR), will have a three-digit capacity to hold the instruction that is being examined and executed. Another register, called the instruction counter (IC), will have a two-digit capacity to hold the address of the next instruction to be brought from storage. When action on one instruction is completed, the control unit will bring the next instruction from the storage address given by the IC and place it in the IR. While this is going on, the number in the IC is increased by 1.

Figure A.5 illustrates this sequence of events for the second step in the problem to compute the sum of $a + b$. The three machine instructions are assumed to be stored at addresses 07, 08, and 09.

In our simple computer it will be possible to manually set a number in the IC while the computer is idle. When we throw a switch, the cyclical action will begin. Action commences by bringing to the IR the instruction found in the cell designated by the initial setting of the IC. At the same time the IC is increased by 1. Now the instruction in the IR is executed. In this way, if the IC is initially set to 07, the computer will automatically execute one instruction after another from sequentially addressed storage positions.

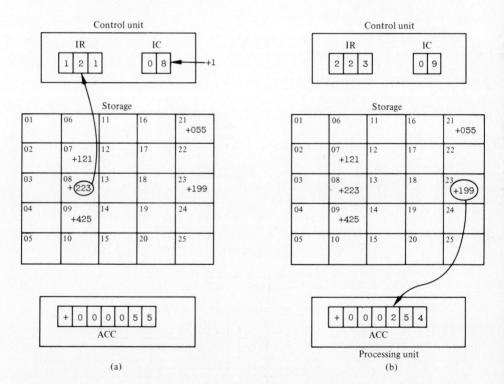

Fig. A.5 (a) The instruction in the IR has just been completed, leaving +000055 in the ACC. The instruction at 08 is being brought from storage to be placed in the IR (destructive read-in). While this is going on, the number in the IC will be incremented by 1. (b) The instruction from 08 is examined and executed, resulting in a new value, +000254, in the ACC.

Input and output units

The input and output devices are designed to function in very simple fashion. We shall imagine that the input unit is capable of reading numbers one at a time from the input device (which might be a punched-card reader). In executing the read instruction,

     7 21

for example, the input unit reads a signed three-digit number, the first one received from the input device. The number so read is transmitted to storage and placed at location 21. Recall that the digit 7 was selected as the code for the read instruction. Figure A.6 schematically represents this input action. Here we can assume that the IC was manually set to 05 to begin this process.

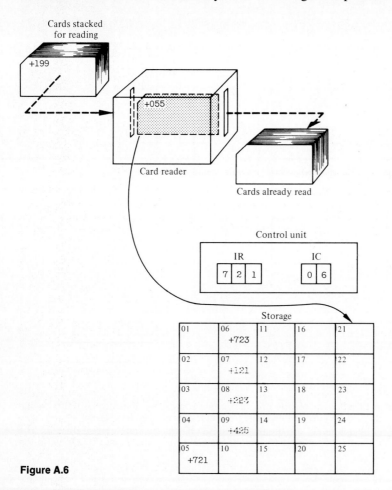

Figure A.6

The next instruction is taken from 06. It might be another input instruction. This time the next number is copied from the input device and placed in storage address 23. In this manner we obtain the values for *a* and *b* so that in the next steps the computer can add them.

If we want to have the computer print the result of the computation, we need an output instruction. Consulting Table A.1, we see that an appropriate instruction would be

8 25

meaning "display on the printer the contents of storage location 25." Supposing that such an instruction is placed at address 10, we see a full sequence of instructions which, if executed, would read data, compute, and print a result. The output step is illustrated in Fig. A.7.

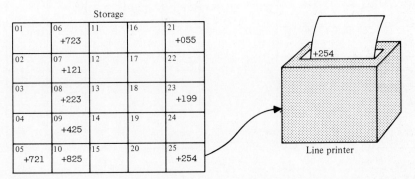

Figure A.7

A *closed loop of instructions*

A computer's power lies in its ability to repeatedly execute simple or complex processes at high speeds. To repeat the simple process we are considering here, perhaps on many pairs of values for *a* and *b*, we can imagine stacking many sets of data to be read. For each set of data we wish to execute the instructions stored in addresses 05 through 10, so that the computer can read the data, compute, and print the resulting sum. Such repetition can be accomplished by placing a *transfer* instruction in address 11. The code digit we have chosen for this is 9 (see Table A.1). The instruction we want is then

   9 05

which would mean "just replace the contents of the IC, now 12, with 05 (the address portion of the instruction in the IR)." No other action is taken. Transfer instructions effectively alter the sequence of instructions being executed. In this case the net effect is to form a "closed loop," repeating instructions located at 05 to 11, inclusive. Figure A.8 diagrams the action in the control unit when a transfer instruction is encountered. In Fig. A.8(a) the instruction from address 11 is brought to the IR, and the contents of the IC are increased from 11 to 12. Execution of a transfer command involves only the control unit. In Fig. A.8(b) the contents of the IC are replaced by the rightmost two digits of the IR.

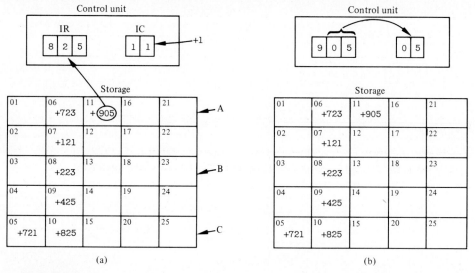

Figure A.8

Figure A.9 summarizes in flowchart representation the algorithm that we have just coded as a machine-language program.

Terminal read process

Under what circumstance will a program loop such as that in Fig. A.9 terminate? When the input stack of cards has been exhausted, the next read instruction cannot be carrried out. We will therefore design our computer so that it will automatically halt when it is asked to execute a read instruction and there are no more cards available to be read.

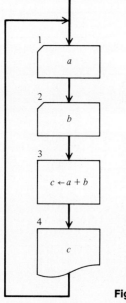

Figure A.9

Exercises

1. Although we have not yet described division in our miniature computer, let us assume that a quotient $p \div q$ (the integral part) may be obtained by the code sequence that corresponds to

   CLA P
   DIV Q

   The resulting quotient will be found in the three lowest-order positions of the ACC.

   Write a sequence of symbolic codes and corresponding machine codes that will compute the value

   $$y = \frac{a - b}{a + b}.$$

   Draw a picture of the storage cells showing all instructions and locations for original or intermediate results. You must make certain decisions, such as where to keep a, b, and y in storage and at what location to begin the program.

   Hint: Before the division can be carried out, both the numerator and the denominator must be computed. At least one of these must be saved, in a place that you will have to designate, while the other is being computed.

2. After completing Exercise 1, write a sequence of instructions that reads a pair of values for a and b from punch cards, computes y, prints it, and returns to read another pair of values.

Table A.2 Code for computing $|a - b|$

Symbolic code		Machine code	
Address name	Instruction	Address†	Instruction
START	RDS A	09	701
	RDS B	10	702
	CLA A	11	101
	SUB B	12	302
	STO C	13	403
	TMI NEG	14	017
AGAIN	PRT C	15	803
	TRA START	16	909
NEG	CLA B	17	102
	SUB A	18	301
	STO C	19	403
	TRA AGAIN	20	915

† We are assuming the following: (1) Instructions begin at 09. (2) A at 01, B at 02, C at 03.

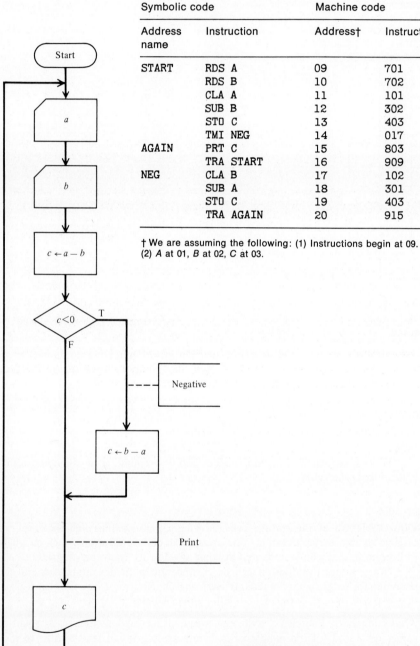

Fig. A.10 Flowchart for computing $|a - b|$.

3. Assume that a product $p \times q$ may be obtained by the code sequence that corresponds to

```
CLA P
MPY Q
```

Write a code sequence to compute the following.

a) $d = \dfrac{a \times b}{c}$ b) $c = \dfrac{a}{b \times c}$

Decisions

We have included a conditional transfer instruction in our miniature computer's order list. We have selected the transfer on the minus, or TMI instruction, with a code 0. Upon executing a TMI, the computer examines the sign of the ACC. If it is negative $(-)$, the instruction is then treated as an *unconditional* transfer, or TRA instruction. That is, the last two digits of the instruction replace the current contents of the IC, thus breaking the normal sequence of instructions. If the sign of the ACC is positive $(+)$, no further action is taken. The computer then goes on to get the next instruction in the normal sequence.

Let us see how we might employ the TMI instruction to compute and print the absolute value of $a - b$, or $|a - b|$, for many pairs of values, a, b. There would be several alternative ways to code this problem. One approach, not the best necessarily, is diagrammed in Fig. A.10 and coded both symbolically and in machine code in Table A.2. Here is one way you can follow this program step by step and gain an added grasp of the process that goes on inside the computer: (1) Draw the storage unit, arithmetic unit, and control unit, as we have done in earlier figures. (2) Enter the instructions in their proper "squares" of storage. (3) Place 09 in the IC. (4) "Turn the switch on" and begin computing with a pair of values for a and b. Try it.

A.7 REFERENCES ON COMPUTER SYSTEM ORGANIZATION

Bell, C. G., J. C. Mudge, and J. E. McNamara, *Computer Engineering: A DEC View of Hardware Systems Design.* Digital Equipment Corporation, Bedford, Mass., 1978.

Organick, E. I., and J. A. Hinds, *Interpreting Machines: Architecture and Programming of the B1700/B1800 Series.* Elsevier-North Holland, New York, 1977.

Tanenbaum, A. S., *Structured Computer Organization.* Prentice-Hall, Englewood Cliffs, N.J., 1976.

APPENDIX B

FLOWCHART CONVENTIONS

In this text, we have tried to follow the flowchart standards of the American National Standards Institute ("Standard flowchart symbols and their use in information processing (X 3.5)" American National Standards Institute, New York, 1970) insofar as they relate to the concepts needed in flowcharts accompanying Fortran programs. We use the following symbols defined in the Standard.

1. *Processing.* The basic rectangular box indicates a processing step, that is, a change in the value, form, or location of data. For Fortran flowcharts, this box ordinarily encloses one or more assignment statements. (See Section 1.3.)

2. *Punched card input.* This box represents input from punched cards. We use this form for all input steps (although actually the input data may be transmitted from a keyboard, or from some other medium, such as mag-

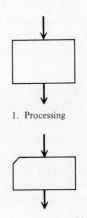

1. Processing

2. Punched card input

netic tape). Inside the box we write the list of items whose values are to be read. (See Chapters 6 and 9.)

3.   *Document output.* This box represents output in the form of a printed document. We use this form for output to be displayed on a line printer or on any other output device such as a typewriter, or a video display terminal. (See Chapters 6 and 9.)

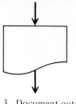

3. Document output

4.   *Decision.* The diamond-shaped box represents a conditional control statement in Fortran. For the logical IF statement, the *Assertion* to be tested is written inside the box, and two flowlines leaving the box (labeled "T" for *true* and "F" for *false*) indicate the alternative paths that the computation may take. (See Chapter 3.)

5.   *Preparation.* We use this shape exclusively for DO statements in this text. At the upper right, inside the box, we indicate the *Label* of the terminal statement. Inside the box we also give the *Index,* the *Initial value,* the *Limit,* and the *Increment* (if required). The flowline leaving the box at the right leads to the group of statements to be repeated under control of the DO statement; this path will be taken so long as the *Index* value is less than or equal to the *Limit.* When the *Index* value exceeds the *Limit,* the flowline at the lower left will be followed. The *Label* of the terminal statement also appears in a Connector symbol at the end of the group of instructions controlled by the DO statement; a flowline leads from this Connector symbol directly back to the box representing the DO statement. (See Chapter 4).

6.   *Predefined process.* This box, distinguished by vertical striping, is used to indicate the activation of a *subroutine* (see Chapter 8). The name of the subroutine and the list of arguments are shown inside the box. The activation of a *function,* since it occurs as a part of the evaluation of an expression, is shown in the context in which it occurs, e.g., inside an ordinary rectangular box for the assignment statement.

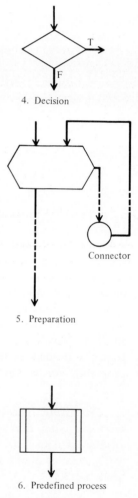

4. Decision

Connector

5. Preparation

6. Predefined process

7. *Multiple decision.* A multiway branch (see Sections 3.1.3 and 3.4) is represented by a diamond-shaped box, supplemented by a system of flowlines, as shown here.

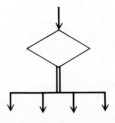

7. Multiple decision

8. *Terminal.* This box is used in two ways in this text. With a flowline leading *from* the box, it indicates the beginning of a program unit (main program or subprogram). For a main program the word "Start" appears inside the box. For a subprogram entry the subprogram name (or entry name) and the list of parameters are shown inside the box.

With a flowline leading *to* the box, it is used for the STOP statement, or for the RETURN statement of a subprogram.

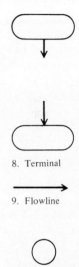

8. Terminal

9. *Flowline.* This is simply a line with an arrow, indicating the sequence in which the statements of a program will be executed.

9. Flowline

10. *Connector.* This symbol, enclosing a label, often indicates a CONTINUE statement. It may indicate any other point in the program where we wish to draw attention to the label of a statement to be executed next.

10. Connector

11. *Annotation.* Descriptive information (sometimes indicating declarations) may be included in a flowchart by means of a symbol of this form.

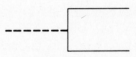

11. Annotation

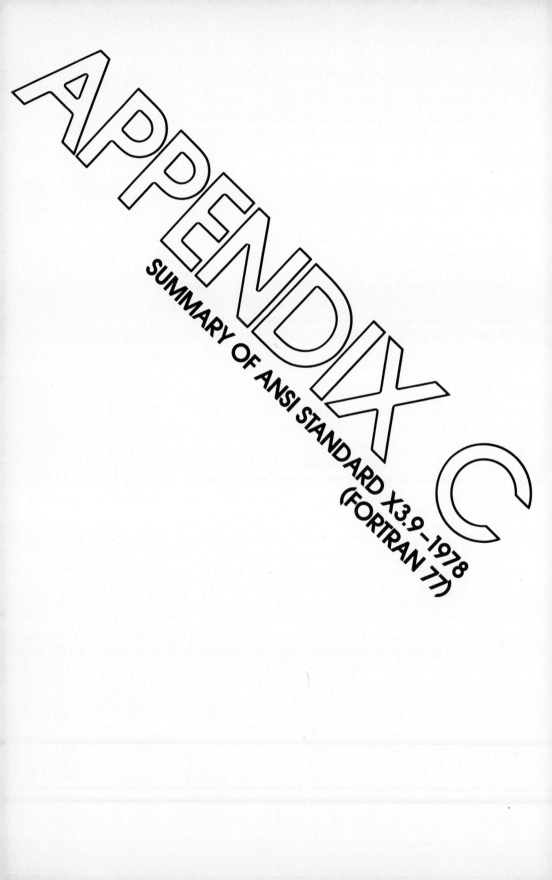

APPENDIX C

SUMMARY OF ANSI STANDARD X3.9-1978 (FORTRAN 77)

An American National Standard for the Fortran language was adopted in 1966. Most processors that were based on this standard used the name Fortran IV. The standard permitted compatible extensions, and by the middle 1970s it became apparent that many of the most widely adopted extensions to Fortran IV could be incorporated into a new Fortran language standard. Accordingly, an updated standard language, known semiofficially as Fortran 77, was announced in 1977 and formally standardized in 1978 by the American National Standards Institute (ANSI). Although compliance with ANSI standards is voluntary, these Fortran standards have strongly influenced the development of processors for the language.

This appendix summarizes the Fortran 77 standard, using rather formal terminology. Many details that are not mentioned in the body of this textbook are covered in this appendix. Thus the appendix is intended mainly to extend the reference value of this book. Like any summary, however, this description is not as definitive as the ANSI standard document itself. Furthermore, the terminology used in this summary deviates occasionally from that used in the official standard.

C.1   INTRODUCTION

The Fortran standard specifies the form and interpretation of a "standard-conforming" Fortran program. A standard-conforming program must use only language elements that are described in the standard. A standard-conforming processor, however, may also provide compatible extensions.

The standard describes a full Fortran language and a subset. A program conforms to the subset if it is composed entirely of language elements from the subset. A subset processor may contain extensions that are part of the full language, but only if they are implemented in a manner compatible with the full language. A subset processor may also include compatible extensions that are not part of the full language.

For example, it is stated that "a statement must not contain more than 1320 characters." This means that if a program includes a longer statement, it is not standard-conforming. It also implies that a standard-conforming processor must accept statements up to 1320 characters long. It does *not* mean that a standard-conforming processor is prohibited from accepting longer statements. Accepting longer statements could be a compatible extension.

Prohibited features thus have the same status with respect to the standard as features that are not mentioned at all. For example, a double precision complex data type is not mentioned. Therefore, such a feature must not be used in a standard-conforming program. A standard-conforming processor may or may not provide it or diagnose its use. A processor may provide such a feature as a compatible extension.

C.2   THE FORTRAN LANGUAGE

C.2.1   Language Elements

A Fortran program is composed of characters. Characters are grouped into lines, lines are grouped into program units, and program units are grouped into an executable program.

Fortran characters

The Fortran character set consists of the 26 letters, 10 digits, and 13 special characters including the blank and the following 12 symbols:

    = + − * / ( ) , . ' $:

The blank character is not significant except (a) in a character constant or a character datum, (b) in an H or apostrophe edit descriptor in a FORMAT statement, and (c) in column 6 of a line to distinguish between an initial line and a continuation line of a statement.

Non-Fortran characters are permitted in certain contexts within a Fortran program, including columns 2 through 72 of comment lines, the characters of a character datum, and file names. However, the use of characters not in the Fortran character set may inhibit portability.

A collating sequence among the characters is partially specified. The letters are ordered from A through Z and the digits from 0 through 9. The blank character is considered less than A and less than zero. The letters and digits do not overlap.

Lines

A line in a Fortran program consists of 72 character positions called columns. A line is a comment line, an initial line of a statement, or a continuation line of a statement.

A line that is entirely blank is a comment line. A line with the letter C or an asterisk in column 1 is a comment line; such a comment line may contain any Fortran characters or non-Fortran characters in columns 2 through 72.

A line that is not entirely blank, and does not have the letter C or an asterisk in column 1, is an initial line if it has a zero or blank in column 6; otherwise, it is a continuation line. Columns 1 through 5 of an initial line must contain a statement label or else must all be blank. Columns 1 through 5 of a continuation line must be blank.

Statements

A statement is written in columns 7 through 72 of one or more lines, the first of which is an initial line, while the remaining ones, if any, are continuation lines. Up to 19 continuation lines are permitted. The continuation lines of a statement must be consecutive lines within the program unit, except that a comment line may precede a continuation line within a statement.

An END statement must not have any continuation lines, and no other statement may have an initial line that looks like an END statement.

A statement is executable or nonexecutable.

Executable statements

The following kinds of statements are executable:

- Arithmetic, logical, and character assignment statements;
- READ, WRITE, PRINT, REWIND, BACKSPACE, ENDFILE, OPEN, CLOSE, and INQUIRE statements;
- DO statements;
- Arithmetic IF and logical IF statements;
- Block IF, ELSE, ELSE IF, and END IF statements;

- Unconditional GO TO, assigned GO TO, and computed GO TO statements;
- CONTINUE statements;
- STOP and PAUSE statements;
- Statement label assignment (ASSIGN) statements;
- CALL and RETURN statements;
- END statements.

Nonexecutable statements

The following kinds of statements are nonexecutable:

- PROGRAM, FUNCTION, SUBROUTINE, ENTRY, and BLOCK DATA statements;
- DIMENSION, COMMON, EQUIVALENCE, IMPLICIT, PARAMETER, EXTERNAL, INTRINSIC, and SAVE statements (these statements, along with the type statements in the following list, are collectively called *specification* statements);
- INTEGER, REAL, DOUBLE PRECISION, COMPLEX, LOGICAL, and CHARACTER type statements;
- DATA statements;
- FORMAT statements;
- Statement function statements.

Note: Although these statements are classified as nonexecutable, they may include expressions that are evaluated each time the program unit is referenced.

Statement labels

A statement may be identified by a statement label, which consists of from one to five digits, with leading zeros and imbedded or trailing blanks ignored.

Any statement may have a label, but the label of a nonexecutable statement except a FORMAT statement must not be referenced. Two statements in the same program unit must not have the same label.

DO *blocks and* IF *blocks*

Statements may be grouped into DO blocks or IF blocks. A DO block consists of all statements in the program unit following a DO statement and ending with the labeled statement that is referenced by the DO statement. An IF block consists of all statements in the program unit following the block IF statement and preceding the corresponding END IF statement.

Program units

A program unit consists of lines containing statements and comments, terminating with a line that is an END statement.

A program unit is a main program, an executable subprogram, or a block data subprogram. An executable subprogram is a function subprogram or a subroutine subprogram.

An executable program is a collection of program units that includes exactly one main program.

Ordering of statements and lines

Comment lines may appear anywhere in a program unit, including ahead of the first statement.

A PROGRAM statement, if present, must be the first statement of a main program. The first statement of a block data subprogram must be a BLOCK DATA statement. The first statement of an executable subprogram must be a SUBROUTINE or FUNCTION statement.

A FORMAT statement may appear anywhere. An ENTRY statement may appear anywhere in an executable subprogram except within a DO block or an IF block.

All specification statements must precede all DATA statements, statement function statements, and executable statements.

All statement function statements must precede all executable statements.

DATA statements may appear anywhere after the specification statements.

Among the specification statements, IMPLICIT statements must precede all others except PARAMETER statements. A PARAMETER statement must precede all other statements containing the symbolic name of a constant whose value is established by that PARAMETER statement.

A symbolic name of a constant, or a variable appearing in a dimension bound expression, must not have its type explicitly declared farther down in the program unit.

The last line of a program unit must contain an END statement.

C.2.2 Storage, Data, and Constants

Storage

The concepts of storage unit and storage sequence do not necessarily imply any particular realization or sequential arrangement of physical storage.

A storage unit is a character storage unit or a numeric storage unit.

Data types

Data is that which occupies storage. Each datum has a type, which is integer, real, double precision, complex, logical, or character.

An integer, real, or logical datum occupies one numeric storage unit. A double precision or complex datum occupies two consecutive numeric storage units.

A character datum occupies one or more consecutive character storage units. A character datum is a fixed-length sequence of individual character items; the length of the sequence is the number of character storage units occupied by the datum.

Variables, arrays, and substrings

A variable is a single datum.

An array is a sequence of data occupying consecutive storage units. Each datum in an array is an array element. All the elements of an array are of the same type. Each element has a unique element position within the sequence of data composing the array. The size of the array is the number of array elements.

A character datum may be a variable, an array element, or a substring. In a character array, all elements are of the same length. Each character item in a character variable or array element has a unique item position within the sequence of items composing the character datum. A substring is a sequence of one or more consecutive character items within a character variable or array element.

All the character items of a character array occupy a single sequence of consecutive character storage units.

Definition status and value of a datum

At any given time during execution of a program, each datum of integer, real, double precision, complex, or logical type, and each character item of a datum of character type, is either defined or undefined. A datum of character type is defined if and only if all its character items are defined. A defined datum has a value, which does not change until the datum becomes undefined or is redefined.

A datum may be initially defined by means of a DATA statement.

The value of an integer datum is an integer (whole number). The value of a real datum is a processor approximation to a real number. The value of a double precision datum is a processor approximation to a real number which is more precise than that of a real datum.

The value of an integer, real, or double precision datum may be positive, negative, or zero. The value zero is considered neither positive nor negative.

A complex datum is an ordered pair of real data; the first element of the pair represents the real part and the second element represents the imaginary part.

The value of a logical datum is true or false.

The value of each character item of a character datum is a representation of a Fortran or non-Fortran character. Blank characters are significant in a character datum.

Constants

A constant is a string of digits and other characters in a program, representing a value that does not change. The form of a constant determines its value and its type.

An integer constant consists of an optional sign followed by a nonempty string of digits, to be interpreted as a decimal number.

A basic real constant consists of a string of digits containing a decimal point, with an optional sign. A real exponent is the letter E followed by an optionally signed integer constant, denoting a power of ten. A real constant is a basic real constant, a basic real constant followed by a real exponent, or an integer constant followed by a real exponent.

A double precision exponent is the letter D followed by an optionally signed integer constant, denoting a power of ten. A double precision constant is a basic real constant or an integer constant, followed by a double precision exponent.

A complex constant consists of an ordered pair of optionally signed real constants, separated by a comma and enclosed in parentheses.

A logical constant has the form .TRUE. or .FALSE..

A character constant consists of a nonempty string of characters enclosed by apostrophes. (The enclosing apostrophes are not part of the value.) An apostrophe within the string is represented by a pair of adjacent apostrophes.

C.2.3 Names

Symbolic names

A symbolic name in a program consists of from one to six alphanumeric characters, the first of which must be a letter. Note that file names, and some other sequences of characters such as format edit descriptors, are not symbolic names even though they may have the same form as a symbolic name.

A symbolic name is the name of a constant, a variable, an array, a common block, a main program, an executable subprogram, a statement function, a block data subprogram, or a procedure.

A symbolic name of a constant is specified in a PARAMETER statement. An array name is declared in an array declarator. A common block name is declared in a COMMON statement.

A main program name appears in a PROGRAM statement. An executable subprogram name is a subroutine subprogram name or a function subprogram name. A subroutine subprogram name is declared in a SUBROUTINE statement, or in an ENTRY statement in a subroutine subprogram. A function subprogram name is declared in a FUNCTION statement, or in an ENTRY statement in a function subprogram. A statement function name appears on the left side of a statement function statement. A block data subprogram name is declared in a BLOCK DATA statement.

A procedure name is a subroutine procedure name, an external function procedure name, an intrinsic function name, or a statement function procedure name. The name of an executable (subroutine or function) subprogram is used as a procedure name in certain contexts, namely, in an executable statement as a reference or as an actual argument, in an EXTERNAL statement, in a type statement, or as a dummy argument. Ordinarily, such a procedure name will also appear elsewhere in the same executable program as an executable subprogram name. However, a procedure name may also refer to a subprogram specified by means other than a Fortran subprogram. A statement function procedure name will also appear as a statement function name in the same program unit.

A subroutine procedure name is used in a CALL statement to reference a subroutine subprogram; an external function procedure name or a statement function procedure name is used in an expression to reference a function subprogram or a statement function.

An intrinsic function name is used in an expression to reference a specific or generic intrinsic function. A name in the "Specific name" or "Generic name" column of the table of intrinsic functions (in Section C.4.4) is classified as an intrinsic function name, except in a program unit in which the name appears in an EXTERNAL statement.

A symbolic name that is not the name of a constant, an array, a common block, a main program, an executable subprogram, a statement function, a block data subprogram, or a procedure, is a variable name. A name that appears in a function subprogram as the function subprogram name (in a FUNCTION or ENTRY statement) is classified as a variable name when it appears elsewhere in the same program unit.

Note that a symbolic name that appears in a program unit only within a dummy argument list and in an actual argument list may be the name of a variable, an array, a subroutine procedure, an external function procedure, or an intrinsic function. If a name appears only in an EXTERNAL statement and in an actual argument list, it may be a subroutine procedure name or an external function procedure name.

Data type of a name

The name of a constant, a variable, an array, a function subprogram, an external function procedure, a statement function procedure, or a specific intrinsic function has a definite data type in a program unit. The name of a common block, a subroutine subprogram, a subroutine procedure, a main program, or a block data subprogram does not have a data type. The name of a generic function has a definite data type for each reference, but its type may vary within a program unit.

The type of the name of a constant, a variable, an array, a function subprogram, an external function procedure, or a statement function may be established explicitly in a type statement. The type of the name of a function subprogram may also be established explicitly in a FUNCTION statement. For a name whose type is not established explicitly in one of these ways, the type is established implicitly, and depends only on the first letter of the symbolic name. The implicit type of a name is established by default or by an IMPLICIT statement. The default implicit type is integer if the first letter of the name is I, J, K, L, M, or N; otherwise, the default implicit type is real. An entity of character type has a length, which is specified explicitly or implicitly along with the type.

The type of a function procedure name determines the type of the value supplied by the procedure when referenced in an expression.

The type of a specific intrinsic function name is given in the table of intrinsic functions (Section C.4.4). The type of a generic function name depends on the type of the argument (as shown in Table 8.1), and may vary within a program unit.

Association

Association provides more than one name for a given datum.

Two variables, array elements, arrays, or substrings are associated if they share at least one character or numeric storage unit. Two entities are totally associated if they both occupy the same storage units. Two entities are partially associated if some, but not all, of their storage units are shared.

An EQUIVALENCE statement causes association of storage in a program unit. A COMMON statement causes association of storage in different program units.

Procedure references cause association between dummy and actual arguments. This does not imply association of storage except when the actual argument is the name of a variable, array element, array, or substring. In a function subprogram, there is an association among all function subprogram names (which appear in the FUNCTION statement and in ENTRY statements in the subprogram) and all local variable names that are the same as any of these function subprogram names.

Associated entities need not have the same type; however, a character entity must not be associated with an entity of any other type.

Partial association may occur between a double precision or complex entity on the one hand and an integer, real, logical, double precision, or complex entity on the other hand. Such association must not occur through argument association, but may be specified by an EQUIVALENCE, COMMON, or ENTRY statement.

Partial association between character entities may occur through argument association, or may be specified by an EQUIVALENCE, COMMON, or ENTRY statement.

Scope of names

The scope of the name of a common block, a main program, an executable subprogram, or a block data subprogram is an executable program. An entity is a global entity if the scope of its name is an executable program. Two global entities in the same program unit must not have the same symbolic name.

The scope of the symbolic name of a constant, a variable, an array, a procedure, or a statement function is a program unit, with the following exceptions: The scope of the name of a dummy argument of a statement function is the statement function statement. The scope of an implied DO variable in a DATA statement is the implied DO list in which it appears. An entity is a local entity if the scope of its name is a program unit.

Two local entities in a program unit must not have the same symbolic name. However, a local entity in one program unit may have the same name as a local entity in another program unit; and a local entity in a program unit may have the same name as a global entity whose name does not appear in that program unit.

A local entity in a program unit must not have the same name as a global entity whose name appears in that program unit, with the following exceptions:

1. A function subprogram name may be the same as the name of a local variable in the same program unit.

2. A common block name in a program unit may be the same as an array name, subroutine procedure name, statement function name, or external function procedure name in the same program unit. A common block name in a program unit may be the same as a variable name in that program unit, except for a variable name that is the same as a function subprogram name in the same program unit. When a common block name in a program unit is the same as the name of a local entity, the appearance of that name in any context other than as a common block name in a COMMON or SAVE statement identifies only the local entity. A common block name must not be the same as the name of an intrinsic function that appears in the same program unit.

An entity may have a name whose scope is less than a program unit. The scope of the name of a dummy argument of a statement function is the statement function statement, and the scope of the name of an implied DO variable in a DATA statement is the implied DO list.

Two or more entities may have the same name if the scope of each is less than a program unit, provided that no part of the program unit is included in the scope of more than one of the entities. Such an entity may also have the same name as a local entity or a common block in the same program unit.

An IMPLICIT statement or a type statement in a program unit, including the length specification for a character entity, also applies to names whose scope is less than the program unit.

C.2.4 Arrays and Substrings

Array names

The symbolic name of an array refers to a sequence of consecutive data called array elements. Each array element may be referenced by the array name qualified by a subscript whose value specifies the position of the particular element within the array. All the elements of an array are of the same type, which is the type of the array name.

Array declarator

An array declarator designates a symbolic name as an array name. It consists of the array name followed by a parenthesized list containing at least one and not more than seven dimension declarators. Each dimension declarator consists of an upper dimension bound expression, optionally preceded by a lower dimension bound and a colon. The upper dimension bound expression in the last dimension declarator for a dummy argument array may be an asterisk.

Each (nonasterisk) dimension bound expression must be composed of integer constants, symbolic names of integer constants, and integer variable names. (No procedure references or array element names are permitted.) Variable names are permitted only in adjustable array declarators. If a lower dimension bound expression is omitted, the default lower bound value is one. The value of each (nonasterisk) upper dimension bound must be greater than that of the corresponding lower bound.

An array name must not appear in more than one array declarator in a program unit. An array declarator may appear in a DIMENSION statement or a type statement. Except for a dummy argument array, the array declarator may appear in a COMMON statement.

Array element names

An array element name consists of an array name followed by a subscript, which is a parenthesized list of subscript expressions (separated by commas), one for each dimension of the array.

Each subscript expression is an integer expression, and may contain array element references or procedure references. The value of this expression must not be less than the corresponding lower dimension bound, nor greater than the corresponding upper dimension bound.

Array element ordering

The elements of an array are ordered according to the sequence of their array element positions. The position of an array element is determined from the subscript expression values along with the dimension bounds, according to the formula

$$P = 1 + \sum_{i=1}^{n} (s_i - j_i) \prod_{m=1}^{i-1} (k_m - j_m + 1),$$

where s_i is the ith subscript expression value, j_i is the ith lower dimension bound, k_i is the ith upper dimension bound, and n is the number of dimensions. (Note that if each s_i equals j_i, then P is one.) If each s_i equals k_i, then the value of P is equal to the number of elements in the array.

Use of array names

An array name may be used (without a subscript) to identify the entire array in certain contexts. These are: (1) in an input or output list; (2) as a dummy argument; (3) as an actual argument in a subroutine or external function procedure reference; (4) in a COMMON statement, a type statement, or an array declarator; (5) as a format identifier in an input or output statement; (6) in an EQUIVALENCE statement; (7) in a DATA statement; (8) in a SAVE statement; (9) as an internal file identifier in a READ or WRITE statement.

Character substrings

The character item positions in a variable or array element of character type are consecutively numbered, in storage sequence order, beginning with position 1. (The characters in a constant are numbered from left to right.) A substring is a sequence of one or more consecutive character items within a character variable or array element.

A substring name consists of a character variable or array element name, followed by a parenthesized substring specification. There must be a colon inside the parentheses; to the left and right are optional substring expressions specifying the smallest and largest item position numbers, respectively, for the substring. If there is no expression to the left of the colon, the default smallest character item position is one; if there is no expression to the right of the colon, the default largest character item position number is the length of the string.

The substring specification expressions, if present, must be of integer type. The smallest character item position must be at least one, and must be less than or equal to the largest item position number, which in turn must not exceed the length of the string.

C.2.5   Specification Statements and Data Statements

DIMENSION *statement*

A DIMENSION statement consists of the keyword DIMENSION followed by a list of array declarators separated by commas. Array declarators may also appear in COMMON statements or type statements.

EQUIVALENCE *statement*

An EQUIVALENCE statement specifies association of storage within a program unit. It consists of the keyword EQUIVALENCE followed by a list of equivalence classes separated by commas.

Each equivalence class is enclosed in parentheses, and consists of two or more variable names, array names, array element names, or character substring names, separated by commas. (When a function subprogram name is also used as a variable name in the same program unit, that name must not appear in an EQUIVALENCE statement.)

Names of character data must not appear in the same equivalence class with data of other types. Character data of different lengths may appear in the same class.

Appearance of names in an equivalence class may cause implied association of other entities whose names do not appear, due to storage sequence rules for array elements, character items in a character datum, items in a common block, and so on. An EQUIVALENCE statement must not contradict other storage sequence specifications implied by such rules.

COMMON *statement*

A COMMON statement specifies association of entities in different program units, and may also contain dimension information. It consists of the keyword COMMON followed by a list of common classes.

Each common class consists of a common block name followed by a list of variable names, array names, and array declarators, separated by commas. The variable names and array names must not be dummy arguments.

Each common block name appears between a pair of slashes. A pair of slashes with nothing between them may also be used to specify the blank common block; and if the first common class in a COMMON statement refers to the blank common block, the first pair of slashes may be omitted.

If a common block name (or omitted name specifying blank common) appears more than once in the COMMON statements of a program unit, the lists of names in all the common classes for that common block name are interpreted as forming a single common class in the order of their appearance.

Names of character data must not be included in the same common class with data of other types.

A common block storage sequence is formed from all the storage units occupied by the variables and arrays whose names appear in a common class. This storage sequence may be extended beyond the last storage unit, if necessary, to include storage units occupied by entities associated by equivalence association. Such associated entities must not occupy storage units that precede the first storage unit of the common block storage sequence.

Within an executable program, all named common blocks with the same common block name (but not the blank common block) are required to have a storage sequence that contains the same number of storage units.

Data in a named common block storage sequence may be initially defined by means of DATA statements in a BLOCK DATA subprogram. Data in the blank common block storage sequence must not be initially defined. Execution of a RETURN or END statement in a subprogram may cause data in named common blocks, but not in the blank common block, to become undefined.

An equivalence class in an EQUIVALENCE statement must not include names of data from more than one common block.

Type statements

A type statement explicitly establishes the type of the name of a variable, an array, a function subprogram, an external function procedure, a statement function, or a symbolic name of a constant.

More than one explicit type specification for a name within a program unit is prohibited. When an explicit specification for a function subprogram name appears in the FUNCTION statement, any other explicit type specification for the name within that program unit is prohibited.

A noncharacter type statement consists of the keyword INTEGER, REAL, DOUBLE PRECISION, COMPLEX, or LOGICAL, followed by a list of variable names, array names, array declarators, function subprogram names, statement function names, function procedure names, or symbolic names of constants (separated by commas).

A character type statement also includes length specifications. It consists of the keyword CHARACTER, followed by an optional length specifier, followed by a list of character variable names, character array names, character array declarators, character function subprogram names, character function procedure names, or symbolic names of character constants (separated by commas). Each name or declarator in the list is followed by an optional length specifier.

If a length specifier immediately follows the keyword, it applies to each name or declarator in the list that does not have its own length specifier. (This first length specifier, if present, may be followed by an optional comma.) Any entry for which no length is specified has the length one by default. Note that all elements of a character array have the same length.

A length specifier consists of an asterisk followed by one of the following: an unsigned, nonzero integer constant; an integer expression enclosed in parentheses; or an asterisk in parentheses. If an integer expression is used, it must be composed of integer constants and symbolic names of integer constants.

The length specifier in a character type statement for a function subprogram name may be a constant or an asterisk in parentheses. In the latter case, the function assumes the length specified in the referencing program unit. In any case, the length specified in the referencing program unit must not conflict with the specification in the subprogram.

The length specifier for a symbolic name of a constant may be an asterisk, indicating that the length is to be determined from the value of the constant specified in the PARAMETER statement.

A character entity whose length specifier is an asterisk enclosed in parentheses must not be used as an operand of a concatenation operator except in a character assignment statement. (The processor may need to determine in advance the length of a character expression, except for assignment.)

IMPLICIT *statement*

An IMPLICIT statement specifies rules for establishing the implicit type of the name of a variable, an array, a function subprogram, an external function procedure, or a statement function, based on the first letter of the name. These rules also establish implicit lengths for character entities. Implicit type rules do not apply to intrinsic function names.

An IMPLICIT statement consists of the keyword IMPLICIT, followed by a list of implicit type specifications separated by commas. Each implicit type specification consists of the keyword INTEGER, REAL, DOUBLE PRECISION, COMPLEX, LOGICAL, or CHARACTER, followed by a parenthesized list of single letters or ranges of letters, separated by commas.

An IMPLICIT statement specifying CHARACTER type may include an asterisk and an integer constant expression denoting the implicit length, between the keyword and the parenthesized list; if the implicit length specification is omitted, the default implicit length is one.

A range of letters is denoted by a pair of letters (in alphabetical order) separated by a minus, and is interpreted as including all letters between those mentioned.

A letter must not appear more than once, as a single letter or within a range of letters, in all the IMPLICIT statements of a program unit.

PARAMETER *statement*

A PARAMETER statement specifies the symbolic name of a constant. It consists of the keyword PARAMETER followed by parentheses enclosing a list of parameter specifications separated by commas. Each parameter specification consists of a symbolic name, an equals sign, and a constant expression, in that order. If the constant expression contains the symbolic name of a constant, the value of that constant must have been established previously in the same PARAMETER statement or a preceding PARAMETER statement in the same program unit. The value of the constant expression is converted, if necessary, to the type of the symbolic name. The value of a symbolic name of a constant must not be specified more than once in the PARAMETER statements of a program unit.

EXTERNAL *statement*

An EXTERNAL statement permits an external procedure name to be used as an actual argument, or it indicates the existence of an external procedure or block data subprogram having the same name as an intrinsic function. If an intrinsic function name appears in an EXTERNAL statement, the intrinsic function is not available for use in the same program unit.

An EXTERNAL statement consists of the keyword EXTERNAL, followed by a list of external procedure names and block data subprogram names, separated by commas. (Note that a statement function name is not permitted.) A symbolic name must not appear more than once in the EXTERNAL statements of a program unit.

INTRINSIC *statement*

An INTRINSIC statement declares a name to be that of a specific or generic intrinsic function. It also permits a specific intrinsic function name to be used as an actual argument. The appearance of a generic intrinsic function name in an INTRINSIC statement does not remove the generic property.

An INTRINSIC statement consists of the keyword INTRINSIC, followed by a list of intrinsic function names separated by commas. A name must not appear more than once in the INTRINSIC statements and EXTERNAL statements of a program unit.

The function names INT, IFIX, IDINT, REAL, FLOAT, SNGL, ICHAR, CHAR, and any of the MAX and MIN functions must not be used as actual arguments. All other specific intrinsic function names (see the table in Section C.4.4) are permitted as actual arguments. Note that generic intrinsic function names that are not also specific intrinsic function names (DBLE, CMPLX, MAX, MIN, LOG, LOG10) must not be used as actual arguments.

SAVE *statement*

A SAVE statement maintains the definition status of entities in a subprogram upon execution of a RETURN or END statement. A program unit may contain more than one SAVE statement.

Entities whose definition status is maintained may include common blocks, variables, and arrays. Variables and arrays within a common block must not be included except by specifying the entire block. A common block specified by a SAVE statement in any subprogram must also be so specified in every subprogram in which the common block appears.

A SAVE statement may consist simply of the keyword SAVE. This specifies that the definition status of all common blocks, variables, and arrays (but not dummy arguments) in the program unit is to be maintained.

The list form of the SAVE statement consists of the keyword SAVE followed by a list of common block names (enclosed between slashes), variable names, and array names, separated by commas. A name must not appear more than once in the SAVE statements of a program unit. The names of dummy arguments, of procedures, or of variables or arrays within a common block must not appear in a SAVE statement.

DATA *statement*

A DATA statement provides initial values for variables, arrays, array elements, and substrings. At the beginning of execution of an executable program, all entities in all program units are undefined except those for which initial values have been provided in DATA statements.

A DATA statement consists of the keyword DATA followed by one or more pairs (optionally separated by commas), each pair consisting of a list of names followed by slashes enclosing a list of constants.

A list of names may include variable names, array names, array element names, substring names, and implied DO lists, separated by commas. The list must not contain names of dummy arguments, functions, or entities in blank common (or entities associated with those in blank common). Entities in (or associated with) a named common block must not appear in a DATA statement except in a BLOCK DATA subprogram. The name of a variable that is also a function subprogram name in the same program unit is also prohibited, along with associated names.

A list of constants consists of items separated by commas; each item is a constant or the symbolic name of a constant, or one of these preceded by a repeat count and an asterisk. A repeat count is a nonzero, unsigned integer constant or the symbolic name of such a constant.

An implied DO list in a DATA statement consists of a list of array element names and implied DO lists, followed by a control part, all enclosed in parentheses. The control part includes an implied DO variable (which must be an integer variable), an equals sign, and two or three expressions separated by commas. The iteration count is established from these expressions exactly as for a DO loop, except that the iteration count must be greater than zero. An implied DO variable in a DATA statement has a scope that is local to the implied DO list. Each of the expressions, as well as each subscript expression in the list part of the implied DO, is an integer constant expression, except that it may contain implied DO variables of enclosing implied DO lists.

In each pair in a DATA statement, there must be a one-to-one correspondence between the names in the list of names and the constants in the list of constants. In this correspondence, an array name in the list of names includes all elements of the array, an implied DO list includes the names of all referenced array elements, and repeat counts are applied to items in the list of constants.

The type of each name must agree with the type of the corresponding constant when either is of type character or logical. A constant of integer, real, double precision, or complex type may correspond with a name of any of these types; type conversion will be applied to the constant if necessary. A character constant will be padded with blanks on the right or truncated from the right, if necessary, to the length of the corresponding character entity in the list of names.

An entity, or two associated entities, must not be initially defined more than once in an executable program.

C.2.6   Expressions and Assignment

Arithmetic expressions

An arithmetic primary is an unsigned arithmetic constant, a symbolic name of an arithmetic constant, a variable reference, an array element reference, a function procedure reference, or an arithmetic expression enclosed in parentheses. An arithmetic primary must be of integer, real, double precision, or complex type.

An arithmetic factor consists of one or more arithmetic primaries separated by the exponentiation operator (double asterisk). In the interpretation of an arithmetic factor containing two or more exponentiation operators, the primaries are combined from right to left.

An arithmetic term consists of one or more arithmetic factors separated by either the multiplication operator (asterisk) or the division operator (slash). In the interpretation of an arithmetic term containing two or more multiplication or division operators, the factors are combined from left to right.

An arithmetic expression consists of one or more arithmetic terms separated by either the addition operator (plus) or the subtraction operator (minus). The first term may optionally be preceded by the identity (unary plus) or the negation (unary minus) operator. In the interpretation of an arithmetic expression containing two or more addition or subtraction operators, the terms are combined from left to right.

Among the arithmetic operators, the exponentiation operator has highest precedence, the multiplication and division operators have intermediate precedence, and the addition and subtraction operators have lowest precedence.

The data type of an expression containing one or more arithmetic operators is determined from the data types of the operands. In an expression consisting of an operand preceded by an identity or negation operator, the type of the expression is the same as the type of the operand. For an expression consisting of a pair of operands separated by an addition, subtraction, multiplication, or division operator, the type of the expression is determined as follows: If both operands are of the same type, the type of the expression is the same also. If either operand is of integer type, the type of the expression is the same as the type of the other operand. If one operand is of real type and the other is of double precision or complex type, the type of the expression is double precision or complex, respectively. An operator must not have one operand of double precision type and the other operand of complex type.

The type of an expression consisting of a pair of primaries separated by an exponentiation operator is determined by the same rules. However, when a complex operand is involved, except for the case of a complex operand raised to an integer power, mathematical considerations require choice of a *principal value* for the result. The principal value is defined as that which would result from evaluating the expression by means of the LOG and EXP intrinsic functions.

Except for a value raised to an integer power, type conversion is applied to the operand (if any) that differs in type from the resulting expression. No type conversion is required when a value of any type is raised to an integer power.

Note that the type of an expression consisting of an operator operating on a single operand or on a pair of operands is determined by the types of those operands—that is, "locally"—and not by the type of any operand in any larger expression containing it.

If the quotient of two expressions of integer type is not a whole number, it is truncated to the next lower integer in magnitude. Note that an integer expression raised to a *negative* integer power is interpreted as the integer 1 divided by the corresponding *positive* power of the expression.

Character expressions

A character primary is a character constant, a symbolic name of a character constant, a character variable reference, a character array element reference, a character substring reference, a character function procedure reference, or a character expression enclosed in parentheses.

A character expression consists of one or more character primaries separated by the concatenation operator (double slash). In the interpretation of a character expression containing two or more concatenation operators, the primaries are combined from left to right. The operands for a concatenation operator must have constant length except in a character assignment statement.

Note that parentheses have no effect in a character expression.

Relational expressions

A relational expression consists of a pair of arithmetic expressions or a pair of character expressions separated by one of six relational operators: .LT. (less than), .LE. (less than or equal to), .EQ. (equal to), .NE. (not equal to), .GT. (greater than), or .GE. (greater than or equal to).

A relational expression involving a pair of arithmetic expressions of different types is interpreted as comparing the difference of the two expressions with zero. Complex expressions may be compared only with the .EQ. and .NE. relational operators. A complex expression must not be compared with a double precision expression.

A relational expression involving a pair of character expressions of different lengths is interpreted as if the shorter operand were extended on the right with blanks to the length of the longer operand.

Logical expressions

A logical primary is a logical constant, a symbolic name of a logical constant, a logical variable reference, a logical array element reference, a logical function procedure reference, a relational expression, or a logical expression enclosed in parentheses.

A logical factor is a logical primary, or the logical negation operator .NOT. followed by a logical primary.

A logical term is a sequence of logical factors separated by the logical conjunction operator .AND.. In the interpretation of a logical term containing two or more logical conjunction operators, the logical factors are combined from left to right.

A logical disjunct is a sequence of logical terms separated by the logical disjunction operator .OR.. In the interpretation of a logical disjunct containing two or more logical disjunction operators, the logical terms are combined from left to right.

A logical expression is a sequence of logical disjuncts separated by either the .EQV. or the .NEQV. operator. In the interpretation of a logical expression containing two or more of these operators, the logical disjuncts are combined from left to right.

Among the logical operators, the logical negation operator has highest precedence, followed by the logical conjunction operator, and then the logical disjunction operator, while the .EQV. and .NEQV. operators have lowest precedence.

Precedence of operators

Precedence within the class of arithmetic operators, and within the class of logical operators, is established by the interpretation rules for expressions. There is only one character operator. A relational expression contains only one relational operator. In an expression containing operators of more than one of these classes, arithmetic operators have highest precedence, followed by character operators, then by relational operators, and finally by logical operators, which have the lowest precedence.

Evaluation of expressions

Any datum referenced as an operand in an expression must be in a defined state at the time the reference is executed, and the type of the datum must agree with the type of the name used to reference it. An integer operand must have an integer value (that is, it must not have a statement label value as a result of the execution of an ASSIGN statement). Any arithmetic operation whose result is not mathematically defined is prohibited in a standard-conforming program.

Side effects of functions must not alter the value of any other entity within the same statement, and must not alter the value of any entity in a common storage area that affects the value of any other function reference in the same statement. In particular, if an actual argument is defined during execution of a function, that argument or any associated entities must not appear elsewhere in the statement. (An exception is made, however, in that function references in the logical expression of a logical IF statement may have side effects that affect the contingent statement. That is, the contingent statement is treated as though it were a separate statement.)

A processor is required to evaluate only as much of an expression as is necessary to determine the value of the expression. For character expressions, a processor needs to evaluate only as many character items of the result as are required by the context.

If a function reference appears in a part of an expression that does not need to be evaluated, all entities that would become defined during execution of the function become undefined when evaluation of the expression is completed.

If a statement contains more than one function reference, the processor is permitted to execute the references in any order, except for the ordering specified for expressions in input or output list elements, logical IF statements, and function argument lists containing function references. Any reordering by the processor must not change the effect of the statement; this requires that any function referenced more than once must produce values that are unaffected by the reordering.

Equivalent expressions

A processor may *evaluate* an expression different in certain respects from that obtained by application of the *interpretation* rules. However, any expression contained in parentheses must be treated as an entity.

For arithmetic expressions, the processor may evaluate any expression that is mathematically equivalent to that obtained from the interpretation rules, provided that the integrity of parentheses is respected. Integer division is not considered mathematically equivalent to real division.†

For relational expressions, the processor may evaluate any expression that is relationally equivalent.

For logical expressions, the processor may evaluate any expression that is logically equivalent, provided that the integrity of parentheses is respected.

Arithmetic, logical, and character assignment statements

An arithmetic assignment statement consists of the name of a variable or an array element of integer, real, double precision, or complex type, followed by an assignment operator (equals), followed by an arithmetic expression.

A logical assignment statement consists of the name of a variable or an array element of logical type, followed by an assignment operator, followed by a logical expression.

---

† It is not clear from the standard whether or not real and double precision expressions are mathematically equivalent.

A character assignment statement consists of the name of a variable, an array element, or a substring of character type, followed by an assignment operator, followed by a character expression. Character positions within the datum designated on the left of the assignment operator must not be referenced by the expression on the right.

Execution of an assignment statement begins with evaluation of the expression to the right of the assignment operator. The rules for evaluation of expressions require that this expression have a defined value. Execution of the assignment statement causes the datum designated by the variable name, array element name, or substring name to the left of the assignment operator to become defined with the value of this expression, after conversion if necessary.

In the case of arithmetic assignment, conversion may consist of type conversion, whose effect is the same as applying the appropriate generic type conversion function. For character assignment, the value of the expression will be padded with blanks on the right or truncated from the right, as necessary to achieve the required length.

Execution of a character assignment statement having a substring name on the left defines only the character items in the positions specified by the substring name. The definition status of other character items of the same character variable or array element is not changed by the execution of the assignment statement.

ASSIGN *statement*

An ASSIGN statement consists of the keyword ASSIGN, a statement label, the keyword TO, and an integer variable name (in that order). The statement label must be the label of an executable statement or a FORMAT statement in the same program unit.

Execution of an ASSIGN statement causes the integer variable to become defined with the statement label as its value. The variable becomes undefined with respect to use in integer (arithmetic) expressions or in any other way, except for reference by an assigned GO TO statement or as a format identifier in an input or output statement. The variable may later be redefined with another statement label value, or with an integer (arithmetic) value.

Events that cause entities to become defined

Execution of an arithmetic, logical, or character assignment statement causes the datum named on the left of the assignment operator to become defined.

As execution of an input statement proceeds, each datum that is assigned a value (of the correct type) from the input medium becomes defined at the time of this assignment.

Execution of a DO statement, and incrementation processing, causes the DO variable to become defined.

Beginning execution of an implied DO list in an input or output statement, and incrementation processing, causes the implied DO variable to become defined.

Data listed in the list of names in a DATA statement become defined at the beginning of execution of an executable program.

Execution of an INQUIRE statement causes entities that are assigned values during execution of the statement to become defined.

Execution of an ASSIGN statement causes the variable in the statement to become defined with a statement label value.

When an entity of a given type becomes defined, all totally associated entities of the same type become defined.

A reference to a subprogram causes a dummy argument to become defined if the corresponding actual argument is defined and if the actual argument has a form compatible with the dummy argument.

When a complex entity becomes defined, all partially associated real entities become defined. If both parts of a complex entity become defined as a result of partially associated real or complex entities becoming defined, the complex entity becomes defined.

Events that cause entities to become undefined

All entities are undefined at the beginning of execution of an executable program, except those initially defined by DATA statements.

When an entity of a given type becomes defined, all totally associated entities of different types become undefined.

Execution of an ASSIGN statement causes the variable in the statement to become undefined for use as an integer, and causes all associated entities to become undefined.

When an entity of type other than character becomes defined, all partially associated entities become undefined, except for partial association between a complex entity and a real or complex entity.

If a reference to a function appears in an expression in which the value of the function is not needed to determine the value of the expression, and if evaluation of the function would cause an argument of the function or an entity in common to become defined, then the argument or the entity in common becomes undefined when the expression is evaluated.

The execution of a RETURN or END statement within a subprogram causes all entities within the subprogram to become undefined, except for the following: (a) entities in blank common; (b) initially defined entities that have neither been redefined nor become undefined; (c) entities specified by SAVE statements; (d) entities in named common blocks that appear in the subprogram and in at least one other program unit that is referencing the subprogram either directly or indirectly. Note that at the beginning of execution of an external function subprogram, all local variables whose names are the same as the function name or an entry name, and any associated entities, are undefined.

When an error condition or an end-of-file condition occurs during execution of an input statement, all the entities in the input list of the statement become undefined.

Execution of an INQUIRE statement may cause entities to become undefined.

When an entity becomes undefined as a result of the foregoing conditions, all totally associated entities, and all partially associated entities of types other than character, become undefined.

C.2.7   Control Statements

The execution sequence

Execution of a program begins with the first executable statement appearing in the main program, and continues with the statements in order of their appearance except when the sequence is interrupted by execution of a procedure reference or a control statement.

A subprogram procedure reference causes interruption of execution of the program unit where the reference appears. As part of the execution of the statement containing the reference, the referenced subprogram procedure is executed. Execution of the referenced procedure begins with the first executable statement following the subprogram header statement or the referenced ENTRY statement. A statement function reference causes execution of the statement function statement as part of the execution of the statement containing the reference.

A control statement is a GO TO, arithmetic IF, RETURN, or STOP statement, an input or output statement containing an error specifier or an end-of-file specifier (statement label), a CALL statement with an alternate return specifier, a logical IF statement whose contingent statement is any of the foregoing, a block IF, ELSE IF, or ELSE statement, a DO statement, the terminal statement of a DO block, or an END statement.

GO TO statements

An unconditional GO TO statement consists of the keyword GO TO followed by the statement label of an executable statement in the same program unit. Execution of an unconditional GO TO statement causes interruption of the sequence of execution of statements; execution continues with the statement having the designated label.

A computed GO TO statement consists of the keyword GO TO, a parenthesized list of statement labels (separated by commas), an optional comma, and an integer expression, in that order. Execution of a computed GO TO statement begins with evaluation of the integer expression. If the value is between 1 and the number of labels in the list, the effect is an unconditional GO TO, to the label whose position in the list corresponds to the value of the expression. Otherwise, the execution sequence continues with the statement following the computed GO TO.

An assigned GO TO statement consists of the keyword GO TO, followed by an integer variable name. (This may optionally be followed by a parenthesized list of labels of statements in the same program unit, separated by commas; an optional comma may appear between the variable name and the left parenthesis.) At the time of execution of the assigned GO TO, the integer variable must be in a defined state (as a result of the execution of an ASSIGN statement) with a value that is the statement label of an executable statement in the same program unit. (If the parenthesized list of labels is present, the value of the integer variable must be one of the labels in the list.) Execution of an assigned GO TO statement has the effect of an unconditional GO TO to the designated label.

Arithmetic IF *and logical* IF *statements*

An arithmetic IF statement consists of the keyword IF, followed by a parenthesized integer, real, or double precision expression, followed by the labels of three executable statements in the same program unit (separated by commas). The expression is evaluated, and the execution sequence continues with the statement having the first, second, or third label, depending on whether the value of the expression is negative, zero, or positive, respectively.

A logical IF statement consists of the keyword IF, followed by a parenthesized logical expression, followed by a contingent statement. The contingent statement must be an executable statement, but it must not be a DO statement, a logical IF statement, or a block IF, ELSE IF, ELSE, END IF, or END statement. The logical expression is evaluated, and the contingent statement is executed if the logical expression is true. If the logical expression is false, the contingent statement is ignored. (Note that the logical expression is permitted to contain references to procedures that may cause side effects that affect the values of expressions in the contingent statement.)

Block IF, ELSE IF, *and* END IF *statements and* IF *blocks*

A block IF statement consists of the keyword IF, followed by a parenthesized logical expression, followed by the keyword THEN. An ELSE IF statement consists of the keyword ELSE IF, followed by a parenthesized logical expression, followed by the keyword THEN. An ELSE statement consists of the keyword ELSE. An END IF statement consists of the keyword END IF.

A block IF statement introduces an IF block. For each block IF statement there must be a corresponding END IF statement, which must appear following the block IF statement in the same program unit.

The nesting level of a given statement in a program unit is (1) the number of block IF statements that have appeared between the beginning of the program unit and the given statement, whose corresponding END IF statements have not appeared; plus (2) the number of DO statements that have appeared between the beginning of the program unit and the given statement, whose corresponding terminal statements have not appeared. A block IF statement and its corresponding END IF statement must appear at the same nesting level, and a DO statement and its corresponding terminal statement must appear at the same nesting level (see note on p. 453).

An IF block consists of all statements in the program unit following the block IF statement and preceding the corresponding END IF statement. An IF block consists of one or more subblocks, delimited by block IF and END IF statements, as well as by ELSE IF and ELSE statements at the same nesting level as the block IF statement. Any number of ELSE IF statements may appear. At most one ELSE statement may appear, and must not precede any ELSE IF statements at the same nesting level. If a block IF or a DO statement appears within a subblock, the corresponding END IF or terminal statement must also appear within the same subblock. Transfer of control into a subblock from outside the subblock is prohibited. The statement label, if any, of an ELSE IF or ELSE statement must not be referenced. A subblock may be empty.

Execution of a block IF or ELSE IF statement begins with evaluation of the logical expression. If the expression is true, the normal execution sequence continues with the statements (if any) in the subblock introduced by the block IF or ELSE IF statement. If the expression is false, control is transferred to the next subblock delimiter statement at the same nesting level. Execution of an ELSE statement has no effect. The last statement of each subblock is *implicitly* followed by a transfer of control to the END IF statement that terminates the IF block.

DO *statement and* DO *blocks*

A DO statement introduces a DO block. It consists of the keyword DO, followed by a statement label and an optional comma, followed by a control part. The control part includes a DO variable, an equals sign, and two or three expressions separated by commas. The DO variable is an integer, real, or double precision variable, and each of the control expressions is an integer, real, or double precision expression.

The statement label references the terminal statement of the DO block, which must appear following the DO statement in the same program unit, and which must be an executable statement but must not be an unconditional GO TO statement, an assigned GO TO statement, an arithmetic IF statement, a RETURN statement, a STOP statement, an END statement, or a DO statement.

A DO block consists of all statements in the program unit following the DO statement and ending with the labeled statement that is referenced by the DO statement. A statement may be the terminal statement of more than one DO block.

The nesting level of a given statement in a program unit is (1) the number of block IF statements that have appeared between the beginning of the program unit and the given statement, whose corresponding END IF statements have not appeared; plus (2) the number of DO statements that have appeared between the beginning of the program unit and the given statement, whose corresponding terminal statements have not appeared. A block IF statement and its corresponding END IF statement must appear at the same nesting level, and a DO statement and its corresponding terminal statement must appear at the same nesting level. (*Note:* A statement that terminates more than one DO block is considered to appear at its actual level as well as at an additional consecutively lower level for each additional DO block that it terminates.)

Transfer of control into a DO block from outside the block is prohibited. *Execution of a* DO *statement* includes all of the following steps:

1. The expressions in the control part are evaluated and converted, if necessary, to the type of the control variable. The (converted) values of the first two expressions become the values of m_1, the initial parameter, and m_2, the terminal parameter, respectively. If there is a third expression, then its value (which must not be zero) becomes the value of m_3, the incrementation parameter; otherwise, the default value of m_3 is one.

2. The DO variable becomes defined, with the value of m_1.

3. The initial value of the iteration count is established, as the value of the expression max (int $((m_2 - m_1 + m_3)/m_3)$,0).

4. Loop control processing, as described in the following paragraph, completes the execution of the DO statement.

Loop control processing consists of testing the iteration count. If it is greater than zero, the normal execution sequence continues with the statements in the DO block. If the iteration count is zero, execution of the DO block is complete. If there is a DO block at the next lower nesting level that shares the same terminal statement, and whose iteration count is not zero, then execution continues with the implicit incrementation processing (described below) for that DO block. If the terminal statement is the last statement in a subblock of an IF block, then execution continues with the implicit transfer of control to the corresponding END IF statement. Otherwise, execution continues with the next statement beyond the terminal statement.

Execution of the statements in the DO *block* must not cause the DO variable to become undefined or to be redefined. When (if ever) the terminal statement is reached, it is executed. The terminal statement is *implicitly* followed by the incrementation processing described in the following paragraph.

Incrementation processing involves the DO variable and the incrementation count for the DO block sharing this terminal statement whose nesting level is highest among those blocks whose incrementation count is not zero. The value of the DO variable is incremented by the value of the incrementation parameter m_3, and the iteration count is decremented by one. Execution then continues with loop control processing for this DO block, as described above.

Note: A DO statement with m_2 less than m_1 was prohibited in the 1966 Fortran standard, but many processors permitted such a statement and interpreted it as though the value of m_2 were replaced by the larger of m_1 and m_2—that is, all loops were executed at least once. In Fortran 77, a loop will be executed "zero times" if m_2 is less than m_1 and m_3 is positive.

Other control statements

CALL and RETURN statements are described in Section C.4.4.

A CONTINUE statement consists of the keyword CONTINUE. Its execution has no effect.

A STOP statement consists of the keyword STOP, optionally followed by a string of not more than five digits or by a character constant. Execution of a STOP statement causes termination of execution of the executable program, and makes the string of digits or the character constant (if any) accessible.

A PAUSE statement consists of the keyword PAUSE, optionally followed by a string of not more than five digits or by a character constant. Execution of a PAUSE statement causes interruption of execution of the executable program in such a way that execution can be resumed, and makes the string of digits or the character constant (if any) accessible.

An END statement consists of the keyword END, written only in columns 7 through 72 of an initial line. An END statement must not have a continuation line. The last line of every program unit must be an END statement. If an END statement is executed, its effect is that of a RETURN statement in a subprogram, or a STOP statement in a main program.

During execution of input and output statements, an error condition or an end-of-file condition may cause interruption of the normal execution sequence. See Section C.3.

C.2.8   Statement Function Statement

A statement function is specified by a single statement that is similar in form to an assignment statement. A statement function is a nonexecutable statement. It must follow all specification statements and precede all executable statements in the program unit.

A statement function statement consists of a symbolic name (which is the statement function name) followed by a parenthesized dummy argument list, followed by an equals sign (assignment operator), followed by an expression.

The dummy argument list contains zero or more dummy arguments (separated by commas); each dummy argument is a variable name, and the same name must not appear more than once in the list.

Both the expression and the statement function procedure name must be of integer, real, double precision, or complex type, or both must be of logical type or both must be of character type.

Variables referenced in the expression may be dummy arguments of the statement function, or variables local to the program unit. The expression must not contain a reference to a statement function procedure unless the statement function statement for that procedure appears earlier in the program unit.

The expression must not include a reference to an external function having side effects that alter the value of a dummy argument of the statement function.

C.3 INPUT AND OUTPUT

C.3.1 Concepts

Input is the transfer of data values from a file to storage. Output is the transfer of data values from storage to a file. Input and output statements control these transfers, and may also specify the representation of the data values on the file. Statements that cause data to be transferred are READ, WRITE, and PRINT statements. File-positioning input and output statements, which control the position of a file, are BACKSPACE, ENDFILE, and REWIND statements. Auxiliary input and output statements, which control the connection between a file and an executable program, are OPEN, CLOSE, and INQUIRE statements.

Files

A file has certain *file properties,* which depend partly on the executable program and partly on the processor, and which may vary from time to time. The properties of a file include a set of allowed access methods, a set of allowed forms, and a set of allowed record lengths. A file may exist or not: Execution of certain statements may cause a file to exist that did not previously exist, or vice versa. A file may be connected to the executable program or not. A file may have a name or not.

A file that is connected may have been preconnected. Such a file may exist or not. If it does not exist, execution of a WRITE, PRINT, ENDFILE, or OPEN statement referencing the file will cause it to exist.

A file that is connected may have become connected by execution of an OPEN statement. Such a file exists.

A file that is not connected may exist or not; however, if it is not a named file, it cannot exist. Execution of an OPEN statement referencing the file will cause the file to become connected and to exist.

A file will cease to exist upon execution of a CLOSE statement specifying STATUS = DELETE. An unnamed file ceases to exist when it becomes disconnected by any means.

Connection properties

When a unit becomes connected to a file, either by preconnection or by execution of an OPEN statement, the following connection properties may be established.

1. An access method, which is sequential or direct, is established for the connection.

2. A form, which is formatted or unformatted, is established for a connection to a file that exists or is created by the connection. For a connection that results from execution of an OPEN statement, a default form is established if no form is specified: The default form is formatted if the access method is sequential, or unformatted if the access method is direct. For a preconnected file that exists, a form is established by preconnection. For a preconnected file that does not exist, a form may be established, or the establishment of a form may be delayed until the file is created (for example, by execution of a formatted or unformatted WRITE statement).

3. A record length may be established. If the access method is direct, the connection establishes a record length, which is the length of each record of the file. A connection for sequential access does not have this property.

4. A blank significance property, which is ZERO or NULL, is established for a connection for which the form is formatted. This property has no effect on output. For a connection that results from execution of an OPEN statement, the blank significance property is NULL by default if no blank significance property is specified. For a preconnected file, the property is established by preconnection. The blank significance property of the connection is effective at the beginning of execution of each formatted input statement. During execution of the statement, any BN or BZ edit descriptors may temporarily change the effect of embedded and trailing blanks.

Internal files

An internal file is a sequence of character storage units. Minor variants of the READ and WRITE statements are used to transfer data to or from an internal file, as though it were a file connected for formatted sequential access. Each record of an internal file is a character variable, array element, or substring, and the record length is the length of the character datum.

Records

A formatted record is a sequence of characters. On a file whose form connection property is formatted, all records are formatted records except that the last record on a file connected for sequential access may be an endfile record. Data values transferred to or from a file of formatted records are edited during transfer—in other words, the representation of the values on the file consists of sequences of characters, related to the actual (numerical, logical, or character) values of the data in a manner determined by an explicit or implicit format specification. An explicit format specification is referenced in a READ, WRITE, or

PRINT statement as a reference to a FORMAT statement or to a character datum
or constant containing a format specification; implicit format specification is specified by an asterisk in place of the format reference in a READ, WRITE, or PRINT
statement, and designates "list directed" formatting that is controlled by the types
of the data values being transferred to or from the file. Implicit format specification must not be used with a file connected for direct access, nor for an internal
file. A file of formatted records may be prepared by means other than the execution of a Fortran program.

An unformatted record is a sequence of processor dependent representations
of data values. On a file whose form connection property is unformatted, all
records are unformatted records except that the last record on a file connected
for sequential access may be an endfile record. Format controlled editing is not
applied during transfer of data values to or from a file of unformatted records.

An endfile record may occur only as the last record of a file connected for
sequential access. An endfile record is written by execution of an ENDFILE statement. It does not necessarily have any concrete physical embodiment: The requirement is that during execution of a READ statement the fact that the file is
positioned at the same point where an endfile record was last written can be detected by the processor.

The length of a record on a file connected for sequential access is established
at the time the record is written. The length of a record on a file connected for
direct access is established at the time of connection, and is the same for all
records of the file; if the data values transferred to the file do not fill a record, the
remainder is filled with blanks if the record is formatted, or is undefined if the
record is unformatted.

Each record of a file connected for direct access has a unique record number, which is established when the record is written and does not change. Records
may be written in any order. There is no way to delete a record, but a record
may be rewritten.

Unit specifier

A unit specifier consists of an external unit identifier or an internal file identifier,
optionally preceded by the keyword UNIT and an equals sign.

An external unit identifier is either (1) an integer expression whose value
is zero or positive; or (2) an asterisk, identifying a particular processor-determined external unit that is preconnected for formatted sequential access. A given
integer value identifies the same external unit in all program units of an executable program. An asterisk must not be used as a unit identifier in a file positioning or auxiliary input or output statement.

An internal file identifier is the name of a character variable, character array, character array element, or character substring.

File position

A file connected for direct access is implicitly positioned during execution of a READ or WRITE statement. Prior to data transfer, the file is positioned at the beginning of the record specified in the control list. This record becomes the current record. If more than one record is read or written, the record numbers of the additional records follow sequentially after the number specified in the control list. After data transfer, if no error has occurred, the file is positioned after the last record read or written and that record becomes the preceding record. The *nextrec* specifier in an INQUIRE statement may be used to determine the record number of the record following the one just read or written.

A file connected for sequential access is implicitly positioned during execution of a READ, WRITE, PRINT, or ENDFILE statement, and may be explicitly positioned by execution of a BACKSPACE or REWIND statement. If the file contains an endfile record, the file must not be positioned after the endfile record prior to data transfer. On input, the file is positioned at the beginning of the next record prior to data transfer; on output, a new record is created. One or more records are read or written. If an endfile record is read (during input), data transfer ceases and the file is positioned after the endfile record. Otherwise, if no error has occurred, the file is positioned after the last record read or written and that record becomes the preceding record. In the case of output, the last record written becomes the last record of the file. Execution of an ENDFILE statement creates an endfile record, and positions the file after the endfile record. Execution of a REWIND statement positions the file at its initial point. Execution of a BACK-SPACE statement causes the file to be positioned before the preceding record, unless the file is at its initial point.

File status specifiers

Any input or output statement (including file positioning and auxiliary input or output statements) may contain an input-output status specifier, ISOSTAT = *ios,* or an error specifier, ERR = *s*; and a READ statement may also contain an end-of-file specifier, END = *s*; where *ios* is the name of an integer datum, and *s* is the label of an executable statement appearing in the same program unit. If an error condition occurs during execution of a statement containing an error specifier, or if an endfile record is read during execution of a statement containing an end-of-file specifier, control is transferred to the statement having the designated label. Execution of any statement containing an input-output status specifier causes the datum *ios* to become defined with a zero value if neither an error condition has occurred nor an endfile record has been read, with a processor-dependent positive value if an error condition has occurred, and with a negative value if no error condition has occurred and an endfile record has been read.

C.3.2 READ, WRITE, and PRINT Statements

Statement forms

A READ, WRITE, or PRINT statement has one of the following forms (where portions appearing in square brackets are optional):

READ (*clist*) [*list*]
READ *fmt* [, *list*]
WRITE (*clist*) [*list*]
PRINT *fmt* [, *list*]

A control list, *clist*, has one of the following forms:

unit, *fmt*, *kwlist*
unit, *kwlist*
kwlist

where *unit* and *fmt* are unit and format specifiers in nonkeyword form, and *kwlist* is a list of specifiers all of which are in keyword form. The control list must include a unit specifier, and may include at most one of each of the following: a format specifier, a status specifier, an error specifier, and either an end-of-file specifier or a record specifier. A format specifier is included for a formatted file. A record specifier is included for a direct access file. An end-of-file specifier may be included in a READ statement for a sequential access file.

The statement forms that do not include control lists must not be used for a direct access file (since the record number specification can be given only in a control list).

Specifiers

A specifier in a READ, WRITE, or PRINT statement is a unit specifier, a format specifier, a record specifier, a status specifier, an error specifier, or an end-of-file specifier. Unit specifiers, status specifiers, error specifiers, and end-of-file specifiers are described above.

A format specifier has the form [FMT =] *fmt*, where *fmt* is one of the following:

1. The statement label of a FORMAT statement in the same program unit;
2. The name of an integer variable that has a statement label value referencing a FORMAT statement in the same program unit;
3. A character constant;
4. A character array name;
5. A character expression that does not involve concatenation of variable length operands; or
6. An asterisk.

A record specifier has the form REC $= rec$, where *rec* is an integer expression whose value is positive, designating a record number in the direct access file.

The input or output list

The *list* of a READ, WRITE, or PRINT statement specifies the data whose values are to be transferred.

A basic list item in a READ statement is a variable name, an array element name, an array name, or a substring name. A basic list item in a WRITE or PRINT statement is any of the foregoing, or any expression except a character expression that involves concatenation of variable length operands. An array name appearing as a basic list item is equivalent to a sequence of basic list items that includes all the array elements in the order of their array positions.

Each item of an input or output list is a basic list item or an implied DO list. An implied DO list consists of a list of basic list items or implied DO lists, followed by a control part, all of which is enclosed in parentheses. The control part includes an implied DO variable, an equals sign, and two or three expressions separated by commas. The sequence of values of the implied DO variable is established exactly as for a DO variable. In an input list, the implied DO variable must not appear as a list item in the same implied DO list. The implied DO list is equivalent to a sequence of items that includes the list items once for each iteration of the implied DO list, with appropriate substitution of values for any occurrence of the implied DO variable.

Execution

Data transfer is specified by the input or output list, along with the format. File positioning may occur even when there are no data values specified by the list. A READ statement transfers data from an internal file, or from a unit connected to an external file. A WRITE or PRINT statement transfers data to an internal file, or to a unit connected to an external file.

A READ statement that does not contain a control list is interpreted as specifying a particular processor-determined unit, which is the same as the unit identified by an asterisk in a READ statement that contains a control list. A PRINT statement is interpreted as specifying some other processor-determined unit, which is the same as the unit identified by an asterisk in a WRITE statement.

A READ, WRITE, or PRINT statement for a formatted file includes a format specifier.

All values needed to determine which entities are specified by a list item are established at the beginning of the processing of that item. All data specified by a list item is transferred prior to the processing of any subsequent list item. A DO variable of an implied DO list becomes defined at the beginning of processing of the items in that implied DO list.

All data referenced in an output list must be defined. A direct access READ statement must specify a record that has previously been written.

Unformatted data transfer causes exactly one record to be read or written. The type of each input list item must correspond to the type of the list item used when the record was written, except that one complex item may correspond to two real items. This correspondence must include the length of character items.

One or more records are written during formatted data transfer; the initiation of new records is controlled by the format. For a direct access file, the record number is increased by one each time a new record is initiated.

A WRITE or PRINT statement may transfer formatted data to a sequential file that is connected to a printer which uses the first character of each record for vertical spacing control. For such devices, vertical spacing before printing is one line (normal) if the first character is blank, two lines if the first character is zero, skip to the first line of next page if the first character is one, and no advance if the first character is plus. A record with no characters has the same effect as a record containing a single blank character.

C.3.3 Explicit Format Specification

Specifying a format

An explicit format is specified by a reference to a FORMAT statement or to a character expression. A FORMAT statement must be labeled, and consists of the keyword FORMAT followed by a format specification enclosed in parentheses. If a format is specified by a reference to a character expression, the expression must have a value consisting of matching left and right parentheses enclosing a valid format specification. Blank characters may precede the left parenthesis, and character positions following the right parenthesis may contain arbitrary characters or may be undefined.

The format specification consists of a list of items, each of which is either an edit descriptor or a format specification enclosed in parentheses and optionally preceded by a repeat count specification (which is a nonzero, unsigned integer constant). The items in the list are separated by commas, except that the comma may be omitted between a P edit descriptor and an immediately following item that is an F, E, D, or G edit descriptor, before or after a slash edit descriptor, or before or after a colon edit descriptor. Each edit descriptor is one of the following:

Iw	$Iw.m$	$'h_1\ h_2\dots h_n'$		$nH\ h_1\ h_2\dots h_n$
$Fw.d$		Tc	TLc	TRc
$Ew.d$	$Ew.dEe$	nX		
$Dw.d$		$/$	$:$	
$Gw.d$	$Gw.dEe$	S	SP	SS
Lw		kP		
A	Aw	BN	BZ	

where h_1, h_2, . . . , h_n are Fortran or non-Fortran characters, and w, m, d, e, n, c, and k are integer constants. (All are unsigned and nonzero except that m, d, or k may be zero and k may be optionally signed.)

The I, F, E, D, G, L, and A edit descriptors may be preceded by a repeat count specification; the others must not be.

Interaction with input or output list

Explicitly formatted input or output involves a sequence of input or output list items, and a sequence of edit descriptors. If the READ, WRITE, or PRINT statement that references the format specification contains an input or output list that specifies at least one list item, the format specification must include at least one I, F, E, D, G, L, or A edit descriptor.

Each input or output list item, taking into account the fact that several list items may be specified by an array name or by an implied DO list, comprises one element of the list sequence, except that each complex item comprises two elements of the list sequence.

Each format specification item that is preceded by a repeat count r has the same effect as if the item were written r times consecutively in the format specification.

The sequence of edit descriptors is as written, from left to right, taking into account all repeat specifications. In effect, the last edit descriptor on the right is followed by an implicit colon.

Each I, F, E, D, G, L, or A edit descriptor (counting repetitions) is associated with one element of the input or output list sequence. The other edit descriptors are not associated with any element of the list sequence.

If the number of associated edit descriptors is less than the number of elements in the list sequence, then a "rescan point" in the format specification is determined as follows: If any item of the format specification is a format specification enclosed in parentheses, then the rescan point is at the beginning of the last such item in the main list, and includes its repeat count (if any). Otherwise, the rescan point is the beginning of the format specification. The total effective format specification is the original format specification, followed by as many repetitions as are required of that portion of the original specification to the right of the rescan point. Each repetition includes the implicit colon at the end. (If repetition is required, the repeated part must contain at least one I, F, E, D, G, L, or A edit descriptor.)

Format control begins with the first edit descriptor in the effective format specification, and continues in sequence.

When an edit descriptor other than an I, F, E, D, G, L, A, or colon is encountered, the appropriate editing is performed without reference to the input or output list sequence.

When an I, F, E, D, G, L, A, or colon edit descriptor is encountered, reference is made to the input or output list sequence. If the sequence has been completed, format control terminates. If there are items remaining in the sequence, then if the edit descriptor is a colon, it is ignored and the next edit descriptor is taken; otherwise, the associated item from the input or output list sequence is edited as required.

Interaction with a file

Each formatted record of a file is a sequence of characters. A field is a part of a formatted record that is transmitted to or from the file as a result of a single edit operation. A field corresponds to one I, F, E, D, G, L, or A edit descriptor and to one item in the list sequence, or to one H or apostrophe edit descriptor (with no corresponding list item). The field width is the number of characters in the field.

Numeric input editing   Leading blanks in a field are not significant. Plus signs are optional. A field of all blanks is interpreted as zero.

An Iw or I$w.m$ edit descriptor is associated with an input list item of integer type. The value of w specifies the field width; m is ignored.

An F$w.d$, E$w.d$, E$w.dE e$, D$w.d$, G$w.d$, or G$w.dE e$ edit descriptor is associated with a real or double precision item in the input list sequence. The input field consists of an optional sign, followed by a string of digits optionally containing a decimal point, optionally followed by an exponent consisting of an E or D followed by an optionally signed integer constant. If no decimal point appears in the input field, the value of d is used to determine the implied position of the decimal point, counting from the last character preceding the exponent if there is one in the field, or from the last character position of the field. If there is a decimal point in the field, it overrides the d specification of the edit descriptor. The input field may contain more digits than are considered significant by the processor.

The kP edit descriptor specifies a scale factor k, which is an optionally signed integer constant. The value of the scale factor in effect at the beginning of execution of an input statement is zero. The effective value of the scale factor does not change during execution of the statement, except when a P edit descriptor is encountered. The scale factor has no effect on input, except for F, E, D, or G editing of a field that does not contain an explicit exponent. If there is no exponent in the input field, it is treated as if the field were followed by the exponent $-k$.

Numeric output editing   A (nonzero) negative value produces a minus sign in the output field; a zero value does not produce a minus sign; a positive or zero value has an optional plus sign. The external representation is right-justified in the field, with leading blanks. If the number of characters exceeds the field width, or if an exponent exceeds its specified length using Ew.dEe or Gw.dEe editing, then the entire output field is filled with asterisks. However, if the field width is not exceeded when optional characters are omitted, the field is not filled with asterisks. (Note that a plus sign is not optional when SP sign control is in effect.)

An Iw or Iw.m edit descriptor is associated with an output list sequence item of integer type. The value of w specifies the field width. The value of m, if present, must not exceed that of w; this value specifies the minimum number of nonblank characters to be transmitted, including leading zeros if necessary. If m is zero, a zero datum will be transmitted as a field of blank characters regardless of the sign control in effect.

An Fw.d edit descriptor is associated with an output list sequence item of real or double precision type. The field width is specified as w, with a fractional part consisting of d digits. The output field consists of blanks, if necessary, followed by a minus sign or an optional plus sign, followed by a string of digits that includes a decimal point and represents the magnitude of the data value, as modified by the scale factor currently in effect, and with the fractional part rounded to d decimal digits.

An Ew.d, Ew.dEe, or Dw.d edit descriptor is associated with an output list sequence item of real or double precision type. The field width is w, with a fractional part consisting of d digits, and an exponent of e digits (if e is specified). The output field consists of an optional sign, followed by an optional zero, a decimal point, d significant digits obtained by rounding the data value, and an exponent.

The exponent may have any of several forms. If e is not specified, the exponent value must not exceed 999; an exponent larger than 99 occupies four character positions including a sign and three digits. If e is specified, the exponent occupies $e + 2$ character positions, including an E or a D (whichever appears in the edit descriptor), a sign, and e exponent digits. If e is not specified and the exponent is 99 or less, the exponent occupies four character positions; either it is in the same form as when the exponent is larger than 99 (with an extra leading zero exponent digit) or it is in the same form as if e were specified with the value 2 (and with an E in the output field for E editing, and with either an E or a D for D editing).

The kP edit descriptor specifies a scale factor k, which is an optionally signed integer constant. The value of the scale factor in effect at the beginning of execution of an output statement is zero. The effective value of the scale factor does not change during execution of the statement, except when a P edit descriptor is encountered.

For F output editing, the scale factor value is added to the exponent of the internal data value.

For E or D output editing, the scale factor must be greater than $-d$ and less than $d + 2$. If $-d < k \leq 0$, there will be exactly $|k|$ leading zeros and $d - |k|$

significant digits after the decimal point. If $0 < k < d + 2$, there will be exactly k significant digits to the left of the decimal point and $d - k + 1$ significant digits to the right of the decimal point (thus a total of $d + 1$ significant digits in the output field).

A $Gw.d$ or $Gw.dEe$ edit descriptor is associated with an output list sequence item of real or double precision type. The field width is specified as w, with a fractional part consisting of d digits, and an exponent of e digits (if e is specified). Editing is the same as F or the same as E, depending on the magnitude of the datum. If the exponent would be between 0 and d inclusive, the F mode is used, but the value of w is decreased by 4 (or $e + 2$ if e is specified) and the value of d is adjusted so that the total number of significant digits, both to the right and to the left of the decimal point, is the original value of d in the G edit descriptor; the scale factor has no effect in this case. If the exponent is negative or is larger than d, then editing (including scale factor effects) is identical to $Ew.d$ or $Ew.dEe$.

Editing of logical data   An Lw edit descriptor is associated with a list sequence item of logical type. The value of w specifies the field width. The input field consists of one or more blanks, an optional period, and a T for true or an F for false; characters in the field after the T or F are not significant. The output field consists of $w - 1$ blanks followed by a T for true or an F for false.

Editing of character data   An A or Aw edit descriptor is associated with a list sequence item of character type. If w is not specified, the field width is the length of the character datum specified as the list sequence item.

If w is present, it specifies the field width. An input field will be padded on the right with blanks or truncated from the *left,* if necessary, to the length of the character datum. A character datum for output will be truncated from the right or padded with blanks on the *left,* if necessary, to the field width w.

Apostrophe editing   Apostrophe editing must not be used on input. The field width is the same as the number of characters in the edit descriptor (interpreted as a character constant). The specified character string is transmitted to the output record, without reference to the output list.

H editing   This form of editing must not be used for input. The nH edit descriptor causes the n characters (including blanks) immediately following the H in the format specification to be transmitted to the output record. The field width is n.

T and X editing   These edit descriptors specify the position, within the record, of the next character to be transmitted. The position may be in either direction from the current position. The specified position may be beyond the end of the record if no characters are actually transmitted from that position.

On output, if a character is transmitted to a position to which another character has already been transmitted, the character transmitted earlier is replaced. If, as a result of T and X positioning, there are positions in a record to which no character is transmitted, such positions are filled with blanks by default.

The T*c* edit descriptor positions the record at its *c*th character.

The TL*c* edit descriptor positions the record backward *c* characters from its current position.

The TR*c* or *n*X edit descriptor positions the record forward *c* (or *n*) characters from its current position.

Slash editing   The slash edit descriptor causes the input or output file to be positioned at the beginning of the next record, which then becomes the current record. For a file connected for direct access, the record number is increased by one.

The number of records read by a formatted input statement can be determined from the following rule: A record is read at the beginning of execution of the statement (even if the input list is empty), each time a slash edit descriptor is encountered in the format specification, and each time a format rescan occurs at the end of the format specification. The number of records written by a formatted output statement can be determined from the following rule: A record is written each time a slash edit descriptor is encountered in the format specification, each time a format rescan occurs at the end of the format specification, and at the completion of execution of the statement (even if the output list is empty). Thus *n* successive slashes between two other edit descriptors cause $n - 1$ blank lines if the records are printed. The occurrence of *n* slashes at the beginning or end of a complete format specification causes *n* blank lines if the records are printed. However, a complete format specification containing *n* slashes and no other edit descriptors (where *n* is zero or greater) causes $n + 1$ blank lines if the records are printed.

Colon editing   The colon edit descriptor terminates format control if there are no more items in the input or output list sequence. If there are more items, this edit descriptor has no effect.

S editing   The S edit descriptor has no effect on input. For output, it affects only I, F, E, D, and G editing. The output fields produced by these edit descriptors include positions in which the processor may insert an optional plus sign. At the beginning of each output statement, the processor option is in effect. An SP (sign print) edit descriptor requires the processor to insert plus signs in those positions; an SS (sign suppress) edit descriptor requires that plus signs in those positions be omitted; and an S (sign optional) descriptor restores the option to the processor.

BN **and** BZ **editing**   These specifiers have no effect on output. On input, they affect only I, F, E, D, and G editing. Blank characters, other than leading blanks, in fields edited by these descriptors may be interpreted as zeros or ignored. At the beginning of execution of each input statement, the interpretation of such blank characters is controlled by the blank significance property of the connection to the file. A BN (blank null) edit descriptor causes blanks to be ignored (except that a field of all blanks has the value zero); a BZ (blank zero) edit descriptor causes blanks to be interpreted as zeros.

C.3.4   List Directed Formatting

List directed formatting is specified by a format specifier consisting of an asterisk.

List directed input

List directed input is the transfer of data values from formatted records to storage under the control of the input list. The characters in one or more records constitute a sequence of separators and representations of data values. A separator is a (maximum length) nonempty string of characters consisting of zero or more blanks and at most one comma or slash. The end of a record has the same effect as a blank character, unless it is within a character constant. Blanks preceding the first data value encountered by an input statement are not considered separators.

Each item of the input list, taking into account the fact that several list items may be specified by an array name or by an implied DO list, comprises one element of the list sequence. Each element of the list sequence corresponds to an item in the record that is a data value, a null value, the form $r * v,$ or the form $r *,$ where v is a data value and r is an unsigned, nonzero integer constant specifying a repeat count. These forms must not contain embedded blanks, except where permitted within a data value.

In general, the form of a sequence of characters acceptable in a field for explicitly formatted input for a list item of a given type is also acceptable for the representation of a data value of the same type for list directed input; there are some exceptions, however. Blanks are never used as zeros in a data value, and embedded blanks are not permitted in a data value except within character values or before and after the real or imaginary part of a complex data value.

A data value corresponding to an integer list item is a string of digits without a decimal point, optionally preceded by a sign, and with no embedded blanks.

A data value corresponding to a real or double precision list item is a *numeric input field,* consisting of a basic part and an optional exponent part, with no embedded blanks. The basic part consists of a string of digits with an optional decimal point, and optionally preceded by a sign. If there is no decimal point, the implied decimal point position is at the right of the string of digits. The exponent part is a signed integer constant, optionally preceded by a D or E.

A data value corresponding to a complex list item is a pair of numeric input fields (representing the real and imaginary parts), separated by a comma and enclosed in parentheses.

A data value corresponding to a logical list item is a sequence of characters consisting of an optional period, a T for true or an F for false, and optional characters that must not include a comma, slash, or blank.

A data value corresponding to a character list item is a nonempty string of characters enclosed in apostrophes. An apostrophe within a data value is represented by a pair of consecutive apostrophes without an intervening blank or end of record. The end of a record is otherwise ignored when it appears within a character data value. A data value will be padded on the right with blanks or truncated from the right, if necessary, to the length of the character datum specified by the list item.

A null value is specified by two consecutive separators with no value between them, by no value preceding the first separator encountered by an input statement, or by the form $r *$. The (internal) datum corresponding to a null value is not changed during input; it retains its previous value (or remains undefined). A single null value may correspond to an entire complex list item, and not to the real or imaginary part separately.

When a slash is encountered within a separator during list directed input, execution of the statement terminates. The effect is to supply null values for any remaining list items.

List directed output

List directed output is the transfer of data values from storage to formatted records under control of the output list. Representations of data values on one or more output records are produced, and (except for character values) are separated by a processor-dependent sequence of characters consisting of blanks and at most one comma. The record structure of the output file is determined by the processor. The processor may begin a new record at any point except within a data value, and under certain conditions may begin a new record within a value of character or complex type.

For a list item of logical type, the data value consists of the character T or F.

For a list item of integer type, a data value is produced in the same form as by Iw editing, for some processor-defined value of w.

For a list item of real or double precision type, the data value is produced in approximately the same form as by Gw.dEe editing, for some processor-defined values of w, d, and e.

For a list item of complex type, two data values of the same form as a real value are produced, enclosed in parentheses and separated by a comma.

For a list item of character type, a data value in "printable" form is produced, which is not necessarily suitable for list directed input. The string of characters is not delimited by apostrophes, apostrophes within the string are represented only by a single apostrophe, and a blank character (for vertical spacing control) is inserted at the beginning of any record that contains the continuation of a character value from a preceding record.

If two or more successive list items have identical values, the processor has the option of producing a single value preceded by a repeat count.

Slashes as separators, and null values, are not produced by list directed output.

Each output record begins with a blank character (to provide vertical spacing control if the record is printed).

C.3.5 OPEN, CLOSE, and INQUIRE Statements

OPEN *statement*

An OPEN statement consists of the keyword OPEN followed by a parenthesized list of specifiers, which must include an external unit specifier and may include at most one of each of the following:

IOSTAT = *iostat,* where *iostat* is the name of an integer datum;

ERR = *s,* where *s* is the label of an executable statement in the same program unit;

FILE = *file,* where *file* is a character expression giving the name of a named file;

STATUS = *status,* where *status* is 'OLD', 'NEW', 'SCRATCH', or 'UN-KNOWN';

ACCESS = *access,* where *access* is 'SEQUENTIAL' or 'DIRECT';

FORM = *form,* where *form* is 'FORMATTED' or 'UNFORMATTED';

RECL = *recl,* where *recl* is an integer expression whose value is positive;

BLANK = *blank,* where *blank* is 'NULL' or 'ZERO'.

Execution of an OPEN statement in a program unit causes connection of the specified unit for purposes of all other program units of the executable program as well. An OPEN statement that causes a unit to remain connected to the same file to which it is already connected must not change the *access, form,* or *recl* specification of the file; the *blank* specification may be changed, however. The meaning of the specifiers is as follows.

If the *file* specifier is given, and the unit is not already connected to a file, then it becomes connected to the specified file, which is created if it does not already exist. If the *file* specifier is given, and the unit is already connected to the specified file, then it remains connected to the same file; if the file does not already exist, it is created. If the *file* specifier is given, and the unit is already connected to a different file, then it is disconnected from the previous file and becomes connected to the specified file, which is created if it does not already exist. If the *file* specifier is omitted, and the unit is already connected to a file, then it remains connected to the same file; if the file does not exist, it is created. If the file specifier is omitted, and the unit is not already connected to a file, then it becomes connected to a processor-determined file, which is created if it does not already exist.

If the *status* specifier is `'OLD'` or `'NEW'`, a *file* specifier must be given. If it is `'OLD'`, the file must already exist. If it is `'NEW'`, the file must not already exist; the file will be created and its *status* will be changed to `'OLD'`. If the *status* is `'SCRATCH'`, a *file* specifier must not be given. The default status is `'UNKNOWN'`.

The default *access* specification for an existing file is the existing property; the default access specification for a file being created is `'SEQUENTIAL'`.

The default *form* specification is `'FORMATTED'` if the *access* is `'SEQUEN-TIAL'`, or is `'UNFORMATTED'` if the *access* is `'DIRECT'`.

The *recl* specifier gives the length of each record in a direct access file. If the *form* is `'FORMATTED'`, the length is measured in characters; if the *form* is `'UNFORMATTED'`, the length is measured in processor-dependent units.

The *blank* specifier determines whether blank characters in numeric input fields in a formatted file are to be treated as zeros or ignored. If this specifier is omitted, a value of `'NULL'` is assumed. (Note that if the file is already connected with a `'ZERO'` *blank* specifier, the value of the specification will be changed even if the specifier is omitted from the OPEN statement.)

CLOSE *statement*

A CLOSE statement consists of the keyword CLOSE followed by a parenthesized list of specifiers, which must include an external unit specifier and may include at most one of each of the following:

IOSTAT = *iostat,* where *iostat* is the name of an integer datum;

ERR = *s,* where *s* is the label of an executable statement in the same program unit;

STATUS = *status,* where *status* is `'KEEP'` or `'DELETE'`.

Execution of a CLOSE statement terminates the connection between the specified external unit and the file to which it is connected. (If the unit is not connected to a file, the CLOSE statement has no effect.) The connection is terminated for purposes of all other program units of the executable program as well. After execution of a CLOSE statement, the unit may be reconnected to the same file or to a different file, and the file (if it is a named file) may be reconnected to the same unit or to a different unit. (If a file is not named, there is in general no way to identify it in order to reconnect it after it has become disconnected.)

If the *status* specifier is `'KEEP'`, the state of existence of the file remains unchanged. If the *status* is `'DELETE'`, the file ceases to exist. `'KEEP'` must not be specified for a SCRATCH file. If the specifier is omitted, the default is `'DE-LETE'` for a SCRATCH file; otherwise, it is `'KEEP'`.

At termination of execution of an executable program, except due to an error condition, all connected units are implicitly closed with the appropriate default *status* specifier.

INQUIRE *statement*

An INQUIRE statement consists of the keyword INQUIRE followed by a parenthesized list of specifiers, which must include either an external unit specifier or a *file* specifier (but not both), and may include at most one of each of the specifiers in the list below.

> IOSTAT = *iostat,* where *iostat* is the name of an integer datum;
>
> ERR = *s,* where *s* is the label of an executable statement in the same program unit;
>
> EXIST = *exist,* where *exist* is the name of a logical datum;
>
> OPENED = *opened,* where *opened* is the name of a logical datum;
>
> NUMBER = *number,* where *number* is the name of an integer datum;
>
> NAMED = *named,* where *named* is the name of a logical datum;
>
> NAME = *name,* where *name* is the name of a character datum;
>
> ACCESS = *access,* where *access* is the name of a character datum;
>
> SEQUENTIAL = *sequential,* where *sequential* is the name of a character datum;
>
> DIRECT = *direct,* where *direct* is the name of a character datum;
>
> FORM = *form,* where *form* is the name of a character datum;
>
> FORMATTED = *formatted,* where *formatted* is the name of a character datum;
>
> UNFORMATTED = *unformatted,* where *unformatted* is the name of a character datum;
>
> RECL = *recl,* where *recl* is the name of an integer datum;
>
> NEXTREC = *nextrec,* where *nextrec* is the name of an integer datum.

If a *file* specifier is given, the INQUIRE statement relates to the specified named file. If no file having the specified name exists, the data referenced by *named, name, sequential, direct, formatted,* and *unformatted* become undefined. If *opened* is set to false, *access, form, recl, nextrec,* and *blank* become undefined.

If a unit specifier is given and the specified unit is not connected to a file, the data referenced by *number, named, name, access, sequential, direct, form, formatted, unformatted, recl, nextrec,* and *blank* become undefined.

If *access* is `'SEQUENTIAL'`, *recl* and *nextrec* become undefined. If *form* is `'UNFORMATTED'`, *blank* becomes undefined.

The datum referenced by *exists* becomes true if a *file* specifier is given and a named file with the specified name exists, or if a unit specifier is given and the specified unit exists; otherwise, the datum becomes false.

The datum referenced by *opened* becomes true if a *file* specifier is given and the specified file is connected to a unit, or if a unit specifier is given and the specified unit is connected to a file; otherwise, the datum becomes false. If *opened* becomes true, *number* is assigned the value of the unit number to which the named file is connected; otherwise, *number* becomes undefined.

The datum referenced by *named* becomes true if the file is a named file; otherwise, the datum becomes false. If *named* becomes true, *name* is assigned the name of the file (which is not necessarily the same as the name given in the *file* specifier).

The datum referenced by *access* is assigned `'SEQUENTIAL'` or `'DIRECT'` according to the access property of the connection. If there is no connection, *access* becomes undefined. The data referenced by *direct* and *sequential* are each assigned `'YES'`, `'NO'`, or `'UNKNOWN'`, indicating whether or not the particular access method is included among the set of allowed access methods for the file (or whether this information cannot be determined).

The datum referenced by *form* is assigned `'FORMATTED'` or `'UNFOR-MATTED'` according to the access property of the connection. If there is no connection, or if the connection is to a file that does not exist and for which no form has been established, *form* becomes undefined. The data referenced by *formatted* and *unformatted* are each assigned `'YES'`, `'NO'`, or `'UNKNOWN'`, indicating whether or not the particular form is among the set of allowed forms for the file (or whether this information cannot be determined).

The datum referenced by *recl* is assigned the record length (measured in characters for formatted records, and in processor-dependent units for unformatted records) if the access method is direct. If the file is not connected for direct access, *recl* becomes undefined.

The datum referenced by *nextrec* is assigned a value one greater than the record number of the last record read or written, if any. If the file is connected but no records have been read or written since it was connected, the datum is assigned the value 1. If the file is not connected for direct access, *nextrec* becomes undefined.

C.4   MAIN PROGRAM AND SUBPROGRAMS

C.4.1   Main Program

A main program is a program unit that does not have a FUNCTION, SUBROU-TINE, or BLOCK DATA statement as its first statement; it may have a PROGRAM statement as its first statement.

A main program must not contain a BLOCK DATA, ENTRY, FUNCTION, RETURN, or SUBROUTINE statement, and must not contain a PROGRAM statement except as its first statement.

There must be exactly one main program in an executable program. Execution of an executable program begins with the first executable statement of the main program. A main program must not be referenced as a (subroutine or external function) procedure.

A PROGRAM statement consists of the keyword PROGRAM followed by a symbolic name. This name must not be used as the name of any other program unit, or of a common block, in the same executable program.

C.4.2 Subprograms

Subroutine subprograms

A subroutine subprogram is a program unit that has a SUBROUTINE statement as its first statement. A SUBROUTINE statement consists of the keyword SUBROUTINE, followed by a symbolic name that is the subroutine subprogram name, optionally followed by a parenthesized list of dummy arguments. (If there are no arguments, the enclosing parentheses are optional.)

Each dummy argument (if any) is the symbolic name of a variable, an array, or a procedure, or is an asterisk indicating an alternate return.

A subroutine subprogram may contain any statement except a BLOCK DATA, FUNCTION, or PROGRAM statement or another SUBROUTINE statement.

A subroutine must not reference itself, either directly or indirectly.

Function subprograms

A function subprogram is a program unit that has a FUNCTION statement as its first statement. A function statement consists of an optional type specification, followed by the keyword FUNCTION, followed by a symbolic name that is the function subprogram name, optionally followed by a parenthesized list of dummy arguments. (If there are no arguments, an empty pair of parentheses must be present.)

A type specifier consists of the keyword INTEGER, REAL, DOUBLE PRECISION, COMPLEX, or LOGICAL, or of the keyword CHARACTER optionally followed by a length specifier (consisting of an asterisk followed by an unsigned, nonzero integer constant, an integer expression enclosed in parentheses, or an asterisk in parentheses). If no type specifier appears in a FUNCTION statement, the function subprogram name may appear in a type statement.

Each dummy argument (if any) is the name of a variable, an array, or a procedure.

The function subprogram name must not appear as a dummy argument name in the FUNCTION statement nor in any ENTRY statement, and it must not appear in any other nonexecutable statement except a type statement in the subprogram.

In a function subprogram, there is an association among all function subprogram names that appear in the FUNCTION statement and in ENTRY statements in the subprogram, and all local variable names that are the same as any of these function subprogram names. During execution of the subprogram, one such local variable, of the same type as the subprogram name used in the procedure reference that caused execution of the subprogram, must become defined; its value when a RETURN or END statement is executed is the value returned to the referencing program.

A function subprogram may contain any statement except a BLOCK DATA, SUBROUTINE, or PROGRAM statement or another FUNCTION statement.

Subprogram entry

An ENTRY statement may cause execution of a subprogram to begin with a statement other than the first executable statement. A subprogram may have zero or more ENTRY statements. An ENTRY statement is nonexecutable, and may appear anywhere within a subroutine or function subprogram except within a DO block or an IF block.

An ENTRY statement consists of the keyword ENTRY, followed by a symbolic name that is a subprogram name, optionally followed by a parenthesized list of arguments. (If there are no arguments, the enclosing parentheses are optional.)

The dummy arguments are of the same form as those for the SUBROUTINE or FUNCTION statement in the subprogram containing the ENTRY statement. The dummy argument list of an ENTRY statement need not agree with that of the FUNCTION or SUBROUTINE statement nor with that of any other ENTRY statement in the same subprogram.

A name that appears as a dummy argument in an ENTRY statement must not appear in the same program unit in an executable statement, or in a statement function statement except as a dummy argument of the statement function, if such appearance would precede its first appearance in the program unit in a FUNCTION, SUBROUTINE, or ENTRY statement.

Function subprogram entry   Each entry name in a function subprogram must be of character type, if and only if the function subprogram name is of character type. All such names of character type must be of the same length.

The entry name must not appear as a dummy argument name in the FUNCTION statement nor in any ENTRY statement, and must not appear in any nonexecutable statement except a type statement in the subprogram. The name of a local variable that is the same as the entry name must not appear in any statement except a type statement, if such appearance would precede the ENTRY statement.

Dummy arguments

A dummy argument is the symbolic name of a variable, an array, or a procedure, or in a subroutine it may be an asterisk indicating an alternate return.

A dummy argument must not appear in an EQUIVALENCE, DATA, PARAMETER, SAVE, or INTRINSIC statement, nor in a COMMON statement except as a common block name.

A dummy argument may be used as an actual argument in a procedure reference in the subprogram.

A dummy argument name of integer type may appear in an adjustable array declarator.

The array declarator for a dummy argument that is an array name may be an adjustable array declarator; in other words, one or more of its dimension bound expressions may contain integer variable names. The name of each such variable must appear in the subprogram either in a common block or in every dummy argument list that contains the array name.

The length specifier for a dummy argument of character type may be an asterisk in parentheses, indicating that the character entity is to assume the length of the actual argument.

If an intrinsic function name appears in a dummy argument list, the name must not be used as an intrinsic function name in the subprogram.

C.4.3 BLOCK DATA Subprogram

A block data subprogram provides initial values for variables and array elements in named common blocks.

A block data subprogram is a program unit that has a BLOCK DATA statement as its first statement. There may be more than one block data subprogram in an executable program, but an executable program must not include more than one unnamed block data subprogram.

Entities not in a named common block must not be initialized in a block data subprogram. More than one named common block may have entities initialized in a single block data subprogram. A named common block must not be specified in more than one block data subprogram in an executable program. A named common block must have a storage sequence of the same length in a block data subprogram as in all other program units in which it appears.

A BLOCK DATA statement consists of the keywords BLOCK DATA, optionally followed by a symbolic name. A BLOCK DATA statement must not appear except as the first statement of a block data subprogram.

A block data subprogram must not contain any other statements except IMPLICIT, PARAMETER, DIMENSION, COMMON, SAVE, EQUIVALENCE, DATA, END, and type statements. A block data subprogram must not contain any executable statements.

C.4.4 Procedures

Subroutine procedure reference

A subroutine is referenced by a CALL statement, which consists of the keyword CALL followed by the symbolic name of a subroutine procedure or subroutine entry, optionally followed by a parenthesized list of actual arguments.

The actual argument list consists of zero or more actual arguments (separated by commas); each actual argument is an expression (except a character expression involving concatenation of variable length operands), the name of an array or a procedure, or an alternate return specifier (consisting of an asterisk followed by the label of an executable statement in the same program unit).

If there are no actual arguments, the parentheses enclosing the list are optional.

Function procedure reference

A function procedure reference appears in an expression in a program unit. It consists of an external function name, an intrinsic function name, or a statement function name, followed by a parenthesized actual argument list. A statement function reference must not appear except in the program unit that contains the statement function statement.

The actual argument list contains zero or more actual parameters (separated by commas); each actual argument is an expression or the name of an array or procedure (except a statement function name). Actual arguments of a statement function must not include array names or procedure names.

If there are no actual arguments, the enclosing parentheses must appear.

Intrinsic functions   Intrinsic functions are predefined functions supplied by the processor. The intrinsic functions include those listed in Table C.1.

An actual argument of an intrinsic function is an expression. (Array names or procedure names are not permitted.) If there are two or more actual arguments, they must all be of the same type.

An intrinsic function may be referenced by a specific name or by a generic name. When a generic name is used, the type associated with the procedure reference may depend on the types of the arguments. Specific names, but not generic names, may be used when an intrinsic function is an actual argument.

If an intrinsic function name appears in the dummy argument list of a subprogram, the name must not be used as an intrinsic function in the program unit.

External functions   An external function procedure name is the same as a function subprogram name in the same executable program. The type of the subprogram name must be the same as the type of the procedure name, and if these are of character type their lengths must agree.

Table C.1 Generic and specific intrinsic function names

Generic name	Specific names
INT	INT, IFIX, IDINT
REAL	REAL, FLOAT, SNGL
DBLE	—
CMPLX	—
—	ICHAR
—	CHAR
AINT	AINT, DINT
ANINT	ANINT, DNINT
NINT	NINT, IDNINT
ABS	IABS, ABS, DABS, CABS
MOD	MOD, AMOD, DMOD
SIGN	ISIGN, SIGN, DSIGN
DIM	IDIM, DIM, DDIM
—	DPROD
MAX	MAX0, AMAX1, DMAX1
—	AMAX0, MAX1
MIN	MIN0, AMIN1, DMIN1
—	AMIN0, MIN1
—	LEN
—	INDEX
—	AIMAG
—	CONJG
SQRT	SQRT, DSQRT, CSQRT
EXP	EXP, DEXP, CEXP
LOG	ALOG, DLOG, CLOG
LOG10	ALOG10, DLOG10
SIN	SIN, DSIN, CSIN
COS	COS, DCOS, CCOS
TAN	TAN, DTAN
ASIN	ASIN, DASIN
ACOS	ACOS, DACOS
ATAN	ATAN, DATAN
ATAN2	ATAN2, DATAN2
SINH	SINH, DSINH
COSH	COSH, DCOSH
TANH	TANH, DTANH
—	LGE, LGT, LLE, LLT

Correspondence between actual arguments and dummy arguments

The actual arguments in a procedure reference must agree in number with the dummy arguments of the subprogram or of the statement function statement.

Corresponding to a dummy argument that is a variable name, the actual argument must be a variable name, an array element name, a substring name, a constant (including the symbolic name of a constant), or an expression other than one of the foregoing. If the dummy argument becomes defined during execution of the procedure, the actual argument must be a variable name, an array element name, or a substring name. The types of the dummy and actual arguments must agree. The length of an actual argument of character type must be greater than or equal to the length of the corresponding dummy argument.

If the actual argument is an expression, it is evaluated at the time the procedure reference occurs. If it is an array element name or a substring name, the expressions that specify the subscript values or the item position numbers in the substring specification are evaluated at the time the procedure reference occurs. These expression values do not change during execution of the procedure, even though they may involve variables that are redefined or become undefined.

Corresponding to a dummy argument that is an array name, the actual argument must be an array name or an array element name. If the actual argument is the name of an array, its size (number of elements) must equal or exceed that of the dummy array. If it is the name of an array element, then the number of elements between it and the end of the actual array must equal or exceed the size of the dummy array. The types of the dummy and actual arrays must agree. If the dummy array is of character type, then if the actual argument is a character array, the total number of character item positions in the array must equal or exceed the total number of character item positions in the dummy array; if the actual argument is a character array element, the total number of character item positions in all the array elements between it and the end of the actual array must equal or exceed the total number of character item positions in the dummy array.

Corresponding to a dummy argument name that is a subroutine procedure name, the actual argument must be a subroutine procedure name.

Corresponding to a dummy argument name that is a procedure name other than a subroutine procedure name, the actual argument name must be an external function name or a specific intrinsic function name.

If two actual arguments, corresponding to two dummy arguments in a procedure, are the same or associated entities in the referencing program unit, then the dummy arguments must not be redefined nor become undefined during execution of the procedure reference. The same restriction applies when an entity in a common block in the procedure and an actual argument corresponding to a dummy argument in the same procedure are the same or associated entities in the referencing program unit.

In a subroutine subprogram, corresponding to a dummy argument that is an asterisk, the actual argument must be an alternate return specifier.

RETURN *statement*

A RETURN statement consists of the keyword RETURN, optionally followed by an integer expression. A RETURN statement must not appear except in a function subprogram or in a subroutine subprogram.

Execution of a RETURN statement or an END statement in a subprogram terminates execution of the subroutine procedure reference or external function reference, and terminates the association between actual arguments and dummy arguments.

Alternate return If no expression appears in a RETURN statement, or if the value of the expression is less than one or greater than the number of asterisk dummy arguments in the SUBROUTINE or ENTRY statement referenced by the currently active CALL statement, then execution of the RETURN statement causes control to resume with the statement following the CALL statement. Otherwise, the value of the expression in the RETURN statement specifies the sequence number within the dummy argument list of the asterisk whose corresponding alternate return specifier (actual argument) contains the statement label of the statement to be executed next.

C.5 SUMMARY OF SUBSET DIFFERENCES

The document that defines Fortran 77 also describes a standard subset. The subset language is intended to enhance portability among processors for smaller computers or for others that do not choose to implement the full language. The following list summarizes the differences between the subset and the full Fortran 77 language.

The characters $ and : are not in the character set.

A statement must not have more than nine continuation lines.

Data statements must follow all declarations and precede all executable statements.

Comments are not permitted between lines of a statement.

Double precision and complex data types are not included.

An array must not have more than three dimensions.

All arrays have an implied lower bound of one for each dimension.

Adjustable dimension declarators must not be expressions.

The statements BLOCK DATA, CLOSE, COMPLEX, DOUBLE PRECISION, ENTRY, INQUIRE, PARAMETER, and PRINT are not included.

A SAVE statement must contain a list of common block names.

A DATA statement must not include an implied DO list.

Type conversion is not permitted in DATA declarations.

DO variables and parameters must be of integer type; expressions are not permitted. This also applies to implied DO lists for input or output.

The control expression of a computed GO TO must be a variable.

List directed input and output is not provided.

An internal file must not be an array.

An external unit identifier must not be an expression.

A format identifier must not be an expression or a reference to a character datum. Character constants are permitted.

Unit and format specifiers do not include the keywords `UNIT =` or `FMT =`.

There is no `IOSTAT` specifier or `ERR` specifier.

The "short form" `READ` and `PRINT` statements are not included.

Constants and general expressions are not permitted in output lists.

An `OPEN` statement is used only to specify unformatted direct access.

Named files are not included.

The format edit descriptors $Iw.m$, $Dw.d$, $Gw.d$, $Gw.dEe$, $Ew.dEe$, Tc, TLc, TRc, S, SP, SS are not included. No more than three levels of format nesting are permitted.

The alternate return feature is not included.

Character functions are not included.

Generic intrinsic functions are not included.

A character length specification must be a constant.

Substrings are not included.

Concatenation is not included.

The intrinsic functions `LEN`, `CHAR`, and `INDEX` are not included.

C.6 MAJOR DIFFERENCES BETWEEN FORTRAN 77 AND THE PREVIOUS STANDARD, ANS X3.9-1966

Note: An extremely important consideration in the development of Fortran 77 was the minimization of conflicts with the previous standard. The differences listed here represent (with only two exceptions) extensions to, rather than conflicts with, ANS X3.9-1966. It should also be noted that Fortran 77 consists of a full language and a subset; differences noted in this list refer to the full language.

"Structured" branching statements   The following statements have been added to the language:

```
IF (e) THEN
ELSE IF (e) THEN
ELSE
END IF
```

For each IF-THEN statement there must be a corresponding END IF statement. Between the IF-THEN and the corresponding END IF there may appear any number of ELSE IF-THEN statements, and at most one ELSE (which must not precede any of the ELSE IF-THEN statements). Groups of statements delimited by IF-THEN and END IF must be properly nested, both with respect to other such groups and with respect to DO loops. Transfer of control into such groups is prohibited.

Character data type   A new data type, consisting of character strings of fixed declared length, has been added to the language. Included are character constants, character variables, and arrays of character data. Operations on character data include concatenation and designation of substrings. Intrinsic functions for conversion between single characters and small integers, for pattern matching, and for determining the length of a string are included.

The Hollerith data type of ANS X3.9-1966 has been deleted. Because this introduces a conflict with the previous standard, it is anticipated that some processors will wish to retain Hollerith data as an extension to Fortran 77; accordingly, the standard includes an appendix with recommendations for the form such an extension should take.

DO loop changes   A DO statement specifying a terminal parameter whose value is less than that of the initial parameter is no longer prohibited. If the incrementation value is positive, such a statement specifies a loop to be executed "zero times." Negative increments are also permitted. The DO variable remains defined at completion. Transfer of control into a DO loop is prohibited (but was permitted under certain conditions by the previous standard).

List directed input and output   A form of input and output is provided, which does not require an explicit format specification. The form of the external representation is determined by the input or output list item.

Expressions   An arithmetic expression may include subexpressions of more than one type. (If an operator has two operands of different types, the operand whose type differs from that of the result is converted before the operator is applied.) A subscript expression may be any integer expression. A DO parameter may be any expression of integer, real, or double precision type.

Compile-time constants   A PARAMETER statement has been provided, which declares the value corresponding to the symbolic name of a constant. Such a name may be used in an expression, in a DATA statement, or in following PARAMETER statements.

Implicit type declaration   An IMPLICIT statement may be used to declare implicit types for variables and array names beginning with certain letters.

Generic intrinsic functions   Many intrinsic (predefined) functions produce a value whose type depends on the type of the function arguments.

Subprogram reference   Subroutines and functions may contain ENTRY statements, and subroutines may have alternate returns.

Array bounds   An array declaration may include both upper and lower dimension bounds; if the lower bound for a dimension is not specified the default is one. Arrays may have up to seven dimensions. The upper bound for the last dimension of a dummy argument array may be an asterisk, designating that the size of the array is to be determined from the actual argument.

Computed GO TO default   If the control expression of a computed GO TO is out of range, execution continues with the statement following the computed GO TO.

Input and output statements   The following features have been included:

An output list may contain constants and expressions.

An input or output statement may contain a character string to be used as the format specification.

End and error condition control for input and output are provided.

Tab format edit descriptors have been added.

Direct access input and output are provided.

A character array may be used as an internal file.

OPEN, CLOSE, and INQUIRE statements are provided.

SAVE statement   Values of entities in a subprogram may be preserved during the time when the subprogram is no longer being referenced, if their names are specified in a SAVE statement.

Fortran character set   The apostrophe and the colon are added to the Fortran character set. The collating sequence is only partly specified.

Comment lines   An asterisk or a C in column 1 designates a comment line.

ANSWERS
TO SELECTED EXERCISES

CHAPTER 2

Section 2.1.5

1. RV: X, BITE, HATE, X3, A1B2, KITE
    IV: LOVE, IJK, MITER, KITE
    RC: 123.4, 3., 0.00003
    IC: 123, 1234, 12345678
    N: $1.98, I*J*K, 3X, LANDSCAPE, POLICEMAN, 3*X, 123,400,000,
          COMPUTER, 1A2B

3. 0.276 E −3, −4.19 E 4, 3.08 E 0, 6.023 E 23

5. 2MARY, POLAR, ABLE, P, N−5, 2Z, I1234TT

Section 2.2.3

1. (a) −1; (b) 0; (c) −4; (d) −1
3. (a) −11; (b) 1.0; (c) 11; (d) 5; (e) 7; (f) −1

4. a) R = A + REAL (I)
   b) W = REAL (I) − 1.3 + REAL (J)
   c) K = INT (REAL (2 / 3) * 6.6) *or* K = 0
   d) I = INT (123456789.0 + B)
   e) OK as is

5. INT (RL − 4.0) * INT (RW − 4.0)

Section 2.3.5

1. a) OK as is
   b) SQRT (REAL (J))
   c) SQRT (REAL (NINT (Y) + 1)) *or* SQRT (ANINT (Y) + 1.0)
   d) ABS (J + 3)
   e) MOD (Y, ANINT (Z))
   f) EXP (REAL (LEG + 3))

3. (a) 720.0; (b) 26.8328; (c) 27

5. INT (15.7 / 1.8)
   MOD (15.7, 1.8)

Section 2.4.3

1. (a), (b), (d)

2. (b) READ *, I1, I2
      PRINT *, I1 / I2, MOD (I1, I2), I1, I2

4. (e) READ *, PUR, BILL
      IPUR = NINT (100.0 * PUR)
      IBILL = NINT (100.0 * BILL)
      ...

Section 2.5.4

1. a) BETA(J)
   b) ALPHA(J + 2)
   c) GAMMA (2 * J − 1)

3. REAL CARTON(5, 4, 17)

5. (a) 1.25; (c) −91.7; (e) 1.35; (g) −6.74; (i) 5

CHAPTER 3

Section 3.1.5

1. a) I .EQ. N
   b) X + Y .GT. 3.4
   c) (G .GE. 3) .OR. (A .EQ. 3.6)
   d) Nonsense
   e) OK as is

3. a) Missing right parenthesis at end
   b) `(A .LT. 99.0) .OR. (B .LT. 99.0)`
   c) Valid, but will always be *false*
   f) OK as is

6. a) Any value except 1 changes to 1.
   b) 0 changes to 3; 3 changes to 0.
   c) Any value except 1 or 2 generates error message and leaves the value unchanged.
   d) Any value except 1 or 2 is left unchanged.

11. (a) Any *Kode* other than 1 is treated as a withdrawal.

15. There should be as many `END IF` statements as `IF...THEN` statements. In making this check, *ignore* `ELSE IF...THEN` statements.

17. a) `WHBASE = MAX (GRPAY − EXEMP, 0.0)` *or*
      `WHBASE = DIM (GRPAY, EXEMP)`
   b) `BIGVAR = MAX (FIRST, SECOND)`
   c) `BIG = MAX (X, Y)`
      `SMALL = MIN (X, Y)`
   d) `BIGVAR = MAX (FIRST, SECOND, THIRD)`
   f) `ABS (A)`

Section 3.2.4

1. True

3. True

5. True

Section 3.4.4

2. If the `GO TO` statements were omitted, the statement `I = 1` following 20 CONTINUE would inevitably be executed. Thus 1 would be assigned as the final value of *I* in all cases.

CHAPTER 4

Section 4.1.4

6. b) The following program will not work:

```
      DO 17 I = 1, N
         J = N + 1 − I
         AUX = A(I)
         A(I) = A(J)
         A(J) = AUX
17    CONTINUE
```

because each pair of elements gets exchanged *twice*—thus each element of *A* is returned to its original value. The correct program interchanges each pair of elements only once. A simple change in the limit parameter of the DO statement will make the program work correctly.

7. a) OK as is

    b) DO 13, I = 1, N

    c) DO 22, JOLLY = 12, 62, I

    d) DO 39, I = 1, NINT (H)

    e) DO 15, KAYONE = K(2), K(3), K(4)

13.
```
      P = 1.0
      DO 987, I = 1, N, 2
         P = P * (Y - X(I))
987   CONTINUE
```

Section 4.2.1

2.
```
      INTEGER ONE(15), OTHER(20)
      READ *, (ONE(I), I = 1, 15)
      READ *, (OTHER(I), I = 1, 20)
      DO 172, I = 1, 15
         DO 171, J = 1, 20
            IF (ONE(I) .EQ. OTHER(J)) PRINT *, ONE(I)
171      CONTINUE
172      CONTINUE
      END
```

This program matches each item of one array against all items of the other array; therefore, a value that appears more than once in the same array will be printed several times. A program to print each matched value exactly once is more challenging.

8. Values of elements of the array A:

-6	-5	-4	-3	-2	-1
-5	-4	-3	-2	-1	0
-4	-3	-2	-1	0	1
-3	-2	-1	0	1	2
-2	-1	0	1	2	3
-1	0	1	2	3	4

The program finds the total of all *positive* values, below the heavy line, in rows L through K. Thus, in case 1 the rows are 3, 4, 5, and 6; the total is 13. In case 2 the rows are 4 and 5, and the total is 3.

CHAPTER 5

Section 5.1.6

3. (a) 27; (b) 14; (c) 28; (d) 3

Section 5.2.6

1. b) STRING(9 : 10)

2. a) QUICK[]BROWN[]FOX

    c) OVER[]THE[]LAZY[]DOG.

    e) Y[][]

3. a) LONGER = LIST(1) // LIST(2) // LIST(3)

c) LIST(2) = LONGER(6 : 9)

CHAPTER 6

Section 6.1.3

1. a) Missing comma in D(I), I

c) JOHNNIE name too long; no parentheses enclosing implied DO.

e) Cannot have constants in an input list.

g) When there is no list, the comma is omitted.

i) OK as is. The list consists of two items, the second of which is the integer 0. However, the programmer may have intended 4.0 instead of 4,0 at the end.

k) The constant 'A[]=' must not appear in an input list; also, the period following this constant was probably intended to be a comma.

2. a) (T(I), I = 2, 50, 2)

c) (R(1, J), J = 1, 5), (R(6, J), J = 1, 5)

3. a) READ *, N, (A(I), I = 1, N)

c) PRINT *, (D(I, L), I = 1, N)

e) PRINT *, CRISS

g) PRINT *, ((CRAZY(I, J), J = 1, 5), I = 1, M, 2)

Section 6.2.8

1. a) (21X, F 10.3)

c) (1X, 3 F20.4)

e) (1X, I6, F10.2 / 1X, I6, 2 F10.2 / 1X, I6, 3 F10.2)

g) ('[]Checker[]is[]off[]the[]board.')

CHAPTER 7

Section 7.1.3

1. a) INTEGER CHEK(8, 8)

c) CHARACTER FIRST(17)*8, SECOND(7)*12 *or* use two separate declarations

e) DIMENSION NEWTON(0 : 49)

3. IMPLICIT LOGICAL (N)
COMPLEX N

5. DIMENSION DEL(50, 50)

7. DIMENSION KEL(10, 30), REL(10, 30)

Section 7.3.2

1. DIMENSION A(8, 8), B(8, 6)
EQUIVALENCE (A, B)

3. EQUIVALENCE (DECK(1, 1), SPADES), (DECK(1, 2), HEARTS),
(DECK(1, 3), DIAMDS), (DECK(1, 4), CLUBS)

5. `DIMENSION RA(3, 5), IA(3, 5)`
   `EQUIVALENCE (RA, IA)`

7. `DIMENSION CUBE(3, 3, 3), KUBE(-2 : 24)`
   `EQUIVALENCE (CUBE(2, 2, 2), KUBE(20)`

CHAPTER 8

Section 8.2.3

1. 36.70   31   17.24   48   831.16   92
7. 0.61605250; 0.34274053; 0.16045898

Section 8.5.4

1. a) B(3) in *Revers;* A(3) in main program
   b) Case 1: 3.0; Case 2: 3.0; Case 3: 5.4

Section 8.6.1

1. `ABLE(I, P) = I * J * IP`
3. OK as is
5. `XXL (J) = I * J * LL`
7. `ZEFF (XX) = A * XX + B`
   `PUTT (Y) = ZEFF (X) / Y`
9. 45.0

Bold numbers refer to the summary of the Fortran 77 Standard in Appendix C.